"Our mission is to improve decision making, stimulate research and inform debate within government and the wider community by providing a quality statistical service"

Social Trends 26

1996 Edition

Editor: JENNY CHURCH

Associate Editor: CAROL SUMMERFIELD

Production team: STEPHEN DREWELL
ALYSON WHITMARSH
ELOISE CRITCHLEY
GAVIN HALES
TIM HARRIS
DAVID SHARP
TONY SYMMONDS
STEVE WHYMAN
PETER WHITE
MARTIN HARGREAVES
CARLTON BROWN
JOANNE YOUNG
ANDY LEACH

London: HMSO

Contents

3604811043

Introduction

Social Trends draws together statistics from a wide range of government departments and other organisations to paint a broad picture of British society today, and how it has been changing. The 13 chapters each focus on a different social policy area, described in tables, charts and explanatory text. *Social Trends* is aimed at a very wide audience: policy-makers in the public and private sectors; market service providers; lawyers; people in local government; journalists and other commentators; academics and students; schools; and the general public.

The editorial team always welcomes readers' views on how *Social Trends* could be improved. Please take a few moments to fill in the readership survey questionnaire you'll find inside the book and send it back to us. We want to make sure that future editions are geared to your needs.

Articles

This year *Social Trends* contains two articles which present data from two different types of longitudinal data sources. The first is on the Office of Population Censuses and Surveys' Longitudinal Study by Jillian Smith. The second looks at the British Household Panel Survey and is written by a team from the ESRC Research Centre on Micro-social Change, led by J Gershuny.

New material and sources

To preserve topicality, over half of the 329 tables and charts in the chapters of *Social Trends 26* are new compared with the previous edition. In addition there is a new chapter on Lifestyles. This builds on the previous Leisure chapter by adding information on time use and reintroducing the section on political participation.

In all chapters, the source of the data is given below each table and chart. *Social Trends 26* also includes at the end of each chapter a list of references directing readers to other published sources of data (both government and non government) and a list of contact telephone numbers. Those using *Social Trends* as a first point of reference should find this particularly useful. Regional and local authority analyses of some of the information in *Social Trends* may be found in the CSO's publication *Regional Trends*, available from HMSO bookshops.

Availability on electronic media

The data contained in the tables and charts in *Social Trends 26* are available on diskette to any reader returning the order form on the back of the readership survey questionnaire. Please let us know if you have not received a copy of the form by calling us on 0171 270 6081.

The first 25 editions of *Social Trends* are already available on CD-ROM and a separate *Social Trends 26* CD-ROM will be available in February. For details on how to order a copy please again contact us on 0171 270 6081.

Contributors

The Editor and Associate Editor wish to thank all their colleagues in the Government Statistical Service and contributors in other organisations without whose help this publication would not be possible. Thanks also go to the CSO Graphic Design Unit.

Appendix

The Appendix gives definitions and general background information, particularly on administrative structures and legal frameworks. Anyone seeking to understand the tables and charts in detail will find it helpful to read the corresponding entries in the Appendix in addition to the footnotes relevant to each table and chart. A full index to this edition is included following the Appendix.

Social Statistics Section
Central Statistical Office
Room 1808
Millbank Tower
Millbank
LONDON SW1P 4QQ

List of tables and charts

Numbers in brackets refer to similar items appearing in *Social Trends 25* Page

Page

Page

Page

10: Housing

11: Environment

Page

Editor's introduction to the articles

While a wide range of information on the changing nature of society can be gathered from administrative records and regular and ad-hoc surveys, these can only provide 'snap-shots' of the population or survey sample at a particular time and therefore describe the broad pattern of change. However, 'snap-shot' information does not provide possibilities for inferring causal sequences: for example, does unemployment effect health? What is the effect of family breakdown on employment and income? These sorts of questions can only be answered by tracking people over time, ie collecting information on the same sample of individuals over a period of time. Such studies are referred to as longitudinal studies. It is hoped that these articles will help raise awareness of the availability and use which can be made of this type of data.

Longitudinal datasets can be constructed in a number of ways. Administrative data can be linked through a unique identifier and the individual's 'life events' therefore connected. Alternatively the same sample of individuals can be surveyed over a period of time. This sample can either be selected from the population of adults, households, etc and then reinterviewed over time, or a cohort can be selected, often at birth, and then information collected from them over time by means of either surveys or from administrative data.

The two articles in this edition of *Social Trends* present data from two different types of longitudinal data sources: the Longitudinal Study (LS), run by the Office of Population Censuses and Surveys and the British Household Panel Survey (BHPS), run by the Economic and Social Research Council's Centre on Micro-social Change. The LS uses a combination of the two main types of longitudinal data described above, by linking together results from a 1 per cent sample of the decennial Population Censuses with registration data such as births, deaths and emigration records. The BHPS collects data through interviews with a sample of individuals who are revisited every year. The LS has particular strengths in its size and long time span which allow people to be followed through their main life transitions. The BHPS, now in its fifth year, interviews a sample of individuals about the detail of their current and past lives. The LS paints a broad picture; the BHPS supplies the detail. Each study has a unique and complementary value for analyses over time.

The OPCS Longitudinal Study

Jillian Smith

Office of Population Censuses and Surveys

Introduction

The Office of Population Censuses and Surveys Longitudinal Study (OPCS LS) is a resource developed over the last twenty years. It incorporates decennial census and event registration records for about 1 per cent of the population of England and Wales. The LS takes as its starting point a sample of records from the 1971 Census of England and Wales of all people born on four calendar dates in any year.

The England and Wales sample of 512,881 persons in 1971 is a representative 1.1 per cent sample of the population, unclustered except by date of birth, and including people in institutions. To maintain representativeness, all new births and immigrants with the four LS birth dates are added to the sample. For each subsequent census, samples drawn on identical criteria have been extracted and each person's census record linked to previous records, where these exist. Deaths and exits from England and Wales are recorded through registration systems. In addition to the census information for LS sample members all information for people living in the same household is also added. As a result, the total sample at the time of the 1991 Census was 543,884 LS members and 1,203,940 other household members. Between 1971 and 1991, 821,681 individuals have been LS members, while for 331,875 people the Study includes information from the 1971, 1981 and 1991 censuses.

A.1

Structure of the OPCS Longitudinal Study

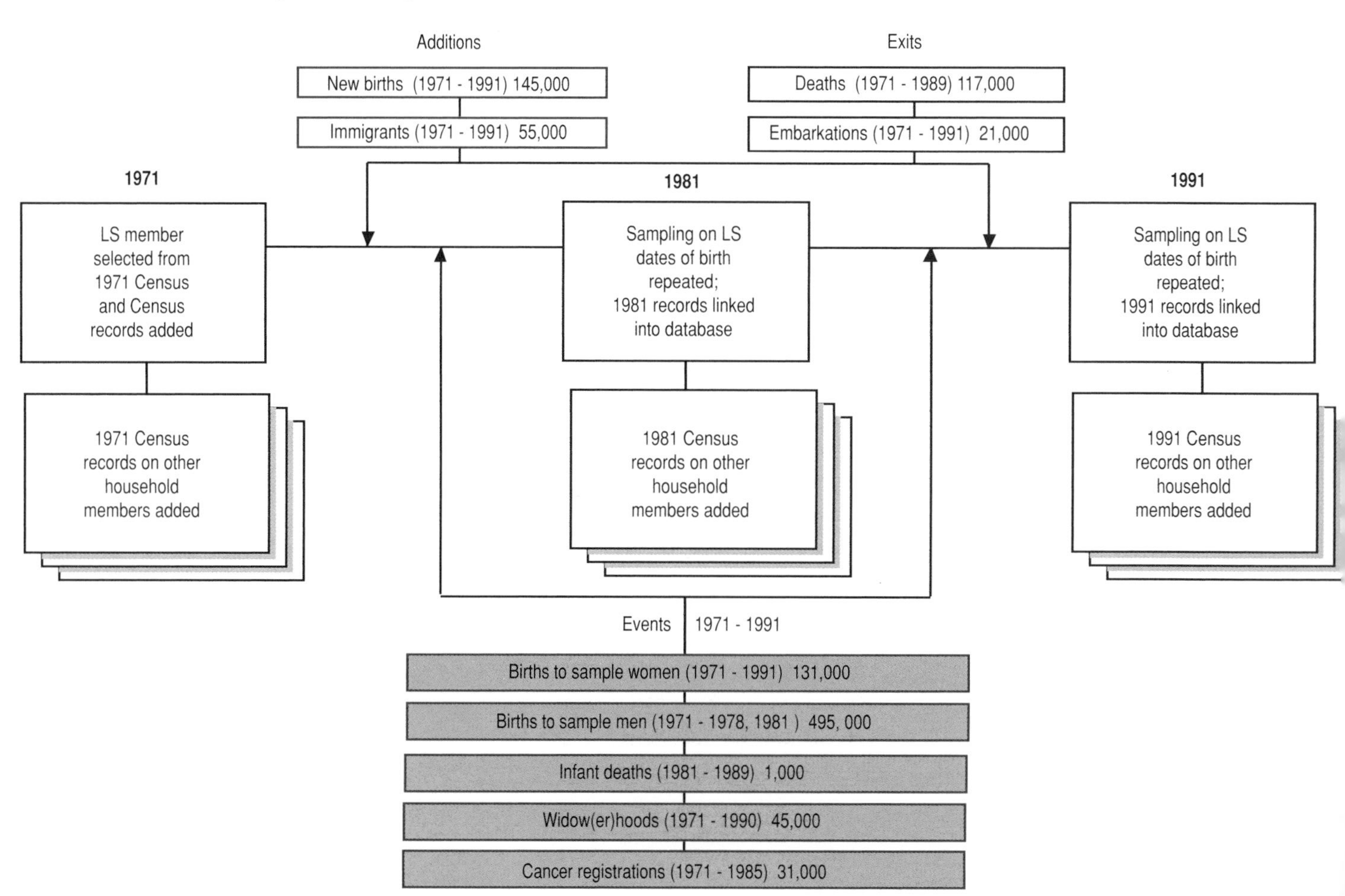

A Scottish longitudinal study, also started in 1971, was discontinued after the 1981 Census for cost reasons. Some limited Scottish information is available where LS members have moved between Scotland and England and Wales[1].

The three censuses which have been included to date (1971, 1981 and 1991) give a wide range of information at three specific points in time. To this a range of OPCS registration data is linked continuously (or 'prospectively') to sample members' records. The registration information, which is routinely collected by OPCS, has been added to LS members' records since 1971, normally every year, but in the case of some events, for limited periods. **Chart A.1** shows the full list of these vital events with their time ranges. Notable exceptions to the list are marriages and divorces, because date of birth, which is crucial for linkage of records, is not collected, and abortions, which are considered too sensitive for inclusion.

The methods used to link census and event information are very complicated and described elsewhere[1]. However, the value of the linked dataset depends upon its completeness and accuracy, which is, in the main, very high. For example, the linkage rate for surviving sample members at the 1981 census was 91 per cent, and that of the 1991 census sample 90 per cent. Identification and linkage rates of the vital events vary considerably depending upon the methods available, but for the crucial identification of new births and deaths they are very close to 100 per cent. Immigration and exits from England and Wales are not systematically registered and are less complete. However, the incorporation of census records into the dataset every ten years provides a regular benchmark against which new births, deaths, immigrations and embarkations, recorded through the previous decade, can be checked.

The structure of the LS lends itself to individual level longitudinal analysis, comparing successive census records or using census data in conjunction with the continuously collected vital events. This makes the LS particularly suitable for the study of mortality over time, which, as will be seen, was a primary reason for the creation of the Study in 1973.

Access to the LS

OPCS collaborates with the Economic and Social Research Council (ESRC) to promote wider use of this complex dataset which is located in a hierarchical data base on the OPCS computer. Data are not disguised or altered in any way but sensitive fields, such as date of birth, are protected by the computer system from access by the user. Sensitive data can be used as source data in analysis. Use of the Study is encouraged by OPCS, subject to the constraints of census and population acts of parliament which safeguard the privacy of the individual and maintain confidence in OPCS and the Census. Data are only accessed on site and all researchers sign a confidentiality undertaking. Projects are reviewed and approved at the start and detail of analysis and output tables is restricted. A small team of skilled research staff is available, based at OPCS and at the ESRC funded Social Statistics Research Unit at City University, to help researchers use the dataset. Technological progress has eased access to the data encouraging greater use, although, of course, the confidentiality constraints mentioned above will always apply.

Standard mortality ratios (SMRs) are calculated by comparing the observed number of deaths in a group (numerator) against an expected number of deaths (denominator), usually that of the relevant wider population, known as the standard population. This ratio, normally expressed as a percentage, is the SMR. Values over 100 indicate raised mortality compared to the standard; values under 100 indicate relatively lower mortality.

Use of the LS

As will be seen below, even in its early days the LS was able to support important analyses which helped to confirm patterns of health variation in England and Wales. As the Study has matured, the range of topics for analysis has widened, and with the new impetus provided by the recent addition of the 1991 Census data, a broad programme of work is now under way.

The following sections of the paper cover programmes of work which have used the LS and demonstrate its particular strengths and versatility. Not all areas of LS work are covered here and references to ethnicity, fertility and cancer mortality analyses are listed in the LS publications list[2].

Socio-economic differences in mortality

From the 1950s to the 1970s there was growing dissatisfaction with routine occupational mortality statistics published in OPCS decennial supplements. Concerns were expressed about the accuracy of the statistics in relation to particular industrial groups such as miners where high death rates were observed. Similar concerns affected the traditional measurement of mortality by social class. The LS was primarily introduced to overcome these difficulties.

The traditional approach suggested that mortality was lowest for social class I and highest for class V, at all ages[3]. It also suggested that differences had widened since the Second World War. These findings led to the establishment of the Black Committee to review this problem in 1978 and provided the main evidence in its report[4].

However, measurement problems associated with the decennial supplement figures cast doubts over the conclusions tha could be drawn from the data. These doubts arose from measurement bias; health selection; the limitation of the available data to men of working ages; and choice of appropriate social classifications. In the 1980s, the LS provided a means of overcoming some of these problems and giving reassurance that the original observations were broadly correct. It also has an important role to play in answering questions about the order of events, such as: do the sick become poor or do the poor become sick or do both happen? (See below.)

In the decennial supplements the mortality rates for occupational and social class groups were calculated using information about occupation collected from death registration and census independently. There are two problems with this approach. First, since occupational data collected at death registration are given by someone other than the person in question, they will be prone to inaccuracies and omissions. Second, the occupational data from the two sources are likely to be inconsistent due to differences in the questions asked about occupation: the census asks about occupation last week, whereas at death registration the informant is asked for last occupation. This source of possible bias is often called the 'numerator/denominator effect'.

In the LS, however, the death record is linked to the census record for each individual. Occupation at the time of the census is therefore available for use in calculating death rates for groups of interest As a bonus, since the LS is itself a fully representative sample of the population of England and Wales, it can provide its own

Social class categories are based on the head of household's occupation as follows:

Class I: Higher managerial, administrative or professional
Class II: Intermediate managerial, administrative, or professional
Class IIIN: Supervisory or clerical, and junior managerial, administrative, or professional
Class IIIM: Skilled manual workers
Class IV: Semi and unskilled manual workers
ClassV: State pensioners or widows (no other earners), casual or lowest grade workers, or long-term unemployed

nternal standard against which to compare nortality rates for any sub-group. By using he same data source, it therefore avoids the o called 'numerator/denominator' bias in he calculation of rates.

By its longitudinal design the LS also rovides a means of measuring and djusting for health selection effects. It has ong been recognised that occupational nortality levels would be influenced by a erson in full health taking a demanding job nd a person in poorer health choosing a ess strenuous occupation or not working at ll. This was known generally as 'health elated selection'. Its effect of depressing bserved mortality rates among the mployed became known as the 'healthy vorker effect'. **Table A.2** shows ratios of age pecific mortality rates for the employed to hat for all men or women in the LS for two ollow-up periods. The later follow-up period, 976-1981, shows generally higher mortality mong the employed relative to all men and vomen, indicating a reduction in the healthy vorker effect over time[5].

Vith the techniques in place to avoid the itfalls of numerator/denominator bias and to dentify health selection effects, the LS could ow be used to measure differences in nortality and assess the extent of bias to vhich the decennial supplement data was rone. **Table A.3** shows the mortality radients calculated for the decennial upplement and from the LS, measured cross four different time ranges. Differences between the LS and decennial upplement data and the techniques of stimation used, mean that broad omparisons only should be made[6]. However, the later LS time periods result in ncreasingly accurate estimates. A steeper nortality gradient emerges, as the health election effect, evident in earlier time anges, wears off.

A.2

Mortality ratios[1] for people employed in 1971: by age at death and gender, 1971 - 1975 and 1976 - 1981

England & Wales — Age specific ratios[1]

	Males		Females	
	1971-1975	1976-1981	1971-1975	1976-1981
Age at death				
20-24	87	60	104	58
25-29	86	86	85	87
30-34	87	89	65	106
35-39	82	89	73	98
40-44	89	91	101	105
45-49	88	97	74	91
50-54	87	93	79	87
55-59	85	95	79	84
60-64	83	94	71	88
65-69	77	90	52	81
70-74	67	85	62	78
75-79	68	85	42	75
80 and over	79	83	38	87

1 Ratio of the age-specific death rates for the employed to that for all men and women in the LS.

Source: Office of Population Censuses and Surveys

A.3

Male mortality[1]: by social class in 1971

England & Wales — SMR

	Decennial supplement	Longitudinal Study			
	1970-1972	1971-1975	1976-1981	1982-1985	1986-1989
Social class in 1971					
I	77	80	69	61	67
II	81	80	78	78	80
IIIN	99	92	103	98	85
IIIM	106	90	95	101	102
IV	114	97	109	113	112
V	137	115	124	136	153
All social classes[2]	100	100	100	100	100

1 Aged 15 to 64.
2 Includes men not assigned to a social class.

Source: Office of Population Censuses and Surveys

A.4

Mortality of 1971 and 1981 census cohorts: by housing tenure, car access and gender

England & Wales Age standardised rate ratios[1]

	Males		Females	
	1971-1981	1981-1989	1971-1981	1981-1989
Owner occupier[2]	100	100	100	100
Private renter	119	119	116	119
LA tenant	126	134	122	132
One or more cars[2]	100	100	100	100
No car	130	141	121	124

1 Standardised using the European Standard Population but, for consistency, figures are based on 100.
2 Base line groups.
Source: Office of Population Censuses and Surveys

The LS figures in Table A.3 also provide part of the answer to the question asked above: do the sick become poor or the poor become sick? Since social class is defined at the start of the study period, the social class differences in mortality measured towards the end of the study period cannot be explained by downward social mobility as people become sick[7].

Further work on the 1980s LS data shows some indication of widening differentials measured by housing tenure and car access as proxies for socio-economic status. **Table A.4** shows rate ratios for all ages by gender. Evidence of a pattern of widening differences seems to be emerging, and further work will seek to confirm this[8].

Inequalities in the health of the elderly

By using occupational information from the census the LS has shown that mortality differentials were still evident at older ages. For example, **Chart A.5** shows that among men aged 75 and over, those allocated to social class V had a 50 per cent higher death rate than men in social class I. As a result, theories of a drift down through the social classes with age because of declining health were questioned. 'Life experience' factors appeared to be a more likely explanation to account for the continued mortality differentials at older ages[9].

A.5

Mortality of elderly males: by social class in 1971, 1976-1989

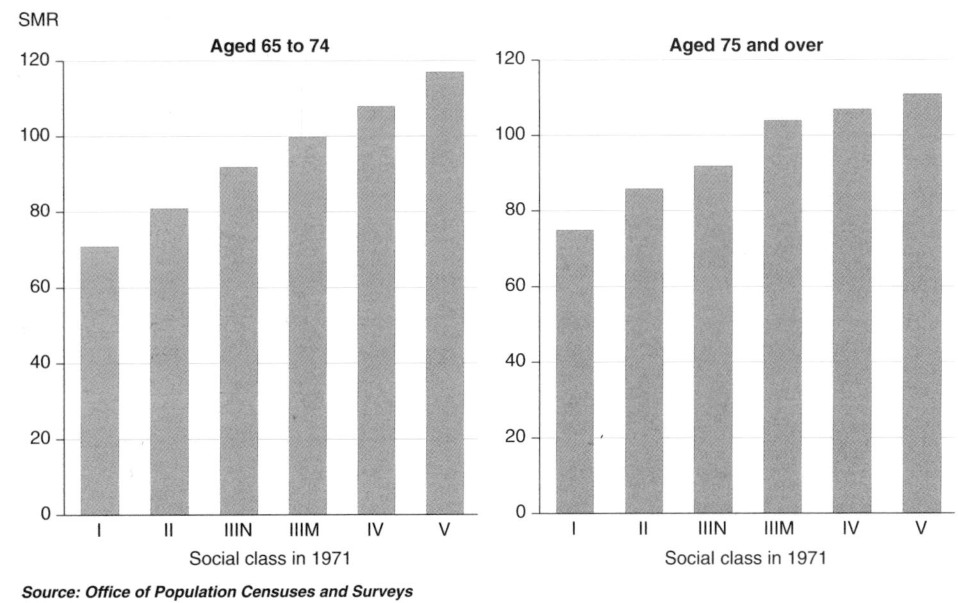

Source: Office of Population Censuses and Surveys

Mortality and the social classification of women

For the study of women's mortality, the fundamental problem has been a lack of occupational information from which to derive social classifications. Women, more than men, move into and out of the labour force, particularly as they have families. As a consequence, at a single point in time many women have no paid work, or work part time, or are in occupations which do not reflect their social class status.

Traditional attempts to overcome this problem have used husband's occupation for married women and own occupation for single, widowed and divorced women[3]. This makes comparisons across all women difficult and disregards the increasingly important contribution of working married women to the economy and well-being of the household. The hunt for better classifications and proxies for economic status has included the use of the LS to explore the effects of marital status, household indices such as housing tenure and access to cars, life-cycle stage (indicated by age of youngest child) and part-time or full-time employment.

The LS has enabled researchers to compare the power of the various indicators and to use them together to construct composite indicators which effectively differentiate the health experience of women. Using mortality data from the latter half of the 1970s, the Study tested a range of possible social indicators for women and found a complicated situation. For married women with an occupational social class, own social class taken together with husband's social class was found to give the greatest variation in mortality. However, for single women the best indicators were own social class and access to a car. 'Unoccupied' married women (comprising housewives, students and the permanently sick), were differentiated by husband's social class, housing tenure and car access. When the age of the youngest child was introduced as a measure of life-cycle stage, age adjusted mortality was found to be lower for housewives with dependent children than for those who were childless or whose children were older. In addition, in certain circumstances, women working part time in non-manual occupations were found to have exceptionally low mortality[10,11].

This work illustrates the ability of the LS to address complex classifications and demonstrates the need for further work in developing social classifications which can encompass the wide range of women's lives.

OPCS are at present completing a review of social classifications in preparation for the 2001 Census, addressing the need for continuity of definitions to match past information and for new approaches which are relevant to changing lifestyles[12].

Mortality and unemployment

Periods of high unemployment over the past twenty-five years have led to many studies of its impact upon health. Early work using LS data from 1971 to 1981 found significantly raised mortality levels for men of employment age who were seeking work at the beginning of the period, as well as for their wives, after controlling for social class. **Table A.6** summarises mortality levels in the 1970s for all men and for men seeking work by social class in 1971[13].

This analysis was repeated for the early 1980s, using a sample of men 'seeking work' at the 1981 census. Between 1971 and 1981 the percentage of men of working age in the LS who were in employment fell from 87 per cent to 81 per cent. However a greater proportion of men reported themselves to be retired or permanently sick, rather than seeking work. This might be the result of an incentive, existing at that time, for people to move from unemployment benefit to invalidity benefit due to the higher rate paid. As a result, although the number of men seeking work was much greater in 1981 than in 1971, they were likely to be a healthier group. Even so excess mortality was again found for those seeking work relative to all men[14]. It is interesting to note, here, the effect which external factors, in this instance benefit levels, can have in determining a different composition within a sample drawn under the same definition at two separate points in time.

A.6

Mortality[1] of all men and men seeking work: by social class in 1971, 1971-1981

England & Wales		SMR
	All men	Men seeking work
I	73	98
II	78	107
IIIN	99	118
IIIM	93	123
IV	103	160
V	120	150
All[2]	100	137

1 Of men aged 15 to 64.
2 Includes men not assigned to a social class.
Source: Office of Population Censuses and Surveys

A.7

Net population change due to inter-regional movement of young women[1], 1970-1971

England & Wales Percentages

	Young women[1]	
	All	In first three years of first marriage
East Anglia	*1.2*	*6.5*
East Midlands	*-0.1*	*3.4*
West Midlands	*-0.8*	*1.8*
South West	*0.7*	*0.5*
Yorkshire & Humberside	*-0.6*	*0.1*
North	*-0.6*	*-1.1*
West	*-0.2*	*-1.2*
South East	*0.3*	*-1.5*
North West	*-0.1*	*-1.9*
England & Wales	*0.0*	*0.0*

1 Aged 20 to 29.

Source: Office of Population Censuses and Surveys

Continuing the development of this topic, work now in progress compares the 1970s decade, 1971 to 1979, with the comparable 1980s period, 1981 to 1989. The analysis again confirms the significantly raised mortality of the unemployed in comparison to all men of working age[15].

Migration and geographic change

The representativeness of the LS for England and Wales allows analysis of both the pattern of migration according to the characteristics of the population and the effect of migration upon different areas.

Early work on migration using the LS looked at the effect on regional populations of change of address in the first years of marriage, finding that migration rates are high at this time in people's lives and also varied by age, housing tenure type and the husband's social class. **Table A.7** shows net population change due to inter-regional migration of women in the first three years of marriage. In addition, the migration of young women had a secondary effect upon regional population trends, as families were started[16].

Some detailed studies of migration flows in the LS have focused upon the flows between the London or South East area and the rest of England and Wales. Longitudinal analysis reveals a complex story.

Work using 1971 and 1981 census data showed that high outward migration of professional and managerial workers from inner London was partially offset by immigration of young people in these groups who had previously been economically inactive and therefore presumably students. In addition, inner London sustained a high level of internal change as people joined and left the labour market. The net result was that the inner London area could sustain a high level of outward migration without a downward shift in occupational structure[17].

When the South East region was compared to the rest of England and Wales, a similar pattern of migration flows was found in relation to social class and economic activity. The South East 'escalator' theory hypothesised that young qualified people tend to come to the South East, train and achieve promotion and leave as middle aged professionals and managers; that few other than the young move into the area, and of these many become unemployed. As a result the South East becomes increasingly middle class but polarised in class structure[18,19,20,21].

When this analysis is extended to separate genders, more interesting detail emerges. Using the 1971 and 1981 LS census data it was discovered that migration to the South East region involved upward mobility for women, whereas migration out of the region often involved an exit from the labour market for women and was strongly to their disadvantage in their own employment careers[22].

An international study in the area of migration looked at comparisons between London, using the LS, and Paris, using the Échantillon Démographique Permanent, a similar study of the French population. This work highlighted the different migration experience of retired people in the two cities. Retirement migration out of London is more likely in the 'well to do' social classes I and II, whereas in Paris it is spread evenly across the social strata. Tenure patterns, conditions of life and attitudes are possible explanations which were examined where the data allowed[23].

The Study has also examined internal migration by ethnic group. Hampered by small sample sizes, it was, nevertheless, shown that the propensity to migrate varied depending upon gender, ethnic group and a measure of estimated reward (defined as gaining of educational qualifications, upward social mobility or entry to white collar occupational status)[24].

Lastly, the Study has taken advantage of the origin of the present national health numbering system to look at migration of a sample of the population which can be traced back to 1939. In 1939 a prewar registration of the population was completed and non-military personnel were issued with a registration number. This number was subsequently used for a large proportion of the population as the NHS number. Since the number was allocated by region, for these people, it is possible to trace their location in 1939. The study, with caveats due to the incomplete sample, looked at migration between 1939 and 1971 and found that, in 1971, movers were more advantaged, in terms of housing tenure and car access, than non-movers. In addition those going to advantaged areas were the most advantaged movers. **Table A.8** shows the percentage of persons who were owner occupiers with access to one or more cars at the 1971 Census, by their migration status[25].

The LS offers unique opportunities for geographic analysis. The relatively large sample, unclustered except by date of birth, means that analysis down to County District level is possible, although at this level of detail, small number problems can arise. The LS also carries the necessary geographic identifiers required on both the census information and on the events data. Most importantly, the LS time dimension allows geographic flows to be studied, greatly enhancing the understanding of both the cause and effect of migration.

A.8

Owner-occupiers with access to cars[1]: by age, gender and mover status[2]

England & Wales Percentages

	Males		Females	
	Non-movers	Movers	Non-movers	Movers
Age at 1971 census				
31-39	*47*	*57*	*46*	*57*
40-49	*41*	*56*	*39*	*51*
50-59	*35*	*48*	*32*	*47*
60-69	*30*	*47*	*23*	*34*
70 and over	*20*	*32*	*15*	*23*
All aged 31 and over	*35*	*50*	*29*	*44*

1 As a percentage of all persons in each age group, gender and mover status group.
2 Movers are those who lived in a different region in 1971 compared with 1939.
Source: Office of Population Censuses and Surveys

The living arrangements of the elderly

The decades covered by the time span of the LS have seen an ageing of the population and, in particular, an increase in the numbers of the very old (85 years and over) who need greater levels of support. In addition people are living in smaller households than previously, which means that support may not be on hand when needed.

With the availability of a range of social classifications, the LS is a useful resource for analysis of the elderly population for whom social class, based on occupation at time of death, may not accurately reflect their status through life. The Study, therefore, offers opportunities to discover whether or not such indicators as housing tenure and social class at census, which are associated with chance of survival at younger age groups, maintain the association at older ages.

A.9

Percentage of married people aged 65 and over in 1971 and still alive in 1981: by gender, age and tenure in 1971

England & Wales Percentages

	Owner occupier	LA tenant	Private renter	All in private households
Males				
Aged 65 to 69	*53.0*	*42.5*	*45.9*	*48.7*
Aged 70 to 74	*40.0*	*31.1*	*30.9*	*36.0*
Aged 75 to 79	*25.0*	*18.3*	*18.0*	*22.0*
Aged 80 and over	*10.0*	*6.8*	*6.8*	*8.6*
Females				
Aged 65 to 69	*68.8*	*63.2*	*63.7*	*66.2*
Aged 70 to 74	*55.2*	*46.0*	*47.2*	*51.2*
Aged 75 to 79	*38.3*	*33.6*	*32.9*	*35.9*
Aged 80 and over	*17.8*	*15.0*	*16.8*	*17.0*

Source: Office of Population Censuses and Surveys

When the LS was used to see how the living arrangements of the 1971 cohort of men and women over 65 years changed over time, a complicated picture emerged associated with gender, marital status, tenure arrangements and life-stage. Tenants of both genders and men in manual or unclassified social class groups in 1971 were more likely to have entered institutions by 1981 than owner-occupiers or men in non-manual occupations. Tenure type was found to be still associated with mortality risk, but the relationship was likely to be weakened by such situations as tenants moving into the owner-occupying households of relations, possibly due to ill health. In addition a cohort effect was apparent due to the relatively high proportion of the very elderly still living in privately rented accommodation which was a common circumstance when they first set up home. **Table A.9** shows survivors in 1981 among men and women aged 65 and over and married in 1971, by tenure in 1971[26].

The Study was used next to look at factors associated with moves into institutions among the elderly. It was found, not surprisingly, that people who in 1971 were not in a family were more likely to be in an institution at the next census. A higher level of moves into institutions was also found for private tenants. **Table A.10** illustrates these points[27].

The final work in this area so far, has been to examine moves by the elderly population into supported private households (defined as households in which the elderly person was living with relatives other than a spouse or unrelated persons) between 1971 and 1981. Models using age, housing tenure, household type and marital status failed to explain such moves and it seems likely that other factors which cannot be identified in the LS, such as health status (for those time periods) and availability of relatives, were important[27].

Work has now started on a further analysis in this area. The inclusion in the 1991 Census of the limiting long-term illness indicator of health status, together with the fertility histories of ever married women collected at the 1971 census, will shed some light on the family situations of the survivors of this group; and further years of mortality data will allow a longer follow-up period to be used.

For this work a particular advantage has been the inclusion in the LS of people living in institutions and the LS's ability to generate social classification proxies relevant to the elderly, such as housing tenure. The work is also an example of the potential to track individual's changing circumstances through time, ultimately to mortality which may be associated with factors in their past lives. At the aggregate level, the changing circumstances of the

A.10

sample over time highlights trends in the population which will have implications for the provision of medical and social services.

The future of the LS

Following the 1991 Census linkage exercise, the LS has been made more flexible and accessible by putting it into a database. This has improved the data preparation process permitting each user to specify their own variables. With support from the ESRC, a large programme of research is now under way. Much of the work explores the latest data available, often making comparisons with earlier time periods. In addition researchers continue to find new ways of using the data and of complementing it with data from other sources. In data management terms, we now stand at the point where plans for linkage of the 2001 Census into the LS will begin. These will be preceded by a review of the Study and justification of its continued value.

The 1991 Census data included new information on ethnicity. For the first time in a census a question on ethnic group was added to that asking country of birth. This will enable identification of second generation members of ethnic groups and add new scope to ethnic studies, including retrospective analysis.

The 1991 Census also asked a new question on limiting long-term illness: 'Does the person have any long-term illness, health problem or handicap which limits his/her daily activities or the work he/she can do? (Include problems which are due to old age).' This question will extend the scope of analysis of the LS in the area of morbidity, previously limited to cancer incidence, and can be used both prospectively and retrospectively.

People aged 65 and over in institutions in 1981: by tenure and household type in 1971

England & Wales Percentages

	Living alone	Married couple living alone	Married couple with children	Lone parent	Not in family/ with others
Males					
Owner-occupier	*6.9*	*2.3*	*1.1*	*3.5*	*7.6*
LA tenant	*4.4*	*3.0*	*0.8*	*2.0*	*14.4*
Private renter	*13.6*	*3.3*	*1.8*	..	*13.2*
All in private households	*8.1*	*2.7*	*1.1*	*5.7*	*10.0*
Females					
Owner-occupier	*8.6*	*4.0*	*1.8*	*3.8*	*8.1*
LA tenant	*10.2*	*5.8*	*2.2*	*4.0*	*7.9*
Private renter	*11.3*	*4.6*	*3.2*	*4.7*	*10.2*
All in private households	*9.9*	*4.6*	*2.2*	*4.0*	*8.2*

Source: Office of Population Censuses and Surveys

As the time span of the data grows the appropriate techniques need to become more sophisticated. Advanced statistical packages (SAS, GLIM and multi-level modelling packages) are now available for use with the source LS data. But most of all the researcher needs to be aware of the nuances which the history and context of the data and its circumstances of collection give to the interpretation of results. This is one challenge of the time dimension.

Creating longitudinal studies takes vision and patience. The LS, with its third census linked, will in future be capable of supporting many analyses anticipated from its early days such as comparison of cohorts across time and the study of longer follow-up periods of mortality analysis. The LS continues to increase its power to monitor health inequality and to support a range of time dependent studies in diverse areas of interest.

References

1 *Longitudinal Study 1971-1991, History, organisation and quality of data:* Hattersley L, Creeser R, *Series LS No 7,* HMSO, 1995

2 *OPCS Longitudinal Study list of publications,* Social Statistics Research Unit, City University, 1995

3 *Occupational Mortality 1970-72, Decennial Supplement*: OPCS, HMSO, 1978

4 *Inequalities in health: The Black Report and the health divide:* Townsend P, Davison N, Whitehead M, Penguin, 1972

5 *Mortality of employed men and women*: Goldblatt P, Fox J, Leon D, *Longitudinal Study 1971-1981: Mortality and social organisation, Series LS No 6,* HMSO, 1990

6 *Mortality of men by occupation*: Goldblatt P, Fox J, *Longitudinal Study 1971-1981: Mortality and social organisation, Series LS No 6*, HMSO, 1990

7 *Variations in health: What can the Department of Health and the NHS Do? A Report produced by the variations sub-group of the Chief Medical Officer's Health of the Nation Working Group,* Department of Health, 1995

8 *Differences in mortality by housing tenure and by car access from the OPCS Longitudinal Study*: Filakti H, Fox J, *Population Trends No 81*, HMSO, 1995

9 *Social class differences in mortality of men: recent evidence from the OPCS Longitudinal Study:* Harding S, *Population Trends No 80, HMSO, 1995*

10 *Mortality and the social classification of women*: Moser K, Pugh H, Goldblatt P, *Longitudinal Study 1971-1991: Mortality and social organisation, Series LS No 6,* HMSO, 1990

11 *Double burden or double blessing? Employment, motherhood and mortality in the Longitudinal Study of England and Wales*: Weatherall R, Joshi H, Macran S, *Social Science and Medicine, Vol 38, No 2*, 1994

12 *Official Social Classifications in the UK,* Rose D, *Social Research Update 9*, University of Surrey, 1995

13 *Unemployment and mortality,* Moser K, Goldblatt P, Fox J, Jones D, *Longituudinal Study 1971-1991: Mortality and Social organisation, Series LS No 6*, HMSO, 1990

14 *Unemployment and Mortality: comparison of the 1971 and 1981 Longitudinal Study census samples*: Moser K, Fox J, Goldblatt P, Jones D, *British Medical Journal, Vol 294, No 6564*, 1987

15 *Economic activity at the 1971, 1981 and 1991 censuses and mortality of the 1981 Longitudinal Study cohort:* Bethune A, forthcoming 1996

16 *The effect of change of address in the early years of marriage on regional populations:* Grundy E, Fox J, *Population Trends, No 38*, HMSO, 1984

17 *Migration and residential social change: a longitudinal analysis of migration flows into, out of and within London 1971-1981*: Hamnett C, *Revue de Géographie de Lyon, Vol 65, No 1, 1990*

18 *Inter-Regional migration and social change: A Study of South-East England based upon data from the Longitudinal Study*: Fielding A, *Institute of British Geographers, Vol 14, No 1,* 1989

19 *Migration and social mobility: South-East England as an Escalator Region:* Fielding A, *Regional Studies, Vol 26.1,* 1991

20 *Social and geographical mobility in the Non-Metropolitan south of England:* Fielding A, *Espaces, Populations, Sociétés,* 1991-2

21 *Migration to and from South East England*: Fielding A, *Final report for the Department of the Environment, 1992*

22 *Geographies of opportunity: a regional analysis of gender-specific social and spatial mobilities in England and Wales 1971-1981*: Fielding A, Halford S, *Environment and Planning A, Vol 25, No 10, 1993*

23 *A comparison of retirement migration from Paris and London:* Cribier F, Kych A, *Environment and Planning A, Vol 25, No 10,* 1993

24 *Race, gender and internal migration within England and Wales:* Robinson V, *Environment and Planning A, Vol 25, No. 10,* 1993

25 *Socio-economic characteristics of interregional migrants in England and Wales*: Leon D, Strachan D, *Environment and Planning A, Vol 25, No 10,* 1993

26 *Longitudinal perspectives on the living arrangements of the elderly*: Grundy E, *Growing Old in the Twentieth Century*, Tavistock, 1989

27 *Socio-Demographic variations in rates of movement into institutions among elderly people in England and Wales: An Analysis of Linked Census and Mortality Data 1971-1985*: Grundy E, *Population Studies, Vol 46, 1992*

British Household Panel Survey

J Gershuny, Nick Buck, Ope Coker, Shirley Dex,
John Ermisch, Stephen Jenkins, Andrew McCulloch
ESRC Research Centre on Micro-social Change

Introduction

The advantages of longitudinal data have already been set out in the Editor's introduction to these articles. But there are some further specific and particular advantages of true 'prospective' panel evidence, and shared to some extent by retrospectively linked administrative panels like the Longitudinal Study of the Census, which relate to the difficulties inherent in collecting evidence retrospectively. Firstly, some classes of data pose recall problems: this applies particularly to evidence about subjective states as we cannot, for example, sensibly ask 'How happy were you in 1991?'. In addition recall of some sorts of objective quantitative information, such as personal income, rapidly becomes unreliable with the passage of time[1]. Secondly, it is in general impractical to establish the past characteristics of units of analysis that no longer exist, particularly households which dissolve and individuals who die.

The British Household Panel Survey (BHPS), is managed by the ESRC Research Centre on Micro-social Change at Essex University; its fieldwork is conducted by NOP under the direction of the Centre. The survey started in September 1991, and has annual 'waves' of data collection; waves one to three (covering a period from 1991 to early in 1994) are already available for analysis, wave four is due to become available early in 1996 and fieldwork for wave five started in September 1995. The ESRC has agreed to fund the data collection up to wave eight (1998-99) and discussions of the possibility of continuing data collection beyond this point are under way.

Wave one consisted of a random sample of private addresses in Great Britain. All members of households at these addresses, together with their natural descendants, constitute the longitudinal sample of the BHPS. In each subsequent wave, the BHPS follows members of the longitudinal sample into their current households; new co-residents who are not longitudinal sample members are also interviewed in order to establish the longitudinal sample members' full household context. These 'cross-sectional' sample members continue to be reinterviewed in subsequent waves, but only for as long as they remain co-resident with a member of the longitudinal sample. These rules, together with some trivial additions, serve to maintain a sample which is representative of the members of the 1991 British population together with their natural descendants. The initial individual response rate was 72 per cent; subsequent wave-on-wave individual response rates were 87 per cent, 90 per cent and 95 per cent respectively for waves two, three and four; we hope to reach 96 per cent by wave five and maintain that rate thereafter. Approximately 7,200 wave one respondents were in wave four.

The Essex Centre carries out a programme of data cleaning and imputation, together with the derivation of sample weights to compensate as far as possible for attrition processes. The information collected in the BHPS covers household composition, employment, income, housing and equipment, consumption expenditures, attitudes and beliefs, heath and well-being, together with additional retrospective data. A brief summary of the contents is given in the box on page 28.

Summary of contents of BHPS questionnaires

Household questionnaire

Personal characteristics of household members
Cohabitation and marital statuses
Relationships between household members
Employment status of household members
Housing and neighbourhood characteristics
Broad household income and expenditure estimates
Household equipment, possession and purchase

Individual questionnaire

More detailed demographic, marital characteristics
Education background and attainment, training record
Employment characteristics of current job
Job satisfaction measures
Continuous employment history since last interview
Incomes from various sources
Continuous record of categories of income types received since last interview
Savings, debt, value of house and car
Financial transfers to and from other individuals within and outside own household
Participation in and time devoted to domestic work, childcare and care of adults
Household decision-making
General Health Questionnaire, health services usage
Values, opinions (social justice, role of state, party politics, parental and gender roles, religion)

Young persons' questionnaire

Spare time (TV use, going out)
Relationships with family and friends
Smoking, drugs, attitudes to health and family life
Well-being and self-image
Social and political awareness
Employment aspirations

Variable components

Wave 1 initial conditions (eg parents' social class)
Wave 2 lifetime marital, cohabitation and fertility
Wave 2 lifetime summary job history
Wave 3 lifetime detailed occupational history
Wave 4 first young persons' survey
Wave 5 personal wealth and debt

Simplifying somewhat, we might think of the BHPS as deriving from just three distinct sources: a 'household questionnaire' containing information about the whole household, which is asked of a reference adult; an 'individual questionnaire' asked of all adult household members aged 16 and over, and including a self-response instrument concentrating on subjective well-being; and a rather innovative 'young person's questionnaire' (for household members aged 11 to 15) which was included in waves four and five and is collected using a self-response instrument responding to a tape-recorded interview.

There is a 'rotating core' of questions asked on the individual questionnaire (including some questions about values which are included every second year), and a variable component which each year collects information which is not regularly repeated. This is either because it is a historical fact that remains unchanged, such as the lifetime histories in waves two and three, or because it is of specialised interest, or because there is a peculiar sensitivity about questions that precludes frequent repetition, such as the wealth data collected in wave five. In this article we provide some examples of the sorts of longitudinal analysis that can be carried out using some of the information contained in the early waves of the BHPS.

Household formation and dissolution

Households change their membership over time: solitary householders may marry and become members of couple households; children are born; aged parents move in with their children; couples separate or divorce; children leave home (and some subsequently return); and people die. These sorts of events pose a problem for analysts of household panel surveys as although individual people may live for a long time, something like 15 per cent of all households in Great Britain change their composition each year. In the panel analyst's jargon, there is in general no 'longitudinal household'[2]. We can of course do some special analyses on just those households that have unchanged membership over time, but many of the more interesting, and policy relevant, things that we want to find out about households may concern, or be a consequence of, changes in household personnel. Paradoxically, to cope with this phenomenon of changing household composition, much of the analysis of household change using panel data must focus on the individual. Rather than taking households as the unit of analysis, we look instead at the causes or consequences of changes in individuals' household contexts or statuses.

In **Table B.1** we use the BHPS to look at mothers changing their household contexts. Estimating annual rates of change by combining changes between waves one and two and waves two and three, we find that 3 per cent of women with children living in a couple become lone parents each year and the household status of a further 2 per cent changes because the child ages beyond dependency or leaves the parental household. Overall, nearly 6 per cent of such women change their household status each year. Calculating similarly, 12 per cent of women cease to be lone parents each year because they form a (usually new) partnership, 1 per cent no longer have any dependent children and around 2 per cent move to other sorts of households, such as to live with their own parents. Overall, almost 15 per cent of lone mothers change their household status within a year. If this departure rate were maintained over time, half of all lone mothers would have a duration of lone parenthood of 4.7 years or less.

B.1

Mothers leaving and entering parenthood, wave one to two and wave two to three

Great Britain — Percentages

	Leaving lone parenthood	Leaving couple with dependent children
Destination		
Lone parent with dependent children	.	3.0
Couple with dependent children	12.1	.
No dependent children	1.3	2.4
Other households	1.5	0.2
No change	85.2	94.4
All	100.0	100.0

Source: British Household Panel Survey, ESRC Research Centre on Micro-social Change

Cohabitation dynamics

Another area in which the BHPS adds significantly to our knowledge of UK demographics concerns the dynamics of cohabiting unions. Combining waves one through three, we found that three fifths of women who entered cohabitation had never been married, a third were widowed, divorced or separated, while the remainder were married in the previous year.

On the other hand, **Table B.2** shows the rates of departure from cohabiting unions. Overall 9 per cent of cohabiting unions dissolve completely each year, while a

B.2

Women leaving cohabitation: by new marital status, wave one to two and wave two to three

Great Britain — Percentages

	Women cohabiting
Marry partner	16
Partnership dissolves	
Never married	6
Widowed, divorced or separated	3
All leaving cohabitation	25

Source: British Household Panel Survey, ESRC Research Centre on Micro-social Change

B.3

Adults who moved house: by type of household change, wave two to wave three

Great Britain

Percentages

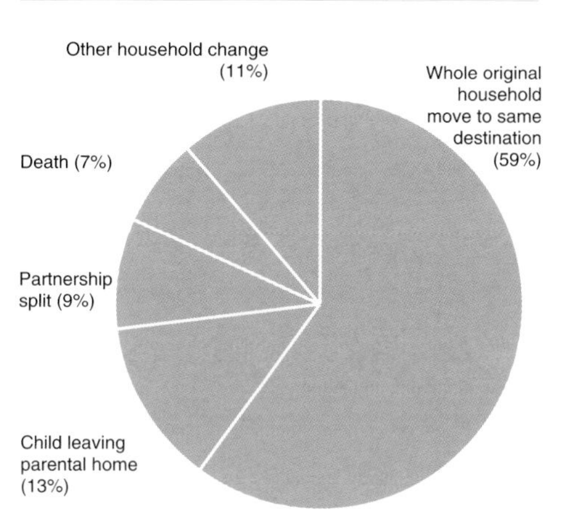

Source: British Household Panel Survey, ESRC Research Centre on Micro-social Change

B.4

Adults changing tenure: by age, wave one to two and wave two to three

Great Britain — Percentages

	Under 35	35 and over
From owner-occupied		
To social housing	*1*	-
To private rented	*3*	*1*
All from owner-occupied	*4*	*2*
From social housing		
To owner-occupied	*4*	*3*
To private rented	*4*	*2*
All from social housing	*8*	*5*
From private rented		
To social housing	*7*	*9*
To owner-occupied	*20*	*8*
All from private rented	*26*	*17*

Source: British Household Panel Survey, ESRC Research Centre on Micro-social Change

further 16 per cent turn into legal marriages. On the assumption of similar rates of departure each year (and that similar rates of departure prevail for men) half of cohabitations would last 2.7 years or less.

Housing dynamics

In relation to housing, one of the major advantages of the BHPS is that it permits a prospective account of housing mobility, rather than the retrospective accounts which are available in some cross-sectional surveys. This allows us both to calculate directly transition rates between different states, such as the major tenures, and also to analyse transitions in terms of associated events and causes.

We can use the BHPS to look at the prospective house movement rates between wave two and wave three. Once again these rates are at the individual level, since we cannot treat the household as a consistent longitudinal unit. Nevertheless we can distinguish between whole household moves and moves involving a splitting of the original household. Overall around 12 per cent of people moved home between wave two and wave three. Somewhat more than half of these moves involve the original household remaining together **(Chart B.3)**. This does not of course include household composition change arising from cases where new members join with the original household at the new location, so that the total level of household composition change associated with mobility is rather greater. Of the factors leading to splits in the original household, splits in married or cohabiting partnerships, children leaving the parental home and other changes each affected around 1 per cent of adults.

Table 10.19 in the Housing chapter analyses adults moving between waves two and three by tenure. We can use these same data to calculate exit rates from each tenure, and the tenure destination from each origin. **Table B.4** shows annual rates, by combining wave one with wave two moves and wave two with wave three moves. Three sectors are distinguished: owner occupation, social housing (including housing associations), and private renting. We also distinguish between younger and older adults. Not surprisingly, private renting has a very much higher exit rate than either of the other tenures, with more than a quarter of younger adults (aged under 35) leaving each year. Even amongst those aged 35 and over, the exit rate is 17 per cent. Amongst the younger renters the major destination is owner occupation, though the flow into social housing remains significant. Amongst older renters the flow into social housing is larger than that into owner occupation. Social housing is substantially more stable, though even here 8 per cent of the younger age group move out each year. Owner occupation is more stable still, and here it is notable both that the flows into social housing are extremely low, and that the exit rate amongst older owners is also particularly low.

While the flows from social housing and owner occupation are relatively small, they can be shown to be related to other life events, and to economic circumstances. Thus in **Table B.5** we show the exit rates from these two tenures amongst those aged 16 to 34 who experience a partnership break, and those who join with a partner. There is a particularly high exit rate from owner occupation associated with partnership breaks, and also to a lesser degree with partnership joins. Leaving social housing is particularly associated with partnership joins.

Table B.6 relates the departure rates from these tenures to the experience of unemployment in the previous year for those aged 16 to 34. While there is no significant association amongst social housing tenants, owners who have experienced unemployment in the past year are significantly more likely to leave the tenure.

Income dynamics

The BHPS also provides information about how individuals' incomes change from one year to another. Given the difficulties of income data collection and the particular unreliability of retrospective recall of income receipts, cross-sectional surveys are unable to establish this sort of evidence. Administrative databases on income in the United Kingdom are neither organised for this type of analysis, nor generally available to analysts.

Information on income mobility is clearly of substantial policy importance. Analyses from cross-sectional surveys, such as the Department of Social Security's (DSS) Households Below Average Income which is based on the Family Expenditure Survey, do not allow us to say how far it is the same people experiencing poverty or low income at each point in time. Neither do they allow us to discriminate between those whose period in low income or poverty is relatively transitory, and those for whom it is a more permanent state. Moreover cross-sectional data do not permit analysis of the factors which lead to income mobility. Panel data allow us to answer questions about the conditions under which individuals move between states. Answering these types of question has been one of the major motivations behind earlier panel studies in other countries, especially the Panel Study of Income Dynamics in the USA[3,4].

The BHPS collects information on income receipts from a wide range of sources from each member of respondent households at each wave. Household income is computed from these individual receipts. Income data are collected so as to be able to compute both latest monthly income and annual income. This means that with the panel data it is possible to measure continuous income over a number of years. In this section we focus mainly on the patterns of change between the first two years to show the levels of mobility, and its association with household and individual characteristics.

B.5

Adults[1] changing tenure[2]: by type of housing and type of partnership change, wave one to two and wave two to three

Great Britain Percentages

	Partnership break	No partnership break	Partnership join	No partnership join	All
From owner-occupied	*25*	*4*	*14*	*4*	*4*
From social housing	*15*	*8*	*26*	*8*	*9*

1 Aged 16 to 34.
2 Percentage of people in each tenure who undergo the experience and move.
Source: British Household Panel Survey, ESRC Research Centre on Micro-social Change

B.6

Adults[1] changing tenure[2]: by unemployment experience and type of housing, wave one to wave three

Great Britain Percentages

	Unemployment experienced	No unemployment experienced	All individuals
From owner-occupied	*10*	*4*	*5*
From social housing	*9*	*10*	*9*

1 Aged 16 to 34.
2 Percentage of people in each tenure who undergo the experience and move.
Source: British Household Panel Survey, ESRC Research Centre on Micro-social Change

B.7

Adults moving between different income groupings: by change in economic status and change in family type, wave one to wave two

Great Britain Percentages

	Family economic status		Family type		
	No change	Change	No change	Change	All adults
Income fell 3 or more quintiles	*1*	*4*	*2*	*4*	*2*
Income fell 2 quintiles	*3*	*7*	*4*	*5*	*4*
Income fell 1 quintile	*17*	*20*	*17*	*24*	*18*
Income in same quintile	*60*	*44*	*58*	*40*	*56*
Income rose 1 quintile	*16*	*17*	*16*	*17*	*16*
Income rose 2 quintiles	*3*	*5*	*3*	*5*	*3*
Income rose 3 or more quintiles	*1*	*4*	*1*	*4*	*1*
All individuals	*100*	*100*	*100*	*100*	*100*

Source: British Household Panel Survey, ESRC Research Centre on Micro-social Change

Given the previously mentioned changeability of household membership, longitudinal analysis must focus on the changes in the levels of household income which individuals experience across time. Any meaningful comparison over time must of course control for the effects of changes in household size and composition since, for example, an increase in income combined with an increase in the number of dependants, might mean an overall decline in spending power. So, to estimate an individual's effective command over goods and services, we adjust household income by an 'equivalence scale' reflecting the household size and composition. In this section we present data on both gross income before tax, and net income after tax, before housing costs. We use the same net income ranking based on individuals and equivalence scale definitions as in the DSS Households Below Average Income statistics[5]. While gross income is adequate for the analysis of income mobility, net income is more appropriate for studies focused on poverty and low income transitions.

To illustrate income mobility, Table 5.19 in the Income and Wealth chapter uses BHPS data to show the movements of individuals between the different quintile groups between 1991 and 1993. This mobility pattern may also be seen in **Table B.7** which shows the distribution of distances of moves measured by quintile group. The last column shows this distribution for all individuals. Overall, over half of people did not move quintile group between wave one and wave two while around a third moved to an adjacent group. As might be expected when looking at changes over only one year, there is substantial short distance mobility, but there is also some longer distance mobility evident.

Income mobility is associated with both changes in the economic status of the family to which the person belongs and with changes in family type. To illustrate this, the first and second columns of Table B.7 contrast individuals where the family economic activity status has changed, for example through job loss or job gain, or a shift between full-time and part-time work for one or more members of the family unit. As might be expected, there is clearly much greater mobility where there has been a change in economic status. More particularly it shows much higher levels of longer distance movement, and also some bias towards downward movement. Once again, when we contrast individuals who have experienced some change in family structure (such as through marriage or cohabitation, splits from a partner, or from the birth of a child) with those with no change, there is a much higher level of income mobility, and particularly more long distance mobility.

B.8

n order to examine factors associated with ncome mobility, we focus only on novements in and out of the lowest quintile roup. We can then classify people into four nobility categories: those in the bottom uintile at both waves; those in the bottom uintile at the first wave, but who escape by he second; those in the top 80 per cent of he distribution at the first wave, but who fall nto the lowest quintile at wave two; and inally those who stay in the top 80 per cent at both waves.

able B.8 shows the distribution of these four roups, by wave one characteristics. Overall around 12 per cent of people were in the bottom quintile at both waves while around 14 per cent were in this quintile at one wave or the other, though not both. Thus the proportion who persistently experience low ncome is substantially less that the size of he group at any point in time. There are marked differences in the rates of low ncome experience and flows in and out of he bottom quintile by both family type and amily economic activity status. Thus, as Table B.8 shows, there are few couples without children who either stay in the owest quintile or experience low income at either wave. By contrast single pensioners and lone parents are very likely to be found n the lowest quintile. Both these groups, but especially lone parents, are very likely to experience persistent low income and, relative to this group, the proportion of upward and downward movers is relatively small. By contrast single non-elderly persons without children, while having a lower than average overall experience of low income, have relatively high income mobility.

Adults moving between different net income groupings: by family type and family economic status, wave one to wave two

Great Britain Percentages

	Stay in bottom quintile	Upward movers	Downward movers	Stay in top four quintiles	All
Family type					
Single pensioner	*27*	*13*	*13*	*47*	*100*
Pensioner couple	*16*	*10*	*6*	*67*	*100*
Couple with children	*11*	*6*	*7*	*76*	*100*
Couple no children	*4*	*4*	*5*	*88*	*100*
Single with children	*39*	*11*	*14*	*37*	*100*
Single no children	*7*	*6*	*9*	*79*	*100*
Family economic status					
Self-employed	*6*	*5*	*9*	*80*	*100*
All employed full time	-	*1*	*3*	*95*	*100*
Couple, one employed full time, one employed part time	*2*	*2*	*6*	*90*	*100*
Couple, one employed full time, one not employed	*6*	*5*	*7*	*82*	*100*
Part-time employment only	*21*	*13*	*11*	*54*	*100*
All aged 60 and over	*24*	*12*	*11*	*54*	*100*
All unemployed	*47*	*22*	*9*	*21*	*100*
Other	*39*	*12*	*15*	*35*	*100*
All adults	*12*	*7*	*8*	*73*	*100*

Source: British Household Panel Survey, ESRC Research Centre on Micro-social Change

Economic activity status is also related to income mobility. Families where all adults were working full time at wave one are generally not found in the lowest quintile at wave one, but also show very low rates of downward mobility. Couples with one full-time and one part-time worker are again unlikely to be found in the lowest quintile, but experience somewhat more downward mobility, as do couples with only one worker. The self-employed show rather higher mobility into the lowest quintile than do employees. It is however families without full-time workers which experience both much higher rates of low income experience and also higher rates of mobility.

B.9

Adults moving between gross income groupings, wave one to wave two to wave three

Great Britain — Percentages

Wave one quintile group	Wave two quintile group	Wave three quintile group: Bottom	Top four	All
Bottom	Bottom	*10*	*3*	*13*
Bottom	Top four	*2*	*5*	*7*
Top four	Bottom	*4*	*3*	*7*
Top four	Top four	*4*	*69*	*73*
All	All	*20*	*80*	*100*

Source: British Household Panel Survey, ESRC Research Centre on Micro-social Change

We can extend this analysis to examine transitions over three waves. For the time being this must be carried out using gross income. A number of extra households from waves one and two are also available for this analysis since, while gross income imputations for households containing individual refusers are available at all waves, corresponding net income imputations are not yet available. We continue to use quintile groups as the unit, and **Table B.9** presents the distribution of movements in and out of the lowest quintile across the three waves.

Using the three waves of data the distinction between the number in low income at all waves and the number of low income households in at least one wave becomes sharper (10 per cent compared with 31 per cent). However the other point that emerges is that the probability of making a move is dependent on previous experience of low income. Thus between wave one and wave two, 9 per cent moved into the lowest quintile, while 34 per cent of those in the lowest quintile moved upwards. However if we examine the individuals in the top 80 per cent of the distribution at both wave one and wave two, then only 6 per cent are found to have fallen into the lowest group. Correspondingly, of the individuals in the lowest quintile at waves one and two, only 24 per cent experienced an upward move.

Employment dynamics

The BHPS data provide a year on year picture of the flows of individuals into and out of various employment states. The majority of employed individuals stay in the same state as they were in one year ago; 90 per cent of those in paid employment at one interview were also in paid employment one year earlier. A selection of the more minor flows are displayed in **Table B.10**. Some of these flows are small for the purposes of carrying out analyses but they can be pooled from a number of waves to provide larger samples. Comparing their status at waves one and two, 4 per cent of men and 3 per cent of women in paid work moved to unemployment over the year. (Unemployment is self-reported.) These are not the total numbers of individuals who experienced unemployment over the year; to these 89 men and 58 women who flowed into unemployment after wave one, it is

B.10

Transitions in employment status: by gender, wave one to two and wave two to three

Great Britain — Percentages

	Wave one to two		Wave two to three	
	Males	Females	Males	Females
Paid employment to unemployed	*4*	*3*	*4*	*2*
Self employed to unemployed	*4*	..	*4*	..
Self employed to employee	*9*	*20*	*8*	*11*
Paid employment to retired	*2*	*1*	*2*	*2*

Source: British Household Panel Survey, ESRC Research Centre on Micro-social Change

ossible to add a further 63 women and 96 nen who experienced unemployment etween the wave one and two interviews, ut who were not unemployed at either nterview. (Between waves two and three, 91 nen and 51 women had this experience of eing unemployed between the waves but vere in another employment state at each vave.) Thus there is a significant addition to he experience of unemployment by ombining the wave record with the ontinuous data from the interval between wo waves. The same phenomenon is isible for some of the other states of conomic activity.

Approximately similar proportions of men vho were employed as were self-employed lowed into unemployment from wave one to wo or two to three, at 4 per cent. Higher roportions of the self-employed at wave one or wave two, became employees by vave two or wave three respectively. Nomen were more likely than men to make his move. A relatively small proportion of nen and women moved from paid jobs to etirement in any one year, at 2 per cent of oth men and women, although onsiderably more moved into retirement rom other states.

Unemployment experiences

Men's experience of unemployment depends on unemployment levels over time, oarticularly for men without higher qualifications. As unemployment has tended, on average, to increase slowly since the 1950s with a more dramatic rise in the late 1980s and early 1990s, successive generations of this less well qualified group of men have experienced increasing levels

Duration of unemployment: by gender, working histories up to wave four

Great Britain

Percentages

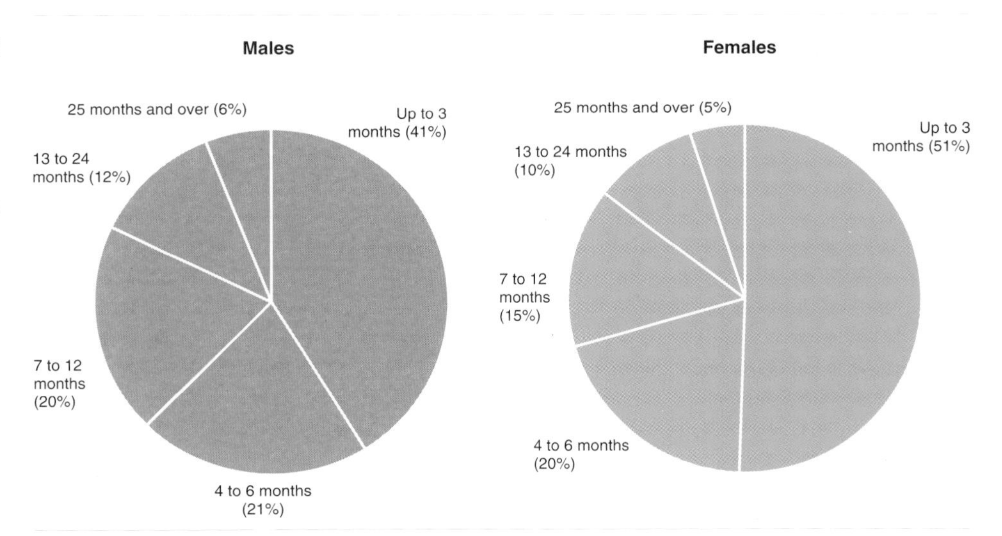

Source: British Household Panel Survey, ESRC Research Centre on Micro-social Change

of unemployment. To a lesser extent, generations of highly qualified men have also experienced rising levels of unemployment.

Just under two thirds of men and over three quarters of women did not record any unemployment periods between waves one and four. Of the men and women who did have a recorded spell of unemployment, the majority only had one spell. Having three or more spells of unemployment was relatively uncommon: 5 per cent of men but only 2 per cent of women recorded such experiences. The durations of the completed recorded periods of unemployment are shown in **Chart B.11**. The distributions of unemployment period durations are similar for men and women. Approximately 60 per cent of the unemployment periods for men and 70 per cent for women lasted for up to six months and 5 to 6 per cent were long-term unemployment durations lasting more than one year.

B.12

Time spent unemployed: by gender, between September 1990 and wave four

Great Britain		Percentages
	Males	Females
No time unemployed	*81*	*91*
Up to one third of time unemployed	*13*	*8*
Between one third and two thirds of time unemployed	*4*	*1*
More than two thirds of time unemployed	*2*	*1*
All	*100*	*100*

Source: British Household Panel Survey, ESRC Research Centre on Micro-social Change

Individuals' experiences of unemployment can be cumulated and the proportions of time spent unemployed from September 1990 to the wave 4 interview can be calculated. These percentages are displayed in **Table B.12**. The majority spent less than a third of this period unemployed. A tiny minority, approximately 1 per cent, had spent over two thirds of this period unemployed.

Uses and future research

The BHPS has always been intended to contribute to the formulation of public policy. Government departments were extensively consulted in the course of its preparation, and researchers from a number of departments were included in the Advisory Committee which established the basic instrument. There are a variety of policy applications. For example, movements in and out of the labour market can be tracked, including the factors influencing women's re-entry into the labour market after a period of caring for small children or elderly dependants. Income dynamics, such as mobility in and out of poverty, can also be examined as well as the related concern of benefit distribution, including the number of times people move in and out of benefit and the periods for which benefit is taken up. The information which BHPS provides on household and family dynamics (and the effect of household formation and dissolution on income) is of some importance in the area of social security policy, particularly in relation to processes by which one parent families are formed and the choices which lone parents make with regard to the labour market and child care. These are of course just examples chosen from among a much wider range of potential applications. The BHPS is a general purpose instrument designed to investigate longitudinal interconnections among very different aspects of individuals and household circumstances. And as the number of waves of data collection increases, so does the scope for investigation of these complex dynamic processes.

References

1 *The Reliability of Recall Data: A Literature Review:* Dex S, *Working papers of the ESRC Research Centre on Micro-social Change Paper 11,* Colchester: University of Essex, 1991; *Retrospective v Prospective Measurement of Life Histories in Longitudinal Research:* Scott J, and Allwin D, *Intersection of Personal and Social History,* Durham: Chapel Hill, 1995

2 *Longitudinal conceptions of households: fertile or futile?* Duncan G J, and Hill M, *Journal of Economic and Social Measurement,* 1985

3 *Slipping into and out of poverty; the dynamics of spells:* Bane M J, and Ellwood D T, *Journal of Human Resources,* 1986

4 *Years of Poverty, Years of Plenty:* Duncan G J, *Ann Arbour: Institute for Social Research,* 1984

5 *Households Below Average Income 1979-1992/93,* HMSO, 1995

Chapter 1 Population

Population change and structure

In mid-1994, the population of the United Kingdom was 58.4 million, one and a half times as many as at the beginning of the century. (Table 1.2)

The counties with the fastest growing populations are Cambridgeshire and Buckinghamshire, while the metropolitan areas tend to have falling populations. (Chart 1.4)

People under 16 and those aged 65 and over together made up more than a third of the UK population in 1994. (Table 1.5)

The number of people aged 80 and over in the United Kingdom more than doubled between 1961 and 1994, to 2.3 million. (Chart 1.1)

Births and deaths

In 1994 there were 751 thousand births and 626 thousand deaths in the United Kingdom. (Chart 1.12)

Death rates for men are generally higher than those for women in all age groups. (Table 1.14)

Migration

The South East lost the largest number of people due to net internal migration in 1994 whilst the South West had the largest gain. (Table 1.15)

World population

The world's population stood at 5.7 billion in mid-1995 and is projected to reach 10 billion in 2050. (Page 46)

1.1

Population aged 60 and over: by age

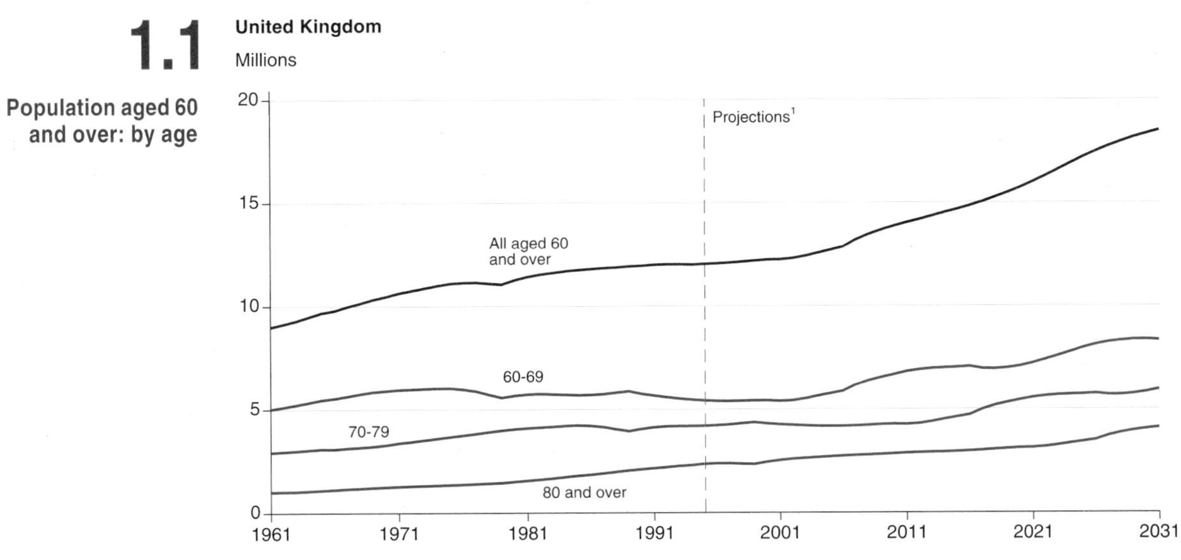

1 1992-based projections.

Source: Office of Population Censuses and Surveys; Government Actuary's Department; General Register Office (Scotland); General Register Office (Northern Ireland)

1.2

Population change[1]

United Kingdom | Thousands

	Population at start of period	Average annual change: Live births	Deaths	Net natural change	Other[2]	Overall annual change
Census enumerated						
1901-1911	38,237	1,091	624	467	-82	385
1911-1921	42,082	975	689	286	-92	194
1921-1931	44,027	824	555	268	-67	201
1931-1951	46,038	785	598	188	25	213
Mid-year estimates						
1951-1961	50,287	839	593	246	6	252
1961-1971	52,807	963	639	324	-12	312
1971-1981	55,928	736	666	69	-27	42
1981-1991	56,352	757	655	103	43	146
1991-1994	57,808	773	642	132	64	196
Mid-year projections[3]						
1994-2001	58,395	776	622	154	49	203
2001-2011	59,800	716	614	102	44	146
2011-2021	61,257	718	635	83	6	89
2021-2031	62,146	703	693	9	0	9

1 See Appendix, Part 1: Population and population projections.
2 Includes net civilian migration and other adjustments.
3 1992-based projections.

Source: Office of Population Censuses and Surveys; Government Actuary's Department; General Register Office (Scotland); General Register Office (Northern Ireland)

1.3

Population[1] of the United Kingdom

Thousands

	1961	1971	1981	1991	1994	2001	2031
England	43,561	46,412	46,821	48,208	48,707	50,023	52,435
Wales	2,635	2,740	2,813	2,891	2,913	2,966	2,977
Scotland	5,184	5,236	5,180	5,107	5,132	5,143	4,998
Northern Ireland	1,427	1,540	1,538	1,601	1,642	1,667	1,831
United Kingdom	52,807	55,928	56,352	57,808	58,395	59,800	62,241

1 Data are mid-year estimates for 1961 to 1994 and 1992-based projections for 2001 and 2031. See Appendix, Part 1: Population and population projections.

Source: Office of Population Censuses and Surveys; Government Actuary's Department; General Register Office (Scotland); General Register Office (Northern Ireland)

Information on the size and structure of the population of the country is vital in understanding many other aspects of society such as the labour market and household composition; it also affects the demand for the provision of various services including health care, social security benefits and education.

Population change and structure

In 1994 the population of the United Kingdom was 58.4 million people, an increase of just over half since the beginning of the century **(Table 1.2)**. The fastest period of growth was in the first decade when the average annual increase was 385 thousand; population growth was again fairly rapid in the 1960s, mainly due to the 'baby boom'. In contrast, between 1971 and 1981 a sharp decrease in births led to the smallest overall average change seen this century of just 42 thousand per year. An even lower annual increase, of 9 thousand per year, is projected for the period 2021 to 2031. The United Kingdom population as a whole is projected to peak at 62.3 million in 2027.

The rate at which the population changes is dependent on the natural change (that is, the difference between the number of births and deaths) and the net effect of migration. Around 85 per cent of the growth in the population over the last 20 or so years is the result of net natural increase. The other factor which contributes to population change is migration; this is dealt with in greater detail later in the chapter.

Between 1961 and 1994 the population of the United Kingdom increased by nearly 11 per cent **(Table 1.3)**. However, there were wide variations between the constituent countries. In Northern Ireland the population rose by 15 per cent, while it increased by 12 per cent in England and 11 per cent in Wales. In Scotland however the population was actually 1 per cent lower in 1994 than in 1961, although it has experienced small increases in each of the last six years. In 1994, 83 per cent of the people in the United Kingdom lived in England, 9 per cent lived in Scotland, 5 per cent in Wales and 3 per cent in Northern Ireland.

Chart 1.4 shows that there have also been wide variations in population change within the four countries of the United Kingdom. The areas which are shaded red on the chart are those in which the population increased between 1984 and 1994; those shaded in blue experienced a fall. While the average annual growth rate for the United Kingdom was 0.3 per cent over this period, East Anglia experienced the highest average annual growth rate of all the regions of more than double this amount at 0.8 per cent, a total gain of 8.5 per cent over the decade. The counties with the biggest population increases were Cambridgeshire and Buckinghamshire. It was the metropolitan areas that tended to lose population; for example, Merseyside lost 0.4 per cent per year. However there were small increases in Greater London and West Yorkshire. Most of the projected population increase up to 2011 is expected to occur in non-metropolitan areas.

In common with most of Western Europe the United Kingdom has an ageing population. In 1961 just under 12 per cent of the United Kingdom's population were aged 65 or over; by 1994 this had increased to 16 per cent (**Table 1.5**). In contrast the population aged under 16 fell from a quarter in 1961 to around a fifth in 1994. This trend is projected to continue, so that in 2031 those under 16 are expected to make up just under 18 per cent of the population while those aged 65 and over will comprise around 23 per cent. Major factors contributing to this include the downward trend in the number of births and increasing longevity.

Chart 1.1 at the front of the chapter shows that the overall numbers of those aged 60 and over has risen by a third since 1961 to 12 million people; this is projected to continue to rise by over half to reach more than 18 million in 2031. However, within this group there has been a sharper increase among the very elderly. The proportion of the over 60s who are aged 80 and over

1.4

Population change: by area, mid-1984 to mid-1994

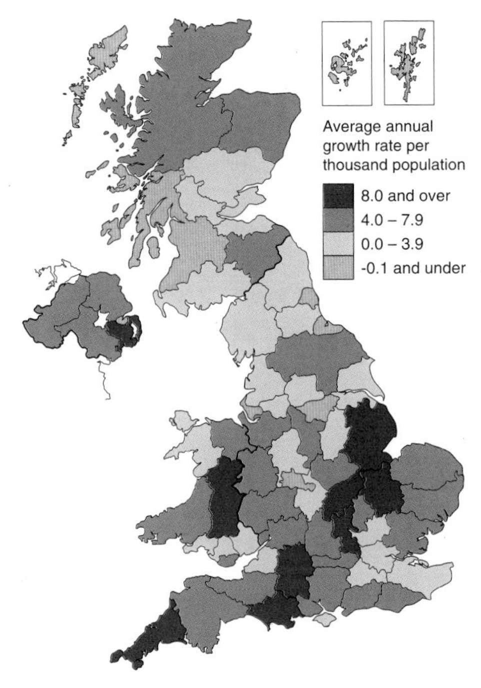

Source: Office of Population Censuses and Surveys; General Register Office (Scotland); General Register Office (Northern Ireland)

1.5

Population[1]: by age and gender

United Kingdom — Percentages

	Under 16	16-39	40-64	65-79	80 and over	All ages (=100%) (millions)
Mid-year estimates						
1961	*25*	*31*	*32*	*10*	*2*	52.8
1971	*25*	*31*	*30*	*11*	*2*	55.9
1981	*22*	*35*	*28*	*12*	*3*	56.4
1991	*20*	*35*	*29*	*12*	*4*	57.8
1994	*21*	*35*	*29*	*12*	*4*	58.4
Males	*22*	*36*	*29*	*11*	*2*	28.6
Females	*20*	*33*	*29*	*13*	*5*	29.8
Mid-year projections[2]						
2001	*21*	*33*	*31*	*11*	*4*	59.8
2011	*19*	*30*	*34*	*12*	*5*	61.3
2021	*18*	*30*	*33*	*14*	*5*	62.1
2031	*18*	*28*	*30*	*16*	*7*	62.2
Males	*19*	*29*	*31*	*16*	*5*	30.9
Females	*18*	*28*	*30*	*17*	*8*	31.3

1 See Appendix, Part 1: Population and population projections.
2 1992-based projections.

Source: Office of Population Censuses and Surveys; Government Actuary's Department; General Register Office (Scotland); General Register Office (Northern Ireland)

1.6

Dependent population[1]: EC comparison, 1994

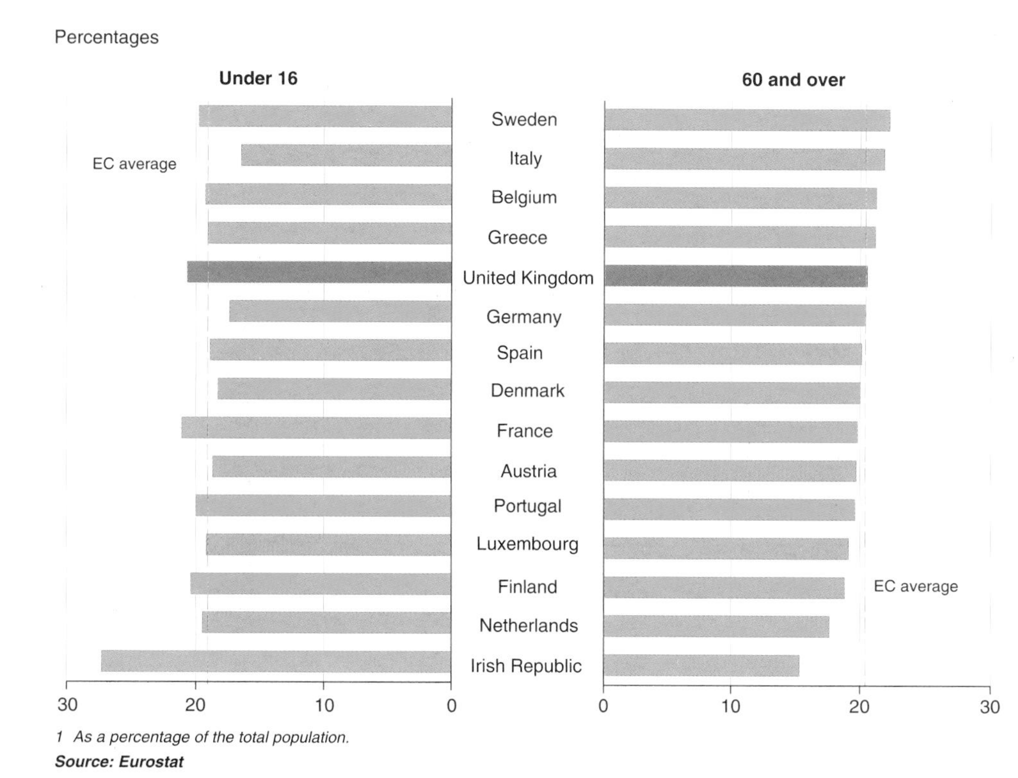

1 As a percentage of the total population.
Source: Eurostat

increased from 11 per cent in 1961, to 19 per cent in 1994 and is projected to increase to 22 per cent by 2031. These projected increases have implications for the provision of pensions and health care. Further information on services provided for the elderly is given in Chapter 8: Social Protection.

The population over retirement age, together with the population under working age, form the dependent population: a crude measure of the number of people who are supported economically by those of working age. **Chart 1.6** compares the proportions of the population which are under 16 and over 60 throughout the European Community (EC). The Irish Republic had the largest proportion of its population in these age groups in 1994, at nearly 43 per cent; Sweden and the United Kingdom had the next highest proportions. The Netherlands had the lowest proportion at just 37 per cent. The Irish Republic had the youngest age structure in 1994, with 27 per cent aged under 16 and just 15 per cent aged 60 and over. On the other hand, Italy had the oldest age structure: the over 60s represented 22 per cent of the whole population while the under 16s comprised around 16 per cent.

The age structure also varies among the different ethnic groups in Great Britain: the ethnic minority population has a younger age structure than the White population. For example, in Spring 1995 the under 30s represented nearly seven in ten of the Pakistani/Bangladeshi group compared with just under four in ten of those in the White group **(Table 1.7)**. Overall people from ethnic minority groups represented just under 6 per cent of the population of Great Britain in Spring 1995.

1.7

Population: by ethnic group and age, Spring 1995

Great Britain Percentages

	Under 16	16-29	30-44	45-59	60 and over	All ages (=100%) (thousands)
Ethnic minority group						
Black[1]	*29.0*	*25.5*	*27.0*	*11.3*	*7.2*	869
Indian	*25.3*	*26.0*	*25.5*	*16.0*	*7.2*	844
Pakistani/Bangladeshi	*40.6*	*26.4*	*19.4*	*9.3*	*4.3*	725
Other[2]	*37.2*	*23.3*	*26.0*	*9.6*	*3.9*	773
All ethnic minority groups	*32.6*	*25.3*	*24.6*	*11.7*	*5.8*	3,211
White	*20.1*	*19.0*	*21.6*	*18.3*	*20.9*	52,844
All ethnic groups[3]	*20.9*	*19.4*	*21.8*	*18.0*	*20.1*	56,072

1 Includes Caribbean, African and other Black people of non-mixed origin.
2 Includes Chinese, other ethnic minority groups of non-mixed origin and those of mixed origin.
3 Includes ethnic group not stated.
Source: Labour Force Survey, Central Statistical Office

The Spring 1994 Labour Force Survey found that almost eight in ten members of the ethnic minority population aged under 25 were born in the United Kingdom compared with just over a fifth of those aged 25 and over. There were higher proportions of people from ethnic minority groups living in metropolitan areas, particularly Greater London and the West Midlands, than in other areas. Information from the 1991 Census shows that outside metropolitan areas the proportion of people from ethnic minority groups is generally small; notable exceptions are Leicester, Slough and Luton.

In 1995 the Office of Population Censuses and Surveys introduced a new socio-economic classification of the areas of Great Britain which provides a simple and effective way of showing characteristics of areas. This classification is used in **Chart 1.8** to show the distribution of these areas throughout Great Britain. According to this classification, just under a fifth of the population live in rural areas which, as might be expected, tend to have a predominance of agricultural work. These areas include the Highlands and Islands of Scotland, the remoter parts of England and Wales and towns in rural areas. A fifth of the population live in urban centres which are typified by higher than average proportions of people using public transport for work and a lower than average proportion of households that have cars. Manufacturing Pennine towns, such as Bolton, and some areas with large concentrations of people from ethnic minority groups, such as Bradford, are included in this classification. Further information on the area classification is given in the Appendix, Part 1: Area classifications.

A breakdown of the economically active population by social class, a classification based on occupational status, is given in **Chart 1.9**. This shows that men are much more likely than women to be in the professional group: nearly 8 per cent of men in the United Kingdom in Spring 1995 were in this group compared with around 2 per cent of women. Women, on the other hand, are more likely to be in the skilled non-manual category: more than a third of women were in this group compared with only a tenth of men.

1.8

Population: by type of area, 1994

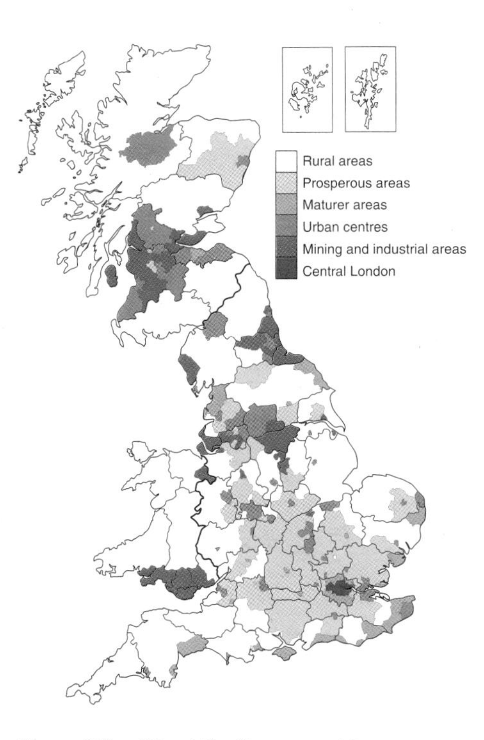

Source: Office of Population Censuses and Surveys; General Register Office (Scotland)

1.9

Population[1]: by social class, Spring 1995

United Kingdom

Percentages

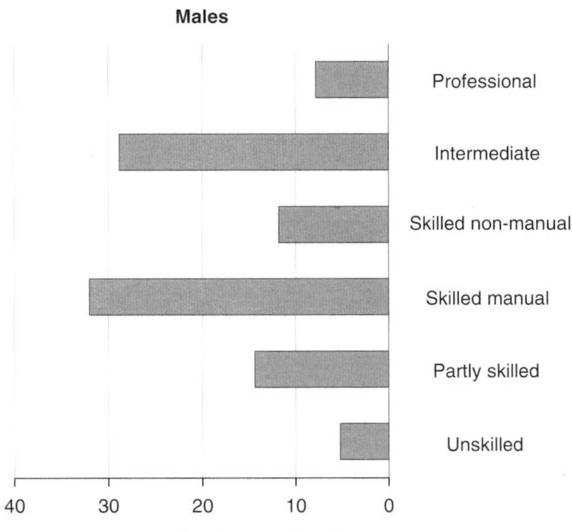

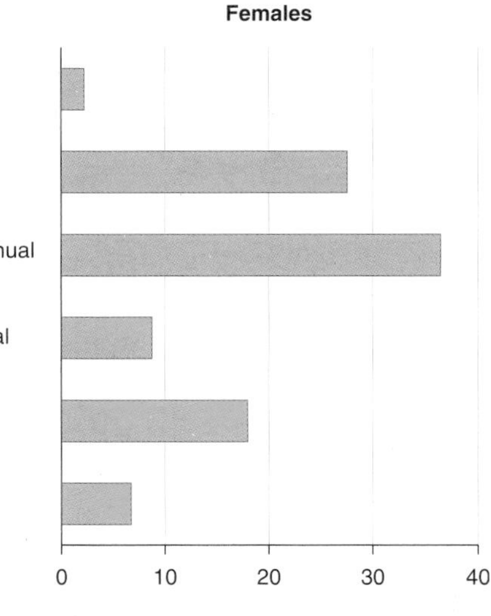

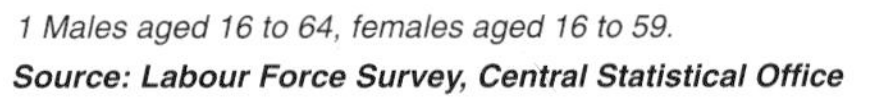

1 Males aged 16 to 64, females aged 16 to 59.

Source: Labour Force Survey, Central Statistical Office

1.10

Marital status of the population: by gender and age, 1993-94

Great Britain Percentages

	16-24	25-34	35-44	45-54	55-64	65-74	75 and over	All aged 16 and over
Males								
Married	*4*	*54*	*76*	*81*	*81*	*79*	*63*	*62*
Cohabiting	*7*	*14*	*6*	*3*	*2*	*1*	-	*6*
Single	*88*	*29*	*12*	*8*	*7*	*6*	*7*	*24*
Widowed	-	-	-	*1*	*4*	*10*	*28*	*4*
Divorced	-	*2*	*4*	*5*	*5*	*3*	*1*	*3*
Separated	-	*1*	*2*	*1*	*1*	*1*	*1*	*1*
All males	*100*	*100*	*100*	*100*	*100*	*100*	*100*	*100*
Females								
Married	*12*	*60*	*73*	*78*	*73*	*52*	*23*	*56*
Cohabiting	*12*	*12*	*4*	*3*	*1*	-	-	*5*
Single	*75*	*19*	*7*	*3*	*5*	*8*	*9*	*18*
Widowed	-	-	*1*	*4*	*14*	*35*	*65*	*14*
Divorced	*1*	*5*	*10*	*10*	*6*	*4*	*2*	*6*
Separated	*1*	*3*	*4*	*3*	*1*	*1*	-	*2*
All females	*100*	*100*	*100*	*100*	*100*	*100*	*100*	*100*

Source: General Household Survey, Office of Population Censuses and Surveys

The 1993-94 General Household Survey found that men formed a larger proportion than women of single people. On the other hand, women made up the largest proportion of the divorced and separated which is due to a higher proportion of men than women remarrying or cohabiting following divorce. Overall nearly seven in ten men and six in ten women were living with a partner in 1993-94 **(Table 1.10)**. Cohabitation is more common among younger age groups; 14 per cent of men and 12 per cent of women aged 25 to 34 were cohabiting in 1993-94. The under 25s are the most likely to be single - overall eight in ten people of that age were single. Further information on cohabitation is included in Chapter 2: Households and Families.

Births and deaths

The total period fertility rate (TPFR) measures the average number of children that would be born to each woman if the current age specific birth rates persisted throughout her child-bearing life. It is a more reliable measure of current fertility than crude birth rates as it is not affected by changes in the size and age structure of the female population. However, trends in the TPFR are affected by the ages at which women have children. The TPFR peaked at 2.95 in 1964 and then fell rapidly to a low point of 1.69 in 1977 since when it has been more stable **(Chart 1.11)**. In 1994 it was 1.75 which was well below the rate of 2.1 which is associated with long-term population

1.11

Total period fertility rate[1]

United Kingdom

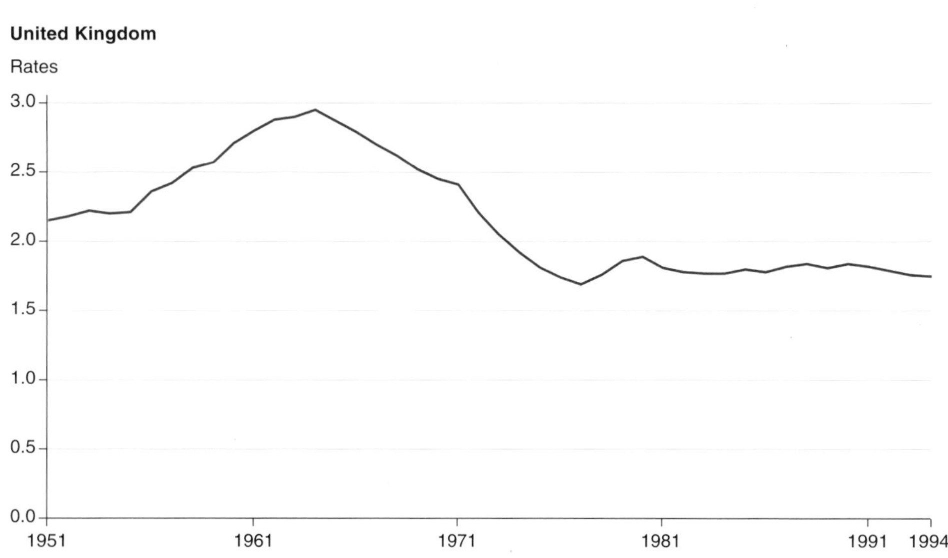

1 The average number of children which would be born per woman if women experienced the age specific fertility rates of the period in question throughout their child-bearing lifespan.

Source: Office of Population Censuses and Surveys; General Register Office (Scotland); General Register Office (Northern Ireland)

replacement. Further information on fertility is also given in the Households and Families chapter.

The annual number of births in the United Kingdom has only exceeded 1 million twice since 1931 - in the post-war baby boom of 1947, and again in 1964 **(Chart 1.12)**. Since the mid-1980s the number of births each year has remained at around three quarters of a million. In 1994 there were 751 thousand births and 626 thousand deaths in the United Kingdom. Deaths have only exceeded births once in recent years, in 1976. Projections from the Government Actuary's Department predict that deaths will again slightly exceed births from 2027.

Between mid-1993 and mid-1994, July was the most common month for births, when there were 66 thousand **(Chart 1.13)**. February was the least common month, but this is due to its shortness; the month with the lowest average births per day was November. In 1994, the most common name given to baby girls in England and Wales was Rebecca, followed by Lauren and Jessica. For baby boys, Thomas was the most common name followed by James and Jack. In Scotland Lauren was the most common girls' name while for boys it was Ryan. The number of deaths at different times of the year is affected by, among other factors, the weather and epidemics. Between mid-1993 and mid-1994 December was the peak month for deaths accounting for 10 per cent of all deaths in the year.

1.12

Births and deaths

United Kingdom

Millions

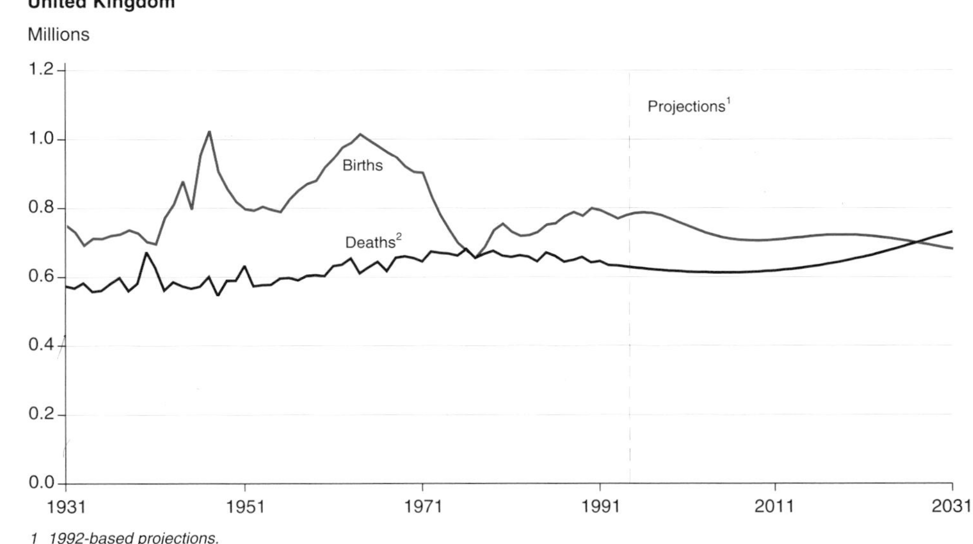

1 1992-based projections.
2 Includes deaths of non-civilians and merchant seamen who died outside the country.
Source: Office of Population Censuses and Surveys; Government Actuary's Department; General Register Office (Scotland); General Register Office (Northern Ireland)

1.13

Births and deaths per month, 1993-1994

United Kingdom

Thousands

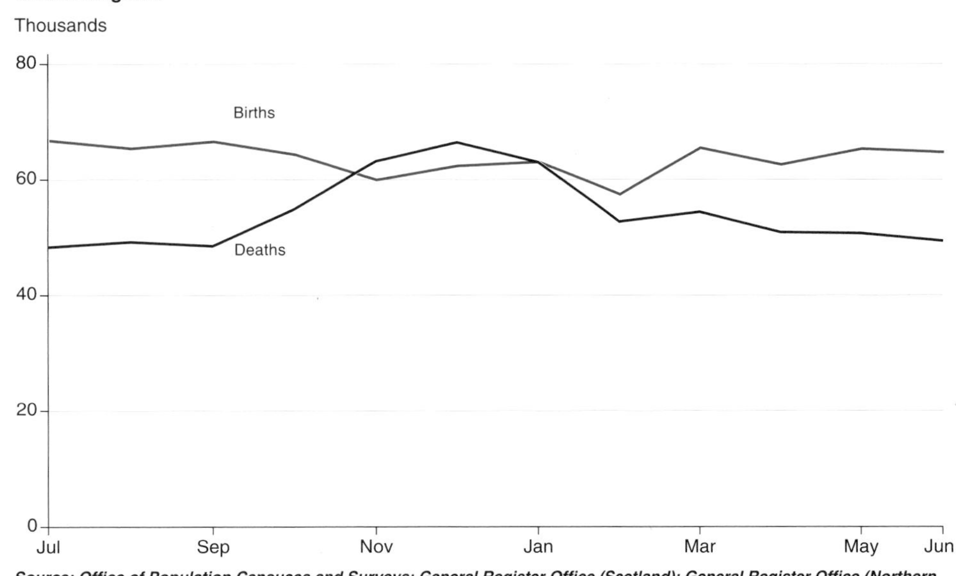

Source: Office of Population Censuses and Surveys; General Register Office (Scotland); General Register Office (Northern Ireland)

1.14

Deaths: by gender and age

United Kingdom								Rates
	Death rates per 1,000 in each age group							All deaths (thousands)
	Under 1[1]	1-15	16-39	40-64	65-79	80 and over	All ages	
Males								
1961	26.3	0.6	1.3	11.7	65.7	193.5	12.6	322.0
1971	20.2	0.5	1.1	11.4	59.9	174.0	12.1	328.5
1981	12.7	0.4	1.0	10.1	56.1	167.5	12.0	329.1
1991	8.3	0.3	1.0	7.3	48.2	148.2	11.1	314.4
1994	6.9	0.2	0.9	6.6	44.7	141.4	10.6	302.1
Females								
1961	18.2	0.7	0.8	6.5	41.0	156.8	11.4	309.8
1971	15.5	0.4	0.6	6.3	35.3	138.0	11.0	316.5
1981	9.6	0.3	0.5	5.8	32.1	126.2	11.4	328.8
1991	6.3	0.2	0.5	4.5	29.1	112.2	11.2	331.8
1994	5.4	0.2	0.5	4.1	27.5	108.6	10.9	323.8

1 Rate per 1,000 live births.

Source: Office of Population Censuses and Surveys; General Register Office (Scotland); General Register Office (Northern Ireland)

In general death rates in all age groups for men are higher than those for women **(Table 1.14)**. There were 5 per cent fewer deaths in 1994 than in 1993, at 626 thousand. Among men the crude death rate, which takes no account of the age structure of the population, fell from 12.6 per thousand population in 1961 to 10.6 in 1994. In 1961 the female crude death rate was 11.4. Since then the gap between the crude death rates for men and women has narrowed and since 1991 the female rate has exceeded that for males. The different age structures for men and women explain this apparent anomaly.

1.15

Migration[1] within the United Kingdom: inter-regional movements, 1994

													Thousands
	Region of origin												
	United Kingdom	North	Yorkshire & Humberside	East Midlands	East Anglia	South East	South West	West Midlands	North West	England	Wales	Scotland	Northern Ireland
Region of destination													
United Kingdom	.	52	92	86	51	253	104	95	105	106	50	49	12
North	46	.	9	4	2	11	3	3	8	40	1	5	1
Yorkshire & Humberside	88	11	.	14	4	22	6	8	16	79	3	5	1
East Midlands	96	4	17	.	7	31	7	14	10	89	3	3	1
East Anglia	60	2	4	7	.	32	4	3	3	56	1	2	-
South East	237	13	24	27	24	.	53	29	30	201	16	17	3
South West	128	3	7	8	4	67	.	14	9	114	9	5	1
West Midlands	85	3	7	11	3	26	12	.	11	74	7	3	1
North West	94	8	15	8	3	26	7	11	.	79	8	6	2
England	103	45	84	79	47	216	91	83	87	.	48	46	9
Wales	52	1	3	3	1	15	8	8	10	50	.	2	-
Scotland	52	6	5	3	2	17	4	3	7	47	2	.	3
Northern Ireland	11	-	1	-	-	4	1	1	1	9	-	2	.

1 Data are based on patient movements recorded by the National Health Service Central Registers at Southport and Edinburgh and the Central Services Agency in Belfast.

Source: Office of Population Censuses and Surveys; General Register Office (Scotland); General Register Office (Northern Ireland)

Migration

Changes in regional populations within the United Kingdom are caused not just by births and deaths, but also by international migration and movements of people within the country. Migration within the United Kingdom, which is shown in **Table 1.15**, is estimated using information on registrations with General Practitioners. In 1994 both England and Northern Ireland experienced a small net loss of population, while Scotland and Wales had small gains. The biggest fall of all the English regions occurred in the South East which lost around 16 thousand people. However, this was less than in the previous two years. The South West had by far the largest net gain of population of 24 thousand; the only other English regions to gain population were the East Midlands and East Anglia.

Migration between the United Kingdom and other countries is estimated using information from three sources: the International Passenger Survey; Home Office data on people who entered the United Kingdom as short-term visitors but were subsequently allowed to stay for a year or more; and estimates of migration between the United Kingdom and Irish Republic. Between 1990 and 1993 an average of 300 thousand people entered the United Kingdom each year to stay - around 9 per cent more than had done so between 1986 and 1989 **(Table 1.16)**. The number of British citizens leaving the country to live abroad each year remained steady over the two periods. The table includes migration between the United Kingdom and the Irish Republic in the figures for EC citizens. Between 1986 and 1989 EC citizens accounted for over a third of the net gain of non-British citizens, compared with under a twentieth in 1990 to 1993.

1.16

Average annual international migration[1] into, and out of, the United Kingdom: by citizenship

United Kingdom — Thousands

	1986-1989			1990-1993		
	Inflow	Outflow	Balance	Inflow	Outflow	Balance
Non-British						
European Community	57	30	27	46	42	4
Old Commonwealth	23	18	5	26	18	8
New Commonwealth	46	15	30	57	15	42
Other foreign	55	38	17	76	42	33
All non-British citizens	180	102	78	205	117	88
British citizens	103	132	-29	103	132	-30
All countries	283	234	50	308	250	58

1 Includes adjustments for people admitted as short-term visitors who are subsequently granted an extension of stay. Also includes migration between the United Kingdom and the Irish Republic which has been included under EC citizenship. See Appendix, Part 1: International migration estimates.

Source: Office of Population Censuses and Surveys

As part of the International Passenger Survey, migrants between the United Kingdom and other countries are asked for the reason why they are visiting (see Appendix, Part 1: International migration estimates). The most common reason stated by immigrants in 1990 to 1993 was to accompany or join a partner in the United Kingdom: a third gave this reason **(Table 1.17)**. However, these figures should be

1.17

Average annual international migration[1]: by main reason for migration

United Kingdom — Thousands

	1986-1989			1990-1993		
	Inflow	Outflow	Balance	Inflow	Outflow	Balance
Work related	41	47	-6	44	62	-18
Accompany/join	72	58	13	79	64	15
Formal study	35	6	29	46	10	36
Other[2]	24	20	4	36	39	-3
No reason stated	60	85	-25	34	52	-18
All reasons	232	216	16	240	227	12

1 Derived from International Passenger Survey migration estimates only. See also Appendix, Part 1: International migration estimates.
2 Includes looking for work.

Source: Office of Population Censuses and Surveys

1.18

UK nationals living in other EC states[1] and nationals of other EC states living in the United Kingdom[1], 1993

Thousands

	UK nationals living in other EC states	EC nationals living in the United Kingdom
Irish Republic	56	466
Italy	28	73
Germany	107	51
France[2]	50	42
Spain	53	32
Greece	21	25
Netherlands	44	22
Portugal	9	15
Sweden	11	12
Denmark	11	9
Finland	2	8
Austria[3]	3	7
Belgium	25	6
All	424	768

1 Data are not available for Luxembourg.
2 Data relate to 1990.
3 Data relate to 1991.
Source: Eurostat

1.19

Acceptances for settlement: by region of origin and category of acceptance

United Kingdom Thousands

	1984	1986	1991	1993	1994
Asia	22.7	22.8	25.2	25.8	25.9
Africa	4.4	4.1	9.6	10.9	11.9
Americas	6.4	6.4	7.2	7.6	7.9
Europe[1]	6.4	5.2	5.6	5.0	4.6
Oceania	6.0	5.4	2.4	2.6	2.8
Other[2]	5.0	3.8	3.9	3.6	1.9
All regions	51.0	47.8	53.9	55.6	55.1
Of which					
Wives	16.7	14.1	19.0	19.1	18.1
Husbands	5.6	6.8	11.6	12.0	12.1
Children	11.1	10.3	9.1	8.6	9.3
Four years' employment	4.0	3.3	3.4	3.8	4.4
Refugees	1.3	1.5	0.8	2.8	2.4
Other	12.4	11.8	10.1	9.3	8.9

1 Includes all EEA countries throughout the period covered. EEA nationals are not obliged to seek settlement and the figures just relate to those who chose to do so.
2 Data for 1984 to 1993 include acceptances where the country was not separately identified. In 1994 these are included in the relevant geographical areas.
Source: Home Office

treated with caution because many people do not give a reason for their migration, other than migration itself.

In 1993 there were over 460 thousand nationals from the Irish Republic living in the United Kingdom; this was more than the total number of UK nationals living in other EC states **(Table 1.18)**. Overall around 420 thousand UK nationals were living in other EC countries; around a quarter were living in Germany, with the Irish Republic and Spain being the next most common places.

In 1994, just over 55 thousand people were accepted for settlement in the United Kingdom **(Table 1.19)**, slightly fewer than the number accepted in 1993. In 1994, 47 per cent of those accepted were from Asia, while 22 per cent were from Africa. Wives and husbands with partners already in the United Kingdom continue to be the most common categories of acceptance, although the number of wives accepted has fallen since 1993 whilst the number of husbands has risen slightly. Over the last ten years, the number of husbands accepted has more than doubled; acceptances of refugees increased by 87 per cent over the same period. On the other hand, acceptances of children have decreased in the last ten years.

World population

In mid-1995 the world population was 5.7 billion and this is projected to rise to 8.3 billion by 2025 and 10 billion by 2050, according to world population indicators compiled by the United Nations **(Table 1.20)**. Although population growth rates worldwide have fallen and are projected to continue to do so, world population is increasing by more than 86 million per year and this is likely to remain at this rate until 2015. While it took 123 years for world population to increase from 1 billion to 2 billion, the succeeding increments of 1 billion took 33 years, 14 years and 13 years respectively. The world's population is expected to break the 6 billion barrier in 1998, just 11 years after reaching 5 billion.

The world is steadily becoming more urbanised. In 1995, around 45 per cent of the world's population lived in cities; by 2015 this is projected to rise to over 56 per cent, with the most rapid rates of urbanisation being in developing countries. In 1975, just over a quarter of the population in developing regions lived in urban areas and this is projected to rise to half by 2015. This change will place enormous strain on existing social services and infrastructure, much of which will not be able to expand at the same rate as that of urbanisation.

1.20

World population indicators

	Population (millions)		Growth rate (percentages)	1995				
				Percentage urban	Infant mortality[1]	Fertility rate per woman[2]	Life expectancy	
	1995	2025	1995-2000				Males	Females
Europe	727.0	718.2	*0.1*	*74*	12	1.6	69	77
European Community								
Austria	8.0	8.3	*0.4*	*56*	6	1.6	74	80
Belgium	10.1	10.4	*0.3*	*97*	6	1.7	74	81
Denmark	5.2	5.1	*0.1*	*85*	7	1.7	73	79
Finland	5.1	5.4	*0.4*	*63*	5	1.9	73	80
France	58.0	61.2	*0.4*	*73*	7	1.7	74	81
Germany	81.6	76.4	-	*87*	6	1.3	74	80
Greece	10.5	9.9	*0.2*	*65*	9	1.4	76	81
Irish Republic	3.6	3.9	*0.3*	*58*	7	2.1	73	79
Italy	57.2	52.3	-	*67*	7	1.3	75	81
Netherlands	15.5	16.3	*0.6*	*89*	6	1.6	75	81
Portugal	9.8	9.7	-	*36*	9	1.6	72	79
Spain	39.6	37.6	*0.1*	*76*	7	1.2	75	81
Sweden	8.8	9.8	*0.4*	*83*	5	2.1	76	82
United Kingdom	58.3	61.5	*0.3*	*90*	6	1.8	74	79
Other Northern & Southern Europe								
Albania	3.4	4.7	*1.0*	*37*	26	2.8	70	76
Bosnia & Herzegovina	3.5	4.5	*4.5*	*49*	13	1.6	70	76
Croatia	4.5	4.2	*-0.3*	*64*	9	1.6	68	76
Estonia	1.5	1.4	*-0.5*	*73*	16	1.6	64	75
Latvia	2.6	2.3	*-0.7*	*73*	14	1.6	63	75
Lithuania	3.7	3.8	-	*72*	13	1.8	65	76
Macedonia	2.2	2.6	*0.8*	*60*	24	2.0	70	76
Norway	4.3	4.7	*0.4*	*73*	7	2.0	74	81
Slovenia	1.9	1.8	-	*64*	7	1.5	69	78
Switzerland	7.2	7.8	*0.8*	*61*	6	1.6	75	82
Yugoslavia (former)	10.8	11.5	*-0.3*	*57*	18	2.0	70	75
Eastern Europe	308.7	299.4	*-0.1*	*70*	17	1.6	64	74
North America	292.8	369.6	*0.9*	*76*	7	2.1	74	80
Canada	29.5	38.3	*1.0*	*77*	6	1.9	75	81
United States	263.3	331.2	*0.9*	*76*	7	2.1	73	80
Africa	728.1	1,495.8	*2.7*	*34*	85	5.6	53	56
Asia	3,458.0	4,960.0	*1.5*	*35*	57	3.0	65	68
Of which: China	1,221.5	1,526.1	*1.0*	*30*	38	2.0	68	72
Latin America and Caribbean	482.0	709.8	*1.7*	*74*	41	3.0	67	72
Oceania	28.5	41.0	*1.4*	*70*	24	2.5	71	76
Of which: Australia	18.1	24.7	*1.2*	*85*	6	1.9	75	81
New Zealand	3.6	4.4	*1.0*	*86*	8	2.1	73	79
World	5,716.4	8,294.3	*1.5*	*45*	57	3.0	64	68
More developed[3]	1,166.6	1,238.4	*0.3*	*75*	9	1.7	71	79
Less developed[4]	4,549.8	7,055.9	*1.8*	*38*	63	3.4	62	65

1 Per thousand live births.
2 Total period fertility rate. The average number of children which would be born per woman if women experienced the age specific fertility rates of the period in question throughout their child-bearing span.
3 Europe, North America, Australia, New Zealand and Japan.
4 Africa, Latin America, Asia (excluding Japan) and Melanesia, Micronesia and Polynesia.

Source: United Nations

References and further reading

The following list contains selected publications relevant to **Chapter 1: Population**. Those published by HMSO are available from the addresses shown on the inside back cover of *Social Trends.*

Annual Report of the Registrar General for Northern Ireland, HMSO
Annual Report of the Registrar General for Scotland, General Register Office (Scotland)
Birth Statistics (Series FM1), HMSO
Control of Immigration: Statistics - United Kingdom, HMSO
Demographic Statistics, Eurostat
Demographic Yearbook, United Nations
First Names, HMSO
General Household Survey, HMSO
International Migration Statistics (Series MN), HMSO
Key Population and Vital Statistics (Series VS/PP1), HMSO
Labour Force Survey, HMSO
Migration Statistics, Eurostat
Mortality Statistics for England and Wales (Series DH1, 2, 3, 4, 5, 6), HMSO
National Population Projections (Series PP2), HMSO
Population Estimates, Scotland, HMSO
Population Projections for the Counties and District Health Authorities of Wales, Welsh Office
Population Projections, Scotland (for Standard Areas), General Register Office (Scotland)
Population Trends, HMSO
Regional Trends, HMSO
Social Focus on Women, HMSO
Subnational Population Projections - England (Series PP3), HMSO
The State of World Population, UNFPA

Contacts

Telephone contact points for further information relating to
Chapter 1: Population

Office of Population Censuses and Surveys	0171 396 2828
General Register Office (Northern Ireland)	01232 252031
General Register Office (Scotland)	0131 314 4301
Government Actuary's Department	0171 242 6828 extn 381
Home Office	0181 760 8631
Central Statistical Office	
Labour market statistics	0171 273 5585
Eurostat	00 352 4301 34567

Chapter 2 Households and Families

Households

More than a quarter of households in Great Britain in 1994-95 consisted of one person living alone, almost double the proportion in 1961. (Table 2.2)

Families

The proportion of dependent children living in one parent families in Great Britain has tripled since 1972; 19 per cent of children lived with just their mother and 1 per cent with just their father in 1994-95. (Table 2.10)

Cohabitation, marriage and divorce

The proportion of unmarried women aged between 18 and 49 who were cohabiting in Great Britain almost doubled between 1981 and 1994-95, to 23 per cent. (Chart 2.13)

The number of first marriages in the United Kingdom fell by nearly two fifths between 1961 and 1993, to 210 thousand; in contrast, there were nearly seven times the number of divorces in 1993 compared with 1961. (Chart 2.17)

Men tend to be older when they first marry than women: the average age for a man was around 28 in England and Wales in 1993, two years older than for a woman. (Page 57)

More than two and a half times as many divorces were granted to women as men in 1993. (Page 59)

Family building

Since 1992 women in their early thirties have been more likely to have a baby than women in their early twenties. (Page 60)

The proportion of live births outside marriage has increased more slowly in recent years; the proportion remained virtually unchanged between 1993 and 1994, at 32 per cent. (Chart 2.25)

2.1

Average household size[1]

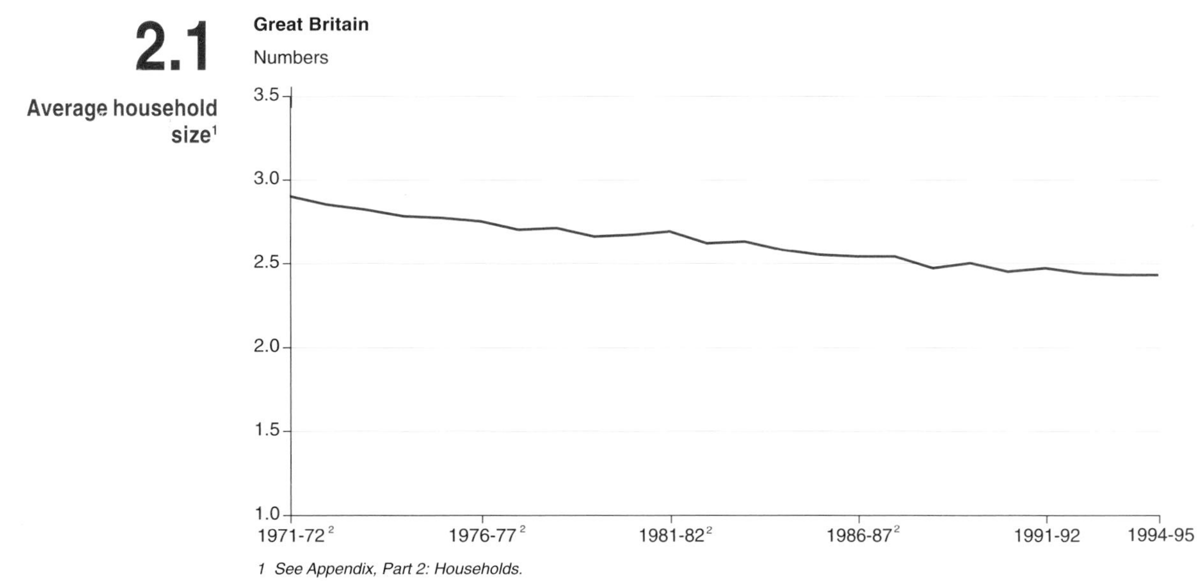

1 See Appendix, Part 2: Households.
2 Data are for calendar years.
Source: General Household Survey, Office of Population Censuses and Surveys

2.2

Households[1]: by size

Great Britain Percentages

	1961	1971	1981	1991	1994-95
One person	*14*	*18*	*22*	*27*	*27*
Two people	*30*	*32*	*32*	*34*	*34*
Three people	*23*	*19*	*17*	*16*	*16*
Four people	*18*	*17*	*18*	*16*	*15*
Five people	*9*	*8*	*7*	*5*	*6*
Six or more people	*7*	*6*	*4*	*2*	*2*
All households (=100%)(millions)	16.2	18.2	19.5	22.4	23.1

1 See Appendix, Part 2: Households.

Source: Office of Population Censuses and Surveys; Department of the Environment

2.3

One person households as a percentage of all households: by gender and whether under or over pensionable age[1]

England & Wales

Percentages

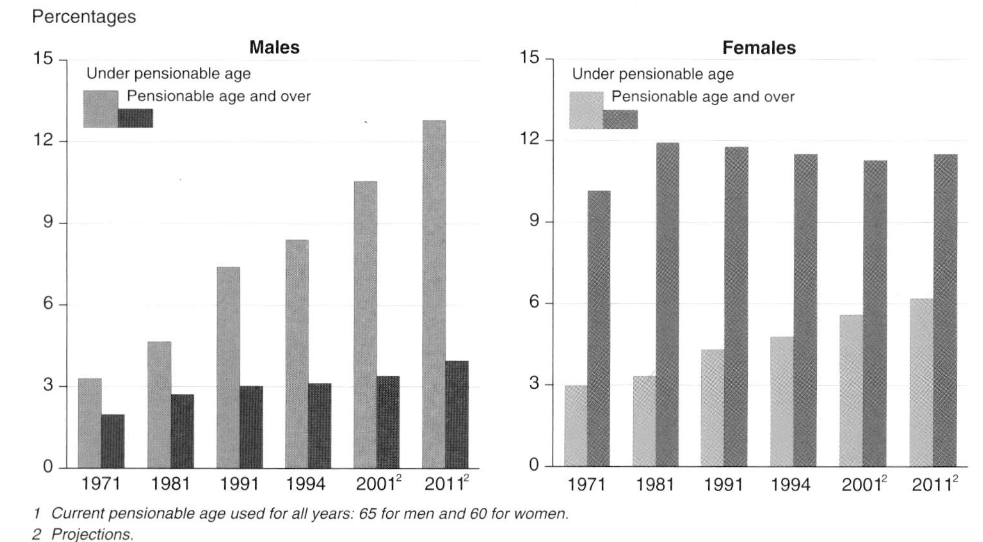

1 Current pensionable age used for all years: 65 for men and 60 for women.
2 Projections.

Source: Department of the Environment

The structure and characteristics of the households and families in which people live affect not only the individuals concerned, but also help us to achieve a wider understanding of society.

Households

The average household size in Great Britain fell to 2.4 in 1994-95, compared with 2.9 in 1971 **(Chart 2.1)**. This is partly due to the increasing elderly population who tend to live alone, but is now also affected by the increasing number of young people, particularly men, living alone. Other factors which lead to smaller household sizes include increasing divorce rates, and falling family sizes as people choose to have fewer children.

In 1994-95 there were 43 per cent more households in Great Britain than in 1961, partly because households now contain fewer people **(Table 2.2)**. Over the same period the proportion of households with five or more people halved. The largest increase has occurred in the number of people living alone: more than a quarter of households in Great Britain were one person households in 1994-95, almost double the proportion in 1961. Households in Northern Ireland tend to be larger than those in Great Britain: in 1994-95 around 15 per cent had five or more members which was about twice the proportion in Great Britain.

The growth in the proportion of one person households is analysed in more detail in **Chart 2.3**. Women over pensionable age formed the largest proportion of people living alone in 1994; this proportion has been relatively stable since 1971, at between 10 and 12 per cent. The recent growth in one person households has been among people under pensionable age, articularly men. This increase is predicted ɔ continue, so that by the year 2011 men nder pensionable age are expected to form ıe largest group of one person households, vertaking women over pensionable age.

s the proportion of one person households as been growing, the proportion of raditional' one family households of a ouple with children has been declining **Table 2.4)**. In 1961, 38 per cent of ouseholds in Great Britain comprised arried couples with dependent children; is proportion fell by 13 percentage points ɔ 25 per cent in 1994-95. Lone parents with ependent children form a small but growing roportion of households, with around 7 per ent of households consisting of lone arents with dependent children in 1994-95. ı Northern Ireland, however, married ouples with dependent children are more ommon; 29 per cent of households were of ıis type in 1994-95.

eople from ethnic minority groups tend to ave more dependent children in their ouseholds which leads to larger average ousehold sizes. In Great Britain in Spring 995 households from the Pakistani/ angladeshi ethnic group were the most kely to consist of six or more people **(Table .5)**. This is partly due to their having on verage more dependent children; in Spring 995 households from this ethnic group had n average of 1.7 dependent children ompared with just 0.6 for all families. eople from the Black ethnic group were the ıost likely to live alone. These differences ıay be influenced by the younger age tructures of the ethnic minority groups and, ɔ a certain extent, cultural differences.

s might be expected, in Northern Ireland atholics tend to live in larger households han Protestants. Again this is related to the umber of dependent children in the household; the average number in a Catholic household was 2.3 in 1994-95 while that for a Protestant was only 1.9.

2.4

Households[1]: by type of household and family

Great Britain — Percentages

	1961	1971	1981	1991	1994-95
One person					
Under pensionable age	*4*	*6*	*8*	*11*	*12*
Over pensionable age	*7*	*12*	*14*	*16*	*15*
Two or more unrelated adults	*5*	*4*	*5*	*3*	*6*
One family					
Married couple[2]					
No children	*26*	*27*	*26*	*28*	*25*
1-2 dependent children[3]	*30*	*26*	*25*	*20*	*20*
3 or more dependent children	*8*	*9*	*6*	*5*	*5*
Non-dependent children only	*10*	*8*	*8*	*8*	*6*
Lone parent[2]					
Dependent children[3]	*2*	*3*	*5*	*6*	*7*
Non-dependent children only	*4*	*4*	*4*	*4*	*3*
Two or more families	*3*	*1*	*1*	*1*	*1*
All households (=100%)(millions)	16.2	18.2	19.5	22.4	23.1

1 See Appendix, Part 2: Households.
2 Other individuals who were not family members may also be included.
3 May also include non-dependent children.
Source: Office of Population Censuses and Surveys; Department of the Environment

2.5

Ethnic group of head of household: by household[1] size, Spring 1995

Great Britain — Percentages

	One person	Two people	Three people	Four people	Five people	Six or more people	All (=100%) (thousands)
White	*28*	*34*	*16*	*15*	*5*	*2*	22,548
Black[2]	*31*	*29*	*20*	*12*	*4*	*4*	379
Indian	*9*	*17*	*20*	*26*	*16*	*12*	265
Pakistani/ Bangladeshi	*8*	*11*	*14*	*21*	*15*	*31*	163
Other[3]	*28*	*23*	*20*	*19*	*6*	*5*	239
All ethnic groups	*28*	*34*	*16*	*15*	*5*	*2*	23,597

1 See Appendix, Part 2: Households.
2 Includes Caribbean, African and other Black people of non-mixed origin.
3 Includes Chinese, other ethnic minority groups of non-mixed origin and people of mixed origin.
Source: Labour Force Survey, Central Statistical Office

2.6

People in households and communal establishments: by type of household and family in which they live[1]

Great Britain					Percentages
	1961	1971	1981	1991	1994-95
One family households					
Living alone	*4*	*6*	*8*	*11*	*11*
Married couple					
No children	*18*	*19*	*20*	*23*	*21*
Dependent children[2]	*52*	*52*	*47*	*41*	*41*
Non-dependent children only	*12*	*10*	*10*	*11*	*8*
Lone parent	*3*	*4*	*6*	*10*	*11*
Other households	*12*	*9*	*9*	*4*	*7*
All people in private households (=100%)(millions)	..	53.4	53.9	55.4	55.9
People not in private households (millions)	..	0.9	0.8	0.8	0.9
Total population (millions)	51.4	54.4	54.8	56.2	56.8

1 See Appendix, Part 2: Households and Families.
2 May also include non-dependent children.
Source: Office of Population Censuses and Surveys

Between 1971 and 1994-95 the number of people living in households in Great Britain grew by about 5 per cent to almost 56 million **(Table 2.6)**. Whereas Table 2.4 showed just over a quarter of households consist of people living alone, Table 2.6 is based on people rather than households; it shows that just over one in ten people live alone. Four in ten people lived in married couple households with dependent children in 1994-95, while more than half lived in this type of household in 1961.

The composition of households can change for a variety of reasons. Members join as people marry or have children, or leave as people separate, children leave home or members die **(Table 2.7)**. The most common types of changes to household composition are children either arriving or leaving.

2.7

Household[1] change: by type of household, 1992 to 1993

Great Britain							Percentage
	No change	Additional children only	Departing children only	Deaths	Separations	Other changes	All change
One person							
Under pensionable age	*87*	-	.	*1*	.	*12*	*10[illegible]*
Over pensionable age	*95*	*0*	.	*4*	.	*1*	*10[illegible]*
Married couple							
No children	*87*	*4*	.	*4*	*3*	*3*	*10[illegible]*
Dependent children[2]	*84*	*7*	*3*	-	*3*	*3*	*10[illegible]*
Non-dependent children only	*70*	*1*	*21*	*2*	*1*	*5*	*10[illegible]*
Lone parent							
Dependent children[2]	*75*	*4*	*4*	*0*	.	*17*	*10[illegible]*
Non-dependent children only	*70*	*0*	*15*	*4*	.	*12*	*10[illegible]*
Other households	*49*	*1*	*1*	*3*	*0*	*47*	*10[illegible]*
All households	*83*	*3*	*4*	*2*	*1*	*6*	*10[illegible]*

1 Households may experience more than one change. Changes are 'ranked' by a measure of importance. See also Appendix, Part 2: Households.
2 May also include non-dependent children.
Source: British Household Panel Survey, ESRC Research Centre on Micro-social Change

amilies

family is defined as a married or
ohabiting couple with or without children, or
lone parent with children. People living
lone are not normally considered to form a
amily.

s children we are nearly all members of
amilies. As young adults we either remain
with our parent(s) as part of the family or
nove away. Around 6 per cent of young
eople aged 16 to 19 in the United Kingdom
ved on their own or with other single
eople without children in Winter 1994-95
Table 2.8). People in their twenties are more
kely to be living with a partner than living
lone. However, men in this age group are
nore likely than women to be living alone
vhereas women are much more likely to be
one parents. A smaller proportion of people
n their thirties and early forties live alone or
s couples with no dependent children than
hose in their twenties; around six in ten
eople in this age group live in couples with
ependent children. As people get older they
re more likely again to live in couple
amilies with no children and, as they pass
heir mid-seventies, to live alone. In
articular almost 70 per cent of women in
his age group lived alone in Winter 1994-
95. This results from the tendency for
vomen to marry older men and outlive their
usbands.

n Winter 1994-95, 27 per cent of families in
Great Britain were couple families with
ependent children and 4 per cent were lone
parent families. However, these proportions
vary between ethnic groups **(Chart 2.9)**. A
nigh proportion, 60 per cent, of families in
Great Britain from the Pakistani/Bangladeshi
ethnic group had dependent children. Also,
s has already been seen, households from
his ethnic group have, on average, the
greatest number of dependent children.

2.8

People in households[1]: by gender, age and family type, Winter 1994-95

United Kingdom Percentages

	One person	Couple: No dependent children	Couple: Dependent children	Lone parent	Other person[2]	All persons (=100%) (millions)
Males						
16-19	*6*	..	..	..	*93*	1
20-29	*23*	*19*	*19*	*1*	*38*	5
30-44	*15*	*19*	*58*	*1*	*6*	6
45-59	*13*	*61*	*22*	*1*	*4*	5
60-74	*20*	*77*	*1*	..	*2*	4
75 and over	*35*	*63*	..	..	*2*	1
Females						
16-19	*8*	*3*	*2*	*3*	*85*	1
20-29	*17*	*22*	*26*	*13*	*23*	4
30-44	*8*	*18*	*57*	*13*	*4*	6
45-59	*13*	*65*	*12*	*3*	*7*	5
60-74	*35*	*60*	..	..	*5*	4
75 and over	*68*	*27*	..	..	*5*	2

1 See Appendix, Part 2: Families.
2 People who were not heads of family unit or dependent children.
Source: Labour Force Survey, Central Statistical Office

2.9

Families with dependent children[1]: by ethnic group, Winter 1994-95

Great Britain

Percentages

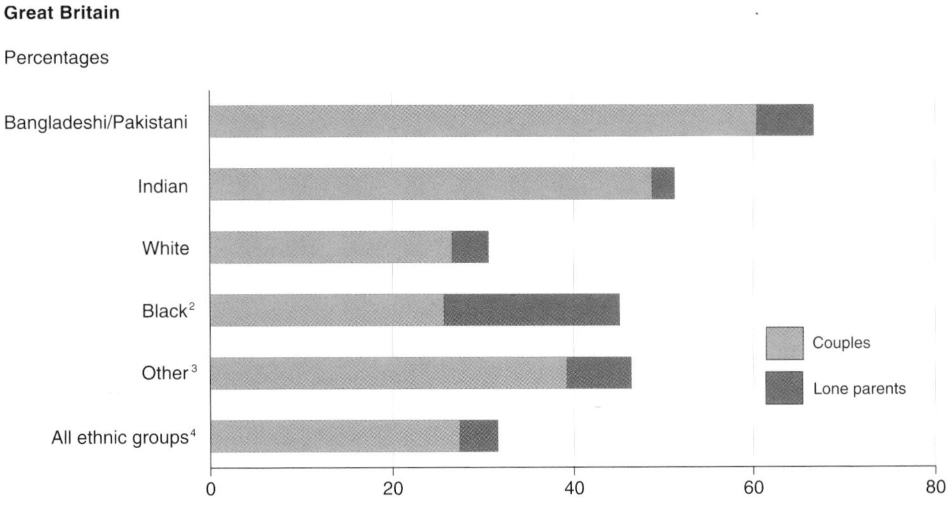

1 As a percentage of all families in each ethnic group. See also Appendix, Part 2: Families.
2 Includes Caribbean, African and other Black people of non-mixed origin.
3 Includes Chinese, other ethnic minority groups of non-mixed origin and those of mixed origin.
4 Includes ethnic group not stated.
Source: Labour Force Survey, Central Statistical Office

2.10

Percentage of dependent[1] children living in different family types

Great Britain — Percentages

	1972	1981	1986	1991	1994-95
Couple					
1 child	*16*	*18*	*18*	*17*	*16*
2 children	*35*	*41*	*41*	*37*	*37*
3 or more children	*41*	*29*	*28*	*28*	*27*
Lone mother					
1 child	*2*	*3*	*4*	*5*	*6*
2 children	*2*	*4*	*5*	*7*	*8*
3 or more children	*2*	*3*	*3*	*6*	*6*
Lone father					
1 child	-	*1*	*1*	-	*1*
2 or more children	*1*	*1*	*1*	*1*	-
All dependent children	*100*	*100*	*100*	*100*	*100*

1 See Appendix, Part 2: Families.

Source: General Household Survey, Office of Population Censuses and Surveys

2.11

Families headed by lone parents as a percentage[1] of all families with dependent children

Great Britain

Percentages

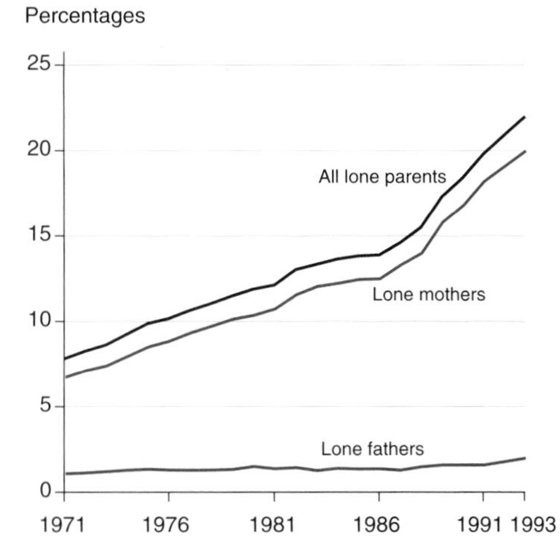

1 Three year moving averages used (apart from 1993).

Source: General Household Survey, Office of Population Censuses and Surveys

Although families from the Black ethnic group have the lowest overall proportion of couples with dependent children, they have the highest proportion of families which are lone parents, at around 20 per cent. In Northern Ireland, a higher proportion of Catholic families contain dependent children than Protestant families.

Most dependent children in Great Britain, four fifths in 1994-95, still live in a family with two parents **(Table 2.10)**. However, this proportion has fallen since 1972 when over nine in ten children lived with two parents. The proportion living in large families with three or more children dropped sharply in the 1970s but has remained steady since, and in 1994-95 was only 27 per cent. The proportion of dependent children living in one parent families has tripled since 1972; 19 per cent of children lived with just their mother and a further 1 per cent with just their father in 1994-95. This reflects the increases in the number of births outside marriage and in divorce during this period (see Chart 2.25 and Chart 2.17).

Similar proportions of children lived in one parent families in Northern Ireland in 1994-95, but a higher proportion of children lived in larger families; 40 per cent lived in couple families with three or more children.

Some children will live in stepfamilies with only one, or perhaps none, of their natural parents. There were about half a million step families in Great Britain in 1991, 1 in 15 of all families with dependent children. This corresponds to just over 1 million dependent children living in step families, around 1 in 12 of all dependent children. There were more than three times as many stepfathers as stepmothers, due to the tendency for children to stay with their mother rather than their father following divorce or separation.

The proportion of families in Great Britain headed by a lone parent increased from nearly 8 per cent in 1971 to 22 per cent in 1993 **(Chart 2.11)**. The proportion of lone mother families increased gradually until the late 1980s, but has since increased more rapidly, so that in 1993 one in five mothers with dependent children was a lone mother. The proportion of lone fathers, on the other hand, has doubled between 1971 and 1993 but still remains small, with 2 per cent of all amilies with dependent children being headed by a lone father. The British Household Panel Survey, which begins on page 27, article gives more information on the duration of lone parenthood.

Nearly two fifths of lone mothers were single in Great Britain in 1994-95 while almost the same proportion were divorced. The gradual increase in the proportion of lone mothers until the mid-1980s was caused mainly by increasing numbers of divorced mothers. Since then the proportion of divorced lone mothers has stabilised, but the proportion of single, never married, mothers has more than doubled. Lone parents tend to have, on average, fewer and younger children than couple parents.

The proportion of lone parent families is greatest in the North West where 30 per cent of families with dependent children were lone parent families in 1994-95 **(Chart 2.12)**. East Anglia had the lowest proportion at only 14 per cent. The 1991 census of population was able to provide information on the prevalence of lone parenthood at county level. This varied considerably from area to area and was found to be highest in Merseyside and Greater London and lowest in Surrey, Buckinghamshire and the Western Isles. Levels of lone parenthood were particularly high in metropolitan counties.

Cohabitation, marriage and divorce

Between 1981 and 1994-95 the percentage of non-married women aged between 18 and 49 who were cohabiting in Great Britain rose from 12 per cent to 23 per cent **(Chart 2.13)**.

Similar information for men has only been available since 1986. Between 1986 and 1994-95 the proportion of non-married men cohabiting increased by 10 percentage points, so that 21 per cent of men aged 16 to 59 were cohabiting in 1994-95.

In addition to the general increase in the proportion of men and women cohabiting, there has also been a trend in Great Britain towards cohabiting for longer periods. Divorced men and women tend to cohabit for the longest; more than a half of those who were divorced and cohabiting had lived with their partner for at least three years.

2.12

Lone parents[1]: by region, 1994-95

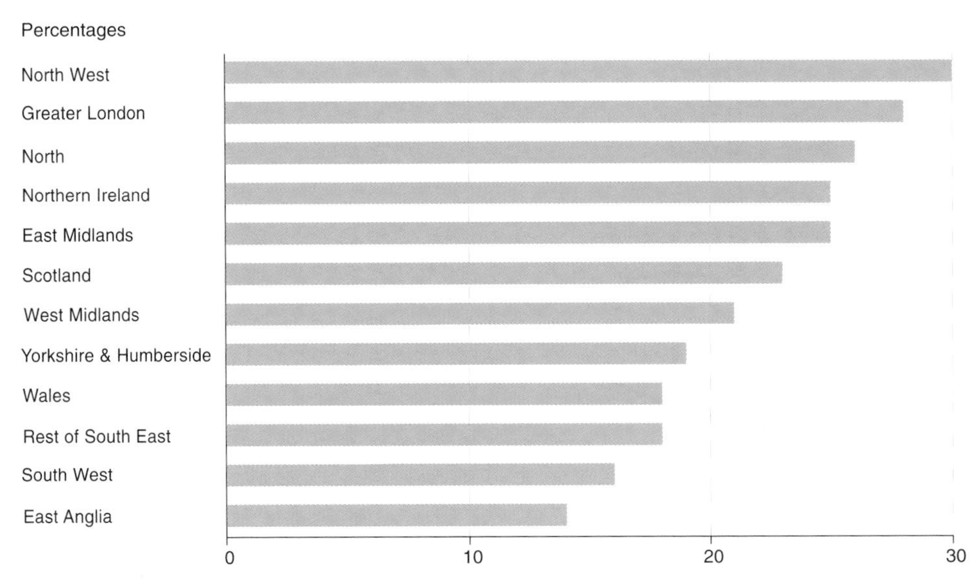

1 Lone parent families with dependent children as a percentage of all families with dependent children in each region.

Source: General Household Survey, Office of Population Censuses and Surveys; Continuous Household Survey, Department of Finance and Personnel, Northern Ireland

2.13

Percentage of women[1] cohabiting

Great Britain

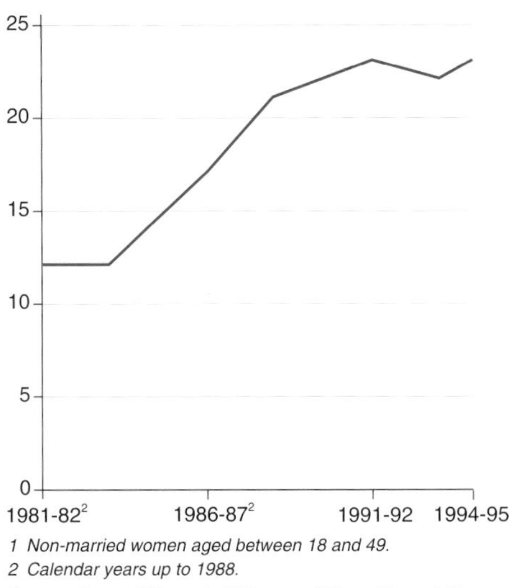

1 Non-married women aged between 18 and 49.

2 Calendar years up to 1988.

Source: General Household Survey, Office of Population Censuses and Surveys

2.14

Percentage of women cohabiting: by age and marital status, 1993-94 to 1994-95

Great Britain					Percentages
	Single[1]	Separated	Divorced	Widowed	All non-married women
16-24	*14*	*8*	..	..	*14*
25-34	*33*	*17*	*29*	..	*30*
35-49	*18*	*7*	*25*	*14*	*19*
50-59	*6*	*5*	*12*	*3*	*8*
All aged 16 to 59	*20*	*10*	*24*	*6*	*19*

1 Never married.

Source: General Household Survey, Office of Population Censuses and Surveys

2.15

People who feel cohabitation[1] is wrong: by gender, 1994

Great Britain		Percentages
	Males	Females
Year of birth		
1960-1978	*7*	*6*
1950-1959	*10*	*8*
1940-1949	*16*	*14*
1930-1939	*23*	*22*
Before 1930	*40*	*34*
All	*17*	*16*

1 Percentage who agreed with the statement that living together outside marriage is always wrong.

Source: British Household Panel Survey, ESRC Research Centre on Micro-social Change

The increase in the number of single women cohabiting has been marked, rising from 9 per cent in 1981 to 24 per cent in 1994-95, while the rise in divorced women cohabiting has been small by comparison. However, divorced women are still more likely to cohabit than single women who have never married. In the period 1993-94 to 1994-95, 19 per cent of non-married women between 16 and 59 were cohabiting **(Table 2.14)**. Just under a quarter of divorced women were cohabiting compared with 20 per cent of single women and 10 per cent of separated women. Among single women, 33 per cent of those aged 25 to 34 were cohabiting, which was about twice the proportion in both the 16 to 24 and the 35 to 49 age groups and almost six times the proportion of women in their fifties. Over a quarter of divorced women between the ages of 25 and 49 were cohabiting; about half as many did in their fifties.

A higher proportion of divorced and separated men were cohabiting than divorced and separated women in 1993-94. In contrast, among single people, a slightly lower proportion of men than women were cohabiting. These differences are partly explained as, overall, more divorced men cohabit with spinsters than bachelors with divorced women.

Younger people have different attitudes to cohabitation than older people. The British Household Panel Survey asked women and men if they thought that 'living together outside marriage was always wrong'. Just over a third of women and two fifths of men who were born before 1930 thought that it was wrong **(Table 2.15)**. These are people in their mid-sixties and older. Younger people were less likely to agree and among those born between 1960 and 1978 less than 8 per cent agreed with the statement. A slightly higher proportion of men than women felt that living together outside marriage is wrong. Nearly half of women born in the 1960s said that they had cohabited at some time in their lives compared with only 19 per cent of those born in the 1940s and 4 per cent born in the 1920s - a reflection of changing attitudes.

While marriage rates decreased in most European Community (EC) countries between 1981 and 1993, there were some exceptions: in both Denmark and Luxembourg marriage rates increased **(Table 2.16)**. The United Kingdom, which in 1981 had the second highest marriage rate among the countries now in the EC, had the fifth highest rate in 1993. Sweden, one of the newest EC members, had the lowest marriage rate, at only 3.9 per thousand population.

In 1993 the United Kingdom had the highest divorce rate in the EC, at almost twice the average. The small increase that the United Kingdom has seen in its divorce rate between 1981 and 1993 has not been reflected in all other countries; in Denmark and Germany divorce rates have fallen. There was also less variation across the EC than in 1981. The differences that do exist may be attributed to the effects of religion, cultural and social differences and legal requirements.

The number of first marriages in the United Kingdom fell by nearly two fifths between 1961 and 1993, to stand at 210 thousand (**Chart 2.17**). In contrast there were nearly seven times the number of divorces in 1993 than there were in 1961. Overall, more than a third of all marriages in 1993 were remarriages. In England and Wales in 1993 first marriage rates for both men and women (per thousand of the single population) were around half those in 1961. Both divorce and remarriage rates increased rapidly in the early 1970s after the *Divorce Reform Act 1969* came into force in 1971. This introduced a solitary ground for divorce, that of irretrievable breakdown of marriage, and played a part in both the increase in divorces and subsequent remarriages. Further information on the effects of this Act and the *1984 Matrimonial and Family Proceedings Act* is given in the commentary around Table 2.20. While remarriage rates have since fallen to half their 1961 level, divorce rates have continued to increase before falling slightly in 1994.

Of the 299 thousand marriages in England and Wales in 1993, just over half involved civil ceremonies. This proportion has risen slightly over the last ten years. In 1993, three quarters of remarriages were by civil ceremonies compared with only just over a third of first marriages.

While the number of first marriages has been falling, the average age of men and women when they marry for the first time has been increasing. The average age of women in England and Wales marrying for the first time was 26 in 1993. Men tend to marry at older ages than women; the average age for a man marrying for the first time was around 28, two years older than a woman.

2.16

Marriage and divorce rates: EC comparison, 1981 and 1993

Rates per 1,000 population

	Marriages		Divorces	
	1981	1993	1981	1993
United Kingdom	7.1	5.9	2.8	3.1
Denmark	5.0	6.1	2.8	2.5
Finland	6.3	4.9	2.0	2.5
Sweden	4.5	3.9	2.4	2.5
Belgium	6.5	5.4	1.6	2.1
Austria	6.3	5.6	1.8	2.0
Netherlands	6.0	5.8	2.0	2.0
France	5.8	4.4	1.6	1.9
Germany	6.2	5.5	2.0	1.9
Luxembourg	5.5	6.0	1.4	1.9
Portugal	7.8	6.9	0.7	1.2
Greece	6.9	6.0	0.7	0.7
Spain	5.4	5.0	0.3	0.7
Italy	5.6	5.1	0.2	0.4
Irish Republic	6.0	4.4	.	.
EC average	6.1	5.3	1.5	1.7

Source: Eurostat

2.17

Marriages and divorces

United Kingdom

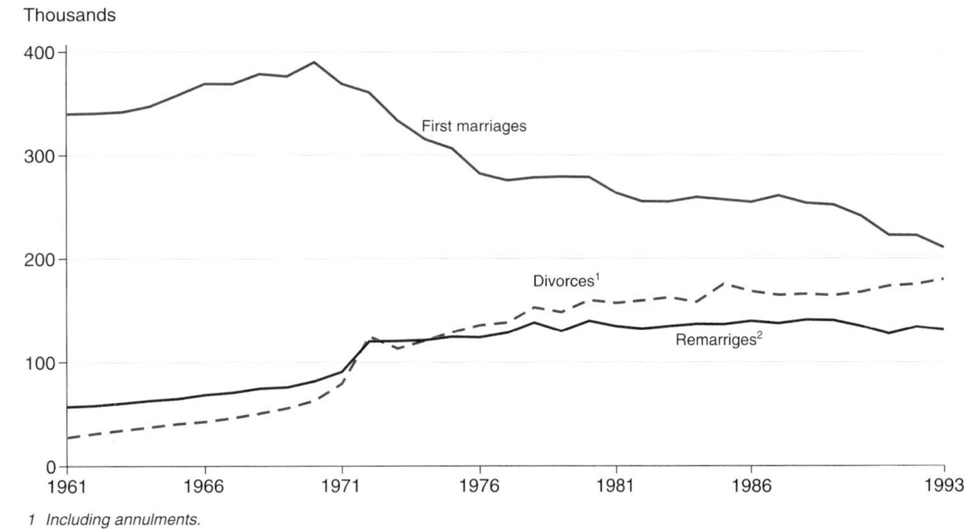

1 Including annulments.
2 For one or both partners.
Source: Office of Population Censuses and Surveys; General Register Office (Scotland); General Register Office (Northern Ireland)

2.18

Age combinations at first marriage, 1993

United Kingdom Percentages

	Age of husband						
	Under 20	20-24	25-29	30-34	35-39	40 and over	All ages
Age of wife							
Under 20	*0.9*	*3.4*	*1.2*	*0.2*	-	-	*5.8*
20-24	*0.9*	*20.9*	*17.4*	*3.3*	*0.5*	*0.1*	*43.1*
25-29	*0.2*	*6.4*	*20.6*	*7.9*	*1.4*	*0.3*	*36.8*
30-34	-	*0.8*	*3.5*	*4.3*	*1.5*	*0.5*	*10.7*
35-39	-	*0.1*	*0.5*	*0.7*	*0.7*	*0.4*	*2.4*
40 and over	-	-	*0.1*	*0.1*	*0.2*	*0.7*	*1.2*
All ages	*2.0*	*31.7*	*43.3*	*16.6*	*4.3*	*2.1*	*100.0*

Source: Office of Population Censuses and Surveys; General Register Office (Scotland); General Register Office (Northern Ireland)

Around 6 per cent of women who first got married in 1993 were under the age of 20 compared with only 2 per cent of men **(Table 2.18)**. However, only 14 per cent of women who married for the first time in 1993 were over the age of 30 compared with 23 per cent of men. Just over 20 per cent of first marriages involved brides and grooms who were both aged between 20 and 24 and in a further 20 per cent both were aged between 25 and 29.

Chart 2.19 shows marriage patterns for people in England and Wales born this century. The trend amongst those born in the first half of the century was of decreasing age at marriage and, among women, increasing likelihood of marrying. About 90 per cent of women born in 1925 were married by the time they were 40, whereas 95 per cent of women born in 1945 were married by this age. Although the 1965 cohort line is incomplete (these people being only in their late twenties in 1994), a smaller proportion of women were married at most ages than those born in 1925 and 1945 - an indication that trends are changing. For men, there is little difference in the proportion married after the age of 40 in each cohort, and at most ages in the later cohorts a smaller percentage of men are married than women.

In 1993, 8 per cent of divorces in the United Kingdom were of marriages that had lasted under three years compared with only 2 per cent in 1981 **(Table 2.20)**. The *Matrimonial and Family Proceedings Act 1984* which reduced the minimum period after marriage that a petition for divorce could be filed had an immediate effect on divorce proceedings in England and Wales. The new law allowed couples to file for divorce after their first wedding anniversary whereas under former legislation they could not usually petition for

2.19

Men and women married by certain ages: by birth cohort

England & Wales

Percentages

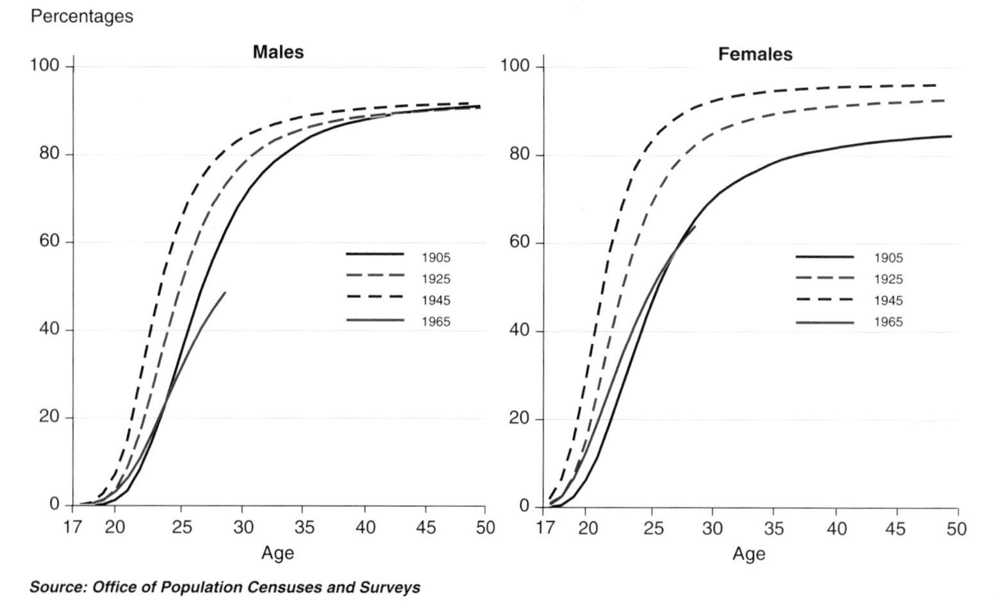

Source: Office of Population Censuses and Surveys

divorce unless their marriage had lasted at least three years. At the other extreme less than 10 per cent of divorces in 1993 were after 25 years of marriage, compared with 21 per cent in 1961. Nearly three in ten divorces took place between the fifth and ninth years of marriage.

Divorces involving children under the age of 16 have become more common in recent years; the number of children under five affected by divorce in England and Wales in 1993 was 55 thousand, almost a quarter higher than in 1983. In comparison, the total number of children under 16 affected by divorce has increased by only an eighth. This may reflect the increase in couples divorcing after fewer years of marriage. In recent years, more than 20 per cent of all divorces involved a husband and wife who were both aged between 20 and 24 when they married.

More than two and a half times as many divorces were granted to women as men in England, Wales and Northern Ireland in 1993: 120 thousand compared with 47 thousand. Where a divorce was granted to the wife, over a half were for unreasonable behaviour and a further fifth for adultery (Chart 2.21). Regardless of the age of the wife divorcing, unreasonable behaviour is the most common reason given but as the age of the wife at divorce increases an increasing proportion are on the grounds of adultery or after two years separation. However, the proportion granted for these two grounds falls for women in their forties and fifties. Also, later in life separation after five years becomes more common. Where the divorce was granted to the husband, the most common ground given was adultery. Jointly awarded decrees are excluded from this analysis.

2.20

Divorce: by duration of marriage

United Kingdom Percentages

	1961	1971	1981	1991	1993
0-2 years	*1*	*1*	*2*	*9*	*8*
3-4 years	*10*	*12*	*19*	*14*	*14*
5-9 years	*31*	*31*	*29*	*27*	*28*
10-14 years	*23*	*19*	*20*	*18*	*18*
15-19 years	*14* (15-24 years)	*13*	*13*	*13*	*12*
20-24 years		*10*	*9*	*10*	*10*
25-29 years	*21* (25 years and over)	*6*	*5*	*5*	*5*
30 years and over		*9*	*5*	*4*	*4*
All durations (=100%) (thousands)	27.0	79.2	155.6	171.1	180.0

Source: Office of Population Censuses and Surveys; General Register Office (Scotland); General Register Office (Northern Ireland)

2.21

Divorces granted: by ground, 1993

England, Wales & Northern Ireland

Percentages

Source: Office of Population Censuses and Surveys; General Register Office (Northern Ireland)

2.22

Fertility rates: by age

Great Britain — Births per 1,000 women

	Under 20[1]	20-24	25-29	30-34	35-39	40 and over[2]	All ages
1961	36.9	173.3	178.2	104.3	49.0	15.1	90.0
1971	50.3	153.8	154.1	77.8	33.1	8.7	83.7
1981	28.3	106.0	129.3	68.4	21.6	4.8	61.5
1986	30.2	92.6	123.4	77.2	24.2	4.7	60.4
1991	33.0	88.7	119.1	85.9	31.6	5.2	63.3
1993	31.0	81.7	113.7	86.3	33.5	6.0	62.1
1994	28.9	78.3	111.6	88.0	35.1	6.2	61.4

1 Births per 1,000 women aged 15 to 19.
2 Births per 1,000 women aged 40 to 44.
Source: Office of Population Censuses and Surveys; General Register Office (Scotland)

2.23

Average age of mother at first birth[1]

United Kingdom

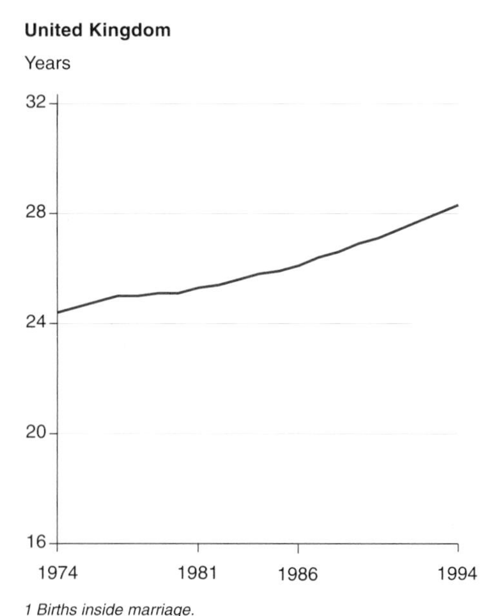

1 Births inside marriage.
Source: Office of Population Censuses and Surveys

Family building

The fall in the overall fertility rate among women during the late 1960s and early 1970s is shown in Chart 1.11 In the Population chapter. **Table 2.22** looks at fertility rates in more detail. In recent years, the overall fertility rate has levelled off, but the rate for women under 30 has carried on falling as they continue to defer childbearing. Since 1992 women in their early thirties have been more likely to have a baby than women in their early twenties. Women aged 25 to 29 are still the most likely to give birth - with a rate of 112 births per thousand women in 1994.

The fertility rate for women in their late thirties increased by two thirds between 1981 and 1994. There have also been increases for those in their early thirties and their early forties over the same period. However, the number of births to women aged 40 and over is small and declines rapidly as their age increases; two thirds of these births occurred to women aged 40 or 41 in the United Kingdom in 1993. The proportion of births to women in this age group which were outside marriage has risen sharply in England and Wales since 1986, to about a quarter in 1994. Around three fifths of these births outside marriage were jointly registered by parents living at the same address, suggesting that they were to cohabiting couples. This figure is greater than the average for all ages (about 55 per cent).

Part of the reason for the decline in the average number of children women will bear may be attributed to the increase in their age at marriage. The average age of mothers at their first birth within marriage increased from 24.4 years in 1974 to 28.3 years in 1994 **(Chart 2.23)**, the highest recorded since 1938.

While the average ages of men and women at marriage have been increasing, the proportion of first births occurring within the first year of marriage in England and Wales has been falling: from 24 per cent in 1986 to under 20 per cent in 1994. This can be mainly attributed to the fall in the proportion of births that occur in the first seven months of marriage, perhaps indicating a fall in marriages because of a prospective birth.

Although most women eventually do have children, there has been a steady rise in the number of women who have never had a child which also contributes to the decline in fertility rates. Only 19 per cent of women born in 1947 were still childless at the age of

30 **(Chart 2.24)**. This proportion increased sharply over time so that over a third of women born in 1962 were still childless at 30, but it is expected that there will be little change among the cohorts born up to 1972. If a woman is childless at the age of 45, this can be taken as an indication that she is unlikely to ever have a child; only 12 per cent of women born in 1947 were still childless by the age of 45 while it is expected that just under 20 per cent of women born in years since 1957 will still be childless when they reach 45.

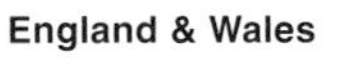

The proportion of live births outside marriage has increased dramatically since the early 1960s, from just over 5 per cent in 1960 to 32 per cent in 1994 **(Chart 2.25)**. Over the last decade the proportion of live births outside marriage has almost doubled. Minor peaks were previously seen during both the First and Second World Wars, although the proportion of live births that were outside marriage only reached one in ten in 1945.

There are regional variations in the proportion of live births that are outside marriage. The highest proportions can be found in the North and North West where 38 per cent of births were outside marriage in 1994. This compares with just under 28 per cent in East Anglia. Proportions in the South West and South East were also relatively low. In Northern Ireland only one in ten live births was outside marriage in 1994. Women who are unmarried tend to be younger, on average, when they have babies than those who are married - 25.7 years compared with 29.6 years in 1994.

2.24

Percentage of women childless at age 30 and 45

England & Wales

Percentages[1]

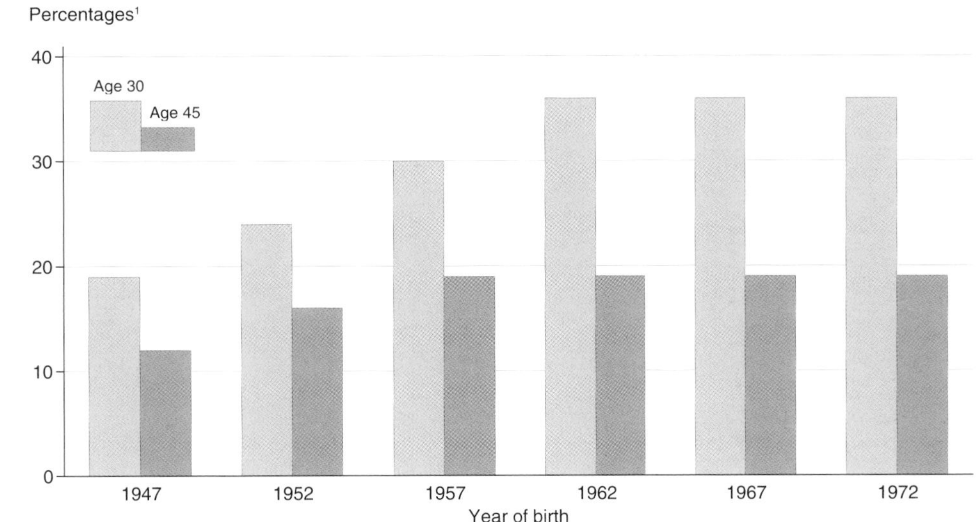

1 Data for age 30 born in 1967 and 1972, and age 45 born in 1952 onwards are projections.

Source: Office of Population Censuses and Surveys

2.25

Live births outside marriage as a percentage of all births

United Kingdom

Percentages

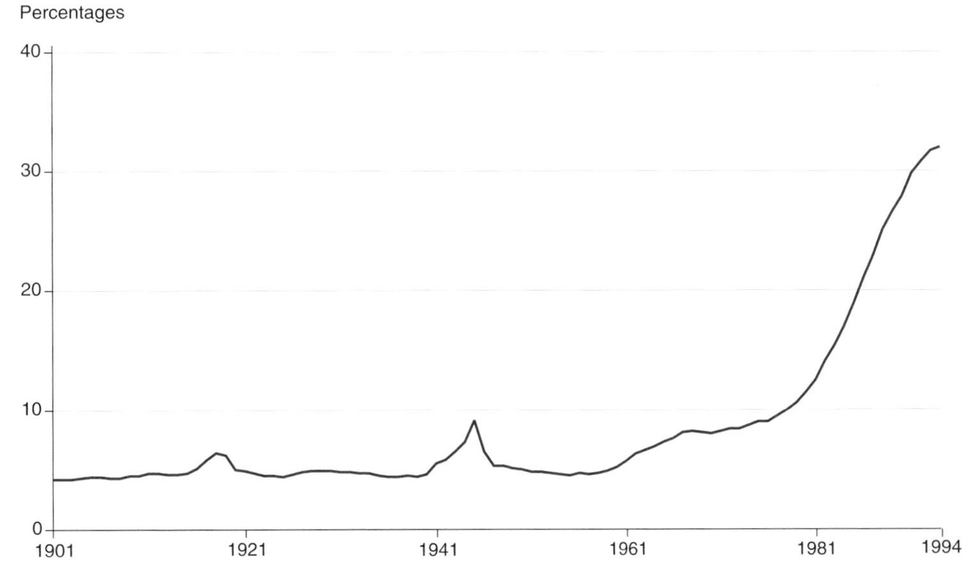

Source: Office of Population Censuses and Surveys

2.26

Conceptions: by marital status and outcome

England & Wales					Percentages
	1971	1981	1991	1992	1993
Inside marriage					
Maternities	*72.6*	*65.9*	*51.9*	*51.2*	*51.2*
Legal abortions[1]	*5.2*	*5.6*	*4.4*	*4.4*	*4.3*
Outside marriage					
Maternities inside marriage	*8.1*	*5.5*	*3.7*	*3.6*	*3.5*
Maternities outside marriage[2]					
Joint registration	*3.5*	*6.8*	*18.9*	*19.9*	*20.2*
Sole registration	*4.1*	*4.8*	*6.0*	*5.9*	*6.0*
Legal abortions[1]	*6.7*	*11.4*	*15.0*	*14.9*	*14.9*
All conceptions (=100%)(thousands)	835	752	854	828	819

1 Legal terminations under the 1967 Abortion Act.
2 Births outside marriage can be registered by the mother only (sole registration) or by both parents (joint registration).
Source: Office of Population Censuses and Surveys

2.27

Abortions: by marital status and age

Great Britain					Percentages
	1971	1981	1986	1991	1994
Single women					
Under 16	*4*	*4*	*4*	*3*	*3*
16-19	*36*	*39*	*34*	*27*	*24*
20-34	*56*	*55*	*60*	*67*	*69*
35-44	*2*	*2*	*2*	*3*	*4*
45 and over	-	-	-	-	-
All abortions[1] (=100%)(thousands)	63.4	96.4	115.2	127.6	118.2
Married women					
16-19	*1*	*2*	*2*	*1*	*1*
20-34	*64*	*67*	*67*	*70*	*68*
35-44	*32*	*30*	*31*	*28*	*30*
45 and over	*1*	*1*	*1*	*1*	*1*
All abortions[1] (=100%)(thousands)	58.6	55.5	47.2	42.0	38.5
All women[2]					
Under 16	*2*	*2*	*3*	*2*	*2*
16-19	*18*	*23*	*22*	*19*	*16*
20-34	*61*	*61*	*63*	*68*	*69*
35-44	*17*	*13*	*12*	*11*	*12*
45 and over	*1*	-	-	-	-
All abortions[1] (=100%)(thousands)	133.1	171.5	181.9	190.6	178.3

1 Includes age not known.
2 Includes women who are widowed, divorced, separated or whose marital status is not known.
Source: Office of Population Censuses and Surveys; National Health Service in Scotland, Common Services Agency

In 1993, 819 thousand women in England and Wales had conceptions which led to maternities or to legal terminations under the *1967 Abortion Act*; around 56 per cent of these conceptions were within marriage **(Table 2.26)**. Twenty five years ago, in 1971, over three quarters of conceptions were within marriage. Despite the increase in conceptions and births outside marriage, there is evidence that most births now occur within stable relationships: the proportion of births outside marriage which were jointly registered in England and Wales has increased from three fifths in 1981 to nearly four fifths in 1993.

Recent results from the Office of Population Censuses and Survey's Longitudinal Study show that half of women in England and Wales who were unmarried at their first birth were married by the time of their second child. Also, for those women who jointly registered a first birth outside marriage, 44 per cent also jointly registered a second. The Longitudinal Study article, which begins on page 16, gives more details of the structure and purpose of the Study.

Married women who conceive are far less likely to have an abortion than unmarried women. A third of conceptions outside marriage resulted in abortion in England and Wales in 1993, compared with less than one in ten of conceptions inside marriage. The number of abortions increased by 43 per cent between 1971 and 1991 in Great Britain, but has since fallen by 6 per cent **(Table 2.27)**. A large proportion of this increase can be attributed to the increase in abortions to single women, which doubled between 1971 and 1991. Abortions now tend to be carried out earlier in pregnancies. In 1993, 89 per cent of abortions in England and Wales were carried out on women under 13 weeks pregnant compared with only 74 per cent in 1971.

The proportion of teenagers conceiving fell in the 1970s but started rising again in the 1980s, so that in 1990 there were 69 conceptions per thousand women aged under 20 in England and Wales. Since 1990 teenage conception rates have fallen, to 60 per thousand in 1993. For those under the age of 16, the conception rate was also lower in 1993 than in 1990, but needs to fall further if it is to meet the Health of the Nation target for England of 4.8 per thousand girls under 16 by the year 2000.

Of the 87 thousand conceptions to teenage women in England and Wales in 1993, around two thirds led to maternities **(Table 2.28)**. This proportion was much lower for girls under the age of 16 where just under half resulted in maternities. Between 1961 and 1994 live births to teenage girls dropped from 60 thousand to 42 thousand, a fall of 30 per cent compared with a fall of only 18 per cent for all live births.

Table 2.29 combines information from the General Household Survey in Great Britain and the Continuous Household Survey in Northern Ireland to look at the types of contraception used by women. Younger women tend to prefer different forms of contraception than older women. For those under the age of 35, the pill is the most popular form, while for those over 35 sterilisation is the most common. Sterilisation was also common among women who had had children, and particularly those who had as many children as they wanted.

The proportion of women aged 16 to 49 using some form of contraception has remained relatively stable since 1976. The pill is still the most common overall, although slightly less so than in 1976. The male condom has increased in usage as has sterilisation.

2.28

Teenage conceptions: by age at conception and outcome, 1993

England & Wales

	Thousands		Rates per 1,000 women	
	Leading to maternities	Leading to abortion	Leading to maternities	Leading to abortion
Age at conception				
13 and under	0.2	0.2	0.5	0.7
14	0.7	1.1	2.4	3.5
15	2.6	2.5	9.3	8.8
All aged under 16[1]	3.5	3.8	3.9	4.2
16	6.5	4.4	23.7	15.9
17	11.3	6.2	39.2	21.5
18	15.8	7.6	52.6	25.2
19	19.5	8.3	62.4	26.7
All aged under 20[1]	56.5	30.2	38.8	20.8

1 Rates for girls aged under 16 and under 20 are based on the population of girls aged 13 to 15 and 15 to 19 respectively.

Source: Office of Population Censuses and Surveys

2.29

Current use of contraception[1]: by age, 1993-94

United Kingdom Percentages

	16-19	20-34	35-49	All aged 16 to 49
Non-surgical				
Pill	*30*	*40*	*9*	*26*
Male condom	*19*	*19*	*14*	*17*
IUD	-	*4*	*6*	*5*
Withdrawal	*2*	*3*	*3*	*3*
Cap	-	*2*	*1*	*1*
Safe period	*0*	*1*	*1*	*1*
Injection	-	*1*	-	*1*
Spermicides	-	*1*	-	-
Surgical				
Female sterilisation	*0*	*5*	*22*	*12*
Male sterilisation	-	*5*	*21*	*12*
At least one method	*41*	*73*	*76*	*73*

1 By women aged 16 to 49.

Source: General Household Survey, Office of Population Censuses and Surveys; Continuous Household Survey, Department of Finance and Personnel, Northern Ireland

References and further reading

The following list contains selected publications relevant to **Chapter 2: Households and Families**. Those published by HMSO are available from the adresses shown on the inside back cover of *Social Trends*.

1991 Census Communal Establishments, Great Britain, HMSO

Annual Report of the Registrar General for Northern Ireland, HMSO

Annual Report of the Registrar General for Scotland, General Register Office (Scotland)

Birth Statistics (Series FM1), HMSO

British Social Attitudes, Dartmouth Publishing

Changing Households: The British Household Panel Survey, ESRC Research Centre on Micro-social Change

General Household Survey, HMSO

Key Population and Vital Statistics (Series VS/PP1), HMSO

Marriage and Divorce Statistics (Series FM2), HMSO

Population Trends, HMSO

Projections of Households in England, HMSO

Regional Trends, HMSO

Social Focus on Children, HMSO

Social Focus on Women, HMSO

Contacts

Telephone contact points for further information relating to **Chapter 2: Households and Families**

Office of Population Censuses and Surveys	
General Household Survey	0171 396 2327
Other inquiries	0171 396 2828
Central Statistical Office	
Labour market statistics	0171 273 5585
Department of the Environment	0171 276 4196
General Register Office (Scotland)	0131 314 4243
National Health Service in Scotland, Common Services Agency	0131 551 8899
General Register Office (Northern Ireland)	01232 252031
Northern Ireland Census Office	01232 526942
Department of Finance and Personnel, Northern Ireland	01232 252508
ESRC Research Centre on Micro-social Change	01206 872957
Eurostat	00 352 4301 34567

Chapter 3 Education

Educational attainment

Four fifths of 18 to 21 year olds have at least one GCSE at grades A to C or equivalent to their credit, compared with two fifths of those in their early fifties. (Chart 3.1)

About 8 per cent of adults have a low level of literacy and about 18 per cent a low level of numeracy in England and Wales. (Table 3.2)

For pupils aged 7 and 14, teacher assessments and tests indicate that girls out-perform boys in mathematics and, to a greater extent, English. (Table 3.4)

Girls are more likely than boys to gain five or more GCSE qualifications at grades A to C, and the differential is widening. They have also overtaken boys in terms of GCE 'A' level success. (Table 3.6)

School pupils and staffing

The pupil-teacher ratio in public sector schools was unchanged in the year to 1994/95 at about 19:1, while that in non-maintained schools decreased slightly to about 10:1. (Table 3.13)

About a quarter of classes in public sector primary schools have more than 30 pupils whereas relatively few secondary school classes are of this size. (Table 3.14)

Further and higher education

The proportion of young people above the school-leaving age who are in full-time education has almost doubled since 1980/81. (Table 3.19)

In the three years to 1993/94 the number of full-time students increased by over 40 per cent in higher education and by more than 50 per cent in further education. (Table 3.21)

3.1

Adults with GCSE grades A to C[1]: by age, 1993-94

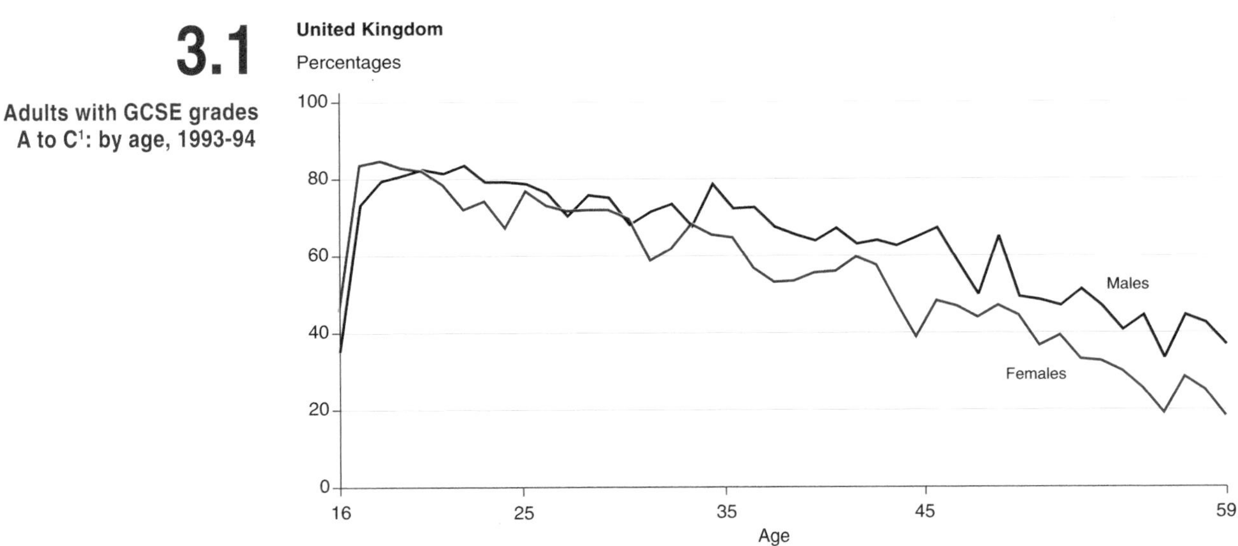

1 One or more GCSE grades A to C or equivalent or better. See Appendix, Part 3: Qualifications.

Source: General Household Survey, Office of Population Censuses and Surveys; Continuous Household Survey, Department of Finance and Personnel, Northern Ireland

Educational provision at a particular period will affect the nation's well-being over future years. For example, Britain's economic position in the next century will be influenced by the quality and relevance of its educational system today.

Educational attainment

The legacy of educational provision over the last fifty years is reflected in the formal educational qualifications of the population. This is encapsulated in **Chart 3.1** which shows the proportions of people of different ages with at least one GCSE grades A to C or the equivalent in past examination regimes. It is notable that among those now approaching retirement, who mostly completed their education in the early 1950s, the proportion is twice as great for men as for women, but the gap has closed in a single generation and in the youngest age groups females are now outperforming males. The chart also shows that the spreading of qualifications to a much wider segment of society is not just a recent phenomenon but has been happening fairly steadily for the last forty years.

A growing cause for concern in recent years has been poor literacy and numeracy amongst adults. The Basic Skills Agency (formerly the Adult Literacy and Basic Skills Unit) has undertaken research to identify the proportion of adults who lack the ability to read, write and speak English, or to use mathematics effectively, at the level necessary to function and progress at work and in society in general. A study which was carried out in England and Wales in 1994 demonstrated that these deficiencies are closely related to, amongst other factors, the age at which people left school. **Table 3.2** shows that, for example, nearly a third of people who left school under the age of 16 have a low level of numeracy, compared with only 3 per cent of those who continued with their education to the age of 21 or beyond.

However, it would be wrong to conclude from these associations that adults' difficulties with basic skills arise mainly from their experiences in the concluding stages of education. On the contrary, there is strong evidence that the seeds of difficulty are sown much earlier. A separate piece of research by the Basic Skills Agency studied a group of 21 year olds for whom information has been collected at various stages in their lives through the 1970 British Cohort Study. This showed that the likelihood of an individual having problems with basic literacy and numeracy skills in adult life is predictable to a considerable extent before education begins: such as the extent to which the parents themselves are qualified.

3.2

Adult literacy and numeracy standards[1]: by age on leaving full-time education, 1994

England & Wales — Percentages

	Low literacy	High literacy	Low numeracy	High numeracy
Age on leaving full-time education				
Under 16	*14*	*9*	*31*	*11*
16	*8*	*19*	*16*	*23*
17-18	*4*	*30*	*8*	*30*
19-20	*3*	*31*	*7*	*40*
21 and over	-	*46*	*3*	*54*
All adults[1]	*8*	*21*	*18*	*25*

1 Percentage of adults aged 22 to 74.

Source: Basic Skills Agency

This last aspect is analysed in **Table 3.3**. For example, those 21 year olds with very poor reading ability were twice as likely as adequate readers (those with no apparent problems) to have parents with no qualifications. Equally, they were only a fifth as likely to have parents with qualifications at degree level.

For those currently at school a system for the regular assessment of pupils in England and Wales is becoming established. Pupils are assessed both by teachers and through formal national tests. The system is primarily intended to help inform teachers and parents about the progress of individual pupils and to promote the accountability of individual schools to parents and others.

Pupil's attainment is shown as a level on the National Curriculum scale. The standards at level two should stretch a typical 7 year old, a typical 11 year old should be challenged by the standards at level four and a typical 14 year old should be on the threshold of levels five and six. **Table 3.4** shows the proportion of 7 year olds and 14 year olds (in those schools that submitted results) in England who reached or exceeded these levels in teacher assessments and tests in 1994. Girls out-performed boys in all subjects except science although even here they out-performed boys in the teacher assessments. Roughly a third of 7 year old boys did not reach level two in writing and spelling. Around half of 14 year old boys were below level five in English tests and slightly less than half were below this level in English as assessed by a teacher. The results for 11 year olds will be published for the first time in 1995, alongside the results for 7 and 14 year olds.

3.3

Reading and numeracy standards of 21 year olds: by educational level of parents[1], 1991

England & Wales Percentages

	Highest qualification of either parent[1]					
	No qualification	Vocational	O level or equivalent	GCE A level or SRN	Degree or Certificate of Education	All qualifications
Reading score						
Very low	*69*	*13*	*12*	*4*	*3*	*100*
Low	*59*	*11*	*17*	*7*	*6*	*100*
No apparent problem	*34*	*17*	*23*	*11*	*16*	*100*
Numeracy score						
Very low	*52*	*17*	*19*	*6*	*4*	*100*
Low	*64*	*11*	*14*	*6*	*5*	*100*
No apparent problem	*36*	*16*	*22*	*11*	*15*	*100*
All 21 year olds	*40*	*16*	*21*	*10*	*13*	*100*

1 When child was aged five.

Source: Basic Skills Agency

3.4

Pupils reaching expected standards[1]: by gender and age, 1994

England Percentages

	Teacher assessment		Tests	
	Males	Females	Males	Females
7 year olds[2]				
English				
Handwriting	*76*	*87*	*76*	*85*
Reading	*76*	*85*	*76*	*85*
Spelling	*67*	*80*	*65*	*77*
Writing	*64*	*76*	*61*	*74*
All elements	*75*	*85*	.	.
Mathematics	*79*	*83*	.	.
of which: arithmetic	*80*	*84*	*80*	*84*
Science	*85*	*87*	.	.
14 year olds[3]				
English	*55*	*72*	*49*	*66*
Mathematics	*62*	*67*	*60*	*63*
Science	*63*	*65*	*64*	*63*

1 Based on results from responding schools only. See Appendix, Part 3: The National Curriculum: assessments and tests.
2 Percentage of pupils achieving level 2 or above at Key Stage 1.
3 Percentage of pupils achieving level 5 or above at Key Stage 3.

Source: Department for Education and Employment

3.5

Pupils[1] achieving GCSE grades A-C[2]: by selected subject and gender

Great Britain Percentages

	Males			Females		
	1988/89[3]	1991/92	1993/94	1988/89[3]	1991/92	1993/94
English	*38*	*41*	*45*	*53*	*57*	*62*
Any science	*35*	*39*	*43*	*33*	*39*	*43*
of which: Biology	*13*	*7*	*7*	*19*	*9*	*8*
Chemistry	*17*	*10*	*9*	*13*	*8*	*7*
Physics	*21*	*11*	*10*	*10*	*6*	*5*
Double award science[3]	*7*	*23*	*32*	*7*	*24*	*34*
Mathematics	*36*	*38*	*42*	*32*	*37*	*42*
Any modern language	*19*	*20*	*25*	*30*	*33*	*40*
of which: French	*17*	*18*	*20*	*27*	*29*	*33*
History	*16*	*15*	*18*	*18*	*20*	*24*
Geography	*21*	*22*	*23*	*18*	*19*	*21*
Craft, design and technology	*19*	*18*	*19*	*5*	*8*	*10*

1 In final year of compulsory schooling.
2 Or equivalent. See Appendix, Part 3: Qualifications.
3 Data are for England only.

Source: Department for Education and Employment; Welsh Office; The Scottish Office Education and Industry Department

External examination results tell a similar story. **Table 3.5** gives the proportions of pupils in their final year of compulsory education who gained GCSE grades A to C (or equivalent) in various subjects in Great Britain. Girls are much more likely than boys to obtain these grades in English, foreign languages and history while boys are more likely to obtain these grades in physics, chemistry and craft, design and technology (CDT). Of course the figures reflect the proportions entering for the different subjects as well as success rates and, as such, they illustrate the extent to which traditional gender differences still persist in the matter of subject choice. However, the proportion of girls who achieved grades A to C in CDT, though small, increased between 1988/89 and 1993/94. Most importantly, perhaps, the proportion of pupils in England with these grades in all core subjects of the National Curriculum (English, mathematics, a science and a modern language) is, overall, much higher for girls than for boys, and the gap has widened over the last five years.

3.6

Qualifications[1] attained: by gender

England Percentages

	Males			Females		
	1980/81	1990/91	1993/94	1980/81	1990/91	1993/94
3 or more GCE A levels[2]	*10*	*13*	*14*	*8*	*14*	*15*
1 or more GCE A level[2]	*16*	*21*	*21*	*15*	*23*	*23*
5 or more GCSE grades A-C[3]	*24*	*36*	*39*	*26*	*44*	*48*
1 or more GCSE grades A-C[3]	*50*	*63*	*64*	*55*	*73*	*75*
1 or more GCSE grades A-G[3]	*87*	*95*	*91*	*90*	*95*	*93*

1 Or equivalent. See Appendix, Part 3: Qualifications.
2 Students at school aged 16 to 18 at start of academic year as a percentage of 17 year old population.
3 Pupils aged 15 at start of academic year as a percentage of the 15 year old school population.

Source: Department for Education and Employment

Table 3.6 shows the percentage of school pupils reaching various levels of attainment for GCSEs and GCE A levels. It shows that the increase in the overall proportion of pupils achieving success in examinations has not been mainly from those getting 'bare minimum' results but from young people with five or more good GCSE grades or GCE A levels. At A level the gender differences are less dramatic than for GCSE but the time trends show the same general pattern: in 1980/81 a smaller proportion of females than males achieved success at GCE A level whereas in the 1990s they have established a consistent lead. In Northern Ireland in 1993/94 almost half of those in year 12 achieved five GCSEs grades A to C which was a higher proportion than in England. At GCE A level, 87 per cent of those in the final year of their course in Northern Ireland achieved a minimum of two passes.

The changes in qualification rates over time, though impressive in themselves, are quite small relative to some of the geographical differences at any one point in time. These are illustrated in **Table 3.7** which shows the proportion of pupils gaining each of three levels of qualifications. The proportion of Scottish pupils receiving their Certificate of Education is very striking (particularly for girls with 'Highers') but it should be noted that the education system and examination structures are different north of the border and the figures are not strictly comparable with those for England and Wales. Within England there is a suggestion of a north-south divide, with Yorkshire and Humberside, the North West and West Midlands having worse results than the rest of the country at GCE A level. The results for Wales are, in general, around the middle of the range set by the English regions.

Another cross-cut of the population which shows up differences in educational attainment is that of ethnic origin. **Chart 3.8** gives the percentage of the working age population who have an educational qualification, analysed by ethnic group. Although, in general, a higher proportion of men than women have a qualification, the difference is smallest among those of Black ethnic origin and largest among those from the Pakistani/Bangladeshi ethnic group. Both men and women from the Black ethnic group are more likely than those of White ethnic origin to have a qualification, although this difference may be a reflection of the younger age structure of the Black population. People of Pakistani/Bangladeshi ethnic origin are the least likely to have a qualification.

3.7

Examination achievements[1] of pupils in schools: by region and gender, 1993/94

Percentages

	2 or more GCE A levels[2]		5 or more GCSEs grades A-C[3]		No graded GCSEs[3]	
	Males	Females	Males	Females	Males	Females
Great Britain	*19*	*21*	*39*	*48*	..	..
North	*13*	*15*	*34*	*43*	*11*	*9*
Yorkshire & Humberside	*14*	*16*	*34*	*43*	*11*	*8*
East Midlands	*19*	*22*	*37*	*45*	*8*	*6*
East Anglia	*20*	*25*	*41*	*51*	*7*	*5*
South East	*21*	*23*	*42*	*50*	*8*	*6*
Greater London	*18*	*20*	*36*	*45*	*10*	*8*
Rest of South East	*23*	*25*	*44*	*53*	*7*	*5*
South West	*22*	*25*	*44*	*54*	*6*	*4*
West Midlands	*16*	*18*	*36*	*45*	*10*	*7*
North West	*13*	*14*	*38*	*46*	*10*	*8*
England	*18*	*20*	*39*	*48*	*9*	*7*
Wales	*20*	*19*	*35*	*44*	*12*	*8*
Scotland	*24*	*31*	*45*	*56*	..	..

1 See Appendix, Part 3: Qualifications.
2 Pupils aged 17 to 19 at the end of the school year in England and Wales as a percentage of the 18 year old population. For Scotland the figures mostly relate to pupils in Year S5 gaining three or more SCE Highers as a percentage of the 17 year old population.
3 Pupils aged 16 at the end of the school year as a percentage of the 15 year old population at start of school year. Scotland pupils are in year S4.

Source: Department for Education and Employment; Welsh Office; The Scottish Office Education and Industry Department

3.8

Percentage of the working-age[1] population with a qualification[2]: by gender and ethnic origin, Spring 1995

Great Britain

Percentages

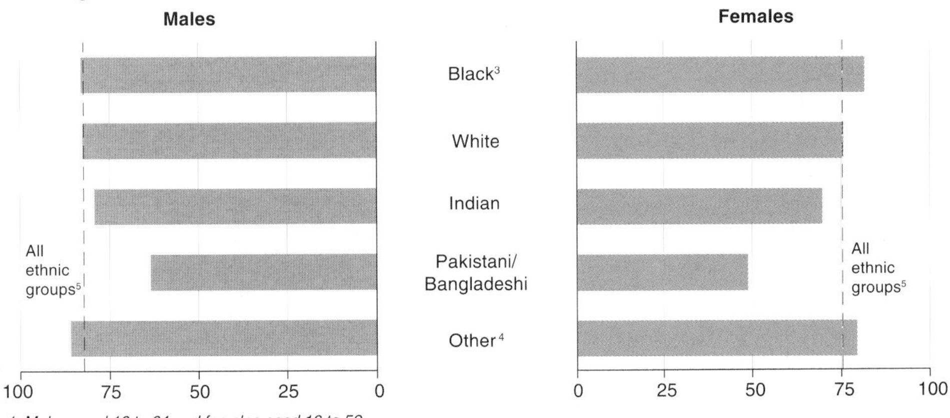

1 Males aged 16 to 64 and females aged 16 to 59.
2 Includes those obtained at school, college, work and from government training schemes.
3 Includes Caribbean, African and other Black people of non-mixed origin.
4 Includes Chinese, other ethnic minority groups of non-mixed origin and people of mixed origin.
5 Includes ethnic group not stated.

Source: Department for Education and Employment, from the Labour Force Survey

3.9

Young people reaching NVQ foundation targets[1]: by age

United Kingdom

Percentages

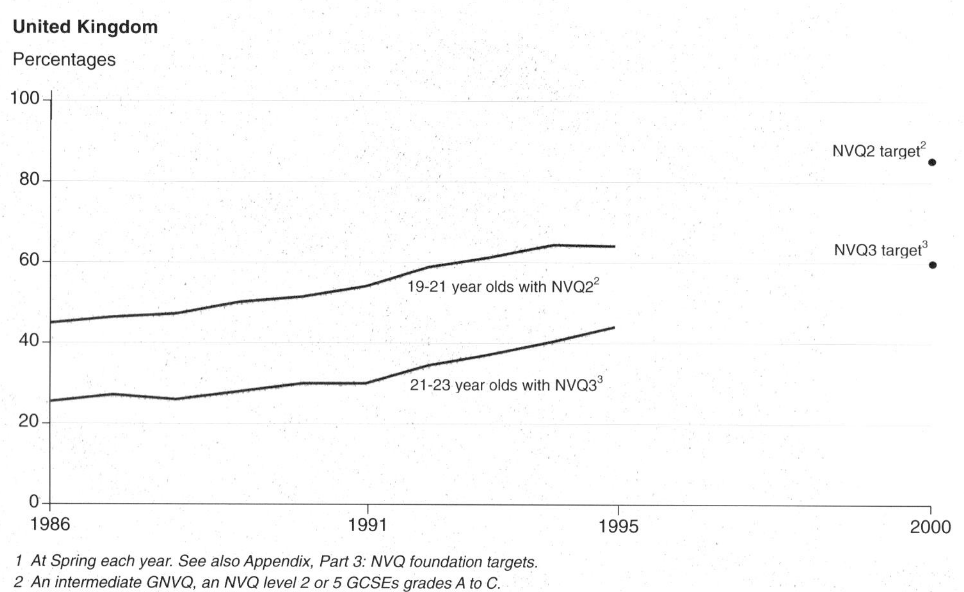

1 At Spring each year. See also Appendix, Part 3: NVQ foundation targets.
2 An intermediate GNVQ, an NVQ level 2 or 5 GCSEs grades A to C.
3 An advanced GNVQ, an NVQ level 3 or 2 GCE A levels.
Source: Department for Education and Employment, from the Labour Force Survey

3.10

School pupils[1]: by type of school[2]

United Kingdom — Thousands

	1970/71	1980/81	1990/91	1993/94	1994/95[3]
Public sector schools[4]					
Nursery[5]	50	89	105	85	86
Primary[5]	5,902	5,171	4,955	5,181	5,251
Secondary					
Modern	1,164	233	94	91	90
Grammar	673	149	156	175	184
Comprehensive	1,313	3,791	2,924	3,033	3,089
Other	403	434	300	288	273
All public sector schools	9,507	9,866	8,533	8,853	8,989
Non-maintained schools					
Pupils aged 10 and under	238	..	266	260	262
Pupils aged 11 and over	383	..	347	342	340
All non-maintained schools	621	619	613	602	602
Special schools[6]	103	148	114	116	116
All schools	10,230	10,633	9,260	9,571	9,707

1 Full-time and part-time pupils are counted as one.
2 See Appendix, Part 3: Main categories of educational establishments and Stages of education.
3 Data for Wales are for 1993/94.
4 Excludes special schools.
5 Nursery classes within primary schools are included in primary schools except for Scotland in 1990/91 when they are included in nursery schools.
6 Includes maintained and non-maintained sector.
Source: Department for Education and Employment; Welsh Office; The Scottish Office Education and Industry Department; Department of Education, Northern Ireland

There has been a strong trend in recent years towards closer integration between academic education and vocational training, symbolised in 1995 by the merger of the training functions of the Employment Department into the Department for Education. The proportions of young people reaching defined levels of qualification have been studied for many years but until the present decade there were no standing arrangements for involving business, the education system and government in setting quantified targets, making coordinated plans for moving towards achieving them and regularly monitoring progress. In 1991, however, the Confederation of British Industry (CBI), with government support, defined some specific goals which should in the national interest be reached before the millennium, and these were revised in 1995.

These goals cover not only examination results in academic subjects but also National Vocational Qualifications (NVQs) gained through occupation-specific courses. The targets for young people are that by the year 2000 at least 85 per cent should reach NVQ level two (NVQ2) and 60 per cent should reach level three (NVQ3). **Chart 3.9** shows that steady progress is being made towards the NVQ3 target but the NVQ2 one remains challenging, with no increase in the proportion reaching this level between 1994 and 1995.

These 'foundation learning targets' for young people are part of a broader programme which also involves 'lifetime learning targets' for the workforce as a whole. For example, one goal is that by the year 2000 some 60 per cent of the whole workforce should be qualified to NVQ level three. By 1995 the proportion stood at 40 per cent, compared with only 30 per cent in 1990. Further material on training is included in the Employment chapter.

School pupils and staffing

In 1993/94, over four fifths of those undertaking full-time education were in schools of one sort or another. **Table 3.10** provides an overview of all schools in the United Kingdom in terms of pupil numbers, and shows how much the institutional pattern has changed over the last quarter of a century. It can be seen that the numbers in public sector nursery schools more than doubled between 1970/71 and 1990/91 due to an increase in the number of pupils attending part-time. Those in grammar and secondary modern schools fell by three quarters and nine tenths respectively over the same period and, although neither of these two types of school is wholly extinct, comprehensive schools now educate more than five out of six of all the pupils in public sector secondary schools.

The numbers in the non-maintained sector have fallen only slightly since 1970/71, accounting for 1 in 16 of all school pupils. Special schools, which provide for children with the most severe special educational needs (SEN) have fewer pupils than in 1980/81. The *Education Act 1981* and the *Education Act 1993* placed a qualified duty on local education authorities in England and Wales to ensure that children with SEN should have their needs met wherever possible in mainstream schools. In Scotland, education authorities are also encouraged to integrate children with special educational needs into mainstream schools wherever possible.

Year to year changes in the numbers of pupils in public sector primary and secondary schools in the United Kingdom are shown in **Chart 3.11**. This illustrates the large scale of the fluctuations in demand which are brought about by changes in birth rates: the number of primary school pupils fell from a peak of 6.1 million in 1973/74 to 4.6 million in 1984/85. There is a time-lag of about five years between the impact of falling rolls on primary schools and that on secondary education, which peaked at 4.6 million in 1978/79 and then fell to 3.5 million in 1990/91. The upward step in secondary school numbers between 1972/73 and 1973/74 reflects the raising of the minimum school-leaving age from 15 to 16 on 1 September 1972.

Demographic factors naturally have their most immediate impact on the educational provision for children under five. In addition there has been a persistent trend towards an ever higher proportion of such children attending schools, particularly public sector primary schools, if only on a part-time basis **(Table 3.12)**. In 1992/93 over a half of three and four year olds attended school compared with around a fifth in 1970/71.

3.11

Public sector school pupils[1]: by type of school

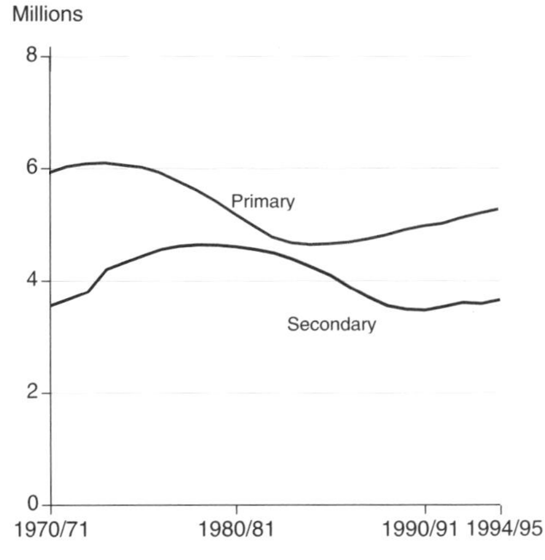

1 Full time and part time.

Source: Department for Education and Employment; Welsh Office; The Scottish Office Education and Industry Department; Department of Education, Northern Ireland

3.12

Children under five in schools[1]: by type of school

United Kingdom — Thousands

		1970/71	1980/81	1990/91	1993/94	1994/95[2]
Public sector schools[3]						
Nursery	- full time	20	22	16	15	15
	- part time	29	67	68	70	70
Primary	- full time	263	281	345	385	399
	- part time	38	167	303	340	351
Non-maintained schools	- full time	19	19	28	29	31
	- part time	14	12	20	22	23
Special schools[4]	- full time	2	4	4	4	4
	- part time	-	1	2	3	3
All schools		384	573	786	867	896

1 Pupils aged under five at December/January of academic year.
2 Data for Wales are for 1993/94.
3 Excludes special schools.
4 Includes maintained and non-maintained sector.

Source: Department for Education and Employment; Welsh Office; The Scottish Office Education and Industry Department; Department of Education, Northern Ireland.

3.13

Pupil/teacher ratios[1]: by type of school

United Kingdom					Ratios
	1970/71	1980/81	1990/91	1993/94[2]	1994/95[2]
Public sector schools[3]					
Nursery	26.6	21.5	21.5	21.6	21.7
Primary	27.1	22.3	21.8	22.2	21.9
Secondary[4]	17.8	16.4	15.0	15.7	15.9
All public sector schools	22.6	19.0	18.3	18.9	18.9
Non-maintained schools[5]	14.0	13.1	10.7	10.3	9.9
Special schools[6]	10.5	7.4	5.7	5.9	6.1
All schools	22.0	18.2	17.0	17.5	17.5

1 See Appendix, Part 3: Pupil teacher/ratios.
2 Excludes sixth form colleges in England and Wales
3 Excludes special schools.
4 Includes voluntary grammar schools in Northern Ireland from 1989/90 (formerly allocated to the non-maintained sector).
5 Excludes independent schools in Scotland in 1970/71 and in Northern Ireland in 1970/71 and 1980/81.
6 Includes maintained and non-maintained special schools.

Source: Department for Education and Employment

3.14

Class sizes[1] in public sector schools: by type of school

England				Percentages
	1980/81	1990/91	1992/93	1993/94
Primary schools				
1-20 pupils	*20*	*12*	*10*	*10*
21-25 pupils	*22*	*23*	*23*	*22*
26-30 pupils	*34*	*43*	*44*	*44*
31 or more pupils	*24*	*22*	*23*	*24*
Number of classes (thousands)	161	147	149	151
Average number in class	26	27	27	27
Secondary schools[2]				
1-15 pupils	*25*	*22*	*20*	*19*
16-20 pupils	*19*	*21*	*19*	*19*
21-25 pupils	*20*	*27*	*28*	*28*
26-30 pupils	*27*	*25*	*27*	*28*
31 or more pupils	*10*	*5*	*6*	*6*
Number of classes (thousands)	171	126	128	130
Average number in class	22	21	22	22

1 Related to one selected period in each public sector school on the day of the count in January.
2 Excludes sixth form colleges.

Source: Department for Education and Employment

Though not in the table it should be noted that the number of under fives in school is approximately matched, and has been ever since 1970, by the number receiving nursery education, principally with registered playgroups or child-minders.

There is some dispute about the educational significance of pupil-teacher ratios and average class sizes but these are widely regarded by parents as key indicators of the quality of education. **Table 3.13** shows the pupil-teacher ratios for all types of institutions. This suggests that the low pupil-teacher ratios for non-maintained schools, at almost half of those for public sector schools, may be one reason why some parents choose these schools for their children. Within the public sector, secondary schools have much lower ratios than primary and nursery schools and, although the differential narrowed in the 1970s, it has been fairly constant since then. Special schools, for obvious reasons, have low ratios, especially in the period since 1980 when they have been providing for pupils with the most severe learning difficulties.

Average class size is obviously closely related to the pupil-teacher ratio and shows similar patterns and trends. **Table 3.14** fills out the picture by showing, for public sector schools only, the distribution of primary and secondary school classes in size bands. Between 1980/81 and 1993/94 the average size of primary and secondary school classes remained almost unchanged. However there has been a slight trend away from very small classes in both primary and secondary schools.

Apart from the changes already mentioned in pupil numbers and staffing, schools have been affected in recent years by various new administrative and financial structures. These include arrangements for local management of schools whereby each school maintained by a local education authority is now given a budget, and responsibility for deciding how to spend it. The final stage of this process, delegating the new functions to special schools, comes fully into effect in April 1996.

A more complete form of devolution which is now available to public sector schools is a move to grant-maintained status. The school's governing body takes sole responsibility for management (within the framework of legislation) and is directly accountable to parents for the way the school is run; the local education authority has only a limited role. Such a move can only take place if approved by a ballot of parents at the school in question. **Chart 3.15** shows that up to 1994 the take-up of grant-maintained status increased each year since 1990 with the proportion more than doubling each year. By January 1994 over 3 per cent of public sector schools in England and Wales were grant-maintained.

School curricula

The National Curriculum, mentioned above in the context of assessment, applies to primary and secondary schools in England and Wales. It is seen as a means of ensuring that all pupils receive a broad and balanced education, and of raising standards in schools. Introduction has been phased over the period since 1989 and will not be completed until the academic year 1997/98. Ten subjects are included: English, mathematics, science, technology, physical education, modern languages, geography, history, art and music. However, modern languages are not required in primary schools and the last four subjects are not required after the third year of secondary schooling. In Wales, Welsh is also included.

Unlike England and Wales, there is no national curriculum in Scotland. Pupils aged 5 to 14 study a broad curriculum based on national guidelines which set out the aims of study, the ground to be covered and the way the pupils learning should be assessed and reported. Post 14 year olds take courses leading to awards in the Scottish Certificate of Education at Standard grade and Higher grade and/or SCOTVEC modules. They can also take the Certificate of Sixth Year Studies in their final year.

Table 3.16 shows the distribution of pupil time by subject group and age in public sector schools in Scotland. At September 1993 English and mathematics each accounted for 13 per cent of total pupil time for 12 and 13 year olds. English, mathematics and science subjects together covered 50 per cent of total pupil time for 16 to 17 year old pupils compared with only 36 per cent for 12 to 13 year olds.

3.15

Percentage[1] of public sector schools with grant-maintained status

England & Wales

Percentages

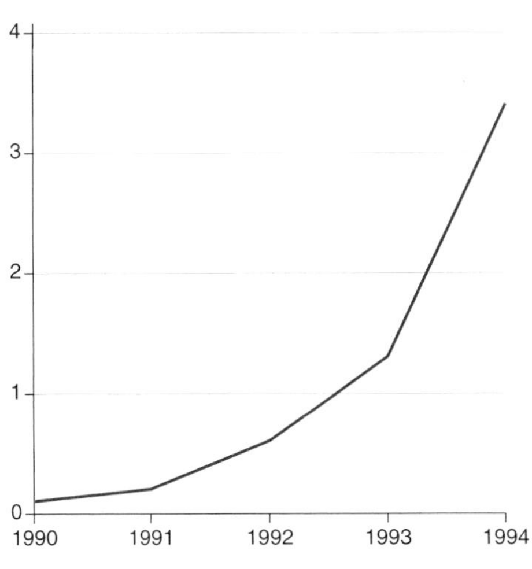

1 At January each year. Excludes sixth form colleges.

Source: Department for Education and Employment

3.16

Time spent on different subjects by pupils in public sector secondary schools: by age, September 1993

Scotland — Percentages

	12-13	16-17
Mathematical studies and applications	*13*	*17*
English	*13*	*17*
Scientific studies and applications	*10*	*16*
Social and environmental studies	*13*	*11*
Physical education	*7*	*6*
Business studies	*1*	*5*
Art and design	*6*	*4*
Computing subjects	*2*	*4*
Modern languages	*11*	*4*
Home economics subjects	*6*	*3*
Technical subjects	*6*	*3*
Religious and moral education	*4*	*2*
Music	*5*	*2*
Other	*4*	*6*
All subjects	*100*	*100*

Source: Scottish Office Education and Industry Department

3.17

Lesson time in public sector[1] primary and secondary schools: by age, January 1994

England				Percentages
	5-7	8-11	12-13	14-16
Hours per week				
25.5 or more	-	-	*5*	*6*
25	*2*	*8*	*37*	*41*
24.5	-	*3*	*12*	*12*
24	*5*	*28*	*23*	*22*
23.5	*4*	*25*	*16*	*15*
23	*13*	*18*	*5*	*4*
22.5	*13*	*8*	-	-
21.5-22	*39*	*8*	-	-
21 or less	*22*	*1*	-	-
Average (hours per week)	22.1	23.5	24.4	24.5
Recommended[2] (hours per week)	21.0	23.5	24.0	24.0

1 Includes grant-maintained schools.
2 It is suggested that schools should consider offering at least 25 hours to pupils in the 14 to 16 age group.
Source: Department for Education and Employment

Perhaps partly in response to the demands of the National Curriculum there has been some increase in recent years in the total amount of lesson time in schools, the 'taught week', excluding registration, breaks and the statutory act of collective worship. Based on advice from the Schools Inspectorate, minimum hours were recommended for England in 1990 which increased with the age of the pupils. **Table 3.17** shows these recommended hours and that on average the actual amount of lesson time pupils receive in public sector schools in England at least matches these recommendations. However, there is some variation between individual schools; for example, 36 per cent of pupils receive less than the recommended teaching time for 8 to 11 year olds.

International comparisons of a more subjective kind are available on the general public's perceptions of the relative importance of different school subjects. The results, summarised in **Table 3.18**, show a large measure of agreement across countries. More than seven in ten people in all the countries shown in the table, with the exception of the United States and the United Kingdom, regarded foreign languages as essential or very important. By contrast the arts received a lower rating everywhere and lowest of all in the United Kingdom. In addition many people in all countries saw mathematics and the native language as being essential or very important.

3.18

Public opinion on subjects regarded as essential or very important in secondary schools[1]: international comparison, 1993/94

					Percentages
	Arts	Sciences	Technology/ technical studies	Foreign languages	Education for citi-zenship[2]
Austria	*43*	*67*	*60*	*91*	*64*
Belgium[3]	*29*	*57*	*53*	*88*	*66*
Denmark	*36*	*46*	..	*79*	*46*
Finland	*31*	*53*	*39*	*87*	*35*
France	*31*	*63*	*47*	*87*	*67*
Netherlands	*31*	*64*	*42*	*85*	*41*
Portugal	*55*	*76*	*66*	*85*	*73*
Spain	*44*	*65*	*63*	*72*	*66*
Sweden	*31*	*65*	*38*	*87*	*70*
Switzerland	*58*	*63*	*52*	*77*	*65*
United Kingdom	*26*	*66*	*57*	*56*	*36*
United States	*47*	*85*	*36*	*53*	*77*

1 Respondents were asked 'The following are examples of things that young people study in secondary school. In your view how important are each of them?'
2 For example, civic or social education.
3 Flemish community.
Source: OECD

Further and higher education

This section deals with education beyond the minimum school-leaving age which in the United Kingdom is 16. Young people's participation rates in the United Kingdom have increased in recent years, and there has been a strong trend towards full-time education **(Table 3.19)**. Broadly speaking, the proportion of young people above the minimum school-leaving age in full-time education has almost doubled since 1980/81. By 1993/94 the proportion undertaking full or part-time education had increased to nearly 50 per cent of 18 year olds and around 40 per cent of 19 to 20 year olds. These figures include employees receiving job-related training at an educational institution; information on job-related training is contained in Table 4.29 in the Employment chapter.

Chart 3.20 shows, for the United Kingdom and some other countries, the proportion of the population participating in education or training at the age of 18. It is striking how much more quickly young people here quit the formal learning environment. By the age of 18 barely half are participating, whereas in France and Germany the proportion is about four fifths. Moreover, a sizeable minority (over a third) of our participants are part time whereas in the other countries almost all education and training for this age group is on a full-time basis. However, nine in ten 16 year olds and nearly eight in ten 17 year olds were in education or training in the United Kingdom. Of the countries shown in the chart, Belgium had the highest proportions.

3.19

Young people in full-time and part-time education: by gender and age[1]

United Kingdom Percentages

	Full time			Part time		
	1980/81	1991/92	1993/94	1980/81	1991/92	1993/94
Males						
16	..	64	71	..	18	15
17	..	46	54	..	20	13
18	..	28	36	..	19	14
19-20	14	21	27	18	14	12
21-24	5	7	10	11	12	10
All males aged 16-24	15	21	26	19	14	11
Females						
16	..	72	77	..	17	15
17	..	54	62	..	14	10
18	..	30	38	..	13	11
19-20	11	20	28	12	14	13
21-24	3	6	9	16	19	17
All females aged 16-24	15	22	27	16	16	15

1 As at 31 August.

Source: Department for Education and Employment

3.20

Percentage of 18 year olds in education and training[1]: international comparison, 1992

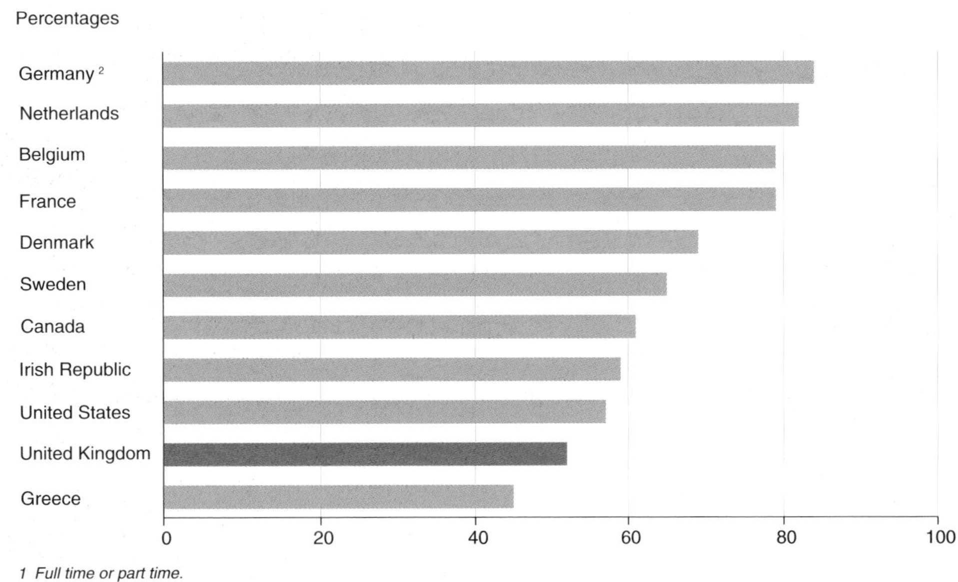

1 Full time or part time.
2 Former Federal Republic.

Source: OECD

3.21

Enrolments[1] in further and higher education: by type of course

United Kingdom — Thousands

	1970/71	1975/76	1980/81	1990/91	1991/92	1992/93	1993/94
Further education							
- Full time[2]	183	318	331	480	550	586	738
- Part time	905	1,423	..	1,759	1,803	1,728	1,756
Higher education							
Undergraduate - Full time	414	464	473	665	748	853	948
- Part time[3]	146	196	248	342	358	456	471
Postgraduate - Full time	43	51	61	84	97	105	116
- Part time[3]	18	23	46	86	98	115	129

1 Home and overseas students. Excludes adult education centres.
2 Data for 1980/81 relate to home students only.
3 Includes Open University.

Source: Department for Education and Employment

3.22

Enrolments in further and higher education: by subject group and gender, 1993/94

United Kingdom — Thousands

	Full time		Part time		All enrol-ments[1]
	Males	Females	Males	Females	
Further education					
Combined and general[2]	131	141	200	359	831
Languages/humanities	35	57	111	251	453
Business and finance	60	84	79	206	429
Engineering and technology	76	5	213	18	312
Sciences	33	59	62	94	248
Education	8	6	25	42	81
Social sciences	3	14	10	46	73
All enrolments[3]	360	379	720	1,033	2,494
Higher education					
Combined and general	61	74	8	11	154
Languages/humanities	66	96	10	14	186
Business and finance	77	76	67	64	285
Engineering and technology	124	23	70	8	225
Sciences[4]	145	121	40	111	416
Education[5]	21	58	15	35	128
Social sciences	57	66	15	21	159
All enrolments[6]	550	514	282	319	1,664

1 Includes students in further education in Scotland whose gender is not recorded.
2 Includes GCSE, CSE and GCE courses.
3 Includes enrolments on unspecified courses.
4 Part time includes nursing and paramedic enrolments at Department of Health establishments.
5 Includes teacher training.
6 Part time includes Open University for which there is no subject breakdown.

Source: Department for Education and Employment

Some young people above the minimum leaving age remain at school. By the age of 18, however, many will have entered either further or higher education. These sectors have both shown spectacular growth during recent years following a period of steady growth for some two decades, with increases in student numbers of the order of two and a half times **(Table 3.21)**. In just the three years to 1993/94 the number of full-time students increased by over 40 per cent in higher education and by over 50 per cent in further education; in each case this was greater than the increase over the whole of the preceding decade.

Overall 70 per cent of further education enrolments, but only 36 per cent of higher education enrolments, are part-time **(Table**

3.22). Among full-time enrolments in both sectors there are roughly equal numbers of men and women. In addition the balance of subjects is not very dissimilar, except that science is relatively more important in higher education where it accounts for 25 per cent of full-time enrolments compared with only 12 per cent in further education. In further education there is a big concentration of male part-timers on engineering and technical courses and of female part-timers on language, humanities, business and finance courses.

However, the healthy growth and widening coverage of the higher education sector should be seen against the background that, compared with other countries, the United Kingdom has fewer of its young people continuing to be educated through their late teens and early twenties, paralleling the low participation rates for 18 year olds already seen in Chart 3.20.

Table 3.23 compares the percentage of the population enrolled in higher education in the United Kingdom with other European Community (EC) countries, where the information is available, in three 'young adult' age groups. The United Kingdom's percentage for 22 to 25 year olds is the second lowest, and less than half that of France and Germany. Its percentage for 26 to 29 year olds is the third lowest, at barely a quarter of the German figure. The comparison is not an exact indication of educational penetration: it is affected by different lengths of course (shorter courses increase the flow of enrolments relative to student years) and a different pattern of study in other EC countries. However, it does illustrate the tendency for formal education to terminate earlier here than elsewhere.

The destinations of first degree graduates following graduation are monitored each year but have shown very little change over the last decade or so, though the absolute numbers have increased by over half **(Table 3.24)**. Of those who graduated in 1993, about one in five went on to further education or training and less than half entered employment in the United Kingdom.

3.23

Enrolment[1] in public and private higher education: by age, EC comparison[2], 1992

Percentages

	18-21	22-25	26-29
Belgium	*31*	*10*	*2*
Denmark	*9*	*20*	*10*
Finland	*15*	*22*	*11*
France	*29*	*14*	*4*
Germany[3]	*10*	*17*	*11*
Greece	*24*	*5*	*1*
Netherlands	*20*	*16*	*5*
Spain	*23*	*15*	*5*
Sweden	*11*	*13*	*7*
United Kingdom	*18*	*7*	*3*

1 Percentage of each age group enrolled.
2 Data are not available for Austria, Irish Republic, Italy, Luxembourg and Portugal.
3 Former Federal Republic.

Source: OECD

3.24

Destination of first degree graduates

United Kingdom Percentages

	Year of graduation			
	1983[1]	1986[1]	1991	1993
United Kingdom employment[2]	*48*	*53*	*44*	*45*
Further education or training	*21*	*19*	*20*	*21*
Believed unemployed	*10*	*7*	*10*	*10*
Overseas graduates leaving the United Kingdom	*4*	*3*	*8*	*10*
Not available for employment	*2*	*2*		
Overseas employment[3]	*2*	*2*	*3*	*2*
Destination not known	*13*	*14*	*13*	*12*
All first degree graduates (=100%)(thousands)	105	112	136	165

1 Data are for Great Britain only.
2 Permanent and temporary.
3 Home students.

Source: Department for Education and Employment

3.25

Student standard maintenance grant and loan[1] in real terms[2]

England, Wales & Northern Ireland

£ thousand at 1995-96 prices[2]

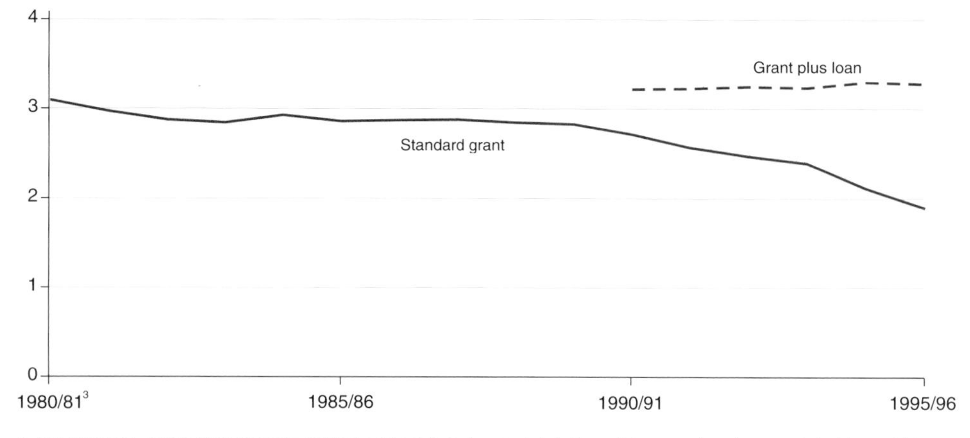

1 See Appendix, Part 3: Student grants and loans. The data for loans relate to those living away from home and studying outside London: the rate for 1995/96 is £1,695 for London and £1,065 for students living at parent's home.
2 Adjusted to 1995-96 prices using the retail prices index.
3 Data for 1980/81 to 1983/84 exclude travelling expenses which, at that time, were a separate payment.

Source: Department for Education and Employment

Finally, an important development in the las fifteen years, at least from the students' point of view, has been the reduction in the real value of student maintenance grants and the introduction of student loans. Between 1980/81 and 1990/91 in England, Wales and Northern Ireland the cash value of the grants increased each year but by less than the rate of inflation (as measured by the retail prices index), causing their value in real terms to fall by an eighth. Sinc 1990/91 even the cash value has not been increased but a loans scheme has been introduced. In 1995/96 this enabled student to augment their grant incomes by about three quarters as much again, giving the possibility of a total income somewhat above the 1980/81 level in real terms. **Char 3.25** shows graphically how the significance of the loan element has increased in recent years.

3.26

Enrolments on adult education courses[1]: by region and gender, 1991 and 1994

Percentages

	1991		1994	
	Males	Females	Males	Females
North	*1.7*	*4.3*	*1.3*	*3.5*
Yorkshire & Humberside	*1.0*	*2.7*	*0.9*	*2.4*
East Midlands	*2.0*	*4.8*	*1.8*	*4.6*
East Anglia	*2.2*	*5.7*	*1.6*	*4.4*
South East	*2.5*	*6.0*	*2.0*	*5.2*
Greater London	*2.8*	*6.6*	*2.3*	*5.5*
Rest of South East	*2.4*	*5.7*	*1.9*	*4.9*
South West	*1.5*	*4.1*	*1.3*	*3.6*
West Midlands	*1.7*	*4.0*	*1.3*	*2.8*
North West	*1.1*	*2.8*	*1.1*	*2.8*
England	*1.9*	*4.6*	*1.6*	*4.0*
Wales	*1.7*	*4.1*	*1.2*	*3.1*

1 Percentage of the population aged 16 and over. See Appendix, Part 3: Adult education.

Source: Department for Education and Employment; Welsh Office

Adult education

Over a third of higher education students and over a half of those in further education are aged 25 and over, most of these being part time. Opportunities for adults to take academic courses have been increasing in recent years; for example the government-financed Open University, which enables students to obtain degrees by studying mainly at home, started its courses in 1971. In 1992/93 there were over 100 thousand students which amounts to 8 per cent of the total in higher education. At a lower level, but catering for much greater numbers, are the part-time day and evening courses provided by adult education centres maintained by local education authorities. The proportions of adults enrolled on these courses in England and Wales are shown in Table 3.26. The proportion has fallen slightly since 1991 but still accounts for well over a million people. The participation rate is generally higher for women than men and is highest in the South East. The lowest rate for both men and women is in Yorkshire and Humberside. Education for adults is also provided by such bodies as the extra-mural departments of universities.

Spending on education

This final section on education concerns financial resources. **Chart 3.27** shows separate figures for government spending in Great Britain on secondary schools on the one hand and primary and nursery schools on the other, expressed on a 'per pupil' basis so as to exclude the effects of the fluctuations in numbers referred to earlier. Secondary school children are more expensive to educate than those at earlier stages, by virtue of their smaller class sizes and more specialised needs. The gap widened after the mid-1980s but since 1990 has narrowed again. In 1993-94 the average spending per nursery and primary school pupil was £1,650 while the equivalent for a secondary school pupil was £2,310. Over the whole period the per capita spending in real terms has increased by around a third. In Northern Ireland in 1993-94 average public spending per primary school pupil was £1,461 and per secondary school pupil, £2,275.

3.27

Average annual public spending per school pupil[1] in real terms[2]: by type of school[3]

Great Britain

£ thousand at 1993-94 prices[2]

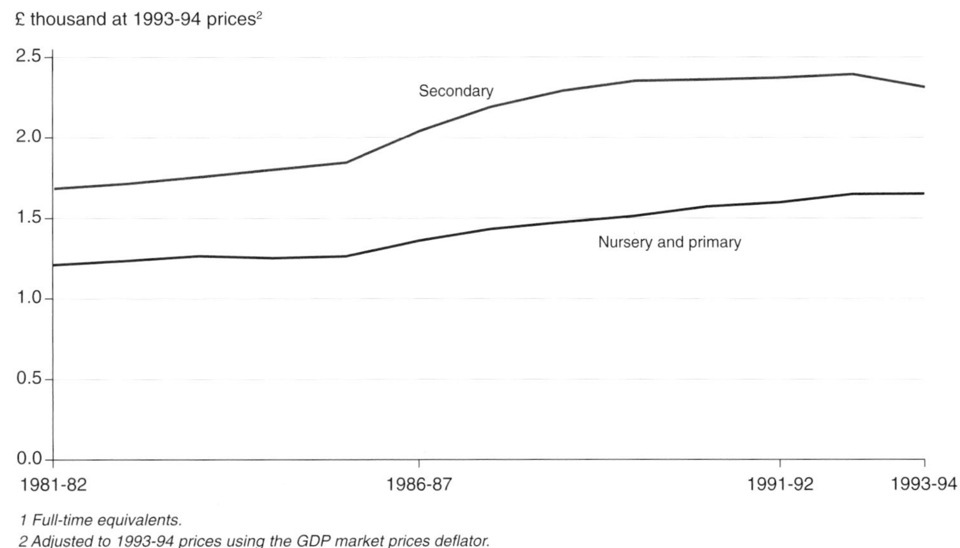

1 Full-time equivalents.
2 Adjusted to 1993-94 prices using the GDP market prices deflator.
3 Excludes grant-maintained schools.
Source: Department for Education and Employment; Welsh Office; The Scottish Office Education and Industry Department

Table 3.28 shows that the disparity between expenditure on primary and secondary education is common to all the G7 countries, and that higher education is invariably the most expensive of all. However the proportionate difference between expenditure on the secondary and higher education sectors is much greater in the United Kingdom than in the other G7 countries and the level of higher education expenditure per student is the third highest, after the United States and Canada.

3.28

Expenditure on education per student in public institutions: by level of education, G7 comparison, 1992

£ thousand

	Primary	Secondary[1]	Higher
United States[2]	3.5	4.0	8.6
Canada	..	..	7.7
United Kingdom[3]	1.9	2.7	6.5
Japan	2.2	2.4	4.4
Germany[4]	1.9	2.7	4.1
Italy	2.5	2.9	3.6
France[5]	1.8	3.4	3.6

1 Includes further education.
2 Includes private higher education.
3 Includes government-dependent private higher education.
4 Former Federal Republic.
5 Includes government-dependent private education.
Source: OECD

References and further reading

The following list contains selected publications relevant to **Chapter 3: Education**. Those published by HMSO are available from the addresses shown on the inside back cover of *Social Trends*.

Annual Report of Her Majesty's Chief Inspector of Schools, HMSO

Annual Survey of Trends in Education, National Foundation for Educational Research

Basic Skills of Young Adults, Adult Literacy and Basic Skills Unit

Department for Education and Office for Standards in Education Departmental Report: The Government's Expenditure Plans, HMSO

Difficulties with Basic Skills, Basic Skills Agency

Education at a Glance, OECD

Education Statistics for the United Kingdom, HMSO

Higher Education Statistics for the United Kingdom, HMSO

Older and Younger: the basic skills of different age-groups, Basic Skills Agency

Regional Trends, HMSO

Social Focus on Children, HMSO

Social Focus on Women, HMSO

Standards and Quality in Education (Report of Her Majesty's Chief Inspector of Schools), HMSO

Statistical Bulletins, from: Department for Education and Employment, The Scottish Office Education and Industry Department, Department of Education, Northern Ireland

Statistics of Education (5 volumes), HMSO

Statistics of Education in Wales, Welsh Office

Taught Time: an interim report, OFSTED

Testing 7 year olds: results of the National Curriculum assessments in England, Department for Education and Employment

Testing 14 year olds: results of the National Curriculum assessments in England, Department for Education and Employment

Contacts

Telephone contact points for further information relating to
Chapter 3: Education

Department for Education and Employment	01325 392658
Department of Education, Northern Ireland	01247 279677
Office of Population Censuses and Surveys	0171 396 2327
The Scottish Office Education and Industry Department	0131 244 0313
Welsh Office	01222 825060
Basic Skills Agency	0171 405 4017

Chapter 4 Employment

The labour force

In 1994, 53 per cent of all women aged 16 and over were economically active, 8 percentage points higher than in 1971. (Page 84)

The proportion of men aged 60 to 64 who were economically active fell to 51 per cent in 1994. (Table 4.4)

Type of employment

In Spring 1995, 25 per cent of employed men in the United Kingdom worked in manufacturing industries compared with only 12 per cent of employed women. (Chart 4.9)

In Spring 1995 there were just over one and a half million temporary workers in the United Kingdom; more than two fifths of these could not find a permanent job. (Table 4.11)

Industrial relations and trade unions

In 1994 the number of working days lost from labour disputes in the United Kingdom was at its lowest level since records began at around 280 thousand. (Chart 4.18)

Unemployment

In Spring 1995, 60 per cent of unemployed men aged 50 to 64 had been unemployed for a year or more compared with 45 per cent of those aged 20 to 29. (Table 4.24)

Employment and training measures

Between 1989 and 1995 the number of apprentices in the United Kingdom fell by nearly half to 191 thousand. (Chart 4.27)

Men are more likely than women to undergo job-related training to improve their chances of promotion whereas women are more likely than men to do so to make their work more interesting. (Page 97)

4.1

Full-time and part-time[1] employment[2]: by gender

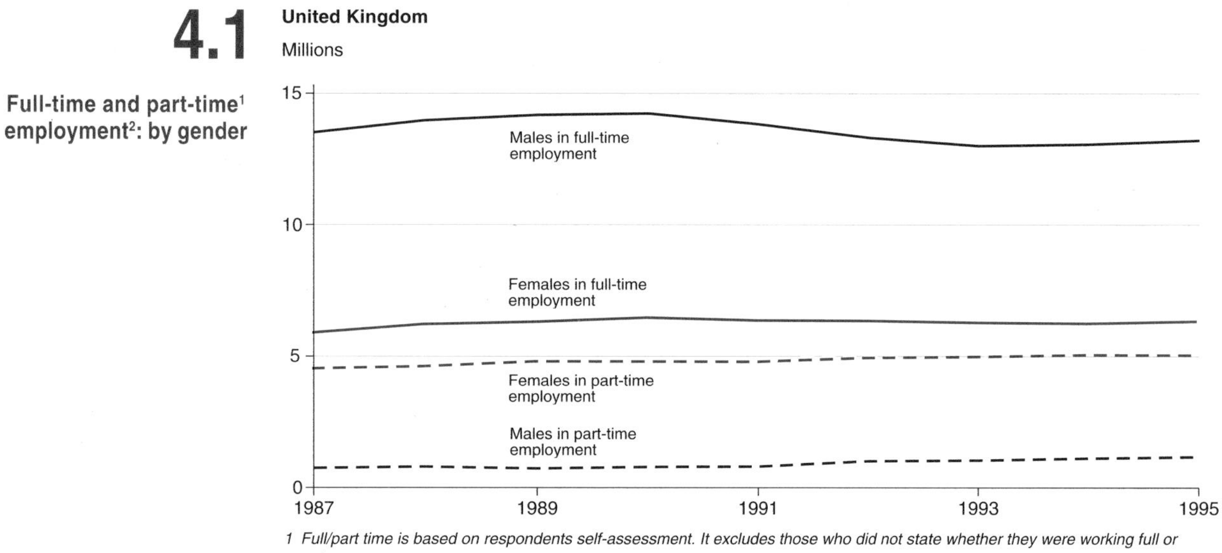

1 Full/part time is based on respondents self-assessment. It excludes those who did not state whether they were working full or part time.

2 At Spring each year. Includes employees, self-employed, those on government training schemes and unpaid family workers.

Source: Labour Force Survey, Central Statistical Office

Glossary of terms

Employees (Labour Force Survey measure) - a count, obtained from household surveys, of persons aged 16 and over who regard themselves as paid employees. People with two or more jobs are counted only once.

Employees in employment (employer survey based measure) - a count, obtained from surveys of employers, of jobs held by civilians who are paid by an employer who runs a PAYE tax scheme. People with more than one job are therefore counted more than once.

The self-employed - a count obtained from household surveys, of persons aged 16 and over who regard themselves as self-employed, ie who in their main employment work on their own account, whether or not they have employees.

Government employment and training programmes - a count, obtained from household surveys, of those who said they were participants on Youth Training, Employment Training, Employment Action or Community Industry or a programme organised by a TEC/LEC.

Work-related government training programmes - a count, obtained from administrative returns, of all participants who receive some form of work experience in the course of their placement but who do not have a contract of employment and are not self-employed.

The labour force in employment - a count, obtained from household surveys and censuses, of employees, self-employed persons, participants in government employment and training programmes, and persons doing unpaid family work.

The workforce in employment - a count of employees in employment (from employer survey based measures), self-employed persons, all HM forces and participants in government employment and training programmes.

The claimant unemployed - a measure, known as the claimant count, and derived from administrative sources, which counts as unemployed those who are claiming unemployment related benefits at Employment Service local offices (formerly Unemployment Benefit Offices).

The ILO unemployed - an International Labour Organisation (ILO) recommended measure, used in household surveys such as the Labour Force Survey, which counts as unemployed those aged 16 and over who are without a job, are available to start work in the next two weeks, who have been seeking a job in the last four weeks or are waiting to start a job already obtained.

The workforce - the **workforce in employment** plus the **claimant unemployed.**

The economically active - the **labour force in employment** plus the **ILO unemployed.**

The civilian labour force - the **labour force in employment** plus the **ILO unemployed** less **HM forces.**

Claimant unemployment rate - the percentage of the **workforce** who are **claimant unemployed.**

ILO unemployment rate - the percentage of the **economically active** who are **ILO unemployed.**

The economically inactive - people who are neither part of the labour force in employment nor ILO unemployed. For example, all people under 16, those looking after a home or retired, or those permanently unable to work.

The population of working age - males aged 16 to 64 years and females aged 16 to 59 years.

Economic activity rate - the percentage of the population in a given age group which is in the labour force.

Some of these terms are covered in more detail in the appendix.

ʼlost people are members of the country's ɪbour force from the time they leave full- me education until they retire. For women, is becoming increasingly important as ɪore and more enter paid employment.

ʼhe labour force

ʼhe age structure of the labour force in ;reat Britain which is shown in **Table 4.2** ʼepends largely on demographic factors, uch as the birth rate in earlier years. All the .abour Force Survey (LFS) estimates from 984 have been revised to take account of ɪe revised population estimates supplied by ɪe Office of Population Censuses and ;urveys following the 1991 Census of ʼopulation. Care should be taken when omparing these figures with those ublished in earlier editions of *Social ʼrends*.

ʼhe decrease in the size of the labour force ged 16 to 24 years since the mid-1980s eflects both a fall in births in the early 970s (see Chart 1.12 in the Population hapter) and an increase in those furthering ɪeir education beyond mandatory schooling see Table 3.21 in the Education chapter).)ver the period 1986 to 1994, the size of ɪis age group in the labour force fell by round a quarter to 4.7 million. It is rojected to fall by a further 0.2 million etween 1994 and 2006 to 4.5 million. The irth rate has also been a factor in the ncrease in the number of people aged etween 25 and 44 in the labour force in the ate 1980s, which is the product of the high irth rates in the early 1960s. This will ventually work its way through to have an ffect on the numbers aged 45 to 59 as they ontinue to increase to more than 9 million y 2006, just under a third of the labour orce.

4.2

Labour force: by age

Great Britain — Thousands

	16-24	25-44	45-59	60-64	65 and over	All aged 16 and over
Estimates						
1984	6,214	12,201	7,077	1,252	429	27,172
1986	6,326	12,788	6,968	1,083	402	27,566
1991	5,684	14,256	7,311	1,102	462	28,815
1992	5,224	14,192	7,596	1,069	501	28,582
1993	4,941	14,258	7,742	1,070	443	28,454
1994	4,710	14,301	7,922	1,051	437	28,421
Projections						
1996	4,404	14,609	8,227	1,049	429	28,717
2001	4,313	14,893	8,748	1,105	409	29,469
2006	4,519	14,609	9,252	1,295	416	30,092

Source: Labour Force Survey, Central Statistical Office

In Spring 1995, nearly 6 per cent of the population of working age in Great Britain were from ethnic minority groups. **Table 4.3** shows that, overall, the percentage of men who were in employment was highest among the White group at 77 per cent,

4.3

Economic status of people of working age: by gender and ethnic group, Spring 1995

Great Britain — Percentages

	White	Black[1]	Indian	Pakistani/ Bangladeshi	Other[2]	All ethnic groups[3]
Males						
Working full time	*72*	*49*	*65*	*41*	*51*	*71*
Working part time	*5*	*8*	*7*	*8*	*8*	*5*
Unemployed	*8*	*21*	*10*	*18*	*12*	*9*
Inactive	*15*	*22*	*18*	*33*	*29*	*15*
All (=100%)(thousands)	16,993	273	306	216	224	18,017
Females						
Working full time	*38*	*37*	*36*	*12*	*30*	*38*
Working part time	*29*	*15*	*19*	*6*	*16*	*28*
Unemployed	*5*	*14*	*7*	*7*	*8*	*5*
Inactive	*28*	*34*	*38*	*75*	*46*	*29*
All (=100%)(thousands)	15,420	296	279	191	238	16,428

1 Includes Caribbean, African and other Black people of non-mixed origin.
2 Includes Chinese, other ethnic minority groups of non-mixed origin and people of mixed origin.
3 Includes ethnic group not stated.

Source: Labour Force Survey, Central Statistical Office

4.4

Labour force economic activity rates[1]: by gender and age

United Kingdom — Percentages

	16-24	25-44	45-59	60-64	65 and over	All aged 16 and over
Males						
Estimates						
1984	*81.8*	*96.1*	*90.0*	*57.5*	*8.7*	*75.9*
1986	*82.6*	*95.9*	*88.8*	*53.8*	*7.9*	*75.2*
1991	*81.2*	*95.7*	*88.1*	*54.2*	*8.6*	*74.9*
1992	*77.5*	*95.1*	*87.5*	*52.8*	*8.9*	*73.9*
1993	*76.1*	*94.5*	*86.3*	*52.2*	*7.4*	*72.9*
1994	*75.1*	*94.1*	*86.1*	*51.0*	*7.6*	*72.6*
Projections						
1996	*72.4*	*94.2*	*86.4*	*50.4*	*7.5*	*72.2*
2001	*70.3*	*94.4*	*85.3*	*49.7*	*7.0*	*71.5*
2006	*69.3*	*94.2*	*83.7*	*49.1*	*6.8*	*70.0*
Females						
Estimates						
1984	*69.1*	*65.6*	*63.3*	*21.8*	*3.1*	*49.2*
1986	*70.6*	*67.4*	*64.0*	*19.1*	*2.7*	*50.0*
1991	*71.3*	*73.0*	*66.9*	*23.9*	*3.1*	*53.1*
1992	*67.5*	*72.8*	*68.4*	*23.4*	*3.6*	*52.8*
1993	*66.0*	*73.6*	*68.5*	*24.7*	*3.5*	*53.0*
1994	*64.6*	*73.5*	*69.3*	*25.3*	*3.2*	*53.0*
Projections						
1996	*63.6*	*74.8*	*70.4*	*26.6*	*3.0*	*53.7*
2001	*63.3*	*77.8*	*71.9*	*29.0*	*2.8*	*55.5*
2006	*63.2*	*81.3*	*72.6*	*31.9*	*2.9*	*56.7*

1 The percentage of the population that is in the labour force.

Source: Labour Force Survey, Central Statistical Office

followed by Indians at 72 per cent. Those of Pakistani or Bangladeshi origin had the lowest rate at 49 per cent. A similar pattern emerges among women of working age. However, while roughly similar proportions of women from the White, Black and Indian ethnic groups were in full-time employment, women of White ethnic origin were far more likely to be working part time. There are large differences in the proportion of women who are economically inactive. Three quarters of women of Bangladeshi and Pakistani ethnic origin were economically inactive which was nearly three times the proportion for women of White ethnic origin. In Northern Ireland, Protestant women were more likely to be in employment and less likely to be inactive than Catholic women.

The economic activity rate is that proportion of the population above the minimum school-leaving age which is in the labour force. The picture for men and women in the United Kingdom is a contrasting one. While the overall rate for men has been falling somewhat and is projected to continue doing so, for women it has been rising **(Table 4.4)**. This increase among women is partly due to an increase in the number of part-time jobs, but also due to women having fewer children, delaying having children and being more likely to return to work after having a child.

In 1994, over half of all women aged 16 and over were economically active, approximately 8 percentage points higher than in 1971. For all women except those aged 16 to 24 and 65 and over, economic activity rates are projected to carry on rising up to 2006 whereas among men the rates are projected to either level off or fall at all ages. Four in every five men aged 60 to 64 were economically active in 1971; the corresponding proportion in 2006 is projected to be one in two. This is a result of the trend towards early retirement.

Among the major industrialised (G7) countries, employment and economic activity rates for older workers (those aged 55 to 64) have fallen over the last 20 years although wide variations exist. In 1994 the highest economic activity rate for older men was in Japan at 85 per cent while the United States had the highest rate for older women at 49 per cent **(Chart 4.5)**. On the other hand

4.5

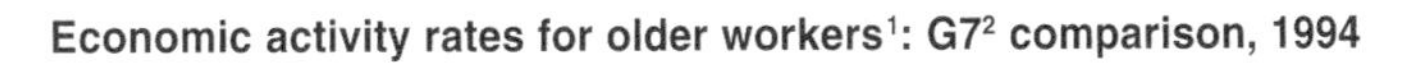

Economic activity rates for older workers[1]: G7[2] comparison, 1994

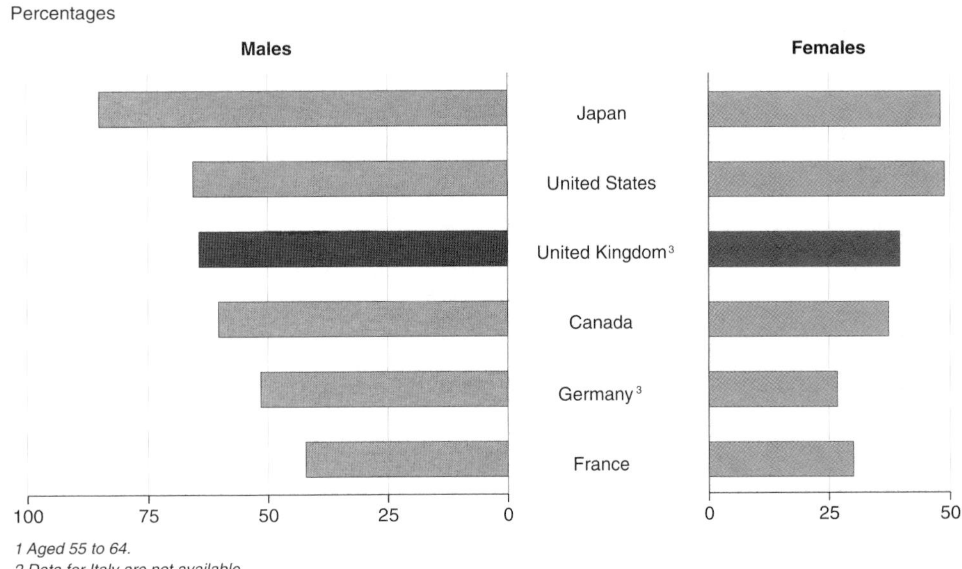

1 Aged 55 to 64.
2 Data for Italy are not available.
3 Data are for 1993.
Source: OECD

he lowest rate for men was in France while ermany had the lowest rate for women. An geing population and ageing labour force re a cause for concern among many ndustrialised nations. Part of the solution to he problem of a growing dependent opulation could be the raising of the etirement age which would reduce pension osts. In 1994 it was announced that the tate retirement age for women in the United ingdom would be raised to 65, the same as or men, between 2010 and 2020. Other ountries considering raising retirement ges are Japan, France and the United tates. The economic activity rates of older vorkers are influenced by other factors such s employers' attitudes, incentives to ncourage deferral of retirement (as in ermany where pension entitlements ncrease between the ages of 65 and 67) nd the attitudes of older workers hemselves.

The difference in the attitudes of workers of ifferent ages in Great Britain to work ommitment in 1994 is shown in **Table 4.6**. A niddle aged employee was more likely to ay that they 'do the best I can even if it nterferes with my life', with around half of all hose aged 45 to 54 questioned agreeing vith this. Younger employees were more ikely to say that they 'would still work even f no financial need'; more than seven in ten 18 to 34 year olds agreed with this. One eason may be the importance they place on the social aspects of a working environment and the opportunity to interact with others. For most age groups, around two thirds of employees said that a 'job is more than just earning a living'. Attitudes of the self-employed were largely consistent with those of employees except that nearly seven in ten were likely to agree with the 'do the best I can even if it interferes with my life' statement compared with under a half of employees. This may be because the link between the work of the self-employed and their income is more direct than that for employees.

4.6

Employees views on work commitment: by age, 1994

Great Britain — Percentages

	18-24	25-34	35-44	45-54	55-59	All aged 16 and over
Would still work if no financial need	*76*	*73*	*70*	*60*	*64*	*69*
Job is much more than just earning a living	*54*	*61*	*67*	*64*	*58*	*62*
Do the best I can, even if it sometimes interferes with my life	*30*	*45*	*49*	*53*	*49*	*46*

Source: British Social Attitudes Survey, Social & Community Planning Research

4.7

UK nationals working in EC states and EC nationals working in the United Kingdom, 1994

Thousands

	UK nationals working in EC states	EC nationals working in the United Kingdom
Belgium	6	3
Denmark	5	8
France	31	35
Germany	62	21
Greece	2	8
Irish Republic[1]	20	230
Italy	2	41
Luxembourg	1	..
Netherlands	25	13
Portugal	1	18
Spain	4	26

1 Data are for 1993.
Source: Eurostat

Employment is not just a national factor as there are a number of European Community (EC) nationals working in the United Kingdom and also UK nationals working in other EC countries. The largest single group of foreign nationals working in the United Kingdom were from the Irish Republic **(Table 4.7)**. However, there has always been a free movement of workers between the United Kingdom and the Irish Republic, even before both countries joined the EC. The country with the second largest number of nationals working in this country in 1994 was Italy, with just over 40 thousand. More UK nationals worked in Germany than any other EC country - over 60 thousand worked there compared with only 1 thousand who worked in Portugal. Further data on the total numbers of foreign nationals living here and UK nationals living abroad can be found in Table 1.18 in the Population chapter.

Type of employment

The type of employment in which people are engaged can vary widely. Over recent years there has been an increase in the number of part-time jobs available in the United Kingdom leading to an increase in economic activity rates of women. In 1994 the majority of employed men in all EC countries were engaged in full-time work **(Chart 4.8)**. However, there are some marked differences in the proportions who work part time. In Luxembourg only just over 1 per cent of employed men were in part-time work compared with 16 per cent in the Netherlands. Women in all EC countries are more likely than men to work part time. The country with the highest proportion of female part-time workers was the Netherlands where over two thirds of women in employment were in part-time work; the United Kingdom had the second highest proportion. Greece had the highest proportion of women workers in full-time employment with over 90 per cent. However only 30 per cent of Greek women were in employment in 1994, compared with 49 per cent in the United Kingdom and 53 per cent in Denmark and Sweden.

The change in the numbers of people in both full-time and part-time work in the United Kingdom is shown in **Chart 4.1**. Since 1987 part-time working has become more common for both men and women. Between 1987 and 1995 the number of women in part-time employment increased by 12 per cent to 5.2 million; among men the number increased by more than half over the same period, but to 1.2 million. However, women's increased economic activity is not just confined to part-time work. Over the same period, the number of women in full-time employment rose by 8 per cent whereas the

4.8

People in full-time and part-time employment: EC comparison, 1994

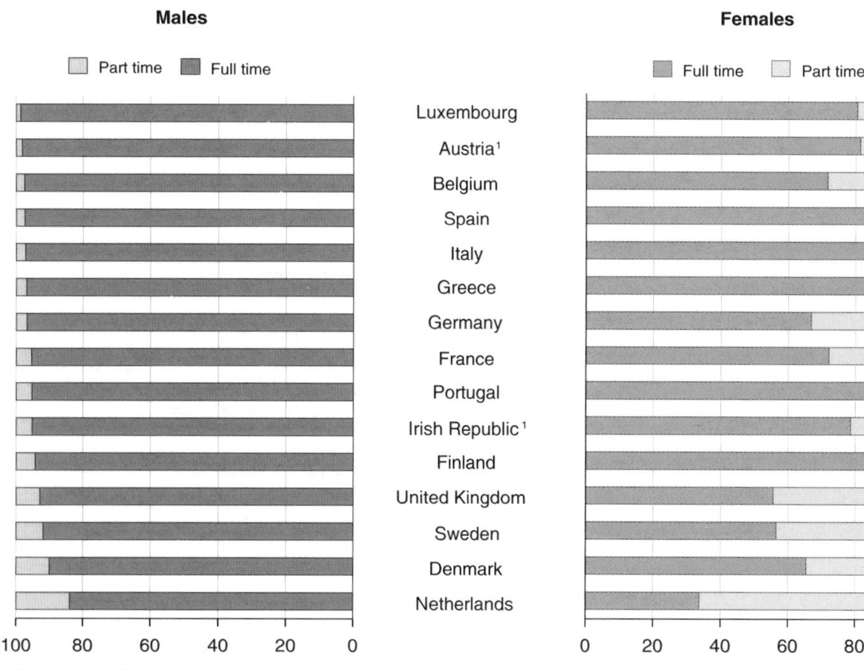

1 Data are for 1993.
Source: Eurostat

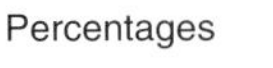

number of men in full-time employment declined by 2 per cent. Between Spring 1994 and Spring 1995 the most notable increase in the number of part-time workers was in the transport industries at 9 per cent. The most significant decrease was in the energy and water supply industries with a fall of 25 per cent.

Men and women predominate in different sorts of industries. Around a quarter of employed men worked in manufacturing industries, compared with just over one in ten employed women **(Chart 4.9)**. Construction is another industry where men far outnumber women. The biggest area for women employees was public administration, education and health: overall nearly four in ten women in employment worked in this area. Women outnumber men by around four to one in the health sector and around two to one in education. However, men still predominate in the higher level jobs in these sectors with only 30 per cent of secondary school head and deputy head teachers being women although they represent nearly half of all teachers in secondary schools in England, Wales and Northern Ireland.

Some occupations tend to be seen as traditionally female areas. In Spring 1995 around a quarter of women in the United Kingdom worked in clerical and secretarial occupations, whereas only 10 per cent of women were in the managerial and administrative occupations **(Chart 4.10)**. By contrast, nearly a fifth of all male employees were managers and administrators, which for men was the largest occupational group. Between 1992 and 1995 there was a 12 per cent fall in the proportion of male employees in craft and related occupations compared with an 18 per cent fall for women.

4.9

People in employment: by gender and industry, Spring 1995

United Kingdom

Percentages

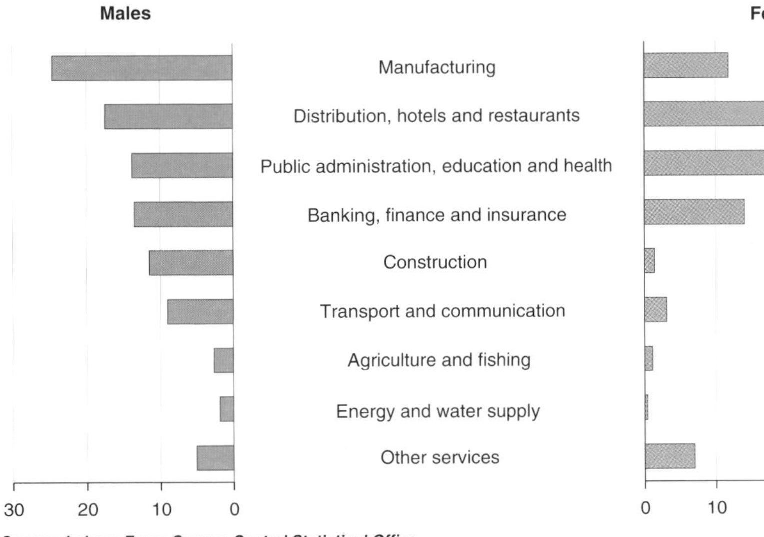

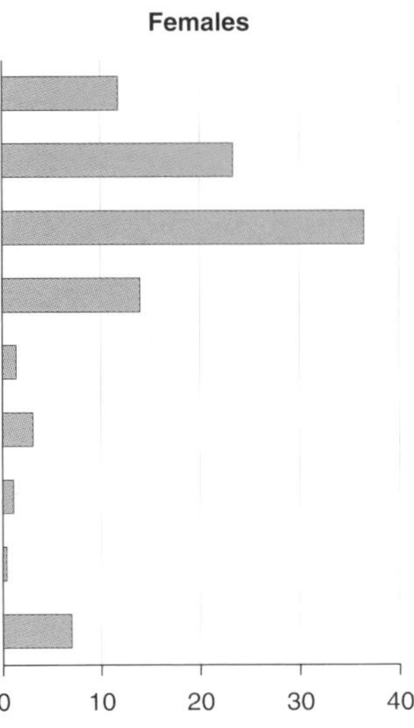

Source: Labour Force Survey, Central Statistical Office

4.10

Employees: by gender and occupation[1], Spring 1995

United Kingdom

Percentages

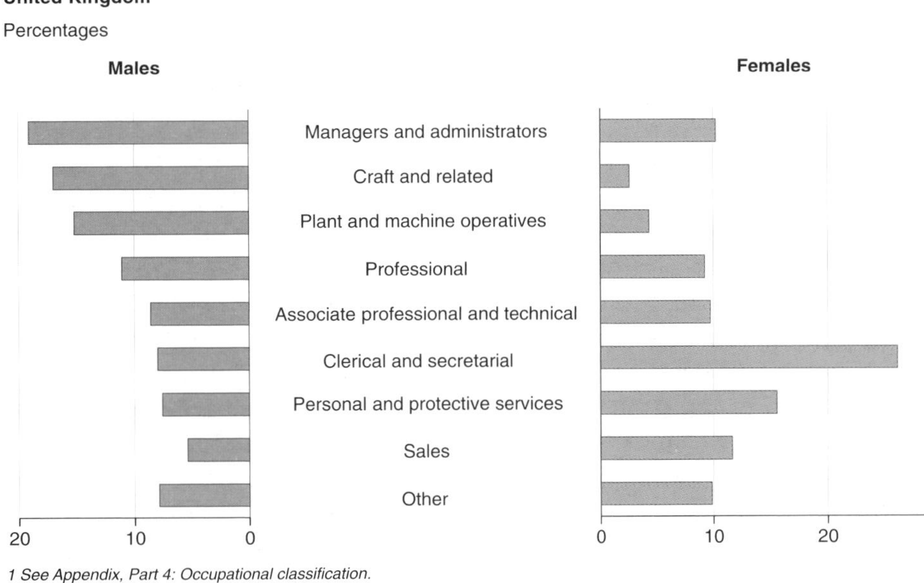

1 See Appendix, Part 4: Occupational classification.

Source: Labour Force Survey, Central Statistical Office

4.11

Temporary[1] employees: by gender and reason for taking temporary job[2], Spring 1995

United Kingdom Percentages

	Males	Females	All
Could not find a permanent job	*51.5*	*37.8*	*44.2*
Did not want a permanent job	*19.2*	*34.5*	*27.4*
Had a contract which included a period of training	*7.3*	*4.3*	*5.7*
Other reasons	*21.9*	*23.3*	*22.6*
All persons in temporary jobs (=100%)(thousands)	720	827	1,547

1 Temporary employees are those who assess themselves to have either a seasonal, temporary or casual job or a job done under contract or for a fixed period.
2 As a main job.

Source: Labour Force Survey, Central Statistical Office

Although jobs are all classified as either full-time or part-time, they are by no means all permanent. In Spring 1995 there were over 1.5 million temporary workers in the United Kingdom, an increase of around 10 per cent on the previous year. Sometimes the nature of the work can lead to it being a short-term contract, such as consultancy work. Some people may prefer the variety and flexibility offered, for example, by agency 'temping' but in other cases they may take temporary work because they cannot find a permanent job. The reasons why people take temporary jobs are shown in **Table 4.11**. More than four in ten of all employees with temporary main jobs in Spring 1995 had them because they could not find permanent work. However, women were nearly twice as likely as men to have a temporary job because they did not want a permanent one. Overall, in Spring 1995 temporary workers represented 7 per cent of all employees.

The British Household Panel Survey reinterviews the same sample of individuals over a period of time and so can show how the employment status of individuals changes from one year to the next. **Table 4.12** shows that around 90 per cent of both men and women who had permanent jobs in 1991 also had a permanent job in 1992. For both genders, the flow from permanent jobs into seasonal or fixed-term contracts was low, particularly in comparison with the flow out of paid work. For people on fixed term contracts, the proportions for those who still had that contract status one year later were relatively low at 30 per cent of men and 27 per cent of women. The main flow from this category was into permanent jobs with 45 per cent of men and 50 per cent of women following this course. Around nine in ten of both men and women who were not working in 1991 were in the same position a year later. Further information on employment dynamics is included in the article on the British Household Panel Survey which begins on page 27.

4.12

Change in contract status, 1991 to 1992

Great Britain Percentages

	1992 status				
	Not working	Permanent job	Seasonal/ casual	Fixed-term contract	All
1991 status					
Males					
Not working	*88*	*8*	*3*	*2*	*100*
Permanent job	*7*	*90*	*1*	*2*	*100*
Seasonal/casual	*39*	*33*	*19*	*9*	*100*
Fixed-term contract	*20*	*45*	*6*	*30*	*100*
Females					
Not working	*91*	*6*	*2*	*-*	*100*
Permanent job	*9*	*88*	*2*	*1*	*100*
Seasonal/casual	*30*	*37*	*28*	*4*	*100*
Fixed-term contract	*16*	*50*	*8*	*27*	*100*

Source: British Household Panel Survey, ESRC Research Centre on Micro-social Change

Time at work

The amount of time that people spend at work during a week varies depending upon many factors such as whether the job is manual or non-manual or what industry it is

n. In the United Kingdom in Spring 1995 there were nearly 20 million people in full-time employment who each worked an average of around 44 hours per week. **Table 4.13** shows the spread of weekly hours usually worked in a week by people in full-time and part-time employment in their main job in the United Kingdom in Spring 1995. The hours include paid and unpaid overtime but exclude meal breaks. For just over three in ten men in full-time employment, the working week was over 48 hours long whereas more than six in ten of their female counterparts usually worked 40 hours or less a week.

Part-time workers are usually defined as those who work no more than 30 hours per week. For these workers, the average hours were around 17 per week with nearly four out of five people in part-time employment usually working less than 25 hours each week. Information on average earnings can be found in Chart 5.6 in the Income and Wealth chapter.

The average hours usually worked per week (including both full-time and part-time work) by employees in the EC in 1994 was just over 37. Of all the member states, the United Kingdom had the highest average hours for men at over 43 hours per week (**Table 4.14**). The weekly average for male employees working full-time varied from over 45 hours in the United Kingdom to just under 39 hours in Belgium, where men worked nearly 15 per cent fewer hours each week. Among women full-time employees, UK women also worked the longest hours at over 40 hours per week. However, the story is very different when part-time work is taken into account. Overall, Greek women work the longest hours at just over 38 per week while their Dutch counterparts worked only two thirds of those hours.

4.13

Total usual hours worked by people in full-time and part-time employment: by gender, Spring 1995

United Kingdom — Percentages

	Males		Females		All persons	
	Full time	Part time	Full time	Part time	Full time	Part time
Under 20	-	62	..	54	-	55
20-24	-	17	1	23	-	22
25-30	1	14	3	17	2	16
31-34	1	2	3	4	2	3
35-40	33	1	56	2	41	3
41-44	15	..	14	..	14	..
45-48	16	..	10	..	14	..
49-59	20	..	8	..	16	..
60 and over	13	..	4	..	10	..
All persons (=100%) (thousands)	13,136	1,082	6,391	5,115	19,527	6,196

Source: Labour Force Survey, Central Statistical Office

4.14

Average hours usually worked[1] per week: by gender, EC comparison, 1994

Hours

	Males			Females		
	Full time	Part time	All	Full time	Part time	All
United Kingdom	45.4	16.0	43.5	40.4	17.9	30.6
Portugal	42.7	26.3	42.4	39.3	20.2	37.9
Greece	41.4	25.6	41.0	39.0	21.5	38.0
Irish Republic	41.6	21.2	40.6	37.8	18.0	33.9
Spain	41.0	19.6	40.6	39.5	17.5	36.3
Luxembourg	40.6	26.7	40.5	37.9	19.7	34.3
France	40.6	22.5	39.8	38.8	22.4	34.2
Italy	39.7	30.1	39.5	36.3	23.0	34.7
Germany	39.9	18.9	39.3	39.2	20.2	33.0
Belgium	38.8	21.1	38.3	36.9	20.9	31.9
Denmark	39.8	14.2	37.1	38.0	21.2	32.0
Netherlands	39.6	18.6	36.3	39.1	17.9	25.2
EC average	41.1	19.5	40.2	38.9	19.7	32.8

1 Employees only. Excludes meal breaks but includes paid and unpaid overtime.

Source: Eurostat

4.15

Employees with flexible working patterns: by gender, Spring 1995

United Kingdom Percentages

	Males	Females	All
Full time			
Flexible working hours	*9.5*	*14.7*	*11.3*
Annualised working hours	*5.6*	*6.8*	*6.0*
Four and a half day week	*3.3*	*3.2*	*3.3*
Term-time working	*1.1*	*4.5*	*2.3*
Nine day fortnight	*0.5*	*0.2*	*0.4*
Job sharing	..	..	*0.1*
All full-time employees[1] (=100%)(thousands)	10,872	5,953	16,734
Part time			
Flexible working hours	*6.9*	*8.8*	*8.5*
Annualised working hours	*3.9*	*5.5*	*5.2*
Four and a half day week	..	..	..
Term-time working	*4.6*	*10.4*	*9.5*
Nine day fortnight	-	..	..
Job sharing	*1.8*	*2.4*	*2.3*
All part-time employees[1] (=100%)(thousands)	817	4,634	5,451

1 Includes employees who did not work flexible working hours or did not state them.

Source: Labour Force Survey, Central Statistical Office

Although employees are usually expected to work a set number of hours per week, there is increasing use of flexible working patterns. Flexible working hours or flexi-time was worked by around 10 per cent of men and 15 per cent of women employees in full-time work in Spring 1995 **(Table 4.15)**. The second most popular form of flexible working for those working full time is annualised working hours. This is when a set number of hours are worked over the course of a year. In Spring 1995, 6 per cent of full-time employees had annualised working hours. The industrial sectors where people work also influences their ability to use flexible working patterns. In banking, financial and business services around 18 per cent of employees worked flexi-time compared with 6 per cent in the distribution, hotels and catering and repairs industries in Spring 1994.

Another working practice is homeworking **(Table 4.16)**. There are a range of different types of worker in this category including farmers, some of the self-employed, people doing piece work and employees who have an arrangement with their employers to regularly do some of their work at home. In Spring 1995 some 0.7 million people worked mainly at home. A further 0.5 million worked in the same grounds or buildings as their home and around 1.6 million used their home as a base. Of those who worked at home, nearly four in ten were manual workers while employers and managers constituted around one in six. Four per cent of women in employment were classed as homeworkers compared with 1 per cent of men. Over three quarters of all homeworkers owned their own business or worked on their own account.

In Spring 1995 the industry with the highest rate of sickness or injury among men was transport and communications where 4.3 per

4.16

Homeworking: by gender and socio-economic group, Spring 1995

United Kingdom Percentages

	Males	Females	All persons
Employers and managers	*22*	*14*	*16*
Professional	*20*	*3*	*8*
Intermediate non-manual	*25*	*17*	*20*
Junior non-manual	-	*18*	*12*
Manual (foremen, supervisors, skilled and own account workers)	*28*	*41*	*37*
Personal service and semi-skilled manual	-	*6*	*5*
Unskilled	-	-	-
All homeworkers (=100%)(thousands)	225	473	697

Source: Labour Force Survey, Central Statistical Office

cent of employees had some time off due to sickness in the reference week (**Chart 4.17**). This compares with an average figure for all industries of 3.7 per cent, virtually the same as in Spring 1994. For women employees, the industry with the highest absence rate was manufacturing at 6.5 per cent. As might be expected absence due to sickness and injury is highest in winter. In Winter 1994, 4.6 per cent of male and 6.2 per cent of female employees were absent for at least one day in the reference week.

Industrial relations and trade unions

Labour disputes may also result in lost working days. **Chart 4.18** shows working days lost due to labour disputes since 1901. In 1918, the then Ministry of Labour decided to try to improve industrial relations, which had been particularly poor during the First World War, by creating Joint Industrial Councils called Whitley Councils after J H Whitley, the Speaker of the House of Commons. Several other measures were introduced but the 1920s were still a period of great industrial unrest, culminating in the General Strike in 1926. The coal industry alone lost 146 million days in this dispute. More recently the number of working days lost reached a secondary peak in 1984 when the miners' strike accounted for over 22 million out of an annual total of just over 27 million days lost. The reasons for stoppages vary: in 1994 the main cause for labour disputes was pay which accounted for 57 per cent of working days lost; in 1993 the main cause was redundancy questions which accounted for 60 per cent of working days lost. In 1994 the number of working days lost was 280 thousand, less than half the previous year's total of 650 thousand and the lowest calendar year total since records began in 1891.

4.17

Percentage of employees absent from work owing to sickness or injury: by gender and industry, Spring 1995

United Kingdom

Percentages

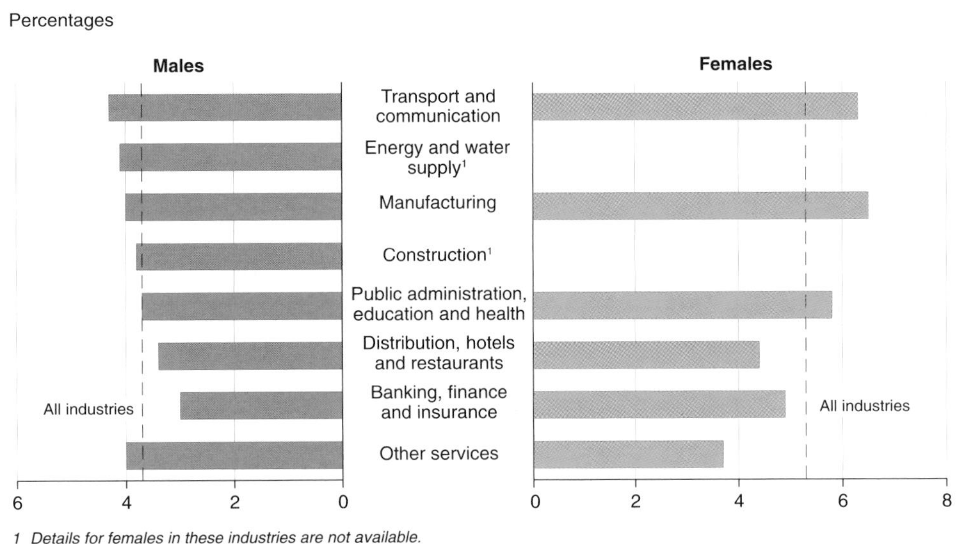

1 Details for females in these industries are not available.

Source: Labour Force Survey, Central Statistical Office

4.18

Labour disputes[1]: working days lost

United Kingdom

Millions

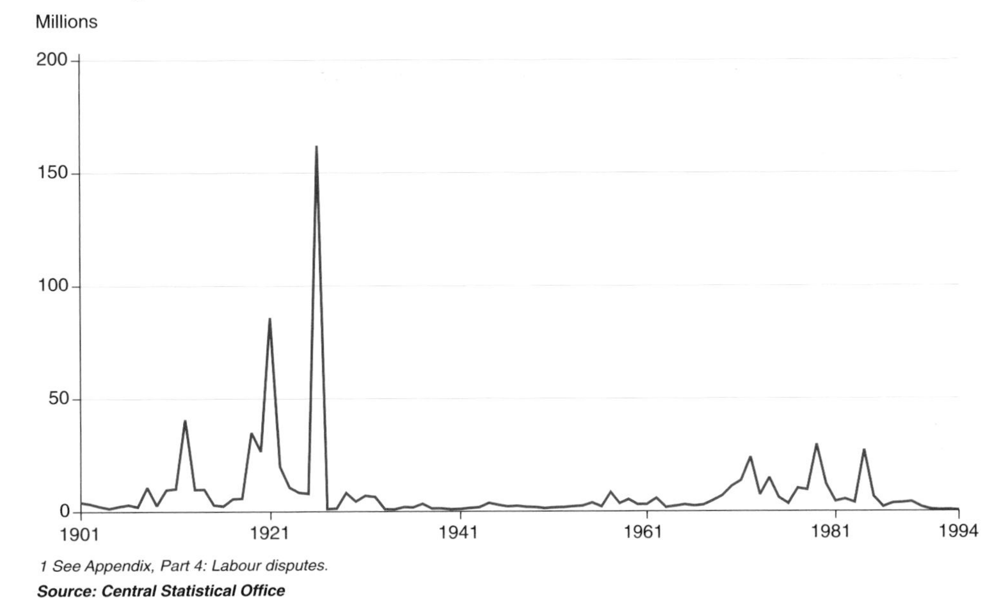

1 See Appendix, Part 4: Labour disputes.

Source: Central Statistical Office

4.19

Trade union membership[1] as a percentage of the civilian workforce in employment: by gender and occupation, Autumn 1994

United Kingdom			Percentages
	Males	Females	All persons
Managers and administrators	*20*	*21*	*21*
Professional	*39*	*59*	*47*
Associate professional and technical	*33*	*53*	*43*
Clerical and secretarial	*35*	*24*	*27*
Craft and related	*29*	*27*	*29*
Personal and protective service	*38*	*24*	*29*
Sales	*13*	*10*	*11*
Plant and machine operatives	*44*	*32*	*41*
Other	*30*	*23*	*26*
All in employment[2]	*31*	*29*	*30*

1 Includes organisations described as staff associations.
2 Includes those who did not state their occupation.
Source: Labour Force Survey, Central Statistical Office

Industrial negotiations generally take place between employers and the workers' representatives, usually trade unions. Over recent years, the level of trade union membership among the workforce has fallen sharply **(Table 4.19)**, as has the number of trade unions. In 1981 there were 414 unions but by 1993 this had fallen by nearly two thirds to 254. This fall in numbers was partly due to mergers. For example, in July 1993 the National and Local Government Officers' Association (NALGO), the National Union of Public Employees (NUPE) and the Confederation of Health Service Employees (COHSE) merged to form the Public Service Union, UNISON. This was the largest trade union in the United Kingdom in 1994 with around 1.5 million members, most of whom are female. The proportion of the workforce who were trade union members continued its recent downward trend in Autumn 1994 when 29 per cent of women and 31 per cent of men were members. In 1994 the rate of union membership was highest among professional occupations at 47 per cent and lowest among sales occupations at just 11 per cent.

4.20

Employees'[1] views of what trade unions should try to do, 1989 and 1994

Great Britain		Percentages
	1989	1994
Protect existing jobs	*28*	*37*
Improve working conditions	*21*	*20*
Improve pay	*28*	*15*
Have more say over management's long term plans	*6*	*14*
Have more say over how work is done day to day	*3*	*5*
Reduce pay differences at the workplace	*6*	*4*
Work for equal opportunities for women	*3*	*2*

1 Employees with a recognised trade union or staff association at the workplace were given a list of things trade unions do and asked 'what, if any, is the most important thing they should try to do at your workplace?'
Source: British Social Attitudes Survey, Social & Community Planning Research

Although the proportion of employees in trade unions has fallen sharply over recent years, the proportion of employees in a trade union who believe that their union is doing its job well is around 60 per cent. The perception of what trade unions should be doing has changed in line with changes in the economic cycle. In 1989, and again in 1994, the British Social Attitudes Survey asked employees with a recognised trade union or staff association at their workplace questions about what trade unions should be doing. In 1989, the protection of jobs and the improvement of pay were considered to be of equal importance. By 1994 more than twice as many employees wanted their union to protect jobs as wanted them to improve pay **(Table 4.20)**. Reasons for this change may include such factors as a belief that trade unions are not as effective as they used to be, that because inflation is perceived to be under control pay rises are not as important and that because unemployment is now more of a fear among working people, job security is seen as a major concern.

Unemployment

The previous sections looked at the economically active who are in employment. This section looks at those who are economically active but unemployed. How unemployment is measured has been a controversial topic for many years. In the United Kingdom two basic measures are used: claimant unemployed and the International Labour Organisation (ILO) definition. The claimant count uses administrative systems to count those people recorded as unemployed at government offices and produces timely statistics relatively easily. The ILO definition covers unemployment based on individuals who are without a job and either available to start work within two weeks and have been seeking a job in the last four weeks or are waiting to start a job they have already obtained. This measure is based on the Labour Force Survey. A more detailed explanation of the two measures is given in the glossary on page 82 at the beginning of this chapter.

These two measures are compared in **Chart 4.21**. For both estimates, the trend has been similar over recent years. A rise in the level of unemployment from the early 1980s until the mid-1980s was followed by a fall until the early 1990s. The level then began to rise once more until around the end of 1992, since when it has been on a downward trend. It is the ILO measure which is used for the rest of this chapter. From Summer 1994 to Summer 1995, ILO unemployment in the United Kingdom fell by 6.4 per cent with the fall for men at 8 per cent being greater than that for women at 3 per cent.

Comparisons with industrial competitors give useful indicators of a country's performance. **Table 4.22** shows how the United Kingdom compares with the other main industrialised (G7) countries in terms of unemployment. In 1994, while the unemployment rate in this country was around 10 per cent, the highest rate of all the G7 countries was in France at over 12 per cent and the lowest was in Japan at around 3 per cent. However, the United Kingdom is one of only three G7 countries that experienced a fall in the rate of unemployment between 1993 and 1994, the other countries being Canada and the United States. The biggest rise was in Italy with more than a 1 percentage point rise.

4.21

Comparisons of alternative measures of unemployment[1]

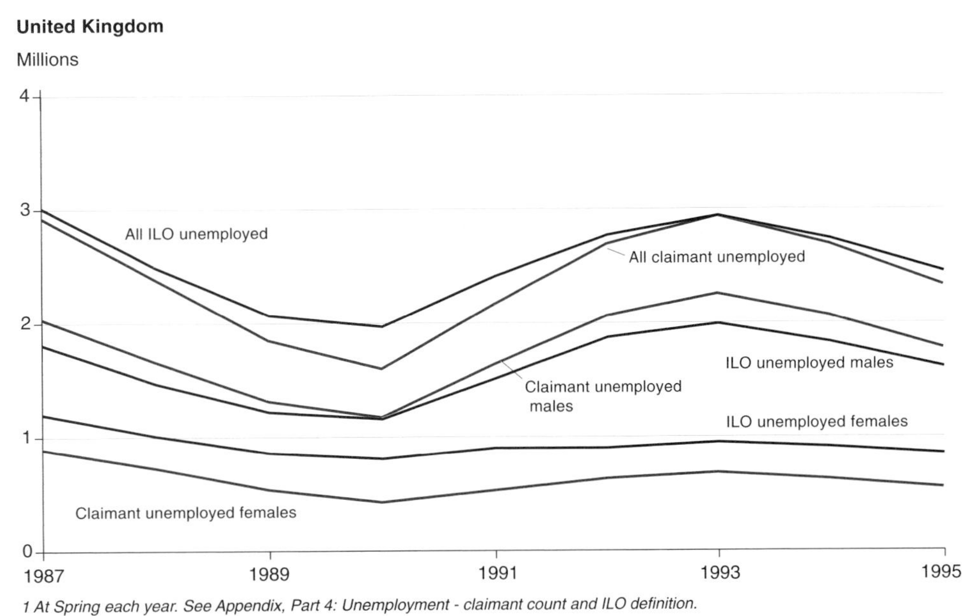

1 At Spring each year. See Appendix, Part 4: Unemployment - claimant count and ILO definition.

Source: Labour Force Survey, Central Statistical Office

4.22

Unemployment rates adjusted to SOEC concepts[1]: G7 comparison

Percentages

	1989	1990	1991	1992	1993	1994
France	..	..	9.5	10.4	11.7	12.3
Italy	10.0	9.1	8.8	9.0	10.3	11.4
Canada	7.5	8.1	10.3	11.3	11.2	10.3
United Kingdom	7.3	7.0	8.8	10.1	10.4	9.6
Germany	..	..	5.6	6.6	7.9	8.4
United States	5.3	5.5	6.7	7.4	6.8	6.1
Japan	2.3	2.1	2.1	2.2	2.5	2.9

1 Except Canada which is based on OECD concepts. See Appendix, Part 4: Unemployment and unemployment rates - SOEC and OECD concepts.

Source: SOEC; OECD

4.23

Unemployment rates[1]: by gender and age

United Kingdom — Percentages

	1991	1992	1993	1994	1995
Males					
16-19	16.5	18.6	22.0	20.9	19.6
20-29	12.3	15.5	16.5	14.9	14.0
30-39	7.8	10.5	10.3	10.2	8.3
40-49	5.8	7.7	8.8	7.6	7.1
50-64	8.4	10.4	11.9	11.0	9.2
65 and over	5.9	4.9	4.6	3.7	2.7
All males aged 16 and over	9.2	11.5	12.4	11.4	10.1
Females					
16-19	13.2	13.8	15.9	16.0	14.8
20-29	9.4	9.4	10.3	9.3	9.2
30-39	6.9	7.5	7.3	7.3	6.5
40-49	4.9	5.1	4.9	4.9	5.0
50-59	5.1	4.5	5.4	5.3	4.2
60 and over	4.4	4.7	4.1	3.0	2.4
All females aged 16 and over	7.2	7.3	7.6	7.3	6.8

1 Unemployment based on the ILO definition as a percentage of all economically active. See Appendix, Part 4: Unemployment - ILO definition. At Spring each year.

Source: Labour Force Survey, Central Statistical Office

Since 1993 the trend in ILO unemployment rates in the United Kingdom for both genders has been downwards. For women, however, unemployment rates have always been lower than those for men **(Table 4.23)**. Unemployment levels for both genders are generally highest among young people, with the unemployed accounting for a fifth of all economically active 16 to 19 year old men in 1995. However, in Spring 1995, of the 124 thousand unemployed 16 to 17 year olds of both genders, around half were in full-time education and seeking part-time jobs.

The duration of a spell of unemployment can vary widely for a variety of reasons, such as skill factors and the type of work sought. **Table 4.24** shows the duration of unemployment for those people who were unemployed in the United Kingdom in Spring 1995. Short-term unemployment was at its

4.24

Duration of unemployment[1]: by gender and age, Spring 1995

United Kingdom — Percentages

	Less than three months	Three months but less than six months	Six months but less than one year	One year but less than two years	Two years but less than three years	Three years or more	All durations[2] (=100%) (thousands)
Males							
16-19	39.9	19.4	22.4	13.5	..	..	164
20-29	18.6	16.4	19.9	18.7	9.3	17.0	541
30-39	14.2	15.7	14.7	17.6	13.6	24.1	345
40-49	14.8	11.9	13.5	15.3	14.3	30.1	256
50-64	15.6	11.2	12.5	18.4	13.7	28.3	293
All aged 16 and over[3]	18.7	14.9	16.6	17.3	11.3	21.0	1,607
Females							
16-19	40.7	22.5	21.1	11.1	..	..	114
20-29	32.8	18.9	18.8	14.6	6.2	8.7	273
30-39	33.8	17.6	16.4	15.1	6.8	10.4	202
40-49	26.9	15.1	17.9	15.2	9.8	14.9	154
50-64	22.3	11.3	16.8	18.2	10.8	20.2	100
All aged 16 and over[3]	31.7	17.4	18.2	14.8	7.2	10.6	846

1 Unemployment based on the ILO definition. See Appendix, Part 4: Unemployment - ILO definition.
2 Includes those who did not state their duration.
3 Includes males aged 65 and over and females aged 60 and over who were unemployed.

Source: Labour Force Survey, Central Statistical Office

highest among 16 to 19 year olds, with around 40 per cent of women of this age being unemployed for less than three months, a similar proportion to their male peers. Long-term unemployment is defined as that which has lasted a year or more. Men are more likely to be long-term unemployed than women. Around half of all unemployed men in Spring 1995 had been unemployed for over a year compared with just under a third of unemployed women. The likelihood of long-term unemployment also increases with age: around 60 per cent of men aged 50 to 64 were unemployed for a year or more compared with only 45 per cent of 20 to 29 year olds.

Unemployment rates also vary between the different areas of Great Britain with inner city areas and former heavy industry areas being particularly affected in recent years. **Chart 4.25** shows county ILO unemployment rates in Spring 1995 for Great Britain. Among the standard regions, unemployment rates were highest in the North, at just under 11 per cent, and lowest in East Anglia, at just over 7 per cent. At a more detailed level, the worst unemployment rates are to be found in Inner London. In Spring 1995 the rate in Hackney was nearly 30 per cent and in Newham was just under 25 per cent. Outside London the highest rate was in Knowsley in Liverpool at just under 19 per cent. Most of the lower rates are found in predominantly rural counties, especially in a large grouping of counties in central and southern England. Oxfordshire had the lowest rate of all the counties at 3.5 per cent.

Table 4.20 showed that people are more concerned about Trade Unions acting to protect jobs than to get pay rises. Redundancy is a real fear among people and the rates for different occupations are given in **Table 4.26**. Overall redundancy rates have shown a downward trend in recent years. In the three months prior to interview in Spring 1995, 220 thousand people in Great Britain were made redundant, of whom 60 per cent were men. In Spring 1995 the highest redundancy rate occurred among people in the craft and related occupations where 16 employees in every thousand were made redundant. This group had the highest redundancy rates in both Spring 1994 and Spring 1995. Redundancies were least likely to occur in the professional occupations.

Older and younger workers were the most likely to be affected by redundancy and men were more likely to be affected than women. In Spring 1995 male employees aged between 16 and 24 were the most likely group to have been made redundant, at around 19 per thousand employees; this differs from Spring 1994 when the highest rate was among men aged over 50. Women aged between 25 and 49 were the group least likely to be made redundant with a rate of 7 per thousand employees compared with 10 per thousand for men in the same age group.

4.25

Unemployment rates[1]: by county[2], Spring 1995

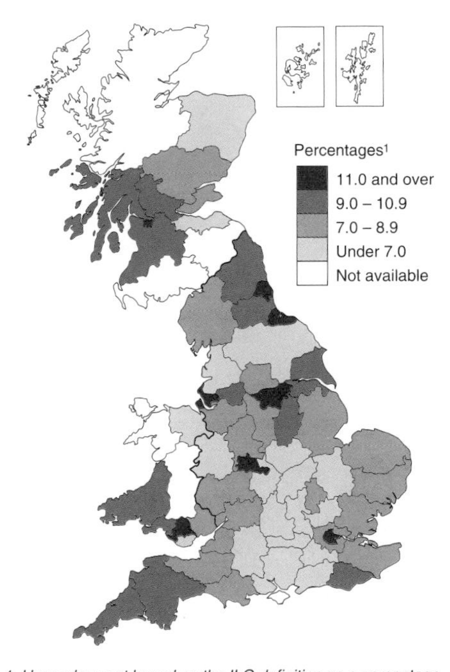

1 Unemployment based on the ILO definition as a percentage of those economically active. See Appendix, Part 4: Unemployment - ILO definition.
2 Regions in Scotland.
Source: Labour Force Survey, Central Statistical Office

4.26

Redundancy rates[1]: by occupation

Great Britain — Rates per 1,000 employees

	1992	1993	1994	1995
Managers and administrators	12.2	8.3	9.8	10.2
Professional	6.3	6.1	4.5	5.3
Associate professional and technical	10.6	8.5	5.7	8.1
Clerical and secretarial	14.7	9.9	7.8	10.6
Craft and related	27.9	20.7	18.2	15.7
Personal and protective services	6.9	6.9	5.8	6.3
Sales	14.8	15.5	10.0	12.6
Plant and machine operatives	22.8	22.7	16.1	12.8
Other	16.4	14.6	9.2	10.4
All occupations	15.1	12.3	9.6	10.2

1 At Spring each year.
Source: Labour Force Survey, Central Statistical Office

4.27

Apprentices: by gender

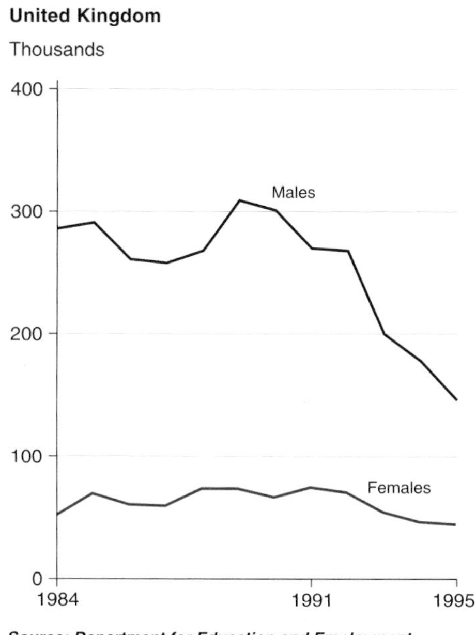

Source: Department for Education and Employment

Employment and training measures

One of the oldest ways in which young workers acquire the skills necessary to do a job is through apprenticeships. Traditionally, these were aimed at young men in manual work where the employer agreed to train the apprentice, who in return agreed to work for the employer once trained. Apprenticeships used to be of seven years duration which was reduced to five after the Second World War. By 1976 over half of all apprenticeships were of four years duration.

Labour Force Survey data for Spring 1994 show that of those apprentices who answered a question about the length of their training, around half were on apprenticeships of more than three years' duration. Since the recent peak in 1989, the number of apprentices has fallen by approximately 50 per cent to 191 thousand **(Chart 4.27)**. This reduction in apprentice numbers has been far greater for men than for women. This is probably because male apprentices are more likely to work in the production and construction industries where the overall fall in employment has been greater than in the service industries. Around half of all women apprentices worked in the personal and protective service occupations in 1995 with the largest group of women apprentices being in hairdressing. In an attempt to increase apprenticeship training of young people at the critical technician/supervisory level, the Government is supporting a new initiative called Modern Apprenticeships - this is mainly for 16 and 17 year olds and covers work areas across industry and commerce.

On-the-job training was the dominant form of training received by young people aged 18 to 19 in employment in 1994, with around three quarters receiving this form of training in England and Wales **(Table 4.28)**. However men were more likely to receive this training than women at 81 per cent compared with 73 per cent. The occupational group most likely to receive this type of training were those in the managers and administrators group where 91 per cent of young people received on-the-job training. Off-the-job training shows a different pattern with 21 per cent of those with GCSEs grades A to C doing training at college compared with only 7 per cent of those with GCE A or A/S levels. Again, the gender difference exists, with 24 per cent of men and 13 per cent of women receiving this type of training. Further information on training and qualifications can be found in Chapter 3: Education.

Training is seen by a large number of employees as an essential investment for the future. In Spring 1995 around 14 per cent of employees of working age received job-related training in the four weeks before they were interviewed in the Labour Force Survey. **Table 4.29** shows the proportions of men and women receiving job-related training. Due to a change in the survey

4.28

Training of young people[1] in full-time employment or on a government training scheme: by qualification level, 1992-1994

England & Wales — Percentages

	GCE A or A/S level	GCSE grades A-C	GCSE other	None/ not stated	All
On-the-job training	*80*	*81*	*73*	*70*	*78*
Off-the-job training					
College	*7*	*21*	*20*	*12*	*19*
Training centre[2]	*19*	*24*	*18*	*18*	*21*
Other location	*2*	*3*	*1*	*4*	*2*

1 Aged 16 in 1990/91 and who completed the Youth Cohort Study questionnaires in Spring 1992, 1993 and 1994.
2 Includes off-the-job training on employers' premises, at a private training centre and at a Government or local authority training centre.

Source: Youth Cohort Study, Department for Education and Employment

questionnaire the figures in this table are not directly comparable with those in Table 4.32 in *Social Trends 25*. A period of training can, of course, last for anything from a day to a period of years. The reasons men and women give for attending training courses differ. Although the most common reason given by both men and women was to learn new skills, men were more likely than women to undergo training because they wanted to improve their chances of promotion. On the other hand, women were more likely to want to make their work more interesting.

4.29

Proportion of employees receiving job-related training[1]: by gender and age

United Kingdom Percentages

	1986	1991	1992	1993	1994	1995
Males						
16-29	*18.1*	*20.3*	*19.5*	*19.2*	*19.5*	*18.1*
30-64	*8.0*	*11.8*	*11.9*	*12.0*	*12.8*	*11.6*
All males aged 16 to 64	*11.4*	*14.7*	*14.3*	*14.3*	*14.9*	*13.6*
Females						
16-29	*14.6*	*17.9*	*18.2*	*18.6*	*21.1*	*18.0*
30-64	*7.2*	*13.3*	*13.1*	*13.4*	*14.1*	*13.6*
All females aged 16 to 64	*9.9*	*14.9*	*14.9*	*15.1*	*16.3*	*15.0*

1 At Spring each year.

Source: Department for Education and Employment, from Labour Force Survey

References and further reading

The following list contains selected publications relevant to **Chapter 4: Employment**. Those published by HMSO are available from the addresses shown on the inside back cover of *Social Trends*.

British Social Attitudes, Dartmouth Publishing
CBI Quarterly Industrial Trends Survey, CBI
Changing Households: The British Household Panel Survey, ESRC Research Centre on Micro-social change
General Household Survey, HMSO
Labour Force Survey Quarterly Bulletin, Central Statistical Office
Labour Market Quarterly Report, Central Statistical Office
Labour Market Trends (incorporating Employment Gazette), Central Statistical Office
Main Economic Indicators, OECD
Northern Ireland Labour Force Survey Statistics Notice, HMSO
Regional Trends, HMSO
Scottish Economic Bulletin, HMSO
Skills Bulletin, Department for Education and Employment
Social Focus on Women, HMSO
Time Rates and Hours of Work, Central Statistical Office
Training Statistics, HMSO
Youth Cohort Study, Department for Education and Employment

Contacts

Telephone contact points for further information relating to **Chapter 4: Employment**

Central Statistical Office	
Labour market statistics	0171 273 5585
Department for Education and Employment	
Training statistics	0114 259 4233
ESRC Research Centre on Micro-social change	01206 872957
Social & Community Planning Research	0171 250 1866 extn 369
Eurostat	00 352 4301 34567

Chapter 5 Income and Wealth

Household income

Real household disposable income per head reached its highest level ever in 1994 - 80 per cent higher than in 1971. (Chart 5.1)

At nearly all ages, women earn less on average than men - the largest difference was for people in their forties at over £140 a week in April 1995. (Chart 5.8)

Taxes

There will be nearly 26 million income tax payers in the United Kingdom in 1995-96 with a total income tax bill of around £72 billion. (Table 5.9)

Amongst the G7 countries, direct taxes and social security contributions as a percentage of personal income was highest in Italy and lowest in the United Kingdom and Japan. (Chart 5.12)

Income distribution

The proportion of people with incomes below half average income rose from 8 per cent in 1982 to 19 per cent in 1993. (Chart 5.17)

Wealth

The distribution of wealth has scarcely changed since 1981 - in 1993, 72 per cent of marketable wealth was owned by the most wealthy 25 per cent of people. (Table 5.21)

Income of the nation

After rising since 1981, GDP fell between 1990 and 1992. Since then it has risen and in 1994 it was above the level seen in 1990. (Chart 5.24)

The South East had the highest GDP per head within the United Kingdom in 1994, while Northern Ireland had the lowest. (Table 5.25)

5.1

Real[1] household disposable income per head

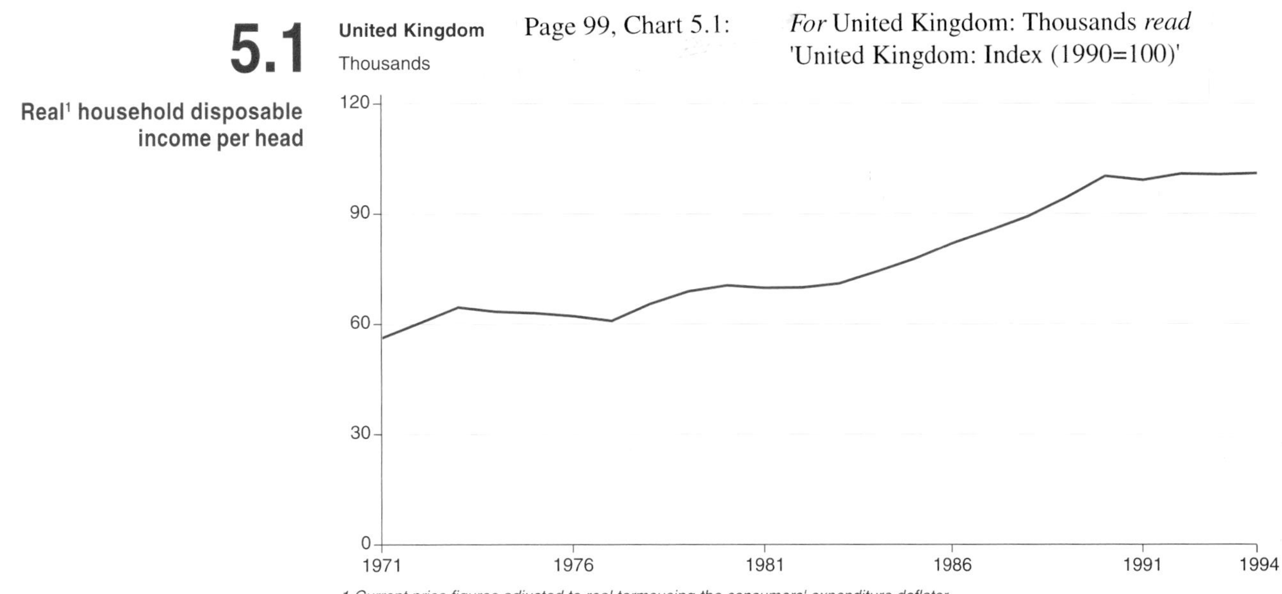

1 Current price figures adjusted to real termsusing the consumers' expenditure deflator.

Source: Central Statistical Office

Income provides the key to the standard of living of individuals and the country as a whole.

Household income

Disposable income is the amount of money people have available to them to spend or invest. It is made up of income from all sources, less taxes on income, national insurance contributions and local taxes. The trend in household disposable income per head in the United Kingdom since 1971 is shown in **Chart 5.1** on the previous page. It is expressed in real terms to allow meaningful comparisons from year to year by adjusting for the effect of inflation. It increased by nearly 80 per cent between 1971 and 1990 and then levelled off, although it reached its highest level ever in 1994.

Households receive income from many sources; aggregate figures for the United Kingdom are summarised in **Table 5.2**. Wages and salaries are by far the largest source of household income, although their share of income fell by 11 percentage points between 1971 and 1994. The proportion of income from private pensions and annuities has more than doubled since 1971, to 11 pe cent in 1994. This is due, amongst other things, to the growing numbers of elderly people in the United Kingdom (see Chart 1. in the Population chapter) and the increase likelihood of them having occupational pensions. The sources of household income vary between the different regions of the United Kingdom **(Table 5.3)**. Wages and salaries are the most important source for a the regions, but in 1993 this varied from 61 per cent of income in Greater London to only 51 per cent in Wales. Occupational and state pensions are of greater importance as an income source in the South West and Wales than elsewhere; this reflects the higher proportions of retired people in these areas. Disposable income varied from 79 per cent of total income in the South East to 87 per cent in Northern Ireland.

The figures in Chart 5.1 and Tables 5.2 and 5.3 represent the aggregate income of the household sector in the United Kingdom as defined in the national accounts (see Appendix, Part 5: Household sector). This covers total income of all people living in households and institutions, and also of

5.2

Household income[1]

United Kingdom — Percentages

	1971	1976	1981	1986	1991	1994
Source of income						
Wages and salaries[2]	*68*	*67*	*63*	*58*	*58*	*57*
Income from self-employment[3]	*9*	*9*	*8*	*10*	*10*	*10*
Rent, dividends, interest	*6*	*6*	*7*	*8*	*9*	*6*
Private pensions, annuities, etc	*5*	*5*	*6*	*8*	*10*	*11*
Social security benefits	*10*	*11*	*13*	*13*	*11*	*13*
Other current transfers[4]	*2*	*2*	*2*	*3*	*2*	*3*
Total household income (=100%)(£ billion at 1994 prices[5])	305	354	386	458	556	564
Direct taxes, etc as a percentage of total household income						
Taxes on income	*14*	*17*	*14*	*14*	*14*	*13*
National insurance contributions[6]	*3*	*3*	*3*	*4*	*3*	*3*
Contributions to pension schemes	*1*	*2*	*2*	*2*	*2*	*2*
Total household disposable income (£ billion at 1994 prices[5])	248	276	310	368	453	466

1 See Appendix, Part 5: Household sector.
2 Includes Forces' pay and income in kind.
3 After deducting interest payments, depreciation and stock appreciation.
4 Mostly other government grants, but including transfers from abroad and non-profit making bodies.
5 Adjusted to 1994 prices using the consumers' expenditure deflator.
6 By employees and the self-employed.

Source: Central Statistical Office

5.3

Sources of household income[1]: by region, 1993

Percentages

	Wages and salaries[2]	Income from self-employment[3]	Income from investments	Occupational and state pensions	Social security benefits	Other income[4]	Total household income (=100%) (£ billion)	Disposable income[5] as a percentage of total
United Kingdom	*56*	*10*	*6*	*17*	*8*	*3*	547	*83*
North	*55*	*9*	*5*	*18*	*10*	*3*	27	*85*
Yorkshire & Humberside	*55*	*11*	*6*	*17*	*8*	*3*	44	*85*
East Midlands	*56*	*12*	*6*	*17*	*7*	*2*	36	*84*
East Anglia	*54*	*12*	*8*	*18*	*6*	*2*	20	*83*
South East	*59*	*10*	*7*	*15*	*6*	*3*	187	*79*
Greater London	*61*	*9*	*7*	*13*	*7*	*4*	76	*79*
Rest of South East	*58*	*11*	*7*	*16*	*6*	*2*	111	*80*
South West	*52*	*12*	*7*	*19*	*7*	*2*	45	*84*
West Midlands	*56*	*10*	*6*	*17*	*8*	*3*	47	*84*
North West	*56*	*8*	*6*	*17*	*10*	*3*	56	*85*
England	*57*	*10*	*7*	*17*	*7*	*3*	461	*82*
Wales	*51*	*10*	*6*	*19*	*11*	*3*	25	*86*
Scotland	*57*	*9*	*5*	*16*	*9*	*4*	48	*85*
Northern Ireland	*54*	*11*	*4*	*15*	*13*	*3*	13	*87*

1 See Appendix, Part 5: Household sector.
2 Includes Forces' pay and income in kind.
3 After deducting interest payments, depreciation and stock appreciation.
4 Mostly other government grants, but including transfers from abroad and non-profit making bodies.
5 Total household income less taxes on insurance, national insurance contributions and contributions to pension schemes.

Source: Central Statistical Office

private trusts. This is a different basis from the next two tables and some of the other charts and tables in this chapter which are based on sample surveys of individuals in households. The surveys collect information about the households that enable analyses of household income by different characteristics, for example by household type **(Table 5.4)**. The importance of the different sources of income varies among the different types of household. Earned income, such as wages and salaries and income from self-employment, is the main source of income for most households. However, retired households and lone parent households depend more on cash benefits, which include state pensions.

5.4

Sources of gross household income: by household type, 1994-95

United Kingdom — Percentages

	Earned income[1]	Investment income[2]	Cash benefits	Total
Retired households[3]	*3*	*45*	*52*	*100*
Non-retired households				
1 adult	*80*	*7*	*12*	*100*
2 adults	*85*	*9*	*6*	*100*
1 adult with children	*32*	*13*	*55*	*100*
2 adults with children	*88*	*4*	*8*	*100*
3 or more adults[4]	*84*	*6*	*10*	*100*
All households	*73*	*11*	*16*	*100*

1 Including wages and salaries, self-employed income and income from 'fringe benefits'.
2 Including occupational pensions and annuities and other income.
3 Households where the combined income of retired members amounts to at least half the total gross income of the household.
4 With or without children.

Source: Central Statistical Office

5.5

Pensioners'[1] gross income: by source

United Kingdom Percentages

	1981	1990-1991	1992	1993
Benefits	*61*	*50*	*50*	*53*
Occupational pensions	*16*	*22*	*24*	*25*
Investments	*13*	*20*	*19*	*16*
Earnings	*9*	*7*	*6*	*6*
Other	-	*1*	*1*	-
All gross income (=100%) (£ per week at July 1993 prices[2])	120.60	163.30	170.40	170.20

1 Pensioner units.
2 Adjusted to July 1993 prices using the retail prices index less local taxes.
Source: Department of Social Security

Table 5.5 shows how the pattern of pensioners' income in the United Kingdom has changed over time. The table measures the income of pensioner units, which are defined as single people over state pension age or a couple where the husband is over state pension age. Benefits still made up over half of a pensioner unit's gross income in 1993, but the proportion of income from occupational pensions has been increasing. The proportion of income from investments rose in the 1980s, but fell in the early 1990s to 16 per cent in 1993: this suggests that changing interest rates have an effect on pensioners' income. Pensioners who retired in the last five years tended to have a higher gross income than those who had retired in earlier years, which is mainly due to higher incomes from earnings and occupational pensions. Recently retired pensioner units received on average £28.70 a week from earnings in 1993 compared with £9.50 for all pensioners, while gross income of recently retired pensioners was £220.50 per week, compared with £170.20 for all pensioners.

5.6

Average earnings[1] and retail prices

United Kingdom
Percentage change over 12 months

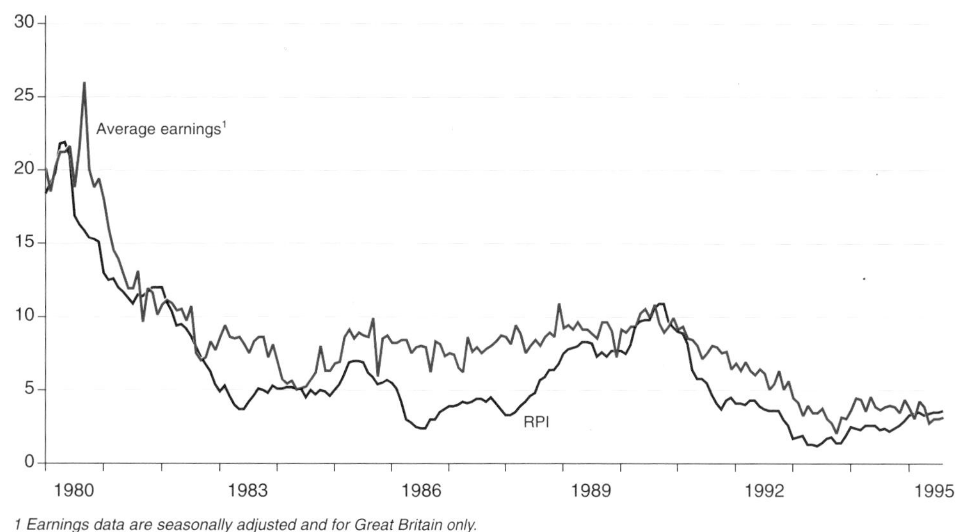

1 Earnings data are seasonally adjusted and for Great Britain only.
Source: Central Statistical Office

As we have already seen, earnings from employment are in general the largest source of a household's income. Earnings change from year to year according to the amount of overtime, bonuses, shift allowances, grade increments and other productivity and incentive payments. In addition, many workers have an annual pay settlement or review. One measure of the changes in earnings is the average earnings index. This is a monthly inquiry of about 8 thousand firms and establishments to find out the amount paid to employees. The annual percentage change in this index is compared to the change in retail prices in **Chart 5.6**. For the majority of the period covered by the chart, increases in earnings have outpaced the increases in retail prices, which means that the real value of earnings has increased. However, for some months in

1995, the increases in retail prices were greater than those in earnings; this is the first time this has happened since 1990.

The New Earnings Survey, an annual survey of employers collecting information on full-time adult employees, is the main source of detailed earnings data. Earnings of people in different occupations have changed in different ways over time. Of the occupations shown in **Table 5.7**, nurses have experienced the greatest percentage increase in their earnings since 1971; the smallest percentage increase was for bricklayers and masons. However, between 1991 and 1995 medical practitioners experienced the greatest percentage increase of 10 per cent in real terms, whereas earnings fell for waiters and waitresses, cleaners, mechanical engineers and solicitors.

Earnings also differ between men and women. At nearly all ages women earn less on average than men **(Chart 5.8)**. The largest difference is for people in their forties, where the gap is over £140 a week. However, women under 18 earn slightly more than men of the same age. The peak earning age for women is in their thirties, while men in their forties earn the most. Factors which have a major effect on women's earnings are having children and caring for them. Women still undertake the majority of caring, particularly for children, and having a family affects women's participation in the labour market; this can take the form of a career break, a move to part-time work or a change in occupation.

The gap between average male and female earnings has stayed fairly constant in real terms since 1971. However, for both men and women who were full-time employees on adult rates, the gap between the highest and lowest earners has widened. After adjusting to April 1995 prices, for men the gap between those in the bottom and top decile groups was £203 in 1971, rising to almost £419 in 1995; for women the gap grew from £122 to £290 over the same period.

5.7

Real[1] gross weekly earnings[2]: by selected occupation

Great Britain — £ per week at April 1995 prices[1]

	1971	1976	1981	1986	1991	1995
Waiter/waitress	108	155	143	156	166	161
Bar staff	119	148	148	165	158	165
Cleaner	113	180	175	185	186	181
Receptionist	117	132	139	158	179	188
Caretaker	163	197	185	203	220	227
Bricklayer/mason	204	252	232	242	256	263
Carpenter/joiner	209	244	230	244	269	274
Nurse	146	194	194	223	308	329
Social worker	209	236	254	273	313	340
Primary teacher	243	295	301	312	370	401
Secondary teacher		327	324	333	403	435
Mechanical engineer	332	377	387	437	510	503
Solicitor	359	392	379	432	610	585
Medical practitioner	515	504	569	612	691	764

1 Adjusted to April 1995 prices using the retail prices index.
2 At April each year. Full-time employees on adult rates whose pay was not affected for the survey period by absence.
Source: New Earnings Survey, Central Statistical Office

5.8

Gross weekly earnings[1]: by gender and age, April 1995

United Kingdom

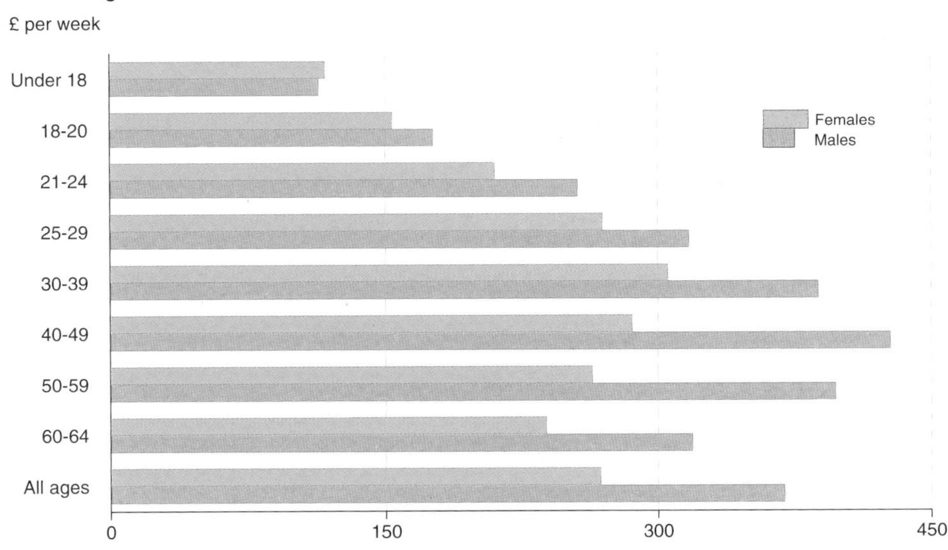

1 Full-time employees on all rates whose pay was not affected for the survey period by absence.
Source: New Earnings Survey, Central Statistical Office

5.9

Income tax payable: by annual income[1], 1995-96[2]

United Kingdom

	Number of taxpayers paying tax at					
	Lower rate (millions)	Basic rate (millions)	Excess over basic rate (millions)	Total tax payable (£ million)	Average rate of tax payable (percen -tages)	Average amount of tax payable (£)
£3,525-£4,999	1.8	.	.	230	*3*	120
£5,000-£7,499	4.1	0.8	.	1,620	*6*	390
£7,500-£9,999	3.8	3.6	.	3,320	*10*	880
£10,000-£14,999	6.1	6.1	.	10,200	*14*	1,680
£15,000-£19,999	4.1	4.1	.	11,500	*16*	2,800
£20,000-£29,999	3.7	3.7	0.2	16,100	*18*	4,290
£30,000-£49,999	1.5	1.5	1.5	12,900	*23*	8,380
£50,000-£99,999	0.4	0.4	0.4	8,200	*29*	19,000
£100,000 and over	0.1	0.1	0.1	8,110	*35*	68,400
All incomes	25.7	20.4	2.2	72,200	*18*	2,810

1 Total income of the individual for income tax purposes including earned and investment income. All figures in the table relate to taxpayers only.
2 Based on projections from the 1993-94 Survey of Personal Incomes.
Source: Inland Revenue

5.10

Net weekly spending power[1]: by gross weekly earnings[2] and type of family, July 1995

Great Britian

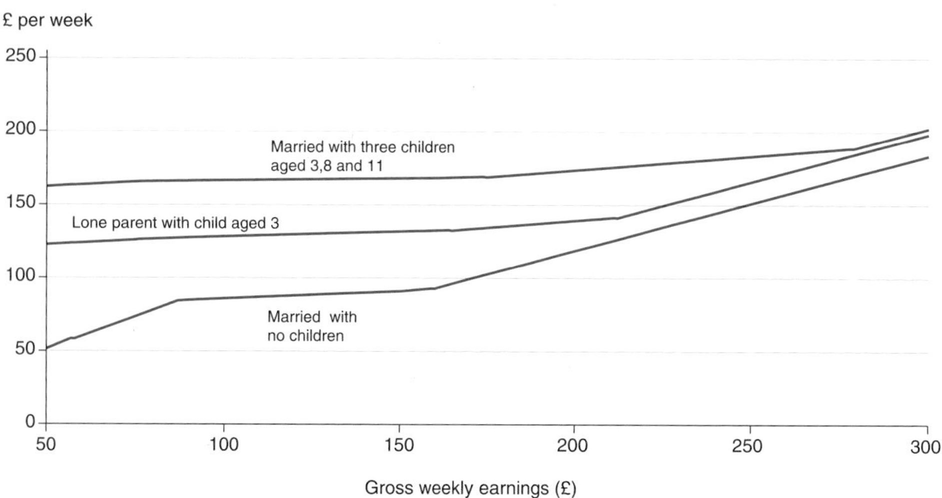

1 Gross earnings less deductions for tax, national insurance, rent and council tax, plus receipts of all benefits which are applicable for a family paying average local authority rent.
2 Gross earnings from full-time work where head of household only is in employment.
Source: Department of Social Security

Taxes

The Inland Revenue have estimated that there will be nearly 26 million taxpayers in the United Kingdom in the tax year 1995-96, with a total tax bill of around £72 billion **(Table 5.9)**. Overall, just over half of the adult population will pay taxes in 1995-96. There are three different rates of tax: lower, basic and higher. Income tax rates have been reduced since 1978-79, particularly for those with higher incomes. The basic rate fell progressively from 33 per cent in April 1978 to 25 per cent in April 1988; the lower rate of 20 per cent was introduced in April 1992. The higher tax rates, which were at a maximum of 83 per cent on earned income between 1974-75 and 1978-79, have been replaced by a single rate of 40 per cent.

The data in the next two items are not estimated from surveys of real families but are modelled. The net income (after tax, National Insurance Contributions, rent and council tax payments have been deducted and receipts of benefits added) for three different family types earning between £50 and £300 per week in July 1995 is shown in **Chart 5.10**. In order to model net income, it is assumed that: there is no income other than the earnings of the head of the household and social security benefits, for which full entitlement is claimed; they have only their personal tax allowances; they live in local authority rented accommodation; and they are not contracted out of the state pension scheme. Average local authority rent and council tax payments are deducted from net income to arrive at net weekly spending power.

Entitlement to certain benefits changes as earnings change. At one time it was possible for an increase in earnings to cause a fall in net income because of the withdrawal of benefits; this was known as the poverty trap.

The effect of the poverty trap has been lessened by social security reforms and, in general, net income increases with gross income. Despite this, the chart is fairly flat in places, showing that in some ranges of income spending power increases only very slowly. Changes in earnings may not lead immediately to changes in benefit entitlement, as family credit is paid at the same rate for six months before being reassessed. At gross earnings of £50 per week the spending power of the three family types varies considerably. The childless couple pays no deductions and receives maximum housing benefit and council tax benefit, leaving them with net income of £50. The family with three children can also claim family credit and child benefit and receive a net income of £161. The difference narrows as earnings increase and income-related benefits taper off, until at earnings of £280 a week and over the three child family loses entitlement to family credit. Their spending power is then just under £20 more than the childless couple, consisting of child benefit partly offset by higher rents and council tax.

A single man on half average earnings, and no other income, will pay 12 per cent of his income in tax in 1995-96, whereas a married man on the same earnings (with a non-earning wife) will pay 8 per cent **(Table 5.11)**. This difference gets smaller as earnings increase. The average proportion of income paid in income tax is expected to rise between 1994-95 and 1995-96, with the biggest increase for a married man on half average earnings.

National Insurance Contributions (NIC) are paid by people earning over a certain amount (£58 per week in 1995-96); most of this money goes into the National Insurance Fund out of which some social security benefits are paid, while the rest of the money goes to the National Health Service.

5.11

Percentage of income paid in income tax and national insurance contributions[1]: by marital status and level of earnings[2]

United Kingdom — Percentages

	1971-72	1981-82	1991-92	1995-96[3]
Single man				
Half average earnings				
Tax	*14.3*	*17.5*	*12.8*	*11.7*
NIC	*7.7*	*7.7*	*6.2*	*6.9*
Average earnings				
Tax	*22.2*	*23.7*	*18.9*	*18.3*
NIC	*5.8*	*7.7*	*7.6*	*8.5*
Twice average earnings				
Tax	*26.2*	*27.3*	*22.0*	*23.3*
NIC	*3.3*	*6.1*	*6.0*	*6.6*
Married man[4]				
Half average earnings				
Tax	*7.5*	*10.5*	*6.5*	*8.4*
NIC	*7.7*	*7.7*	*6.2*	*6.9*
Average earnings				
Tax	*18.8*	*20.2*	*15.7*	*16.7*
NIC	*5.8*	*7.7*	*7.6*	*8.5*
Twice average earnings				
Tax	*26.8*	*25.1*	*20.4*	*22.5*
NIC	*3.3*	*6.1*	*6.0*	*6.6*

1 Employees' contributions. Assumes contributions at Class 1, contracted in, standard rate.
2 Average earnings for full-time adult male manual employees working a full week on adult rates.
3 1994-95 based projections.
4 Assuming wife not in paid employment.

Source: Inland Revenue

The rates of NICs were simplified from five bands to two in 1989. The NIC rate for employees depends on whether they are contracted out or not - that is if the employee is entirely covered by the state pension scheme or whether the job has been contracted out of the earnings-related part of the state scheme by his employer. Rates are calculated as a percentage of gross earnings and in 1995-96 are only paid on the first £440 of weekly earnings. The rates for those who are not contracted out are 2 per cent on the first £58 and 10 per cent on the balance and for those who are contracted out the rates are 2 per cent and 8.2 per cent respectively. The single and married men on average earnings shown in the table both pay a higher proportion of their income in NICs than their counterparts on half, or twice, average earnings.

5.12

Direct taxes and social security contributions[1] as a percentage of personal income: G7 comparison, 1993

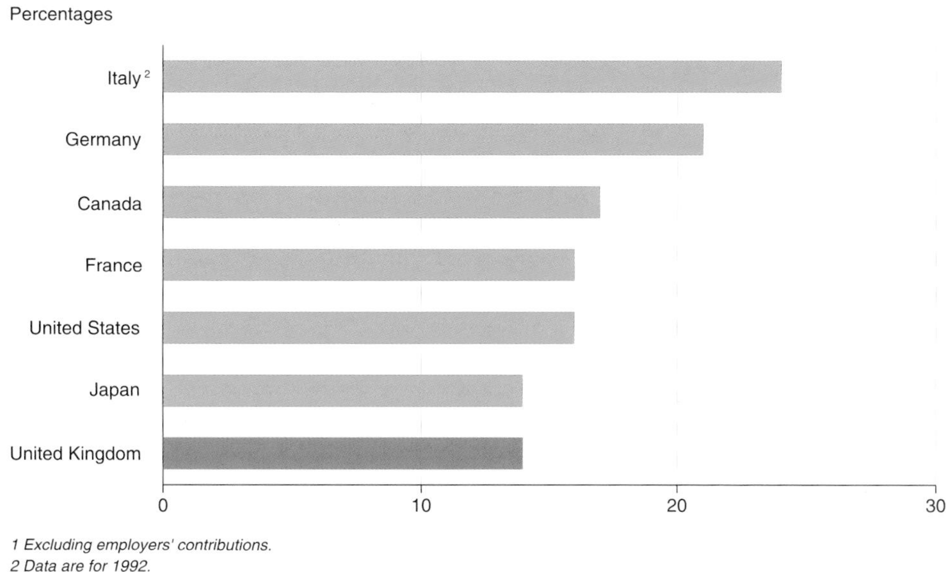

1 Excluding employers' contributions.
2 Data are for 1992.
Source: OECD

5.13

Taxes and benefits[1]: by income grouping[2], 1994-95

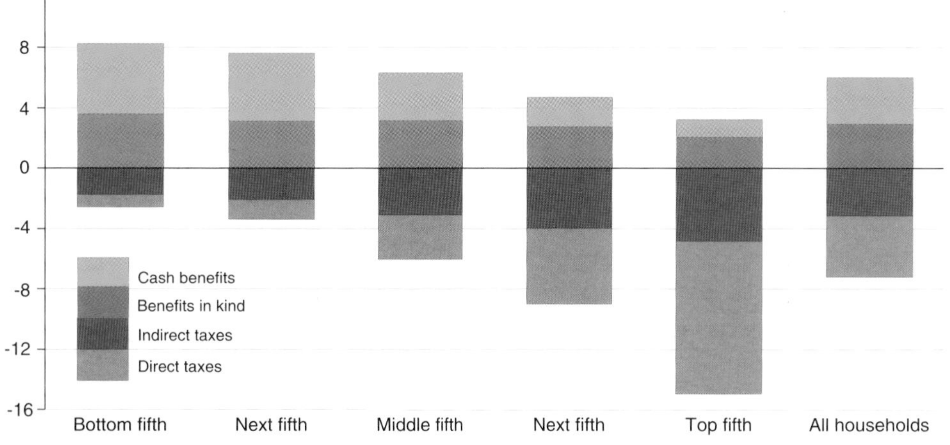

1 Average taxes and benefits per household.
2 Equivalised disposable income has been used for ranking the households into quintile groups. See Appendix, Part 5: Equivalisation scales.
Source: Central Statistical Office

In **Chart 5.12** direct taxes and social security benefits as a percentage of total personal income for the Group of Seven (G7) countries are compared. These countries are the major industrialised countries and together account for around two thirds of the world's Gross Domestic Product. In 1993 deductions were highest in Italy at 24 per cent, while Japan and the United Kingdom had the lowest rates at 14 per cent.

When making international comparisons it is necessary to make adjustments to definitions and coverages. This means that the United Kingdom figures used here are not strictly comparable with figures used elsewhere in this chapter. For example, the community charge is classified as a direct tax here, but not in Table 5.2. A number of other factors must also be taken into account when making these comparisons, particularly the differing balance between direct and indirect taxation used by different countries. There are also considerable differences in government involvement in the provision of services and financial support (for example, medical care and pensions) which are free or subsidised at the point of use.

Income distribution

Most government income is raised from households through direct and indirect taxes and social security contributions; much of its spending then benefits households. Some households will be taxed more than they benefit, and others will benefit more than they are taxed - this is the principle of redistribution of income. As we saw earlier in this chapter, households initially receive income from various non-government sources: from their employment; from occupational pensions; from investments; and from other households - this is called original income. Cash benefits from the state (for example, retirement pensions and income support) are added to original income to give gross income. This income is then reduced by income tax payments, NICs and local tax payments (such as council tax) to leave disposable income. The deduction of payments of indirect taxes, such as VAT, results in post-tax income. Households benefit from government expenditure on services such as education and health and adding in the value of these gives a household's final income.

The redistribution statistics in the tables and charts in this section are generally presented by quintile group of household income. Households are classified into quintile groups based on their equivalised household income. Equivalisation takes into account the size and composition of the household in order to recognise differing demands on resources. For example, to achieve the same standard of living, a household of five would need a higher income than a single person household. (See Appendix, Part 5: Equivalisation scales.)

Chart 5.13 summarises the average taxes paid and benefits received by the households in each quintile group. Those households at the top of the income distribution pay the most taxes, both directly and indirectly, and receive the least cash benefits. However, as a proportion of their disposable income, households in the top quintile pay less in indirect taxes (15 per cent) than those in the bottom quintile (30 per cent).

5.14

Redistribution of income through taxes and benefits[1], 1994-95

United Kingdom £ per year

	Quintile groups of households[2]					
	Bottom fifth	Next fifth	Middle fifth	Next fifth	Top fifth	All households
Average per household						
Wages and salaries	1,180	3,830	10,230	17,820	28,250	12,260
Imputed income from benefits in kind	10	20	100	310	950	280
Self-employment income	260	510	1,050	1,550	6,160	1,910
Occupational pensions, annuities	280	780	1,300	1,520	2,220	1,220
Investment income	170	260	500	800	2,420	830
Other income	140	200	190	250	340	230
Total original income	2,040	5,600	13,380	22,250	40,330	16,720
plus Benefits in cash						
Contributory	1,930	2,290	1,620	1,050	680	1,510
Non-contributory	2,730	2,180	1,540	900	490	1,570
Gross income	6,700	10,080	16,540	24,200	41,510	19,800
less Income tax[3] and NIC[4]	270	760	2,300	4,360	9,350	3,410
less Local taxes[5] (gross)	570	550	630	680	790	640
Disposable income	5,860	8,760	13,610	19,150	31,370	15,750
less Indirect taxes	1,740	2,070	3,090	3,960	4,810	3,130
Post-tax income	4,120	6,700	10,520	15,190	26,570	12,620
plus Benefits in kind						
Education	1,600	1,250	1,390	1,200	670	1,220
National Health Service	1,790	1,720	1,660	1,460	1,270	1,580
Housing subsidy	80	80	40	20	10	50
Travel subsidies	50	60	60	90	130	80
School meals and welfare milk	80	20	10	10	-	30
Final income	7,720	9,840	13,690	17,970	28,640	15,570

1 See Appendix, Part 5: Redistribution of income.
2 Equivalised disposable income has been used for ranking the households into quintile groups. See Appendix, Part 5: Equivalisation scales.
3 After tax relief at source on mortgage interest and life assurance premiums.
4 Employees' national insurance contributions.
5 Gross council tax, rates and water charges. Rates in Northern Ireland.
Source: Central Statistical Office

In 1994-95 original income for households in the bottom fifth of the distribution was about £38 thousand less than for those in the top fifth **(Table 5.14)**. After adding cash benefits and benefits in kind and deducting direct and indirect taxes the difference was reduced to £21 thousand. It is households in the lower quintile groups on whom the bulk of the state benefits are targeted. Benefits are looked at in more detail in Chapter 8: Social Protection.

Decile or quintile group - the main method of analysing income distribution used in this chapter is to rank units (households, individuals, etc) by a given income measure, and then to divide the ranked units into groups of equal size. Groups comprising 20 per cent of units are known as 'quintile groups' and those comprising 10 per cent of units are known as 'decile groups'. Thus the 'bottom quintile group' is the 20 per cent of units with the lowest incomes.

5.15

Household disposable income: by quintile grouping and household type, 1994-95

United Kingdom Percentages

	Quintile groups of households[1]					
	Bottom fifth	Next fifth	Middle fifth	Next fifth	Top fifth	All house-holds
Retired households[2]	*41*	*45*	*24*	*14*	*10*	*27*
Non-retired households						
1 adult	*12*	*10*	*11*	*14*	*21*	*14*
2 adults	*9*	*11*	*19*	*25*	*36*	*20*
1 adult with children	*14*	*8*	*4*	*2*	*1*	*6*
2 adults with children	*18*	*18*	*29*	*27*	*22*	*23*
3 or more adults[3]	*6*	*8*	*13*	*18*	*10*	*11*
All households	*100*	*100*	*100*	*100*	*100*	*100*

1 Equivalised disposable income has been used for ranking the households into quintile groups. See Appendix, Part 5: Equivalisation scales.
2 Households where the combined income of retired members amounts to at least half the total gross income of the household.
3 With or without children.
Source: Central Statistical Office

Decile and quintile points - the term 'quintile point' is used to refer to that income which forms the maximum of one quintile group and the minimum of the next. Thus the 'bottom quintile point' is that income below which 20 per cent of units fall.

It is important to look at what types of households are in which quintile income groups. The bottom fifth contains more retired households than any other type of household, while the top fifth contains more two adult households **(Table 5.15)**. Both retired and lone parent family households are more concentrated in the lower quintile groups than the other household types. In 1994-95, households in the bottom fifth had an average of 0.5 economically active people, whereas households in the top fifth had 1.6.

These analyses by the Central Statistical Office are based on data from the Family Expenditure Survey (FES) and look at the current picture of income redistribution. The Department of Social Security (DSS) analyse the FES data focusing on households below average income and changes over time (see Appendix, Part 5: Households Below Average Income). The methodology used differs in several respects from that used by the Central Statistical Office; in particular it is based on groups of individuals rather than households (see Appendix, Part 5: Difference between Households Below Average Income and Redistribution of Income series). The total equivalised income of a household is used to represent the income level of every individual in that household; individuals are ranked according to their total household income. The Institute for Fiscal Studies extended the DSS analysis to examine longer term trends in the income distribution using the same methodology.

Between 1971 and 1993 average (median) real household disposable income rose by 45 per cent **(Chart 5.16)**. However, the incomes at the illustrated decile points have diverged from the median over time, increasing the gap between those with high and low incomes. Income at the ninth decile in 1971 was just over three times that for the first decile; in 1993 it had increased to over four times that for the first decile.

5.16

Real[1] household disposable income[2]

United Kingdom
£ per week

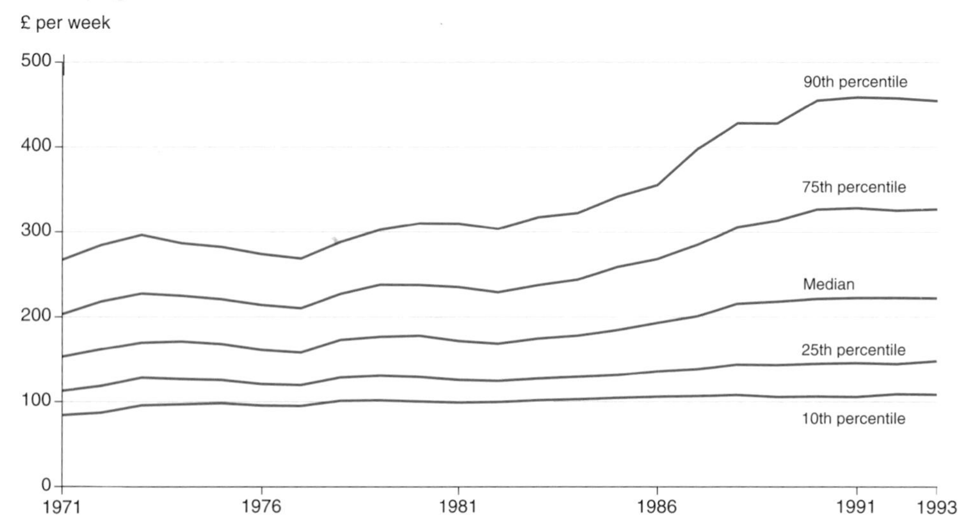

1 Before housing costs, at January 1995 prices deflated by the retail prices index less local taxes.
2 Equivalised disposable household income has been used for ranking the individuals. See Appendix, Part 5: Equivalisation scales.
Source: Institute for Fiscal Studies

Income distribution may also be analysed by examining the number of individuals whose income lies below various fractions of average income. The proportions of people in the United Kingdom with income below either 40, 50 or 60 per cent of the average remained fairly steady from 1961 to the early 1980s, but since then they have risen **(Chart 5.17)**. The proportion of people with income below half average income has risen since 1982 to 19 per cent in 1993. Chart 5.16 indicates that this was the same period during which the top decile point of income rose much faster than the bottom decile point.

In **Chart 5.18** the changes between 1981 and 1992-1993 in two different measurements of disposable income are compared: income before housing costs (BHC) and income after housing costs (AHC) are deducted. BHC income is the sum of income from all sources less deductions. AHC income is BHC income less gross housing costs. Incomes under these two measurements provide complementary indicators of changes in living standards over time. Growth in income measured before housing costs are deducted could overstate improvements in the living standards of low income groups if higher housing benefit is paid only to offset higher rents. On the other hand, income growth measured after housing costs are deducted could understate improvements in living standards, if higher housing costs reflected improved housing.

The higher the income the higher the rise in real terms between 1981 and the period 1992 to 1993. The income of the top fifth increased by 45 per cent in real terms, whereas the income of the bottom fifth increased by 9 per cent before housing costs were taken into consideration, and by only 1 per cent after their deduction. The chart does not monitor how the income of individual households has changed over time, but compares the income of groups of households in the period 1992 to 1993 with the income of groups in 1981 in the corresponding part of the income distribution.

5.17

Percentage of people whose income is below various fractions of average income[1]

United Kingdom

Percentages

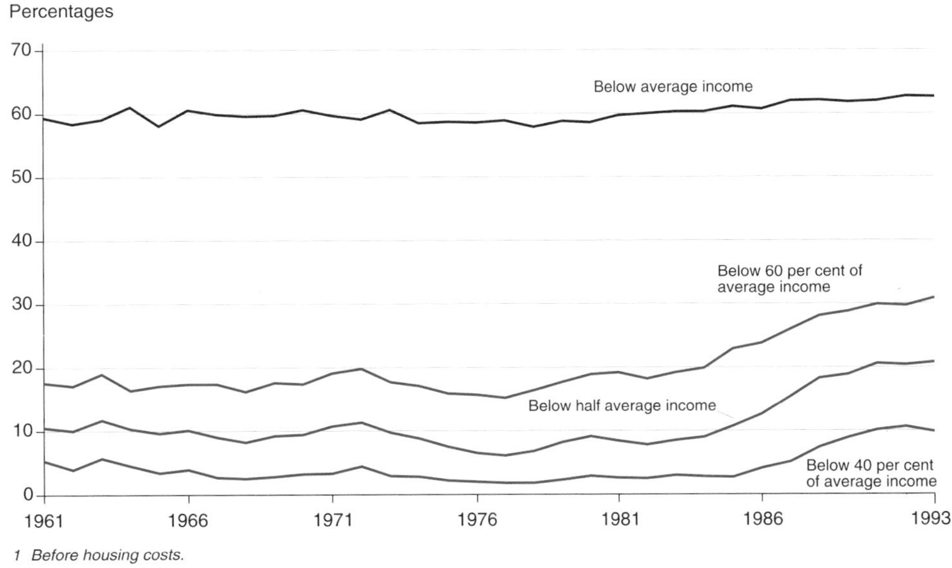

1 Before housing costs.

Source: Institute for Fiscal Studies

5.18

Change in real income[1]: by income grouping, 1981 to 1992-1993

United Kingdom

Percentages

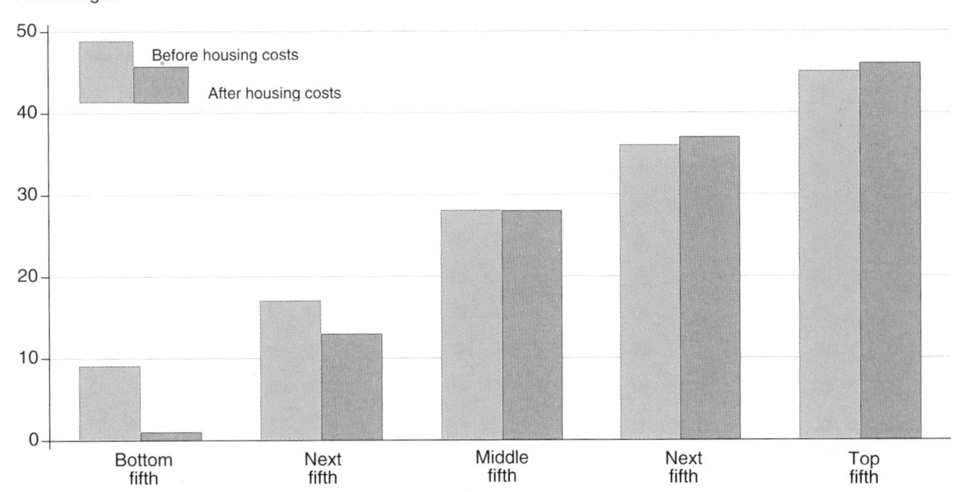

1 Equivalised disposable income has been used for ranking the individuals into quintile groups. See Appendix, Part 5: Households Below Average Income and Equivalisation scales.

Source: Department of Social Security

5.19

Adults moving between different household income[1] groupings, 1991 to 1993

Great Britain — Percentages

	Income fell 4 or more deciles	Income fell 2-3 deciles	Income stable[2]	Income rose 2-3 deciles	Income rose 4 or more deciles
1991 income grouping					
Lowest decile	.	.	*67.2*	*19.1*	*13.7*
2nd decile	.	.	*76.3*	*14.8*	*8.9*
3rd decile	.	*12.1*	*64.8*	*14.1*	*9.1*
4th decile	.	*14.0*	*62.1*	*16.4*	*7.4*
5th decile	*5.0*	*14.2*	*59.9*	*15.1*	*5.8*
6th decile	*8.4*	*12.0*	*59.3*	*18.1*	*2.1*
7th decile	*8.6*	*14.7*	*63.3*	*13.4*	.
8th decile	*12.2*	*15.7*	*62.5*	*9.6*	.
9th decile	*10.7*	*16.8*	*72.5*	.	.
Highest decile	*11.9*	*12.3*	*75.8*	.	.
All deciles	*5.7*	*11.3*	*66.3*	*12.1*	*4.6*

1 Equivalised disposable income has been used for ranking the adults. See Appendix, Part 5: Equivalisation scales.
2 Income did not change, or it fell by one decile or increased by one decile.
Source: British Household Panel Survey, ESRC Research Centre on Micro-social Change

The British Household Panel Survey re-interviews the same sample of households over a period of time and so can show how the income of the same households change from one year to the next. For this analysis, each adult was ranked in 1991 according to the income of its household and then classified into decile groups. In 1993 the same analysis was carried out. It is then possible to identify adults who have moved from one income group to another **(Table 5.19)**.

Two thirds of the adults experienced little income mobility between 1991 and 1993 (ie their household income did not move by more than one decile group). The proportion of adults who moved more than one decile group downwards was about the same as those who moved upwards (about 17 per cent for both). However, the opportunities for substantial change depend somewhat on the initial starting point. Those in the lowest two decile groups cannot fall further (though they may of course experience a drop in living standards). Further information on income mobility is contained in the article on the British Household Panel Survey which begins on page 27.

5.20

Composition of the net wealth[1] of the personal sector

United Kingdom — Percentages

	1971	1981	1991	1994
Life assurance and pension funds	*15*	*16*	*27*	*33*
Dwellings (net of mortgage debt)	*26*	*36*	*37*	*28*
Stocks, shares and unit trusts	*23*	*8*	*8*	*10*
National Savings, notes and coin and bank deposits	*13*	*10*	*9*	*9*
Shares and deposits with building societies	*7*	*8*	*8*	*8*
Non-marketable tenancy rights	*12*	*12*	*8*	*7*
Other fixed assets	*10*	*10*	*5*	*5*
Other financial assets net of liabilities	*-6*	*-*	*-2*	*-*
Total (=100%)(£ billion at 1994 prices[2])	1,172	1,416	2,529	2,551

1 See Appendix, Part 5: Net wealth of the personal sector.
2 Adjusted to 1994 prices using the consumers' expenditure deflator.
Source: Central Statistical Office

Wealth

The value of the net wealth held by the personal sector in 1994 was £2,551 billion **(Table 5.20)**. Net wealth has been increasing since 1971; its highest point was in 1993. The personal sector consists mainly of individuals living in households and institutions, but also includes unincorporated private businesses, life assurance and pension funds. The percentage of net wealth held in dwellings has declined since 1988 as house prices have fallen. The fall in the percentage of net wealth held in stocks, shares and unit trusts between 1971 and 1981 was mainly due to a large fall in share prices during the early 1970s and to the change in the pattern of investment from direct investment in securities and equities to indirect through life assurance and pension funds.

Wealth is much more unequally distributed than income and this has not changed much over the years. Marketable wealth is assets which can be sold or cashed in, for example, shares or dwellings. Adding non-marketable assets such as occupational and state pension rights to marketable assets evens out the distribution of wealth a little, increasing the share of the bottom half from 8 per cent to 18 per cent **(Table 5.21)**. The majority of people hold the highest proportion of their wealth (between 40 and 60 per cent) as residential property. Only those whose wealth is greater than £500 thousand (about 1 per cent of the population) hold more of their wealth in shares than in any other form. Therefore, if the distribution of wealth is adjusted by deducting the value of dwellings, the distribution is even more concentrated in the upper part of the distribution. Wealth in Table 5.21 differs from net wealth of the personal sector shown in Table 5.20 - see Appendix, Part 5: Distribution of personal wealth.

Data on income and data on wealth are collected from different sources and there is little information about the links between the two. The Institute for Fiscal Studies have investigated these links and shown that income and wealth are highly correlated. Other factors also influence the wealth of an individual, for example, age. In 1991-92, average marketable wealth was highest for those aged between 55 and 59.

5.21

Distribution of wealth[1]

United Kingdom — Percentages

	1976	1981	1986	1991	1993
Marketable wealth					
Percentage of wealth owned by:					
Most wealthy 1%	*21*	*18*	*18*	*17*	*17*
Most wealthy 5%	*38*	*36*	*36*	*35*	*36*
Most wealthy 10%	*50*	*50*	*50*	*47*	*48*
Most wealthy 25%	*71*	*73*	*73*	*71*	*72*
Most wealthy 50%	*92*	*92*	*90*	*92*	*92*
Total marketable wealth (£ billion)	280	565	955	1,711	1,809
Marketable wealth plus occupational and state pension rights					
Percentage of wealth owned by:					
Most wealthy 1%	*13*	*11*	*10*	*10*	*10*
Most wealthy 5%	*26*	*24*	*24*	*23*	*23*
Most wealthy 10%	*36*	*34*	*35*	*33*	*33*
Most wealthy 25%	*57*	*56*	*58*	*57*	*56*
Most wealthy 50%	*80*	*79*	*82*	*83*	*82*
Total marketable wealth (£ billion)	472	1,036	1,784	3,014	3,383

1 Applies to adult population aged 18 and over. Estimates for 1976, 1981, 1986 and 1991 are based on the estates of persons dying in those years. Estimates for 1993 are based on estates notified for probate in 1993-94. Estimates are not strictly comparable between 1993 and earlier years.

Source: Inland Revenue

As mentioned earlier, pension rights have an effect on the distribution of wealth. The membership of pension schemes varies by gender and type of employment, as seen in **Table 5.22**. Employees are more likely to

5.22

Membership of a current pension scheme: by gender and whether working full or part time, 1993-94

Great Britain — Percentages

	Employed			Self-employed	
	Occupational pension	Personal pension	Any pension	Personal pension	All employed
Males					
Full time	*60*	*29*	*89*	*66*	*85*
Part time	*16*	*8*	*24*	*31*	*25*
Females					
Full time	*54*	*22*	*77*	*46*	*74*
Part time	*19*	*12*	*32*	*27*	*31*

Source: General Household Survey, Office of Population Censuses and Surveys

5.23

Households owning stocks and shares[1]: by age of head of household, 1993-94

Great Britain

Percentages

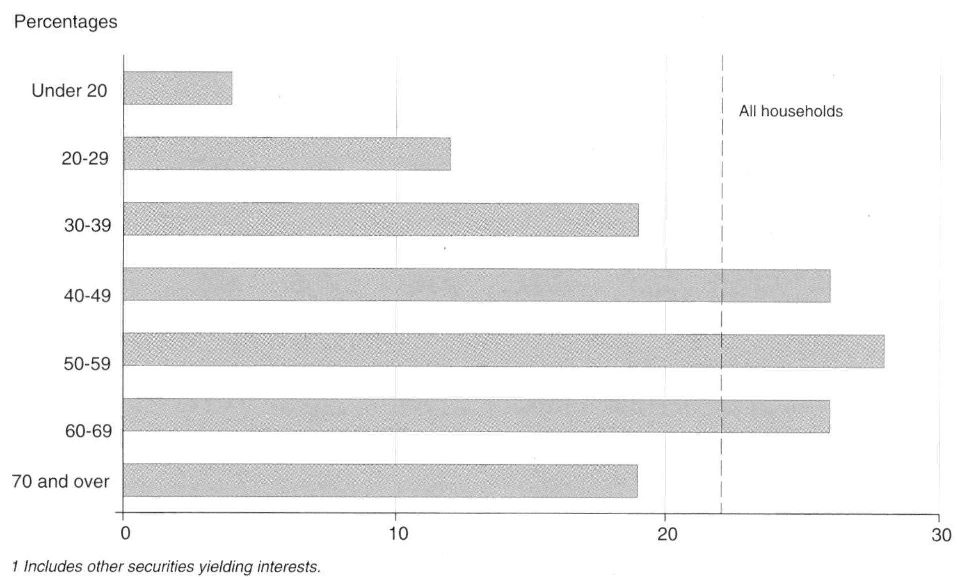

1 Includes other securities yielding interests.

Source: Family Resources Survey, Department of Social Security

belong to a pension scheme than those who are self-employed. The proportion of people who are members of their employers' pension schemes decreased from 61 per cent in 1983 to 58 per cent in 1993-94. Membership of employers' pension schemes varies with socio-economic group. Around three quarters of both professional and intermediate non-manual workers were members of their employers' pension scheme in 1993-94, compared with only two fifths of semi-skilled or unskilled workers. This difference is partly explained by availability of pension schemes to employees in certain occupations.

The Family Resources Survey (FRS), which began in April 1993, is a new survey collecting information on the living standards and circumstances of private households in Great Britain. It shows that in 1993-94 households where the head was aged between 40 and 69 were more likely to own stocks and shares than those in other age groups (**Chart 5.23**). In addition to the FRS, surveys have been carried out to determine the number of individuals who own shares; in 1979 there were approximately 3 million individuals in Great Britain who held shares directly which rose to 10 million in 1993. It is thought that the number of shareholders peaked in 1990 following the privatisation of the electricity companies (see Appendix, Part 5: Share ownership). Information on savings is shown in Chapter 6: Expenditure.

5.24

Gross domestic product[1]

United Kingdom

Volume index (1990=100)

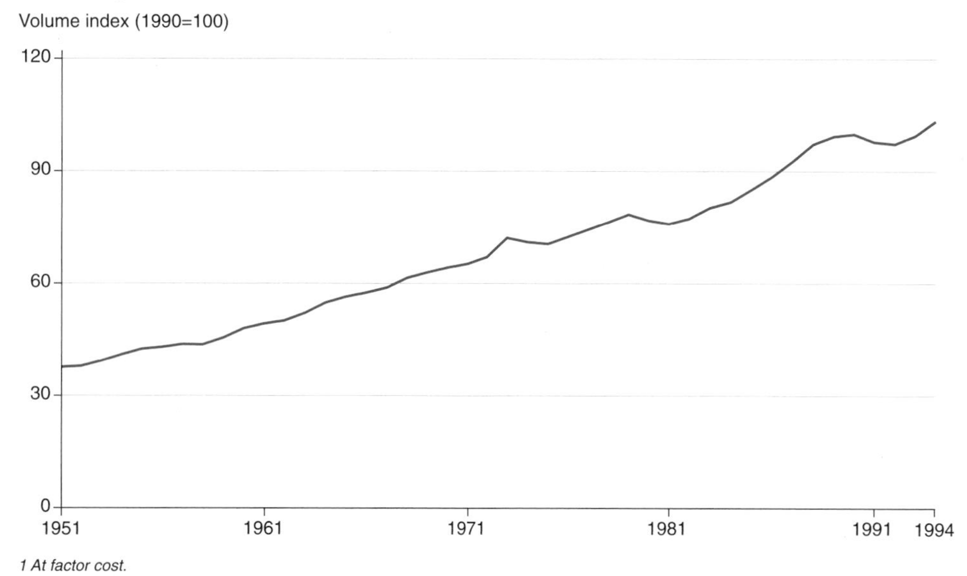

1 At factor cost.

Source: Central Statistical Office

Income of the nation

The income of the nation as a whole comprises the income of individuals and the income (for example profits) of organisations. The standard measure of economic activity in the United Kingdom is Gross Domestic Product (GDP) at constant prices and factor cost; this measure has had the effects of taxes and subsidies and changes in prices taken out. In **Chart 5.24** it is presented as an index using 1990 as the base year. Over the period 1951 to 1994, GDP has grown at an average rate of about 2.4 per cent per annum. There have been three significant dips against the trend.

'hese are explained by the oil price rises in ne mid-1970s, and the two recessions of ne early 1980s (also characterised by a harp oil price increase) and early 1990s. ;DP has been growing again since 1992.

n **Table 5.25** GDP is presented for the onstituent regions of the United Kingdom. ;DP for the continental shelf is excluded rom this table because it cannot be ttributed to a particular region, for example North Sea oil. The GDP per head for each egion is expressed as an index based on ne UK average in each year throughout the eriod shown. In 1994 the South East had he highest GDP per head while Northern reland had the lowest. East Anglia xperienced the fastest growth since 1981 vhile the North and North West showed the lowest growth.

n **Chart 5.26** the countries of the European Community are ranked by their GDP per nead in 1994. These data, although shown n sterling, have been calculated using ourchasing power parities. These provide a etter basis for making international comparisons than exchange rates because hey adjust for the differences in the price evels between countries. For example, if a articular commodity, such as bread, is more xpensive in one country than another, ncomes would need to be higher in that country to reach the same standard of living. The GDP per head of Luxembourg (which nas a small public debt and almost full mployment) was highest in 1994 - more than twice that of Greece which had the owest. The United Kingdom had the ninth nighest.

5.25

Gross domestic product at current factor cost: by region

Index per head (UK=100)

	1971	1981	1986	1991	1994
United Kingdom[1]	100	100	100	100	100
North	87	94	90	89	89
Yorkshire & Humberside	93	92	95	92	89
East Midlands	97	97	98	98	96
East Anglia	95	97	102	101	101
South East	112	117	116	117	117
South West	95	93	94	95	95
West Midlands	103	91	91	93	93
North West	96	95	94	90	90
England	102	102	102	102	102
Wales	87	84	85	85	85
Scotland	94	97	95	97	100
Northern Ireland	78	79	79	82	82

1 United Kingdom less continental shelf.

Source: Central Statistical Office

5.26

Gross domestic product per head: EC comparison, 1994

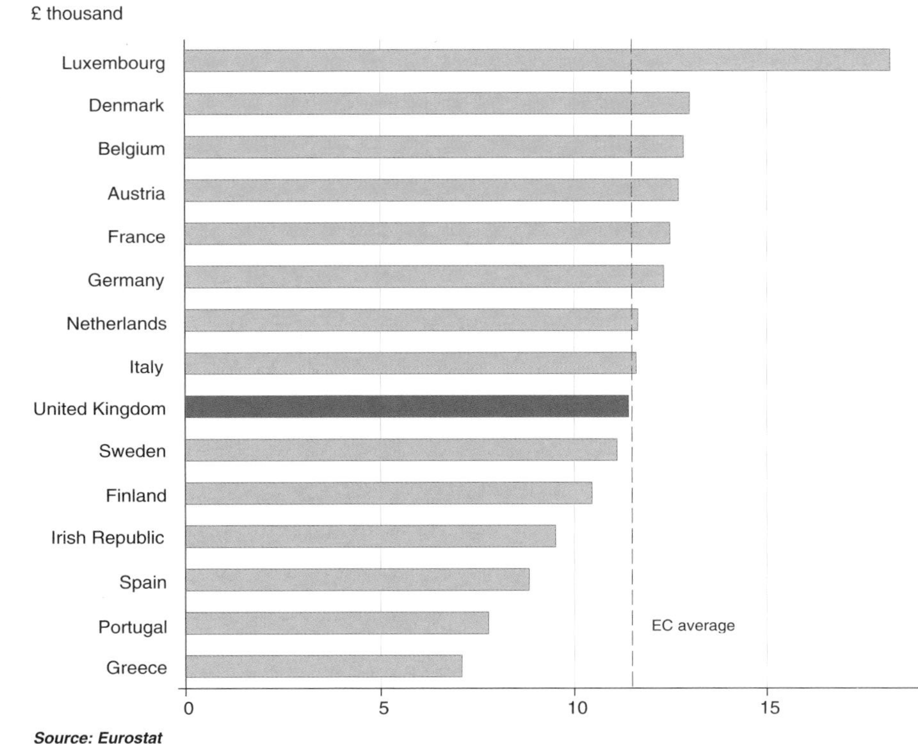

Source: Eurostat

References and further reading

The following list contains selected publications relevant to **Chapter 5: Income and Wealth**. Those published by HMSO are available from the addresses shown on the inside back cover of *Social Trends*.

Changing Households: The British Household Panel Survey, ESRC Research Centre on Micro-social Change

Economic Trends, HMSO

Family Resources Survey, Department of Social Security

Family Spending, HMSO

Fiscal Studies, Institute for Fiscal Studies

For Richer, For Poorer, Institute for Fiscal Studies

General Household Survey, HMSO

Households Below Average Income, A Statistical Analysis, HMSO

Inland Revenue Statistics, HMSO

Inquiry into Income and Wealth, Joseph Rowntree Foundation

Labour Market Trends (incorporating Employment Gazette), Harrington Kilbride

New Earnings Survey, HMSO

Regional Trends, HMSO

Share Ownership - The Share Register Survey Report, HMSO

Social Focus on Women, HMSO

Social Security, Departmental Report, HMSO

Social Security Statistics, HMSO

Tax/Benefit Model Tables, Department of Social Security

The Distribution of Wealth in the UK, Institute for Fiscal Studies

United Kingdom National Accounts (The CSO Blue Book), HMSO

Contacts

Telephone contact points for further information relating to
Chapter 5: Income and Wealth

Central Statistical Office	
Average earnings index	01928 792442
Effects of taxes and benefits	0171 217 4217
National accounts	0171 270 5944
New earnings survey	01928 792164
Personal sector accounts	0171 217 4203/4349
Regional accounts	0171 217 4197
Retail prices	0171 217 4310
Share register survey	0171 217 8236
Department of Social Security	
Family Resources Survey	0171 962 8092
Households Below Average Income	0171 962 8214
Inland Revenue	0171 438 7370
Office of Population Censuses and Surveys	0171 396 2327
ESRC Research Centre on Micro-social Change	01206 872957
Institute for Fiscal Studies	0171 636 3784
Eurostat	00 352 4301 34567

Chapter 6 Expenditure

Household and personal expenditure

Food as a proportion of total household expenditure has nearly halved since 1971, to just 11 per cent in 1994. (Chart 6.1)

Households spent an average of £2.05 a week on the National Lottery in the first quarter of 1995, well under half the amount they spent on cigarettes. (Page 117)

Students spent about £23 a week on entertainment in 1992/93, over half of which went on alcohol and tobacco. (Page 118)

Households with a car make a higher proportion of their food purchases at major supermarket chains than those without a car, at 73 per cent compared with 60 per cent in 1994-95. (Page 119)

Nearly half of couple households with dependent children had a home computer in 1994-95 compared with only a fifth of those without dependent children. (Table 6.8)

Prices

Over time the purchasing power of the 1961 pound has shrunk in value so that it now takes over £11 to buy the equivalent amount of goods. (Chart 6.15)

Consumer credit and household saving

There were 817 million credit card transactions in 1994 compared with only 451 million in 1986; over the same period the value of these transactions has increased from £13.2 billion to £37.8 billion. (Page 124)

Public expenditure

Nearly six in ten people supported increasing taxes to fund higher levels of spending on the health service, education and pensions in 1994. (Page 127)

6.1

Household[1] expenditure on selected items

United Kingdom

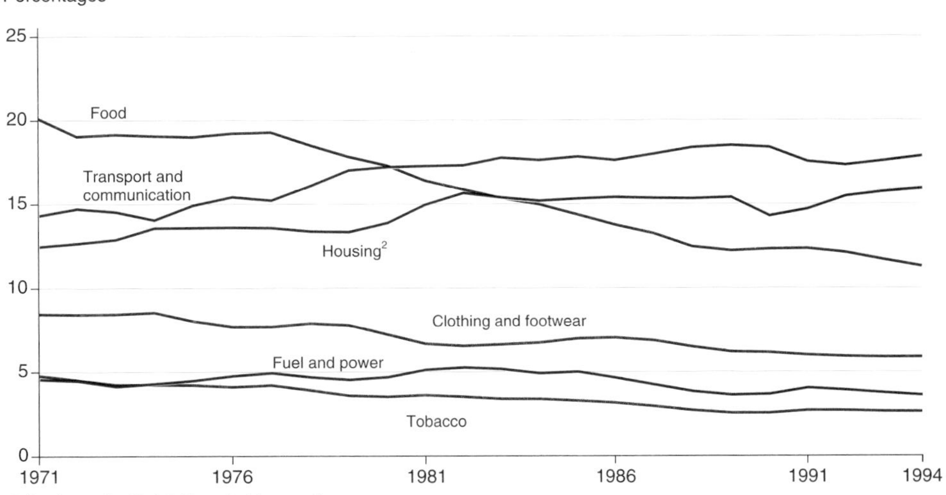

1 See Appendix, Part 6: Household expenditure.
2 Includes domestic rates, but excludes community charge and council tax.
Source: Central Statistical Office

The way in which people choose to use their incomes can have a significant impact on the country's economy, whilst changes in prices affect their purchasing power.

Household and personal expenditure

Total household expenditure in the United Kingdom rose by three quarters between 1971 and 1994 at constant prices, that is after allowing for inflation **(Table 6.2)**. Among the categories shown in the table, the only ones where expenditure decreased at constant prices over the period were tobacco, reflecting the fall in smoking which is shown in Chart 7.19 in the Health chapter and books, magazines and newspapers. The categories which experienced the fastest growth, nearly quadrupling between 1971 and 1994, were UK tourists' expenditure abroad and monetary services, which includes contributions to life assurance and pension funds. Information from the International Passenger Survey shows that when UK tourists went abroad in 1994 they spent an average of £363 per visit, about £32 a day.

These differing trends mean that the composition of household expenditure has changed over the last 20 or so years. **Chart 6.1**, at the beginning of this chapter, shows that the proportion of household expenditure which is spent on food has nearly halved since 1971, to just 11 per cent in 1994. The proportion accounted for by some of the other essentials, such as fuel and power and clothing and footwear, also fell over the same period. On the other hand, housing now accounts for a larger share than in 1971; this is partly due to the number of owner-occupiers continuing to increase as well as the rise in rents.

Table 6.3 shows the spending patterns of households in the different regions of the country, using data from the Family Expenditure Survey (FES). As one might expect, it was households in the South East who spent the most in 1994-95; at an average of £319 a week per household this was almost two fifths more than the amount spent in Wales which had the lowest expenditure. Households in Northern Ireland spent a higher proportion of expenditure on food than any of the English regions, Wales or Scotland. Within this category Northern Ireland households also spent the most on meals out: at £8.40 a week. The proportion of spending on motoring and fares was highest in the East Midlands. However, the

6.2

Household expenditure[1]

United Kingdom Index (1990=100)

	Indices at constant prices (1990=100)					£ billion (current prices)
	1971	1981	1986	1991	1994	1994
Housing	68	81	93	100	104	66.6
Motor vehicles	48	62	83	91	101	52.9
Food	87	91	95	100	104	47.4
Recreation and cultural services	31	58	76	99	112	37.2
Catering	56	58	73	93	96	36.9
Household goods and services	59	68	85	98	111	27.2
Alcohol	73	93	98	96	95	25.8
Clothing and footwear	52	67	92	100	114	24.7
Monetary services	27	36	68	99	101	16.9
Fuel, light and power	86	94	103	108	107	14.9
Other travel	67	71	84	97	103	14.0
Tobacco	136	121	101	98	86	11.0
Post and telecommunications	33	63	80	100	115	7.9
Books, newspapers and magazines	101	97	92	95	97	5.4
Other goods and services	26	54	72	98	97	29.3
Less expenditure by foreign tourists, etc	48	72	94	86	104	-11.3
Household expenditure abroad	34	66	78	97	130	13.8
All household expenditure	59	72	85	98	104	420.4

1 See Appendix, Part 6: Household expenditure.

Source: Central Statistical Office

6.3

Household expenditure: by region, 1994-95

Percentages

	Food	Housing	Leisure goods and services	Motoring and fares	Household goods and services	Alcohol and tobacco	Clothing and footwear	Fuel, light and power	Other goods and services	Average expenditure (=100%) (£ per week)
United Kingdom	*18*	*16*	*16*	*15*	*13*	*6*	*6*	*5*	*5*	283.58
North	*19*	*15*	*15*	*13*	*13*	*9*	*7*	*5*	*4*	239.64
Yorkshire & Humberside	*18*	*15*	*15*	*14*	*14*	*7*	*7*	*5*	*4*	274.23
East Midlands	*17*	*15*	*14*	*20*	*12*	*7*	*6*	*5*	*4*	296.07
East Anglia	*19*	*17*	*15*	*15*	*15*	*5*	*5*	*4*	*4*	257.08
South East	*17*	*18*	*17*	*15*	*13*	*5*	*6*	*4*	*5*	319.42
South West	*17*	*18*	*16*	*15*	*13*	*6*	*6*	*4*	*5*	276.80
West Midlands	*18*	*16*	*15*	*15*	*14*	*6*	*6*	*5*	*4*	259.93
North West	*18*	*15*	*17*	*13*	*14*	*7*	*6*	*5*	*5*	271.87
England	*18*	*17*	*16*	*15*	*13*	*6*	*6*	*4*	*5*	286.91
Wales	*19*	*15*	*14*	*17*	*12*	*7*	*6*	*6*	*4*	230.73
Scotland	*18*	*15*	*18*	*15*	*13*	*7*	*7*	*5*	*4*	280.53
Northern Ireland	*21*	*11*	*14*	*15*	*11*	*7*	*9*	*5*	*4*	295.33

Source: Family Expenditure Survey, Central Statistical Office

figure of 20 per cent shown in the table should be treated with caution as it has a large sampling variability and therefore may not indicate the underlying pattern of expenditure, which is likely to be about 17 to 18 per cent.

The National Lottery began in November 1994. The FES allows us to look at expenditure on National Lottery tickets in the first quarter of 1995 when an average of only £2.05 a week was spent by households in the United Kingdom, well under half the amount they spent on cigarettes and less than 1 per cent of their total weekly expenditure. The amount spent varied between the different social classes: households headed by a skilled manual worker spent the most at an average of £3.13 a week, while those headed by a retired or unoccupied person spent the least at only £1.42 **(Chart 6.4)**. But not everyone spends money on the lottery: altogether some three in ten households recorded no expenditure on the National Lottery during their two week diary keeping period in the first three months of 1995. Household winnings from the National Lottery averaged 80 pence per week.

6.4

Household expenditure on the National Lottery: by social class of head of household, January to March 1995

United Kingdom

£ per week

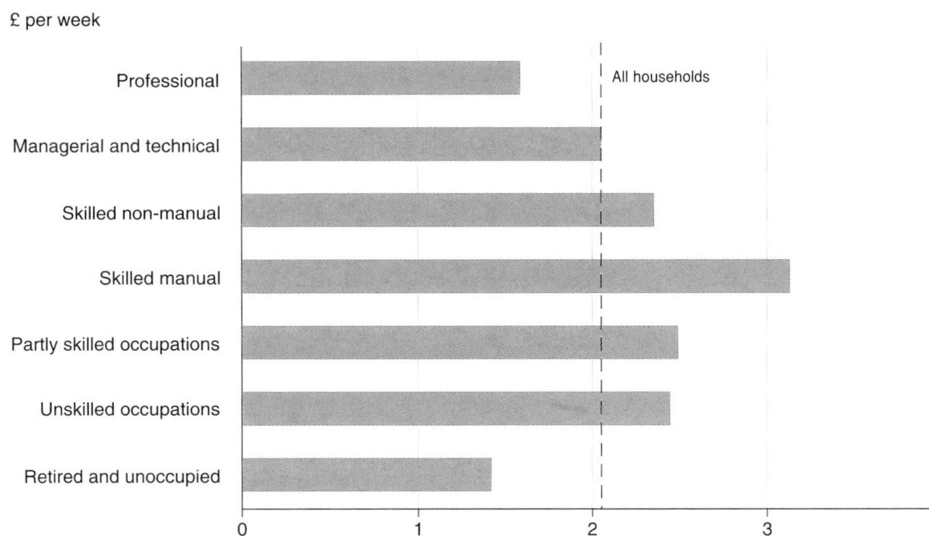

Source: Family Expenditure Survey, Central Statistical Office

6.5

Household expenditure of pensioners[1]: by type of household, 1994-95

United Kingdom Percentages

	1 adult		2 adults		
	State pensions[2]	Other	State pensions[2]	Other	All pensioner households
Food	*25*	*25*	*17*	*20*	*21*
Household goods and services	*17*	*14*	*20*	*14*	*16*
Leisure goods and services	*13*	*14*	*17*	*17*	*16*
Housing	*17*	*15*	*18*	*12*	*15*
Motoring and fares	*4*	*10*	*8*	*17*	*12*
Fuel, light and power	*11*	*8*	*7*	*5*	*7*
Alcohol and tobacco	*5*	*6*	*3*	*6*	*5*
Clothing and footwear	*4*	*4*	*5*	*4*	*5*
Other goods and services	*4*	*5*	*4*	*5*	*4*
All household expenditure (=100%)(£ per week)	75.51	144.83	142.91	236.83	146.41

1 Households where the head of household is over retirement age and is in receipt of a state pension. See Appendix, Part 6: Pensioner households.
2 At least three quarters of the total household income is derived from state pensions and other benefits.

Source: Family Expenditure Survey, Central Statistical Office

Different types of households have different spending patterns. **Table 6.5** looks at the expenditure of pensioner households; these are defined for the purposes of this table as those where the head of household is over retirement age and receiving a state pension. Overall the average expenditure of a pensioner household was just over half that of an average household in 1994-95. Pensioner households mainly dependent on state pensions or benefits have a lower income than those who receive their main income from personal pensions and consequently they also spend less: total expenditure was around 50 per cent less among one adult pensioner households and 40 per cent less for couples. Their spending patterns also differ: those relying on state pensions spend proportionately more on housing and fuel and power and less on motoring and fares.

6.6

Expenditure of non-mature students[1]: by type of accommodation, 1992/93

United Kingdom £ per week

	Living with parents	College provided	Private rented	All accommodation
Basic expenditure				
Housing (including fuel)	9	35	41	35
Food/kitty	14	14	18	16
Course expenses	6	6	6	6
Parental board	21	4	3	5
Travel to/from college	8	1	5	4
Travel to/from parents	-	2	2	1
All basic expenditure	59	61	74	67
Other expenditure				
Entertainment[2]	20	22	25	23
Leisure travel/vehicles	7	8	9	8
Clothes	7	5	5	5
Post/telephone	1	2	2	2
Insurance	-	1	2	2
Miscellaneous	21	15	17	17
All other expenditure	56	53	60	57
All expenditure	114	114	134	124

1 Term-time expenditure of home students, aged under 26 at the start of their course, studying full time at public sector institutions. See also Appendix, Part 6: Student expenditure.
2 Includes CDs, tapes and videos.

Source: Research Services Limited for Department for Education and Employment

Students tend to have very different spending priorities to the rest of the population. In 1992/93, Research Services Ltd carried out a survey for the now Department for Education and Employment which asked students about their expenditure during the academic year. Some of the results for students under the age of 26 are given in **Table 6.6**. Those who lived in privately rented accommodation spent more than those who lived at home or in college-provided accommodation. The largest category of expenditure for all these three groups was housing, if parental board is included. The second highest category of expenditure was entertainment. At around £23 a week, this was almost 50 per cent more than spending on food. Male students spent, on average, nearly 50 per cent more than female students on entertainment. Over half of entertainment spending amongst both males and females was on alcohol and tobacco. Females, however, spent more than males on clothes.

'he FES also collects information on the ypes of shops at which households do their rocery shopping. Overall households spent round 70 per cent of their food expenditure t large supermarket chains in 1994-95 **Table 6.7)**, compared with around 50 per ent in 1987. Of all the grocery products shown in the table, convenience foods are he most likely to be bought at these upermarkets whereas milk is the item which is by far the most likely to be bought t other outlets, presumably reflecting the xistence of a doorstep delivery service. High income households spend a high proportion of their food expenditure at large supermarket chains, spending 79 per cent of heir food expenditure there in 1994-95, compared with only 62 per cent of the food spending by pensioner households. Car ownership is a major influence on where people buy their food as many large supermarkets are either on the edge of, or outside, towns: overall households with a car spent 73 per cent of their food expenditure at major supermarkets compared with 60 per cent for households which did not have a car.

Table 6.2 showed that expenditure on household goods and services has ncreased faster than overall household expenditure over the last 20 or so years; this s reflected in the ownership of consumer durables which is shown in **Table 6.8**. By 1994-95 ownership of colour TVs in Great Britain had virtually reached saturation point. The presence of dependent children in a household tends to indicate that it is more likely to have consumer durable goods; one person households are far less likely to have consumer durables than other types of households, including lone parent families. This is due to the large number of pensioner households in this group which are far less likely than others to have such household goods.

6.7

Percentage of food expenditure made from large supermarket chains: by type of household, 1994-95

Page 119, Table 6.7: *For* Great Britain *read* 'United Kingdom'

Great Britain — Percentages

	High income[1]	Pensioner[2]	Other[3]	All households
Convenience foods	*89*	*78*	*83*	*83*
Non-alcoholic drinks	*86*	*76*	*78*	*78*
Bread, cereals, biscuits, cakes	*81*	*67*	*74*	*74*
Fresh fruit and vegetables	*83*	*53*	*66*	*67*
Uncooked meat	*74*	*55*	*65*	*65*
Uncooked fish and shellfish	*66*	*51*	*64*	*63*
Fresh milk	*32*	*32*	*35*	*35*
Other dairy products	*86*	*72*	*81*	*81*
Other meat and meat products	*84*	*62*	*76*	*75*
Other	*83*	*71*	*76*	*76*
All food	*79*	*62*	*70*	*70*

1 Those households with income in the top 4 per cent of the distribution.
2 At least three quarters of household income derived from benefits and at least one person over the national insurance retirement age.
3 Those households which equate to those covered by the retail prices index.
Source: Family Expenditure Survey, Central Statistical Office

6.8

Households with consumer durables: by type of household, 1994-95

Great Britain — Percentages

	One person	Couple with no dependent children	Couple with dependent children	Lone parent family	Other	All house-holds[1]
Colour television	*92*	*99*	*99*	*97*	*97*	*97*
Black and white television only	*5*	*-*	*1*	*2*	*2*	*2*
Telephone	*85*	*97*	*93*	*83*	*91*	*91*
Washing machine	*71*	*96*	*99*	*93*	*88*	*89*
Deep-freezer/ fridge-freezer	*74*	*94*	*97*	*90*	*87*	*88*
Video recorder	*48*	*85*	*96*	*85*	*77*	*77*
Microwave oven	*47*	*72*	*82*	*66*	*62*	*67*
Tumble drier	*27*	*54*	*72*	*55*	*44*	*50*
CD player	*25*	*49*	*67*	*49*	*45*	*47*
Home computer	*8*	*21*	*48*	*24*	*21*	*24*
Dishwasher	*6*	*22*	*32*	*13*	*14*	*19*

1 Includes a small number of same gender couples.
Source: General Household Survey, Office of Population Censuses and Surveys

6.9

Consumer confidence: the right time to make a major purchase[1]

Great Britain

Percentages

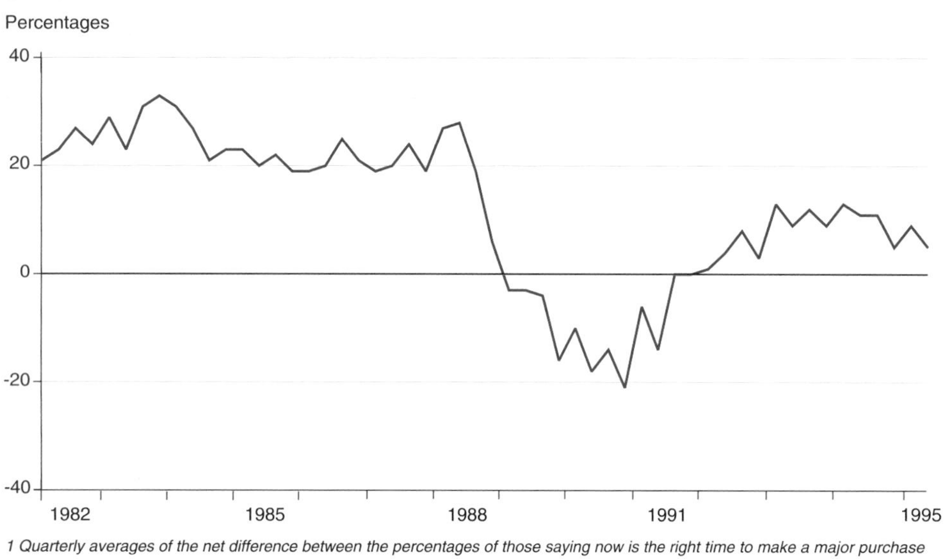

1 Quarterly averages of the net difference between the percentages of those saying now is the right time to make a major purchase and those thinking the purchase should be postponed.

Source: The Gallup Organization for the European Commission

6.10

Retail prices index[1]

United Kingdom

Percentage change over 12 months

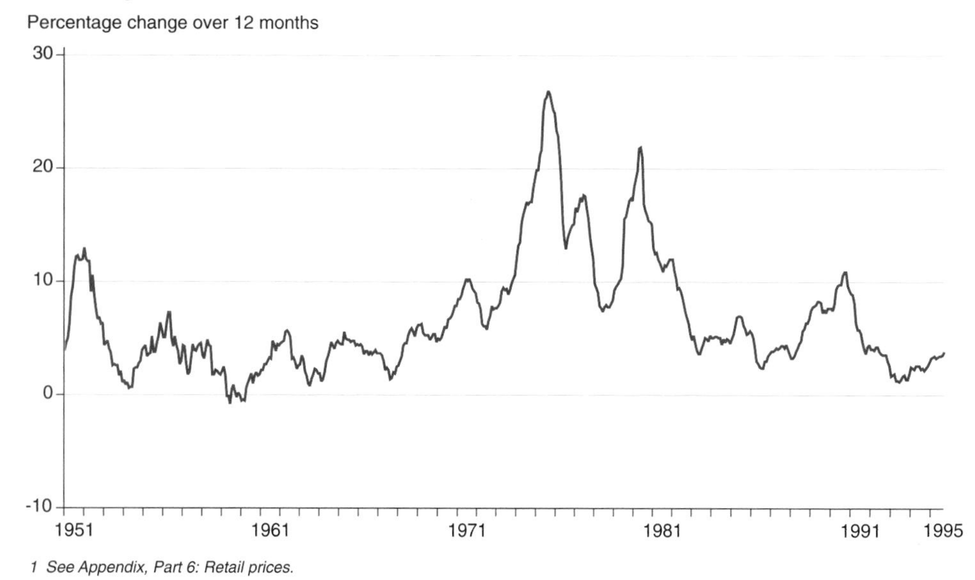

1 See Appendix, Part 6: Retail prices.

Source: Central Statistical Office

How people feel about the general economic environment of the country and their own particular situation, such as job security, can affect their decisions on whether to make major purchases. The Gallup Organization has collected information, for the European Commission, which asks people whether it is the right time to make a major purchase. This information is used in **Chart 6.9** to give a guide to consumer confidence by taking the difference between the percentage of those who said now is the right time to make a major purchase (such as washing machines, televisions or furniture) and those who said that the purchase should be postponed.

The chart demonstrates the volatility of consumer confidence, with swings from optimism to pessimism and back again. After a period of optimism throughout most of the 1980s, confidence began falling in the middle of 1988, reaching a trough in 1990. Interestingly, this shows that this measure of consumer confidence generally precedes the movements in the economic cycle which peaked at the end of 1988. The recession did not bottom out until 1992, but consumer confidence began rising again in 1991 although the peak was well below the level recorded in the 1980s. More recently, since the middle of 1994 the indications are that consumer confidence may be on a downward trend again with fewer people thinking that it is the right time to make a major purchase.

Prices

The rate of growth in retail prices in the United Kingdom, often referred to as the rate of inflation, is measured by the retail prices index (RPI). The index monitors the change from month to month in the cost of a representative 'shopping basket' of goods and services of the sort bought by a typical household. As the RPI is often used to uprate certain payments in line with inflation, such as wages, rents and social security benefits, it affects the lives of millions of people. The change in the RPI over the previous 12 months is shown in **Chart 6.10**. Since 1951 this has ranged from a fall of 0.8

per cent in June 1959 to a rise of 26.9 per cent in August 1975. The biggest drop ever recorded was a fall of 28 per cent in January 1922 reflecting the depression which followed the post-war boom. Since October 1992 the Government has had an explicit inflation objective to keep the measure of the RPI which excludes mortgage interest payments (sometimes called underlying inflation) in the range of 1 to 4 per cent; in September 1995 it was 3.1 per cent.

Chart 6.11 shows the changes in consumer prices between September 1994 and September 1995 for the major industrialised (G7) countries. International comparisons of consumer prices should be made with care as they are affected by differences in national definitions and concepts, particularly in the treatment of housing costs. The data in the chart exclude housing costs as this is felt to be the best available basis of comparison. The highest rate of price inflation among the G7 countries on this basis in the 12 months to September 1995 was recorded in Italy where prices rose by 5.6 per cent; this compares with 3.1 per cent in the United Kingdom which came second in the ranking. In Japan the rate actually fell by 0.2 per cent.

Annual changes in the prices of the various categories of goods and services in the United Kingdom can be seen in **Table 6.12**. Between 1993 and 1994 the all items RPI increased by 2.4 per cent, but within this the cost of tobacco rose by 7.5 per cent while the price of leisure goods fell by 0.6 per cent. In the United Kingdom the 'basket' is composed of more than 600 separate goods and services for which the changes in prices are measured in about 180 towns and cities around the country, leading to around 150 thousand price quotations each month. The composition of the 'basket', that is the relative importance or weight attached to

6.11

Change in consumer prices[1]: G7 comparison, September 1995

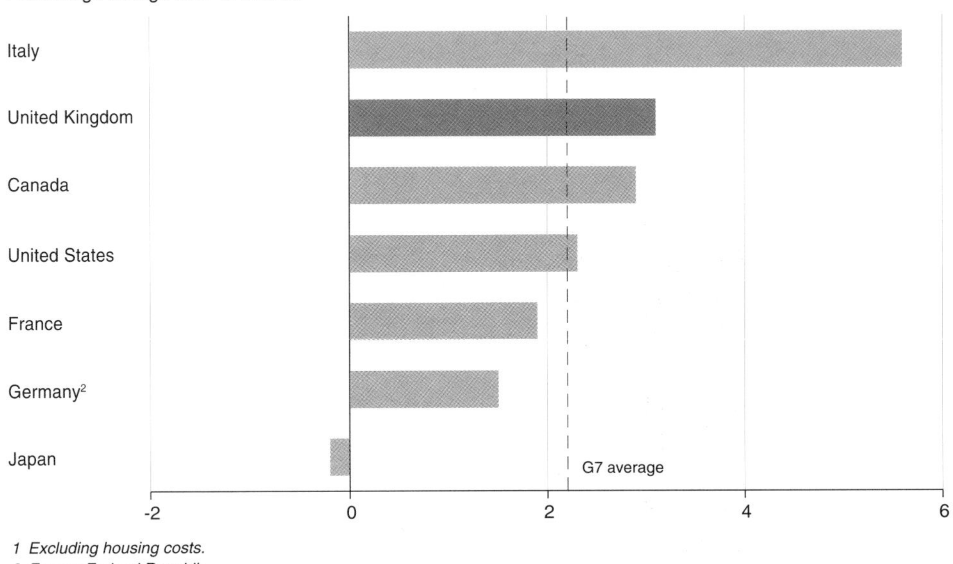

1 Excluding housing costs.
2 Former Federal Republic.
Source: Central Statistical Office

6.12

Index of retail prices: rates of change[1]

United Kingdom Percentages

	1989	1990	1991	1992	1993	1994	1994 (weights)
Housing	*20.3*	*21.0*	*-1.8*	*-0.7*	*-5.4*	*3.3*	158
Food	*5.6*	*8.1*	*5.2*	*2.1*	*1.8*	*1.0*	142
Motoring	*5.5*	*6.1*	*7.4*	*6.8*	*4.3*	*3.5*	142
Household goods	*4.0*	*4.8*	*6.2*	*3.3*	*1.2*	*0.3*	76
Alcoholic drink	*5.6*	*9.7*	*12.4*	*6.4*	*4.5*	*2.5*	76
Leisure services	*6.5*	*8.2*	*11.5*	*8.1*	*4.5*	*3.7*	71
Clothing and footwear	*5.3*	*4.6*	*3.0*	*0.3*	*0.8*	*0.5*	58
Leisure goods	*3.2*	*4.7*	*4.7*	*2.6*	*1.4*	*-0.6*	48
Household services	*5.3*	*6.3*	*8.3*	*5.8*	*3.6*	*0.1*	47
Catering	*6.3*	*8.5*	*10.0*	*6.3*	*5.2*	*4.2*	45
Fuel and light	*5.6*	*8.0*	*7.9*	*2.2*	*-1.3*	*4.4*	45
Personal goods and services	*6.8*	*7.5*	*8.7*	*6.6*	*4.0*	*3.7*	37
Tobacco	*2.9*	*6.8*	*14.3*	*11.0*	*8.5*	*7.5*	35
Fares and other travel costs	*7.2*	*7.1*	*9.8*	*6.2*	*5.2*	*2.6*	20
All items	*7.8*	*9.5*	*5.9*	*3.7*	*1.6*	*2.4*	1,000
All items except housing	*5.4*	*6.9*	*7.6*	*4.7*	*3.1*	*2.3*	842
All items except mortgage interest payments	*5.9*	*8.1*	*6.7*	*4.7*	*3.0*	*2.3*	956

1 Percentage changes on the previous year. See also Appendix, Part 6: Retail prices.
Source: Central Statistical Office

6.13

Cost of groceries

United Kingdom			Pence
	1914[1]	1947[1]	1995
500g beef	5	7	236
500g bacon	5	8	152
250g cheese	2	2	115
250g butter	6	4	78
1kg potatoes	1	1	77
Large loaf (800g)	1	2	74
1kg sugar	2	3	72
125g tea	2	4	63
Half dozen eggs	3	4	59
500g margarine	3	4	50
1 pint milk	1	2	36
Total of above items	30	41	1,011

1 Prices given are to the nearest decimal equivalents.

Source: Central Statistical Office

6.14

Length of time necessary to work to pay for selected commodities and services[1], 1971 and 1995

Great Britain								Hours and minutes
	Married couple with husband only working[2]				Single female parent with child			
	1971		1995		1971		1995	
	Hrs	Mins	Hrs	Mins	Hrs	Mins	Hrs	Mins
500g back bacon (home produced)		35		21		52		25
500g pork sausages		21		11		32		13
250g of butter (Danish)		14		7		20		9
500g old potatoes, loose, white		2		3		3		4
500g of cod fillets		28		24		41		28
500g chicken		22		9		33		11
1 pint of beer (draught bitter)		14		13		20		15
20 cigarettes (king size filter)		22		22		33		26
Ford Escort	2,193	43	1,846	14	3,258	31	2,181	59
Colour television licence	19	21	12	25	28	45	14	40
Return rail ticket from London to Edinburgh (2nd/Standard class)[3]	20	48	8	37	30	54	10	11
Copy of Social Trends	5	15	5	1	7	47	5	56

1 Length of time necessary for a person on average hourly adult earnings for all industries and services to work so that his/her net income pays for the various goods. The earnings figures are based on full-time employees on adult rates whose pay was not affected for the survey period by absence.

2 Married man with non-earning wife and two children under 11.

3 Standard return in 1971; Supersaver in 1995.

Source: Central Statistical Office; Inland Revenue

each of the various goods and services it contains, is revised every year to reflect the changes in household expenditure patterns. For example, out of a total weight of 1,000, food accounted for 250 in 1971 but only 142 in 1994, in line with the fall in the proportion of expenditure accounted for by food seen in Chart 6.1.

As well as the weights changing each year, some items are taken out of the index and others are added to reflect the changing spending habits of society. For example, ice cream was added in 1952; televisions, brown bread and coffee were introduced in 1956 when rabbits and candles came out; in the 1970s, mushrooms, wine, yoghurt, mortgage interest payments and continental quilts were included for the first time; in 1987 CDs and CD players were added but it was not until 1991 that the 7" single was removed from the index; and in 1994 the shampoo and set was replaced by highlights.

Before 1947 the 'cost of living index for the working classes' was the forerunner of today's RPI. The items chosen were very basic, with foodstuffs accounting for three fifths of the total. Since then the food category has moved from containing just basic food products to a wider range of convenience and processed products. Despite these changes it is possible to compare the prices of basic foods over the period. Prices of a typical grocery shopping list are shown in **Table 6.13**. For only six shillings (30 pence in today's money) all these items could have been bought in 1914. The cost of this particular shopping list has increased nearly 34 times in the 81 years, but some items have increased more than others: for example, the price of potatoes rose 124 times while the cost of butter only increased 13 times.

An alternative way to analyse price levels and changes over time is to relate them to earnings by calculating how long someone would have to work to pay for certain goods and services. This is done in **Table 6.14** which compares the net income of a married man with two children and whose wife was not earning with a female lone parent. In general the length of time necessary to work to pay for the items shown in the table fell between 1971 and 1995 indicating that the increase in prices was lower than the increase in the families' incomes. However, there is also greater income parity between the two groups between 1971 and 1995. For example, the female lone parent would have had to have worked 33 minutes in 1971 to buy the equivalent of 500g of chicken, half as long again as the married man, whereas n 1995 she would only have needed to work or 11 minutes, a fifth as long again as the married man.

The RPI is also a measure of purchasing power: as prices increase so the amount of goods and services which can be purchased with a given sum of money decreases. **Chart 6.15** illustrates the erosion of the purchasing power of the pound since 1961: over time the £1 has shrunk in value so that it was only worth the equivalent of 9 pence in 1994. In other words to purchase what £1 could buy in 1961 you would now have to spend over £11. However as incomes have increased at a faster rate, actual purchasing power has increased.

6.15

Purchasing power of a 1961 pound

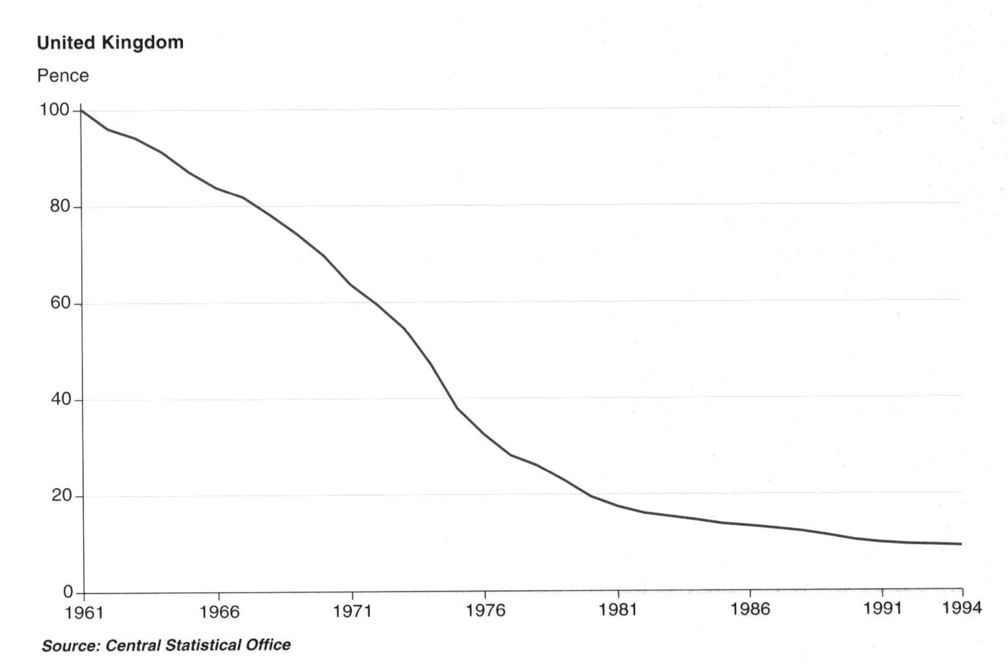

Source: Central Statistical Office

Consumer credit and household saving

The amount of consumer credit outstanding in the United Kingdom in real terms (that is after allowing for inflation) increased rapidly between 1987 and 1989, and then fell slightly up to 1993 before rising again **(Table 6.16)**. The definition of credit used in the table excludes mortgage borrowing. The figures are compiled on a slightly different basis from those in Table 6.15 in *Social Trends 25* which is the reason that these figures are slightly higher.

The bulk of consumer credit is financed by bank loans. However, the importance of this source of credit has been declining since 1987 while lending through bank credit cards has increased in importance. This is due to the growing number of people who use credit cards to pay for goods and services. Information from the Association for Payment Clearing Services indicates that 38 per cent of adults in Great Britain had a credit or charge card in 1994; this compares with 30 per cent in 1984. In addition, data compiled by the Credit Card Research

6.16

Composition of consumer credit

United Kingdom — Percentages

	1987	1991	1992	1993	1994
Bank loans[1]	*63*	*63*	*63*	*59*	*57*
Bank credit card lending	*16*	*18*	*18*	*20*	*20*
Other specialist lenders[2]	*12*	*11*	*10*	*13*	*14*
Retailers	*6*	*5*	*5*	*5*	*5*
Insurance companies	*3*	*2*	*2*	*3*	*2*
Building Society loans[3]	-	*1*	*1*	*1*	*2*
Credit outstanding at end of year (=100%)(£ billion at 1994 prices[4])	51.8	58.8	55.7	54.6	58.3

1 Banks and all other institutions authorised to take deposits under the Banking Act 1987.
2 Finance houses and other credit companies (excluding institutions authorised to take deposits under the Banking Act 1987).
3 Building Society unsecured loans to individuals or companies (ie Class 3 loans as defined in the Building Societies Act 1986).
4 Adjusted to 1994 prices using the retail prices index.

Source: Central Statistical Office

6.17

Net lending to consumers[1]

United Kingdom

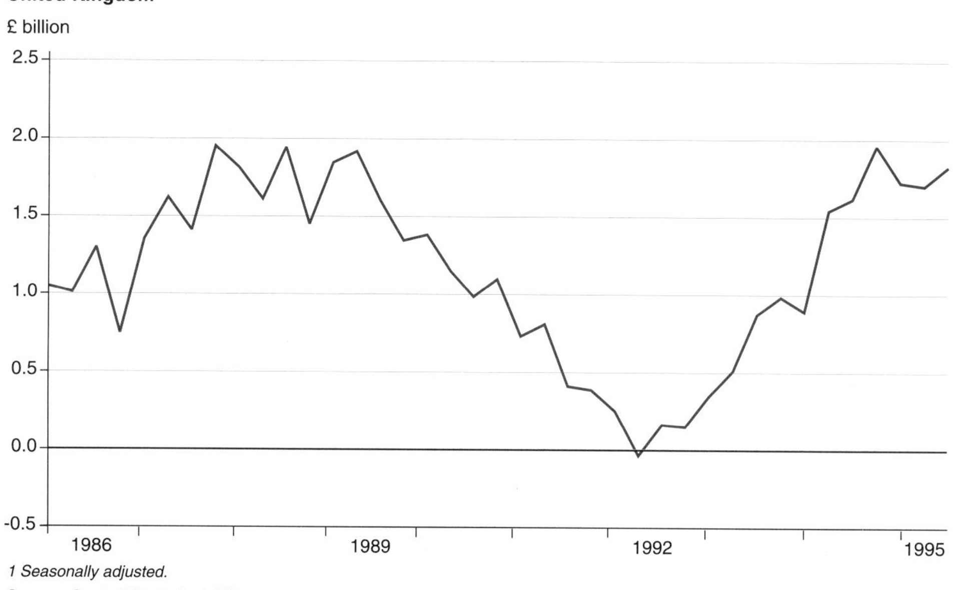

1 Seasonally adjusted.

Source: Central Statistical Office

Group and British Bankers' Association show that there were 817 million transactions by credit cards carrying the Visa or Mastercard logos in 1994 compared with only 451 million in 1986; over the same period the value of these transactions increased from £13.2 billion to £37.8 billion. The average transaction with a credit card was £45 in 1994, accounting for 12 pence in every £1 spent with retailers.

Whereas Table 6.16 covers the total indebtedness of consumers, the amount of net lending to consumers in the United Kingdom each quarter is illustrated in **Chart 6.17**; this provides the best measure of the current growth in consumer credit in this country. Its movements also mirror the effects of the economic cycle. Net lending to consumers fell from nearly £2 billion in the last quarter of 1987 to a small net repayment in the second quarter of 1992 reflecting the fall-off in consumers' expenditure during the last recession, high interest rates and unemployment. Since then it has recovered again - to £1.8 million in the third quarter of 1995.

Table 6.18 uses data from the FES to show the proportion of expenditure on selected items in 1994-95 financed through credit or hire purchase agreements, loans, budget or option accounts and shop or mail order clubs; payments by credit card and loans from employers, friends or relations are not included with these formal loans. As might be expected, the proportion of expenditure financed by these forms of credit was higher for the more expensive purchases: 89 per cent of expenditure on motor vehicles was financed in this way compared with only 38 per cent for audio-visual purchases, such as televisions and video recorders.

In general younger people are more likely to use credit than older people. For example, around two thirds of the expenditure by heads of household under the age of 30 on major electrical appliances was financed by one of the above forms of credit in 1994-95; this was more than double the proportion among those aged 60 and over.

The proportion of adults in Great Britain with a building society account increased rapidly during the 1970s and 1980s but has since levelled off. On the other hand the

6.18

Credit expenditure[1] as a percentage of total household expenditure on selected items: by age of head of household, 1994-95

Great Britain Percentages

	Under 30	30-39	40-49	50-59	60 and over	All ages
Motor vehicles	*94*	*85*	*91*	*88*	*64*	*89*
Major electrical appliances	*67*	*60*	*56*	*48*	*31*	*53*
Personal computers	*63*	*58*	*49*	*44*	..	*50*
Furniture and carpets	*57*	*55*	*52*	*44*	*33*	*49*
Audio-visual equipment	*60*	*50*	*32*	*29*	*16*	*38*

1 Includes expenditure through loans, hire purchase, credit sale agreements, budget or option accounts, shop clubs and mail order clubs; excludes credit card expenditure and loans from employers, friends or relatives.

Source: Family Expenditure Survey, Central Statistical Office

roportion who had a National Savings ccount has halved from one in five adults in 978 to only one in ten in 1993. **Table 6.19** hows that people in work are more likely han those out of work to hold most forms of avings. Retired people tend to hold ifferent forms of savings to younger people: hey are far more likely to hold the more raditional forms of savings such as Premium Bonds or National Savings Certificates.

nformation from the British Household Panel Survey indicates that savings behaviour is strongly related to age: regular savers are most likely to be between 30 and 50 years of age; the over 60s are less likely o save at all while the under 30s tend to be occasional savers, often with a particular goal in view. Changes in family or employment circumstances also affect saving: an additional child in the family ncreases the likelihood of stopping saving; getting married improves the chances of people saving while getting divorced or separated reduces it. In addition, as the ength of unemployment increases so does the probability of stopping saving, while starting a job improves the odds of someone starting to save.

Chart 6.20 shows household saving as a percentage of household disposable ncome. From 1986 to 1990, a period of growing inflation, the savings ratio was negative indicating that total household expenditure exceeded disposable income. In the latest period between 1993 and 1994 the ratio fell from 4.0 per cent to 2.5 per cent, again reflecting household spending ncreasing at a faster rate than household income. Household saving is not measured directly in the UK national accounts but is derived as a residual from two much larger figures which means that the estimates may be subject to a wide margin of error.

6.19

Type of savings[1]: by working status and gender, 1993[2]

Great Britain Percentages

	Employed: Full time	Employed: Part time	Retired	Not working	Males	Females	All adults
Bank account	*89*	*83*	*81*	*70*	*83*	*79*	*81*
Building society account	*69*	*71*	*68*	*55*	*64*	*66*	*65*
Premium bonds	*29*	*28*	*39*	*20*	*28*	*28*	*28*
Company shares[3]	*16*	*11*	*13*	*5*	*14*	*9*	*12*
Government privatisation shares	*12*	*8*	*14*	*6*	*13*	*8*	*10*
National Savings Bank Investment/Ordinary account	*10*	*12*	*10*	*9*	*10*	*10*	*10*
Unit or investment trusts	*10*	*8*	*12*	*5*	*11*	*7*	*9*
National Savings certificates/ bonds	*5*	*7*	*14*	*6*	*8*	*7*	*7*
Personal equity plan	*8*	*5*	*7*	*3*	*8*	*4*	*6*

1 Held by adults.
2 Fieldwork took place in February and March 1993.
3 Excludes government privatisations.
Source: Building Societies Association

6.20

Household saving[1] as a percentage of household disposable income

United Kingdom

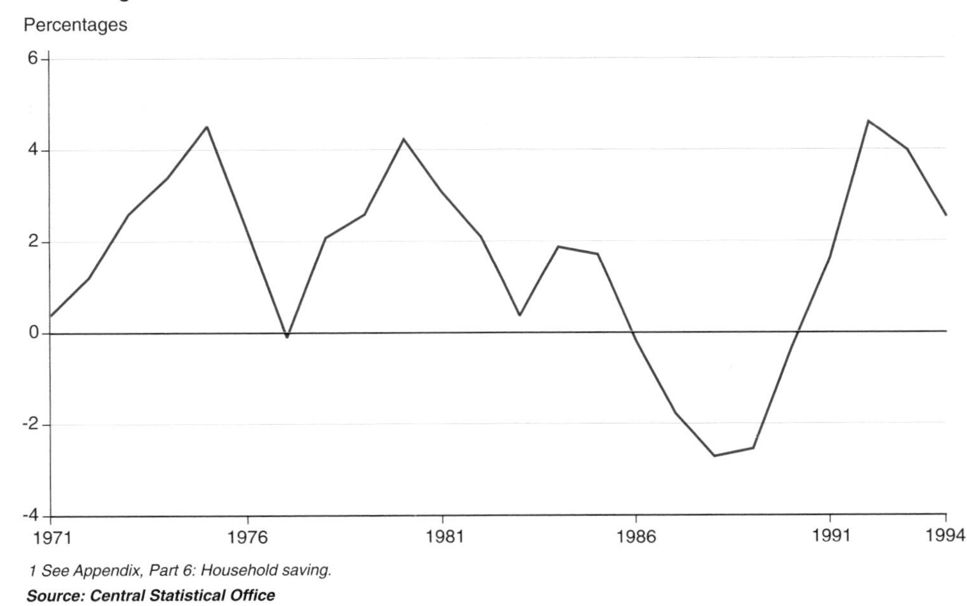

1 See Appendix, Part 6: Household saving.
Source: Central Statistical Office

6.21

General government expenditure as a percentage of GDP[1]

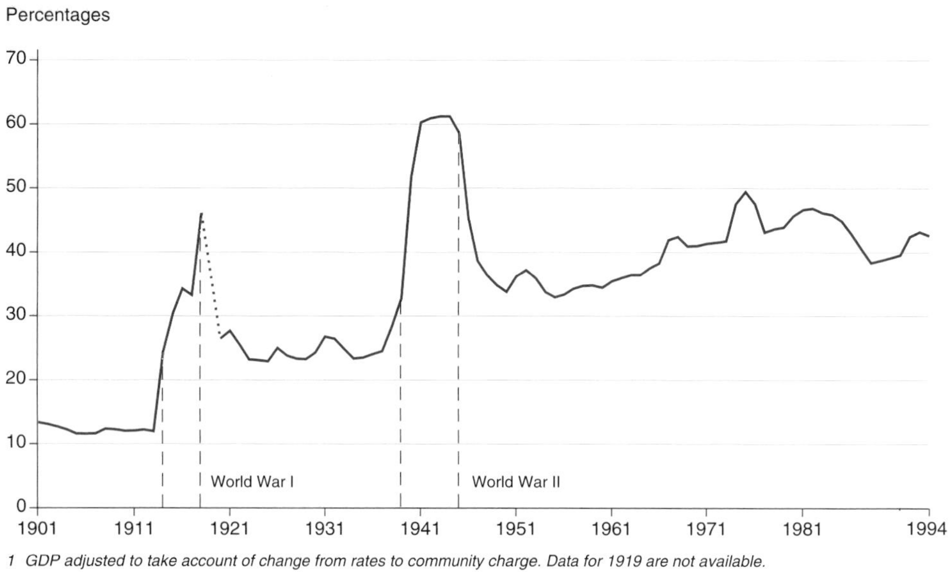

1 GDP adjusted to take account of change from rates to community charge. Data for 1919 are not available.

Source: Central Statistical Office

Public expenditure

So far in this chapter attention has been focused on individuals and households. In this final section expenditure by government, both within this country and in the European Community, is examined. One of the Government's objectives is to reduce public spending as a share of national income over time. **Chart 6.21** shows that the peaks in general government expenditure as a percentage of GDP (the GGE ratio) coincided with wars, particularly the two World Wars. Although the ratio fell back at the end of each World War, it never dropped as far as its pre-war levels. During the early 1950s the ratio rose at the time of the Korean War and other minor peaks occurred in 1968, 1975 and 1982. It then fell steadily to its lowest level for 22 years in 1988, before rising again and levelling off in the last few years.

In real terms, that is after allowing for the effect of inflation as measured by the GDP deflator, GGE increased by a quarter between 1981 and 1994 **(Table 6.22)**. Social security has accounted for the highest proportion of expenditure throughout the period shown in the table, but even so it has increased from just over a quarter of GGE in 1981 to just over a third in 1994. Health and education are the next largest items of expenditure: the proportions allocated to both these functions have remained stable during the 1990s. It is defence which has not only accounted for a declining proportion of GGE but also has fallen in cash terms since 1992.

6.22

General government expenditure: by function

United Kingdom — Percentages

	1981	1986	1991	1992	1993	1994
Social security	*27*	*31*	*32*	*33*	*34*	*34*
Health	*11*	*12*	*14*	*14*	*13*	*14*
Education	*12*	*12*	*13*	*13*	*12*	*13*
Defence	*11*	*12*	*10*	*10*	*9*	*8*
Public order and safety	*4*	*4*	*6*	*5*	*5*	*5*
General public services	*4*	*4*	*5*	*5*	*4*	*4*
Housing and community amenities	*6*	*5*	*4*	*4*	*4*	*4*
Transport and communication	*4*	*2*	*3*	*3*	*2*	*2*
Recreational and cultural affairs	*1*	*2*	*2*	*2*	*2*	*2*
Agriculture, forestry and fishing	*1*	*1*	*1*	*1*	*2*	*1*
Other expenditure	*19*	*16*	*11*	*11*	*12*	*13*
All expenditure (=100%) (£ billion in real terms[1])	224.6	241.0	250.9	268.1	278.3	285.7

1 Adjusted to 1994 prices using the GDP market prices deflator.

Source: Central Statistical Office

The British Social Attitudes Survey has asked people their opinions on public spending since 1983. The first impression is that the public are in favour of the traditional welfare state, the bulk of which (health, education and pensions) they can all expect to benefit from at some stage in their lives. The percentage of people who supported increasing taxes to fund higher levels of spending on these three areas almost doubled between 1983 and 1993, before falling back slightly in 1994 to 58 per cent. However, nearly nine in ten people would like more spending on the health service and three quarters supported more spending on education and pensions **(Table 6.23)**. In contrast support for spending on unemployment benefits is lower and has been more variable over time. Indeed it fell by around 10 percentage points between 1993 and 1994 to 36 per cent, almost certainly due to the drop in the level of unemployment.

Of course a level of self interest will be reflected in people's opinions: older people are especially likely to support spending on health care while people with young families are particularly concerned about education. The most marked difference is in attitudes to social security benefits: over one in five of households in the lower half of the income distribution put benefits as their first or second priority for extra spending whereas only 5 per cent of those in the top half of the distribution did so.

The United Kingdom is one of the net contributors to the European Community (EC) budget, which means that it pays more than it receives back. This is because its share of gross contributions in respect of the Common Agricultural Policy (CAP) is greater than its share of receipts under CAP. In addition the United Kingdom receives no benefit from Cohesion Fund payments, which are only available to the poorer member states (Greece, the Irish Republic, Spain and Portugal). The United Kingdom's net contribution is, however, significantly reduced by an abatement of its gross contributions. The total of the abatement which has been made available to the United Kingdom since the Fontainbleu agreement in 1984 will be more than £17 billion by the end of 1995. Overall the total amount of EC expenditure doubled between 1981 and 1994 at constant prices, partly due to the enlargement of the EC from 10 to 12 member states in 1986. The changing priorities of the Community have led to support for agriculture falling from some three fifths of the total budget in 1981 to a little over half in 1994 **(Table 6.24)**.

6.23

Attitudes[1] to government spending, 1994

Great Britain — Percentages

	More	Same as now	Less	Can't choose/ not answered	All
Health	*87*	*10*	*1*	*2*	*100*
Old age pensions	*74*	*22*	*1*	*2*	*100*
Education	*74*	*22*	*2*	*2*	*100*
Police and law enforcement	*72*	*23*	*2*	*3*	*100*
Environment	*49*	*43*	*3*	*6*	*100*
Unemployment benefits	*36*	*43*	*17*	*4*	*100*
Military and defence	*19*	*45*	*32*	*5*	*100*
Culture and the arts	*12*	*42*	*42*	*4*	*100*

1 Respondents were asked 'Please show whether you would like to see more or less government spending in each area'.

Source: British Social Attitudes Survey, Social & Community Planning Research

6.24

European Community expenditure: by sector

Percentages

	1981	1986	1991	1993	1994
Agricultural Guarantee	*62*	*64*	*58*	*54*	*55*
Structural funds					
Agricultural guidance	*3*	*2*	*4*	*5*	*4*
Regional policy	*14*	*7*	*12*	*15*	*11*
Social policy	*3*	*7*	*8*	*8*	*7*
Other	.	.	*3*	*4*	*5*
All structural funds	*20*	*16*	*26*	*32*	*27*
Research	*2*	*2*	*3*	*4*	*4*
External action	*4*	*3*	*4*	*4*	*5*
Administration	*5*	*4*	*5*	*5*	*5*
Other	*6*	*10*	*4*	*2*	*2*
All expenditure (=100%)(£ billion)	9.8	23.2	37.6	48.4	45.9

Source: European Commission

References and further reading

The following list contains selected publications relevant to **Chapter 6: Expenditure**. Those published by HMSO are available from the addresses shown on the inside back cover of *Social Trends.*

British Social Attitudes, Dartmouth Publishing
Business Monitor MM23 (Retail Prices Index), HMSO
Consumers' Expenditure, Business Monitor MQ24, HMSO
Economic Trends, HMSO
Family Spending, HMSO
Financial Statement and Budget Report, HMSO
General Household Survey, HMSO
Monthly Digest of Statistics, HMSO
Retail Prices 1914-1990, HMSO
Regional Trends, HMSO
Social Focus on Women, HMSO
Student Income and Expenditure Survey, Research Services Limited
The Community Budget: The facts in figures, European Commission
Travel Trends, HMSO
United Kingdom National Accounts (The CSO Blue Book), HMSO

Contacts

Telephone contact points for further information relating to
Chapter 6: Expenditure

Central Statistical Office	
Consumer's expenditure	0171 217 4318
Consumer credit	0171 217 4388
Family Expenditure Survey	0171 217 4207
General government expenditure	0171 270 6168
Household saving	0171 217 4203
Labour market statistics	01928 794903
Retail prices	0171 217 4310
Inland Revenue	0171 438 7370
Office of Population Censuses and Surveys	0171 396 2327
Building Societies Association	0171 734 0655
Gallup	0181 336 6400
Research Services Ltd	0181 861 6000
Social & Community Planning Research	0171 250 1866 extn 369
European Commission	00 322 2959829

Chapter 7 Health

The nation's health

We are continuing to live longer. Based on the projected mortality rates for 1996 a baby girl can expect to live to 80 compared with 49 at the beginning of this century. (Table 7.3)

Around one in ten people aged 16 and over in England in 1993 reported suffering from high blood pressure. (Table 7.7)

Around one in six adults in England reported that they suffered from 'quite a lot' or 'a great deal' of stress in the four weeks before they were interviewed in 1993. (Page 136)

Prevention

In 1993-94 just under two thirds of adults in the professional class with some natural teeth had a regular dental check-up compared with under two fifths of those in the unskilled manual group. (Table 7.16)

Diet

Between 1986 and 1994 our consumption of butter fell by almost two fifths while that of low and reduced fat spreads increased almost two and a half times. (Page 138)

Social habits and health

The number of cigarette smokers in Great Britain continues to decline: in 1972, 52 per cent of men smoked cigarettes compared with 28 per cent in 1994-95. (Chart 7.19)

Causes of death

Death rates from heart disease and lung cancer for men aged under 65 have almost halved during the past two decades. (Chart 7.22)

Death rates from cancer in the United Kingdom were among the highest in the European Community in 1992. (Table 7.23)

7.1

Death rates[1] for people aged under 65: by gender

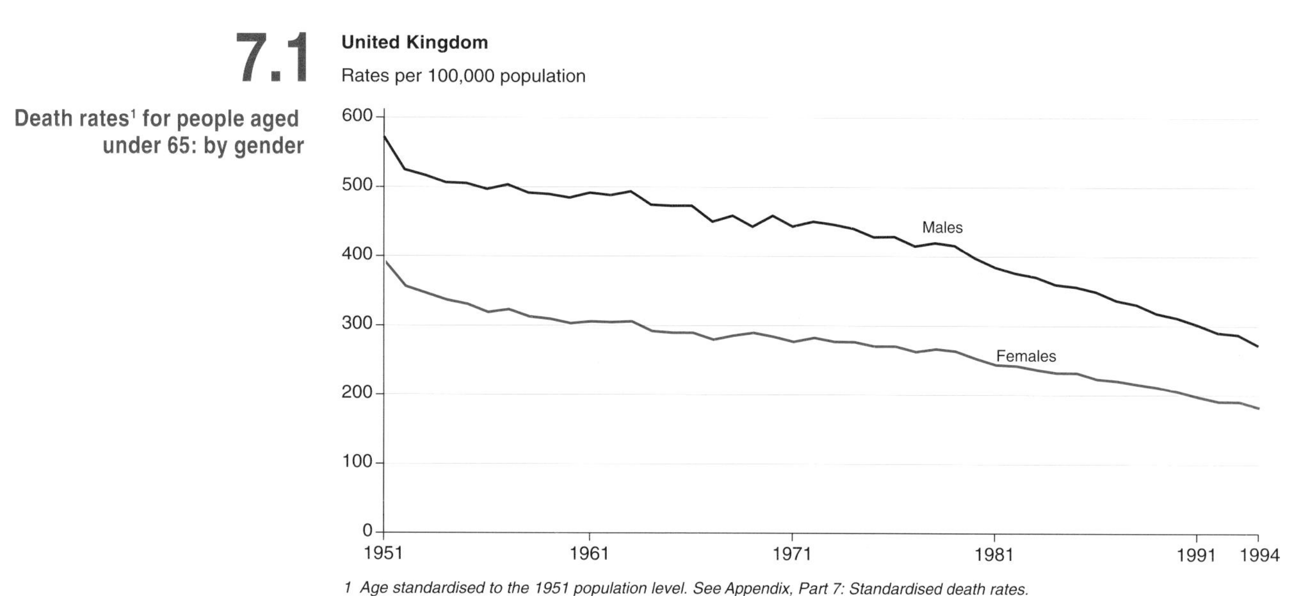

1 Age standardised to the 1951 population level. See Appendix, Part 7: Standardised death rates.

Source: Office of Population Censuses and Surveys; Welsh Office; General Register Office (Scotland); General Register Office (Northern Ireland)

7.2

Infant mortality

United Kingdom

Rates per 1,000 live births

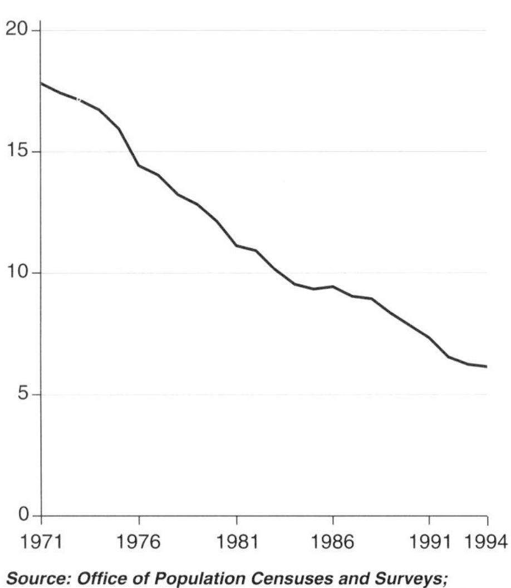

Source: Office of Population Censuses and Surveys; General Register Office (Scotland); General Register Office (Northern Ireland)

Good physical and mental health has an important effect on our overall quality of life.

The nation's health

One indicator which gives an overall measure of the health of the nation is death rates and, in particular, death rates for the under 65s can be taken as an indicator of premature deaths. In 1951 the death rates within this age group were just under 6 per thousand men and almost 4 per thousand women in the United Kingdom; by 1994 they had fallen by more than half to just under 3 and 2 per thousand respectively **(Chart 7.1)**.

As can be seen from Table 1.14 in the Population chapter, the most notable falls in deaths rates have occurred among children. Between 1971 and 1994 death rates for children between the ages of one and fifteen in the United Kingdom more than halved. Even more dramatic has been the fall in infant mortality. In 1994 there were just over 6 deaths per thousand live births in the United Kingdom compared with almost three times that number in 1971 **(Chart 7.2)**. Rates of infant mortality, that is deaths under one year of age, dropped dramatically during the first half of the century. Since then it has continued to fall, but at a slower rate. Rates of infant mortality vary, among other things, with the mother's country of birth. Data produced by the Institute of Public Health at Surrey University show that for births in England and Wales between 1989 and 1991 the rate of infant mortality for mothers born in Pakistan, at 13 per thousand live births, was almost double that for mothers born in the United Kingdom. In addition, rates for mothers born in the Commonwealth countries of the Caribbean and Africa (excluding East Africa) were both one and a half times the rate for mothers born in the United Kingdom.

Falling death rates at nearly all ages mean that our life expectancy is continuing to increase. Since the beginning of the century life expectancy has risen by over a half so that the expectation of life at birth in 1993 was over 73 for males and almost 79 for females **(Table 7.3)**. Despite the continuing overall upward trend in life expectancy, there were actually small reductions (no more than a tenth of a year in most cases) at some ages between 1992 and 1993 which were due to the mild influenza epidemic early in 1993. Life expectancy is currently increasing by around two years every decade.

7.3

Expectation of life[1]: by gender and age

United Kingdom — Years

	1901	1931	1961	1991	1993	1996	2001	2021
Males								
At birth	45.5	57.7	67.8	73.2	73.6	74.4	75.4	77.6
At age								
1 year	54.6	62.4	69.5	73.8	74.1	74.8	75.7	77.9
10 years	60.4	65.2	69.9	73.9	74.2	75.0	75.9	78.0
20 years	61.7	66.3	70.3	74.2	74.5	75.3	76.1	78.2
40 years	66.1	69.3	71.4	75.1	75.4	76.3	77.2	79.3
60 years	73.3	74.3	74.9	77.7	77.8	78.6	79.5	81.4
80 years	84.9	84.7	85.2	86.4	86.4	86.8	87.2	88.2
Females								
At birth	49.0	61.6	73.6	78.7	78.9	79.7	80.6	82.6
At age								
1 year	56.8	65.3	75.1	79.2	79.3	80.1	80.9	82.8
10 years	62.7	67.9	75.4	79.4	79.5	80.3	81.1	83.0
20 years	64.1	69.0	75.6	79.5	79.6	80.4	81.2	83.1
40 years	68.3	71.9	76.3	80.0	80.1	80.9	81.7	83.5
60 years	74.6	76.1	78.8	81.9	81.9	82.6	83.3	84.9
80 years	85.3	85.4	86.3	88.3	88.3	88.8	89.1	90.0

1 Total number of years which a person might expect to live. See Appendix, Part 7: Expectation of life.

Source: Government Actuary's Department

Measuring the more detailed changes in the state of our health can be difficult. It is possible to use administrative records or clinical records but these will only record illnesses which result in a visit to a doctor or a hospital. In order to provide a fuller picture, the Health Survey for England collects information on various aspects of the health of adults aged 16 and over through interviews, measurements and blood tests. Comparable data are not currently available for Wales, Scotland and Northern Ireland although similar surveys are under way or are being developed. Only data from the English survey are therefore shown here.

In 1993 the survey found that over three quarters of men and women rated their health as either 'good' or 'very good'. However, four in ten of both men and women reported having at least one long-standing illness or disability **(Table 7.4)**. As might be expected, this proportion increased dramatically with age; around a quarter of those aged 16 to 44 had a long-standing illness or disability compared with nearly two thirds of those aged 65 and over. The most common type of disability or long-standing illness was that affecting the musculo-skeletal system, such as rheumatism and arthritis.

7.4

Long-standing illness or disability[1]: by gender and age, 1993

England — Percentages

	Males				Females			
	16-44	45-64	65 and over	All aged 16 and over	16-44	45-64	65 and over	All aged 16 and over
Musculo-skeletal system	9.6	22.8	26.4	16.7	8.2	22.7	38.8	18.9
Heart and circulatory system	1.7	14.9	34.2	11.6	2.6	13.5	26.2	10.8
Respiratory system	8.7	7.5	13.5	9.2	8.5	7.9	9.2	8.5
Digestive system	2.7	5.8	8.6	4.7	2.4	5.5	9.4	4.8
Endocrine and metabolic system	1.3	5.2	7.5	3.6	1.4	5.5	7.9	4.0
Nervous system	3.0	3.3	3.6	3.2	3.6	4.8	3.9	4.0
Genito-urinary system	0.4	1.6	4.6	1.5	2.1	2.6	1.9	2.2
Eye complaints	1.3	2.0	5.6	2.3	0.7	1.2	6.3	2.1
Mental disorders	1.0	1.9	1.4	1.4	1.4	3.1	2.0	2.1
Ear complaints	1.3	2.1	5.0	2.2	0.9	2.0	4.4	2.0
Skin complaints	1.5	1.7	1.0	1.5	1.7	1.0	1.9	1.5
Neoplasms and benign growths	0.3	1.1	2.1	0.9	0.5	2.0	2.5	1.3
Blood and related organs	0.1	0.2	0.8	0.3	0.5	0.5	1.8	0.8
Infectious disease	0.3	0.1	0.4	0.3	0.2	0.2	0.3	0.2
Other complaints	-	-	0.1	0.1	0.1	0.1	0.2	0.1
Any long standing illness or disability	26.2	46.3	63.4	39.1	26.7	47.3	62.7	40.3

1 Percentage in each age group reporting each long-standing illness or disability.

Source: Health Survey for England, Department of Health

7.5

Notifications of selected infectious diseases

United Kingdom

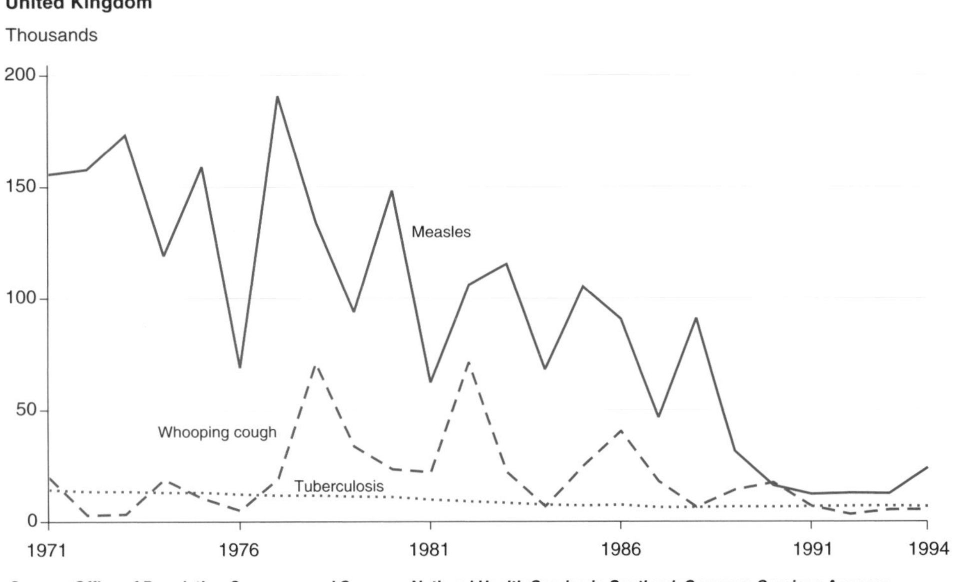

Source: Office of Population Censuses and Surveys; National Health Service in Scotland, Common Services Agency; Department of Health and Social Services, Northern Ireland

Immunisation, antibiotics and improved living conditions have all played a part in bringing many diseases under control. For some diseases, however, large year to year fluctuations in the number of notifications continue. In 1994 there were over 23 thousand notified cases of measles in the United Kingdom - almost double the number in 1992 but less than an eighth of the number recorded in the epidemic of 1977 **(Chart 7.5)**. A nationwide measles and rubella campaign was undertaken in November 1994 to avert a predicted measles epidemic. The campaign achieved a very high coverage of over 90 per cent since when confirmed cases of measles have fallen to historically low levels.

Notified cases of tuberculosis (TB) more than halved from 14 thousand in 1971 to just under 6 thousand in 1987, but then rose slightly to 6.5 thousand in 1993. This increase was in line with observations by the World Health Organisation which noted an increase in the incidence of this disease throughout Europe and the USA. In order to control this increase a number of steps were taken including the setting up of an inter-departmental working group by the Department of Health which is considering improved screening procedures and follow-up of homeless people with TB. In 1994 the number of TB notifications fell to just over 6 thousand. An ongoing immunisation programme for children is designed to help curb the spread of infectious diseases (see Table 7.14).

7.6

Body mass[1]: by gender and age, 1993

England — Percentages

	16-24	25-34	35-44	45-54	55-64	65-74	75 and over	All aged 16 and over
Males								
Underweight	*14*	*5*	*2*	*2*	*3*	*3*	*4*	*5*
Desirable	*59*	*46*	*36*	*29*	*26*	*28*	*38*	*38*
Overweight	*21*	*39*	*48*	*52*	*51*	*54*	*46*	*44*
Obese	*5*	*10*	*14*	*16*	*20*	*15*	*11*	*13*
All males	*100*	*100*	*100*	*100*	*100*	*100*	*100*	*100*
Females								
Underweight	*18*	*10*	*6*	*3*	*2*	*4*	*7*	*7*
Desirable	*54*	*54*	*48*	*41*	*35*	*34*	*35*	*44*
Overweight	*20*	*25*	*29*	*37*	*39*	*41*	*42*	*32*
Obese	*8*	*11*	*17*	*19*	*24*	*21*	*16*	*16*
All females	*100*	*100*	*100*	*100*	*100*	*100*	*100*	*100*

1 Body mass index. See Appendix, Part 7: Body mass index.

Source: Health Survey for England, Department of Health

Some aspects of our health can, at least in part, be controlled by lifestyle. For example, our diet and the amount of exercise we take can have some effect on our weight which in turn can affect our health. The most widely used measure of obesity is body mass index (BMI) which is calculated as weight (kg)/ height (m)^2. However, it should be noted that the index tends to give an inflated measure of fatness to those with muscular physiques who are relatively heavy although lean.

Almost three fifths of men and just under half of women aged 16 and over in England were classed as overweight or obese in 1993. However, a higher proportion of women than men were considered obese - 16 per cent compared with 13 per cent. **Table 7.6** shows that for both men and women obesity is most prevalent for those in the 55 to 64 age group; a fifth of men and almost a quarter of women in this age group were obese. Comparisons with the Dietary and Nutritional Survey of British Adults, carried out by the Office of Population Censuses and Surveys, show that the proportion of adults who are overweight and obese is increasing: in 1986-87, 37 per cent of men were overweight and 8 per cent were obese compared with 44 per cent and 13 per cent respectively in 1993. In Wales (where data are self-reported) a half of men and just under two fifths of women aged 18 to 79 were classified as overweight or obese in 1993.

A number of diseases can be related to being underweight, overweight or obese, including hypertension and cardiovascular disease (CVD). For younger men and women being overweight or obese is known to increase the likelihood of having a CVD. For middle-aged women being underweight or obese increases the risks. A number of other factors affect the likelihood of having a CVD condition although their significance depends on age and gender. They include: having a parent who died from a CVD condition; being economically inactive; and being physically inactive. In 1993 a quarter of both men and women aged 16 and over in England reported that they had had at least one CVD condition at some time in their life. High blood pressure was the most commonly reported CVD condition: around 8 per cent of men and 10 per cent of women reported suffering from high blood pressure at the time of interview **(Table 7.7)**. Like all CVDs, prevalence generally increases with age.

Another disease over which we have an element of control is lung cancer; an estimated 80 per cent of deaths from this disease are attributable to smoking. In 1990 there were around 43 thousand new cases of lung cancer - the same number as in the previous year. Using records from the various health authorities within the United Kingdom it is possible to analyse the incidence of lung cancer on a regional basis **(Chart 7.8)**. The latest data are in respect of 1989; they are based on ratios which age-standardise the population of each region and take the United Kingdom average incidence as 100. Registrations in Scotland

7.7

Percentage[1] of adults who had selected cardiovascular diseases[2]: by gender and age, 1993

England — Percentages

	16-24	25-44	45-64	65-74	75 and over	All aged 16 and over
Males						
High blood pressure	*0.3*	*1.8*	*10.8*	*26.5*	*20.6*	*8.5*
Angina	*0.0*	*0.3*	*4.0*	*11.2*	*7.4*	*3.1*
Diabetes	*0.2*	*1.0*	*4.3*	*6.6*	*8.2*	*3.0*
Abnormal heart rhythm	*0.3*	*1.0*	*2.7*	*6.9*	*5.9*	*2.4*
Heart attack	*0.0*	*0.1*	*1.0*	*3.1*	*2.5*	*0.9*
Stroke	*0.0*	-	*0.3*	*2.7*	*4.0*	*0.7*
Heart murmur	*0.4*	*0.4*	*0.6*	*1.9*	*0.2*	*0.6*
Other heart trouble	*0.3*	*0.2*	*0.7*	*1.8*	*1.5*	*0.6*
Females						
High blood pressure	*1.0*	*2.4*	*13.5*	*24.1*	*27.5*	*10.3*
Angina	*0.0*	*0.2*	*2.3*	*7.6*	*11.9*	*2.7*
Abnormal heart rhythm	*0.7*	*1.6*	*2.6*	*4.0*	*3.4*	*2.2*
Diabetes	*0.3*	*0.8*	*2.6*	*4.8*	*4.7*	*2.1*
Heart murmur	*0.5*	*0.9*	*1.0*	*0.8*	*1.0*	*0.9*
Heart attack	*0.1*	*0.1*	*0.7*	*1.5*	*1.3*	*0.5*
Stroke	*0.0*	*0.0*	*0.4*	*0.5*	*1.4*	*0.3*
Other heart trouble	*0.1*	*0.4*	*0.7*	*1.4*	*2.2*	*0.7*

1 Of each age group.
2 Includes related conditions. At the time of interview for blood pressure; in the year before interview for all other conditions.
Source: Health Survey for England, Department of Health

7.8

Lung cancer: by region, 1989

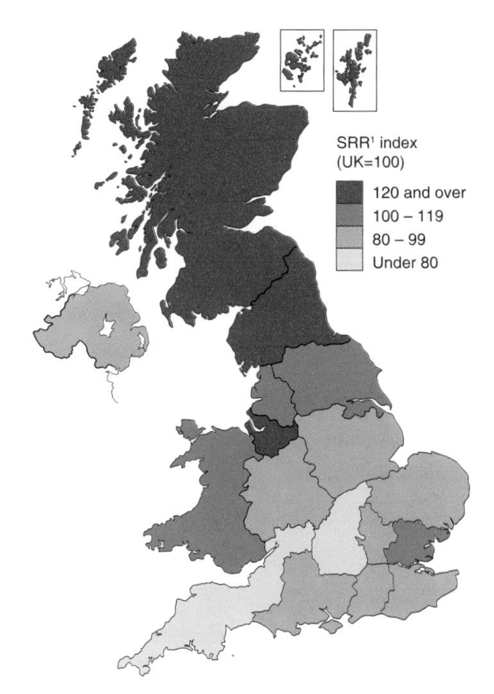

1 See Appendix, Part 7: Standardised registration ratios.
Source: Office of Population Censuses and Surveys; National Health Service in Scotland, Common Services Agency; The Queen's University of Belfast

7.9

New episodes[1] of asthma

England & Wales

Rates[2] per 100,000 population

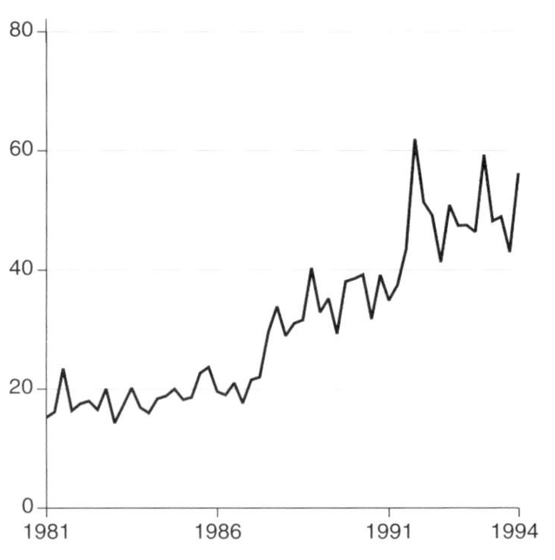

1 A diagnosis for the first time or a previously diagnosed asthmatic person having a new attack.
2 Average weekly rates by quarter.

Source: The Royal College of General Practitioners

and the Northern Health Authority were almost a quarter above the United Kingdom average while those in the South Western Health Authority were a third below. Trends in deaths from lung cancer among the under 65s are shown in Chart 7.22.

Despite the overall improvement in our health, the incidence of some medical conditions appears to be increasing. In 1994 in England and Wales an average of 49 new cases of asthma per 100 thousand population were reported each week - a similar rate to the previous year but much higher than the 18 cases per 100 thousand reported in 1981. It is unlikely, however, that the incidence of asthma has increased by as much as the numbers suggest; an increased tendency for doctors to report respiratory conditions as asthma, greater awareness among the public and greater expectations of therapeutic intervention are all likely to have had an effect. Mean weekly incidence rates for each quarter (as used in **Chart 7.9**) during the last 14 years show that rates are generally highest in the October to December quarter. Detailed analysis of weekly data also show peaks in mid-summer (the hay fever season). The incidence of new attacks in the summer of 1995 was less than in the previous two years.

The prevalence of asthma in 1991-92 in England and Wales among children under 15 was more than twice as high as among people aged 15 and over. Deaths from the condition rose up to the second half of the 1980s then fell: there were 2.1 thousand deaths in 1991 compared with 1.7 thousand in 1994. The underlying cause or causes of asthma have not been established although air pollution is among the factors which can bring on or exacerbate attacks.

The incidence of AIDS (Acquired Immune Deficiency Syndrome) is also continuing to increase. The Public Health Laboratory Service and the Scottish Centre for Infection and Environmental Health recorded 1,785 new cases of AIDS in the United Kingdom in 1994 - in 1986 there were just 298 new cases. Around seven in ten of the cases recorded up to June 1995 were acquired as a result of sexual intercourse between men while one in eight were acquired as a result

7.10

AIDS cases and related deaths and reports of HIV-1 infected persons: by probable exposure category and gender, to end June 1995[1]

United Kingdom Numbers

	AIDS				Reports of HIV-1 infected persons[2]	
	Cases		Related deaths			
	Males	Females	Males	Females	Males	Females
Probable HIV exposure category						
Sexual intercourse						
Between men	8,101	.	5,725	.	15,001	.
Between men and women	782	627	433	333	2,000	2,280
Injecting drug use (IDU)	449	202	292	118	1,885	859
Blood						
Blood factor						
(eg haemophilia)	493	6	424	5	1,218	11
Blood/tissue transfer						
(eg transfusion)	39	71	26	48	77	85
Mother to child	81	82	42	40	152	149
Other/undetermined	100	18	76	9	621	115
All categories	10,045	1,006	7,018	553	20,954	3,499

1 Cumulative reported cases and deaths up to the end of June 1995.
2 Includes 49 reports where the gender was not stated; also includes those individuals who progressed to AIDS.

Source: PHLS Communicable Disease Surveillance Centre

of heterosexual contact **(Table 7.10)**, though numbers in the latter category are rising. The majority of the latter are presumed to have acquired the infection while in countries such as those in sub-Saharan Africa where the prevalence of the Human Immunodeficiency Virus (HIV) is high. Only 6 per cent of AIDS cases recorded up to June 1995 were acquired as a result injecting drug misuse. In Scotland, however, almost two fifths of infections are reported to have been acquired this way.

In the United Kingdom the incidence of reported AIDS cases in 1994 was 29.3 per million population but there have been marked variations in the prevalence of AIDS by gender and region. Over the course of the epidemic in the United Kingdom, for every female reported to have AIDS there have been ten males. Of the 11 thousand cases reported, over two thirds have come from South East England. Future incidence of AIDS will be a reflection of often undiagnosed infections which take place many years earlier; from 1991 to 1994 the number of new diagnoses of infection was fairly constant at just under 2.5 thousand per year, most of which will not yet have progressed to AIDS.

Some diseases can only be transmitted through sexual contact. Although not all sexually transmitted diseases (STDs) will be treated at an STD or genito-urinary medicine clinic, attendances give a good indication of trends for each condition. In 1994 wart virus appeared to be the most common complaint for men while candidiasis was the most common disease among women **(Table 7.11)**.

The number of new cases of some STDs appear to have fallen dramatically; in 1986 around 46 thousand new cases of gonorrhoea were seen at STD clinics compared with 12 thousand cases in 1994. The incidence of gonorrhoea in England is now at its lowest level for some 75 years. On the other hand the incidence of some STDs has been rising; the number of new cases of wart virus in the United Kingdom increased by nearly a fifth for men and two fifths for women between 1986 and 1994.

Not all medical problems, of course, have physical effects. Between April and September 1993, 10 thousand people aged 16 to 64 and living in private households in Great Britain were asked about the presence of 14 symptoms of neurotic disorders. The most commonly found symptoms were fatigue and sleep problems each of which affected around a quarter of those surveyed; irritability and worry both affected around a fifth. Other symptoms included depression, anxiety and obsessions. Overall, around one in eight men and one in five women aged 16 to 64 reported that they had suffered from a neurotic disorder in the week before interview **(Table 7.12)**.

Employment status is a major factor linked to the prevalence of neurotic disorders; around a quarter of unemployed people had a neurotic disorder in the week before interview compared with around only one in eight of those working full time. For women, the rate for depressive disorders was five times higher for those who were unemployed than for those who were working full time.

7.11

New cases seen at sexually transmitted diseases clinics: by gender

United Kingdom — Thousands

	1986	1991	1994
Males			
Wart virus	46	55	55
Non-specific urethritis	..	58	53
Chlamydia	..	19	19
Herpes	11	12	13
Candidiasis	13	11	11
Gonorrhoea	28	12	8
Syphilis	2	1	1
Trichomoniasis	1	-	-
Females			
Wart virus	30	39	42
Non-specific urethritis	..	19	18
Chlamydia	..	22	21
Herpes	9	12	16
Candidiasis	56	54	60
Gonorrhoea	18	8	4
Syphilis	1	-	1
Trichomoniasis	14	6	5

Source: Department of Health; Welsh Office; National Health Service in Scotland, Common Services Agency; Department of Health and Social Services, Northern Ireland

7.12

Percentage of adults[1] with a neurotic disorder[2]: by employment status and gender, 1993

Great Britain — Percentages

	Males	Females	All adults
Working full time	*10*	*16*	*12*
Working part time	*12*	*17*	*16*
Unemployed	*20*	*38*	*26*
Economically inactive	*20*	*22*	*21*
All	*12*	*20*	*16*

1 Aged 16 to 64 and living in private households.
2 In the week before interview.

Source: Survey of Psychiatric Morbidity, Office of Population Censuses and Surveys

7.13

Adults[1] who had experienced high stress levels[2]: by gender and social class of head of household, 1993

England

Age standardised ratios[2]

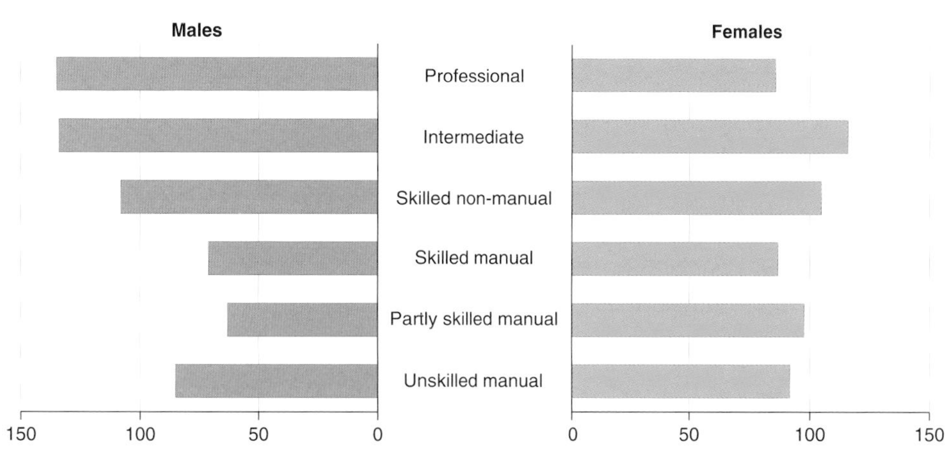

1 Aged 16 and over.
2 Respondents were asked 'In general, how much stress or pressure have you experienced in your daily living in the last four weeks?'. See also Appendix, Part 7: High stress levels and age standardised ratios.

Source: Health Survey for England, Department of Health

7.13 shows how stress is related to social class. The data are based on indices which adjust for the age variation in stress levels experienced and take the likelihood of the average adult aged 16 and over experiencing a high stress level to be 100. Men in the professional and intermediate groups were over a third more likely than the average person to experience a high stress level while men in the partly skilled manual group were a third less likely. As mentioned, stress levels also vary according to age: the peak age for men is 35 to 44 when a quarter suffered a high stress level; for women the peak is 35 to 54 when a fifth were affected to the same degree.

7.14

Immunisation of children[1]

United Kingdom			Percentages
	1981	1991-92[2]	1993-94[2]
Diphtheria	*82*	*94*	*95*
Tetanus	*82*	*94*	*95*
Poliomyelitis	*82*	*94*	*95*
Whooping cough	*46*	*88*	*93*
Measles, mumps, rubella[3]	*54*	*91*	*91*

1 See Appendix, Part 7: Immunisation.
2 Scotland data are for 1992 and 1994.
3 Includes measles only vaccine. Combined vaccine was not available prior to 1988.

Source: Department of Health; Welsh Office; National Health Service in Scotland, Common Services Agency; Department of Health and Social Services, Northern Ireland

Stress, on the other hand, is often associated with work-related factors. The 1993 Health Survey for England asked adults aged 16 and over if they had experienced stress in the four weeks prior to interview. Around a quarter said that they had experienced no stress at all while just under one in six said that they had experienced 'quite a lot' or 'a great deal'. Unlike neurotic disorders, the overall prevalence of stress among men and women was similar.

Work-related stress has been found to be related to a high pace of work, low work variety and a lack of control over the work. For example, only 6 per cent of men with a low work pace had suffered quite a lot/a great deal of stress compared with 37 per cent of those with a high work pace. **Chart**

Prevention

As mentioned earlier, some aspects of health can be controlled by taking preventative measures such as immunisation. Over the years there have been a number of campaigns to encourage parents to have their children immunised. Consequently over nine in ten children in the United Kingdom reaching their second birthday in 1993-94 had been immunised against those diseases shown in **Table 7.14** by their second birthday. The proportion immunised against whooping cough in 1993-94 was more than double the proportion in 1981 although this was particularly low because of fears over vaccine safety. In addition, immunisation against haemophilus influenzae type b was introduced into the childhood immunisation programme in 1992.

By 1993-94, more than three quarters of children aged two in Great Britain had been immunised against it by their second birthday. Not only children, of course, are immunised. For example, vaccination against influenza is recommended for adults who are at increased risk of complications should they develop influenza.

Breast cancer was one of the most common causes of death for women aged under 65 in 1994 in the United Kingdom. In England, as part of their Health of the Nation strategy, the Government set a target of reducing deaths from this disease in the population invited for screening by at least a quarter between 1990 and 2000. The NHS breast screening programme was introduced between 1988 and 1990. It invites women aged 50 to 64 for mammographic screening every three years; in addition mammography is available to women aged 65 and over three yearly on request. All screening centres have now completed their first round of screening and are now inviting women for their second screen. Similar programmes have been set up in Wales, Scotland and Northern Ireland. In 1993-94 over 1.6 million women in the United Kingdom were invited for screening and cancers were detected in 5.5 in every thousand women screened **(Table 7.15)**.

A separate screening programme exists for cervical cancer which in England alone affects around 4.5 thousand women each year. Around a third of these die from the disease. The programme invites women aged 20 to 64 to be screened every five years. In 1993-94 over eight in ten women subject to call or recall within the cervical screening programme in England had been screened within the previous five and a half years. For women screened every five years, the incidence of the disease can be reduced by over 80 per cent.

Regular visits to the dentist for a check-up can help improve dental health. In 1993-94 around half of all adults with some natural teeth in Great Britain said that they visited the dentist for a regular check-up. However, this proportion varies markedly according to socio-economic group: almost two thirds of those in the professional group had a regular check-up compared with less than two fifths of those in the unskilled manual group **(Table 7.16)**. Overall, attendance at the dentist for a regular check-up by women exceeded that for men by 15 percentage points.

Of particular importance for future dental health is the condition of children's teeth today. As might be expected, children are more likely to visit a dentist for a check-up if their mother attends regularly. Hence three quarters of children whose mothers visit the dentist on a regular basis, last visited the dentist for a check-up compared with just over half of children whose mothers only go when they experience trouble with their teeth. In Northern Ireland 38 per cent of men and 58 per cent of women had a regular check-up.

7.15

Breast cancer screening, 1991-92 and 1993-94

United Kingdom		Thousands
	1991-92	1993-94
Invited for screening	1,444	1,609
Screened	1,060	1,209
Cancer detection rates[1]	6.2	5.5
Death rates[2]	46.8	45.2

1 Per 1,000 women screened.
2 Per 100,000 women aged 20 to 74. See Appendix, Part 7: Death rates for breast cancer.

Source: Department of Health; Office of Population Censuses and Surveys; Welsh Office; National Health Service in Scotland, Common Services Agency; Department of Health and Social Services, Northern Ireland

7.16

Percentage of adults[1] who visit the dentist for a regular check-up: by socio-economic group, 1983 and 1993-94

Great Britain		Percentages
	1983	1993-94
Professional	*69*	*64*
Employers and managers	*61*	*62*
Intermediate and junior non-manual	*58*	*55*
Skilled manual[2]	*39*	*44*
Semi-skilled manual and personal service	*36*	*41*
Unskilled manual	*29*	*38*
All adults[1]	*48*	*51*

1 Aged 16 and over with some natural teeth.
2 Includes own account non-professional.

Source: General Household Survey, Office of Population Censuses and Surveys

7.17

Changing patterns in consumption of foods at home

Great Britain

Indices (1971=100)

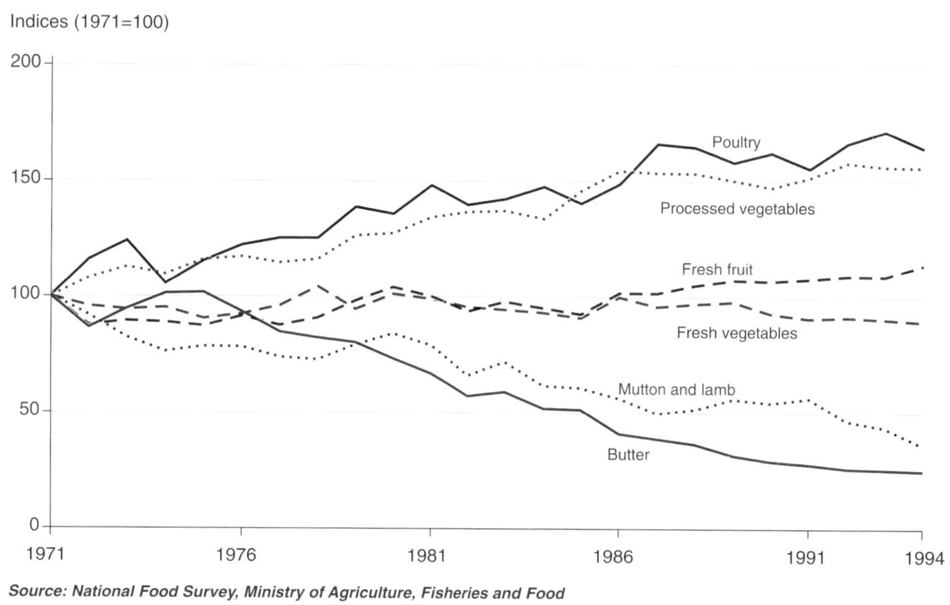

Source: National Food Survey, Ministry of Agriculture, Fisheries and Food

Diet

Some control over our health can be gained by choosing a healthy diet. Since the early 1970s we have made a number of changes to our diet. The consumption of red meats (such as mutton and lamb) has been falling while that of poultry has been rising **(Chart 7.17)**. Our consumption of fresh vegetables (excluding potatoes) fell by around 10 per cent between 1971 and 1994: in 1971 we each ate nearly 800 grams of fresh vegetables per week compared with just over 700 grams in 1994. On the other hand, consumption of processed vegetables has increased by more than half since 1971. The average percentage of energy derived from fat and from saturated fatty acids continues to decline. In 1994 our consumption of butter was only three fifths of what it was 1986 while, over the same period, our consumption of low and reduced fat spreads increased almost two and a half times. In 1994 we each ate an average of 645 grams of fresh fruit per week - 13 per cent more than in 1971.

The changes in our diet described above suggest that we may be taking note of 'healthy eating' messages. Current advice is that we should eat more fruit, vegetables and starchy foods rich in fibre and less fat, salt and sugary foods. The Health Survey for England asked adults about their eating habits of selected foods which fell into each of these categories. **Table 7.18** shows that those aged 65 and over are more likely than younger people to use solid cooking fat, add salt when cooking and to usually drink whole milk. However, those in the 16 to 24 age group were the most likely to eat confectionery on at least five to six days each week.

7.18

Eating habits[1]: by age, 1993

England — Percentages

	16-24	25-44	45-64	65-74	75 and over	All aged 16 and over
Ate vegetables or salad[2]	*65*	*74*	*83*	*83*	*78*	*77*
Usually drank skimmed and semi-skimmed milk	*61*	*65*	*66*	*56*	*38*	*62*
Ate fruit[2]	*41*	*48*	*62*	*66*	*65*	*55*
Ate high fibre cereal	*26*	*36*	*45*	*49*	*46*	*40*
Usually ate wholemeal bread	*18*	*26*	*31*	*36*	*32*	*28*
Used solid cooking fat	*14*	*13*	*15*	*22*	*31*	*16*
Ate confectionery[2]	*38*	*20*	*14*	*25*	*28*	*22*
Took sugar in coffee[3]	*58*	*43*	*42*	*45*	*52*	*45*
Added salt in cooking	*65*	*60*	*74*	*80*	*83*	*69*

1 Percentage of all in each age group except where otherwise stated.
2 On at least five to six days a week.
3 Percentage of those who drank coffee.

Source: Health Survey for England, Department of Health

Social habits and health

It is widely accepted that smoking damages health. **Chart 7.19** illustrates the fall in the proportions of both men and women in Great Britain who smoked cigarettes. In 1972, 52 per cent of men and 41 per cent of women smoked cigarettes; by 1994 this had fallen to 28 per cent of men and 26 per cent of women. However, the rate of decrease has slowed in recent years. People in the 20 to 24 age group are the most likely to smoke cigarettes; around two fifths of both men and women in this age group smoked compared with less than a fifth of those aged 60 and over.

As well as the overall reduction in the proportion who smoked, there has also been a reduction in the proportion smoking cigarettes with middle range tar yields. In 1986, 40 per cent of smokers bought cigarettes in this category but by 1994-95 this had fallen to just 2 per cent. This was at least in part due to manufacturers reducing the tar yields of their cigarettes so as to move them into a lower category. In Northern Ireland 29 per cent of men and 27 per cent of women smoked in 1994-95 while average weekly consumption was 128 cigarettes for men and 106 for women. This is higher than in Great Britain where the corresponding averages were 114 and 97 respectively. In England the Government's Health of the Nation target is to reduce the percentage of adults who smoke cigarettes to no more than 20 per cent by the year 2000. Wales and Scotland have their own local targets.

Medical advice is that light to moderate drinking of alcohol is unlikely to damage health and may even be of health benefit to certain groups. However, sustained consumption at higher levels progressively increases the risk of raised blood pressure, stroke, some forms of coronary heart disease, various cancers and cirrhosis of the liver. Women generally drink far less than men. Fourteen per cent of women aged 18 and over in Great Britain in 1994-95 had not had an alcoholic drink within the previous 12 months compared with 7 per cent of men. A further 44 per cent of men and 58 per cent of women consumed only low amounts (less than 11 units per week for a man and 8 units per week for a woman).

Over one in four men and over one in eight women drank in excess of what were then regarded as the sensible levels which were 21 units a week for a man and 14 for a woman **(Chart 7.20)**. This is most noticeable among younger people: over a third of men and a fifth of women aged 18 to 24 drank more than these sensible levels. The proportion of men drinking over this sensible level remained virtually unchanged between 1986 and 1994-95 while the corresponding proportion for women increased from 11 per cent to 13 per cent. Six per cent of men and 2 per cent of women drank more than 50 and 35 units respectively of alcohol per week which is regarded medically as definitely dangerous to health. In Northern Ireland 21 per cent of men and 7 per cent of women aged 16 and over drank more than these sensible levels in 1994-95.

7.19

Cigarette smoking[1]: by gender

Great Britain

Percentages

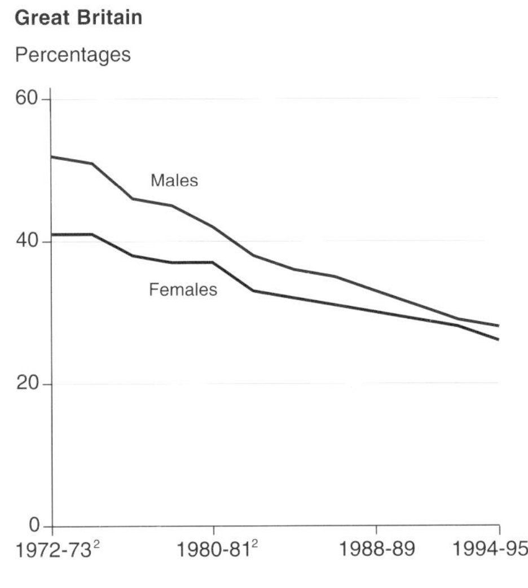

1 By people aged 16 and over, except 1972 which is aged 15 and over. Data are collected every two years.
2 Prior to 1988 data are for calendar years
Source: General Household Survey, Office of Population Censuses and Surveys

7.20

Consumption[1] of alcohol above sensible[2] levels: by gender and age, 1994-95

Great Britain

Percentages

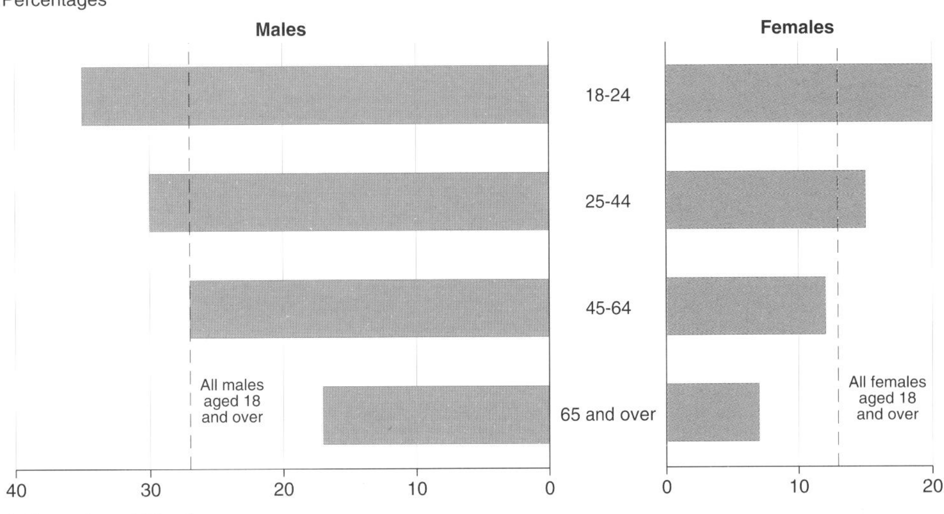

1 By people aged 18 and over.
2 Maximum sensible levels in 1994-95 were 21 units per week for a man and 14 for a woman.
Source: General Household Survey, Office of Population Censuses and Surveys

7.21

New users[1] of drug misuse services: by gender and age, October 1993-March 1994

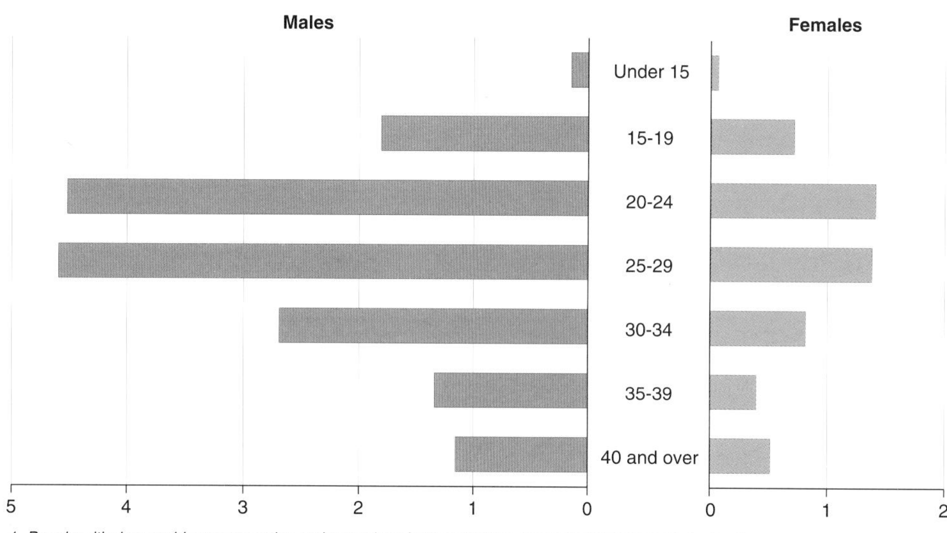

1 People with drug problems presenting to the services for the first time, or after an absence of six months or more.
Source: Department of Health

Drug misuse is associated with a range of illnesses such as life-threatening infections, physical injury, obstetric problems and psychiatric complications, including suicide. During the six month period ending 31 March 1994 over 21 thousand people with a drug problem sought the help of the drug misuse services in Great Britain, either for the first time or after an absence of six months or more **(Chart 7.21)**; three quarters of them were male and over half of both males and females were in their twenties. Heroin was the most common drug misused - 45 per cent used it while 18 per cent used methadone and 10 per cent took amphetamines. The chart probably represents only a small proportion of people misusing drugs: it only records 'new' attenders and excludes those attending on a regular basis, those attending services which are not yet included in central records (such as some needle exchange schemes) and those who do not seek help from any of the available services.

7.22

Death rates[1] for people aged under 65: by gender and selected cause of death

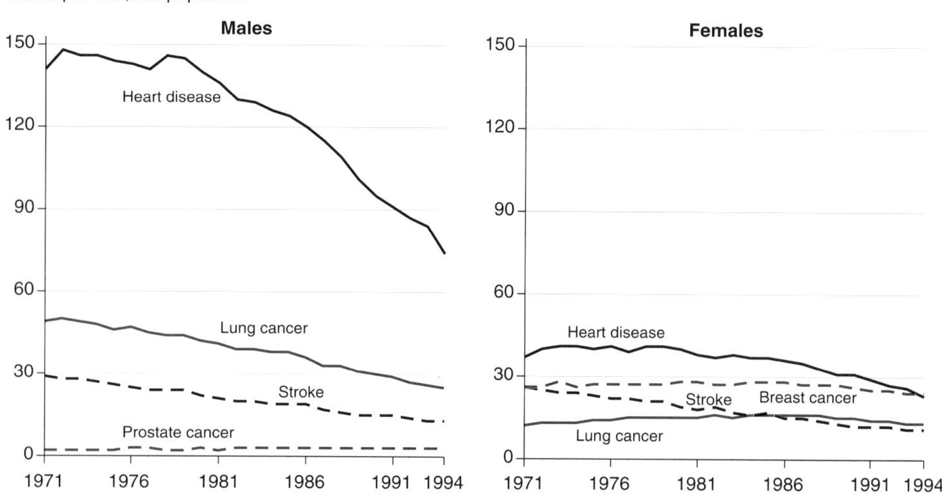

1 Age-standardised to the 1971 population level. See Appendix, Part 7: Standardised death rates.
Source: Office of Population Censuses and Surveys; General Register Office (Scotland); General Register Office (Northern Ireland)

Causes of death

While Chart 7.1 showed that overall death rates for men and women aged under 65 have fallen fairly consistently since the early 1950s, **Chart 7.22** illustrates some of the common causes of death for men and women of the same age. For men aged under 65 in the United Kingdom, death rates for the three most common causes of death shown in the chart have all fallen since the early 1970s. In particular the death rate from heart disease has fallen from 148 deaths per 100 thousand population in 1972 to exactly half that rate in 1994. The rates of male deaths from lung cancer and stroke also halved over the same period. Among women, the death rate for breast cancer has been falling, albeit slowly, since the mid-1980s. Death rates for heart disease almost halved between 1979 and 1994 while those for strokes fell by more than a half.

Death rates from different causes vary between the countries of the European Community (EC). For example, in 1992 the death rate from cancer for women in Denmark was nearly double that in Greece while the rate in the United Kingdom was the third highest in the EC (**Table 7.23**). Among men, the death rate for diseases of the circulatory system in Finland was more than double that in France. Again, the rates in the United Kingdom were among the highest, this time the fifth highest. In all EC countries women have lower overall mortality rates than men.

In 1992 there were almost 5 thousand suicides by those aged 16 to 74 in England and Wales. However, during the 1980s the proportion of suicides attributable to males increased; in 1982 just under two thirds of suicides were to males compared with three quarters in 1992. A study by the Office of Population Censuses and Surveys has shown that the risk of committing suicide varies according to occupation. **Table 7.24** shows that between 1982 and 1992 the highest risk occupation for a male was a vet with over three times the expected number of suicides. Of the occupations shown in the table, farmers accounted for the largest number of suicides - 487 out of a total of 34 thousand over the 11 year period. For a number of reasons occupation data for women are not as complete or as accurate as those for men. However, the study shows that for women, as for men, the highest risk occupations are those in the professional and intermediate classes. Easy access to a method of suicide may well have some effect on the figures. For vets, pharmacists and medical practitioners, poisoning was the most common method used while for farmers it was firearms.

7.23

Death rates[1] for selected diseases: EC comparison, 1992

Rates per 100,000 population

	Malignant neoplasms		Diseases of the circulatory system		Cerebrovascular disease	
	Males	Females	Males	Females	Males	Females
Austria	257	157	473	316	102	80
Belgium[2]	312	160	379	239	80	66
Denmark	272	204	443	263	81	65
Finland	232	135	535	289	104	83
France	295	129	255	151	61	44
Germany	273	162	473	300	99	79
Greece	218	113	395	300	125	126
Irish Republic	271	187	504	302	85	78
Italy[3]	284	146	376	248	105	81
Luxembourg	303	160	413	272	112	102
Netherlands	295	160	370	214	74	63
Portugal	222	126	447	317	231	176
Spain[3]	255	119	335	242	97	82
Sweden	197	143	421	244	74	61
United Kingdom	275	182	450	266	91	80
EC average	273	151	395	251	94	77

1 Age standardised.
2 Data are for 1989.
3 Data are for 1991.
Source: World Health Organisation

7.24

Highest[1] risk occupations for men[2] from suicide, 1982-1987 and 1988-1992

England & Wales Proportional mortality ratios[3]

	1982-1987	1988-1992
Vet	342	361
Pharmacist	204	199
Dental practitioner	205	194
Chemical scientist and engineer	145	156
Forestry worker	182	155
University academic staff	109	152
Farmer	205	145
Medical practitioner	180	144
Hotel porter	176	102
Librarian, information officer	230	84

1 Over the period 1979 to 1990 (excluding 1981). Occupations with less than 20 suicides were excluded.
2 Aged 16 to 64.
3 See Appendix, Part 7: Proportional mortality ratios.
Source: Office of Population Censuses and Surveys

References and further reading

The following list contains selected publications relevant to **Chapter 7: Health.** Those published by HMSO are available from the addresses shown on the inside back cover of *Social Trends*.

Annual Report of the Registrar General for Northern Ireland, HMSO

Annual Report of the Registrar General for Scotland, General Register Office (Scotland)

Asthma, an Epidemiological Overview, Department of Health

Communicable Disease Statistics (Series MB2), HMSO

General Household Survey, HMSO

Health and Personal Social Services Statistics for England, HMSO

Health and Personal Social Services Statistics for Northern Ireland, DHSS, Northern Ireland

Health and Personal Social Services Statistics for Wales, Welsh Office

Health briefings on aspects of health and NHS activity in Scotland (various), National Health Service in Scotland, Common Services Agency,

Health Survey for England, HMSO

Mortality Statistics for England and Wales (Series DH1, 2, 3, 4), HMSO

National Food Survey, HMSO

On the State of the Public Health, HMSO

Population Trends, HMSO

Scotland's Health, A challenge to us all, HMSO

Scottish Health Statistics, National Health Service in Scotland, Common Services Agency

Statistical Publications on aspects of Health and Personal Social Services activity in England (various), Department of Health

Tackling Drugs Together, HMSO

The Prevalence of Psychiatric Morbidity among Adults living in Private Households, HMSO

World Health Statistics, WHO

Contacts

Telephone contact points for further information relating to
Chapter 7: Health

Department of Health	
Demographic statistics	0171 972 5561
Drug misuse/legal status	0171 972 5547
Health service indicators	01532 545555
Ministry of Agriculture, Fisheries and Food	0171 270 8563
Office of Population Censuses and Surveys	
General Household Survey	0171 396 2327
Other inquiries	0171 396 2828
Government Actuary's Department	0171 242 6828
General Register Office (Scotland)	0131 314 4243
National Health Service in Scotland, Common Services Agency	0131 551 8899
General Register Office (Northern Ireland)	01232 252031
Welsh Office	01222 825080
Department of Health and Social Services, NI	01232 522800
Public Health Laboratory Service	0181 200 6868
Royal College of General Practitioners	0121 426 1125
World Health Organisation	00 4539 17 14 82

Chapter 8 Social Protection

General

Expenditure on social protection benefits in the United Kingdom increased by about two thirds in real terms between 1980-81 and 1993-94, to nearly £170 billion. (Page 145)

Three in four households in Great Britain received some type of social security benefit in 1993-94. (Table 8.4)

The top 500 charities (in terms of voluntary income) in the United Kingdom spent nearly £1 billion on health in 1992-93. (Table 8.7)

The sick and disabled

In Great Britain in 1994, 44 per cent of adults questioned were either very or quite satisfied with the National Health Service compared with 38 per cent who were either very or quite dissatisfied. (Page 150)

The number of people with private medical insurance in the United Kingdom rose sharply between the late 1970s and the late 1980s; since then the figure has fallen slightly to 6.8 million in 1994. (Chart 8.18)

The elderly

About 800 thousand meals per week were served to mainly elderly people in their homes or luncheon clubs in England by local authorities or the independent sector in 1994. (Page 154)

Children and families

The average length of time spent by a woman in hospital for childbirth has fallen from 5.3 days in 1981 to 2.9 days in 1993-94. (Table 8.25)

Around 38 thousand children in England, Wales and Northern Ireland were on a child protection register in 1994. (Table 8.27)

8.1

Residents in residential homes for the elderly and adults with a physical or sensory disability

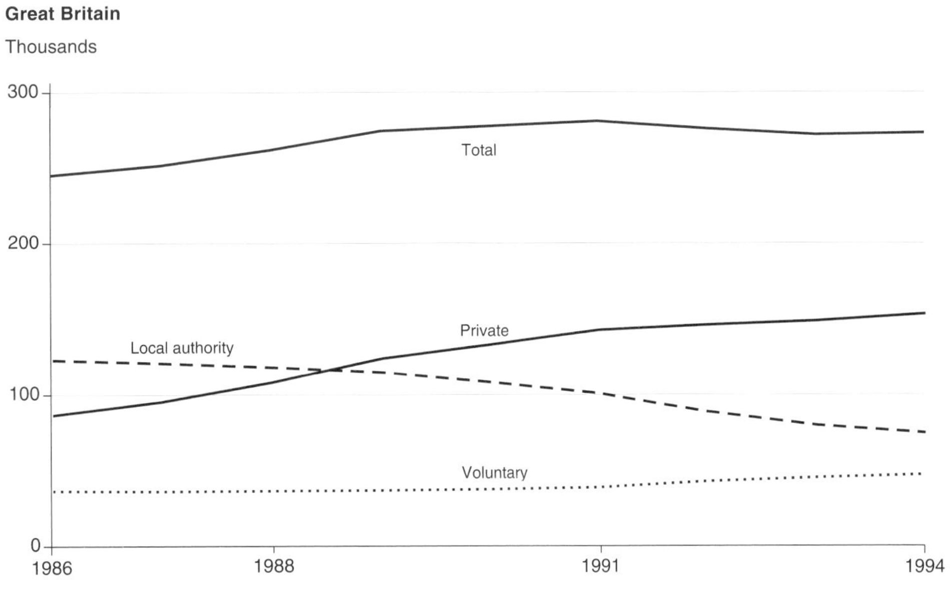

Great Britain

Thousands

300
200
100
0
Total
Private
Local authority
Voluntary
1986
1988
1991
1994

Source: Department of Health; Welsh Office; National Health Service in Scotland, Common Services Agency

8.2

Expenditure on social protection benefits: by function, 1993-94

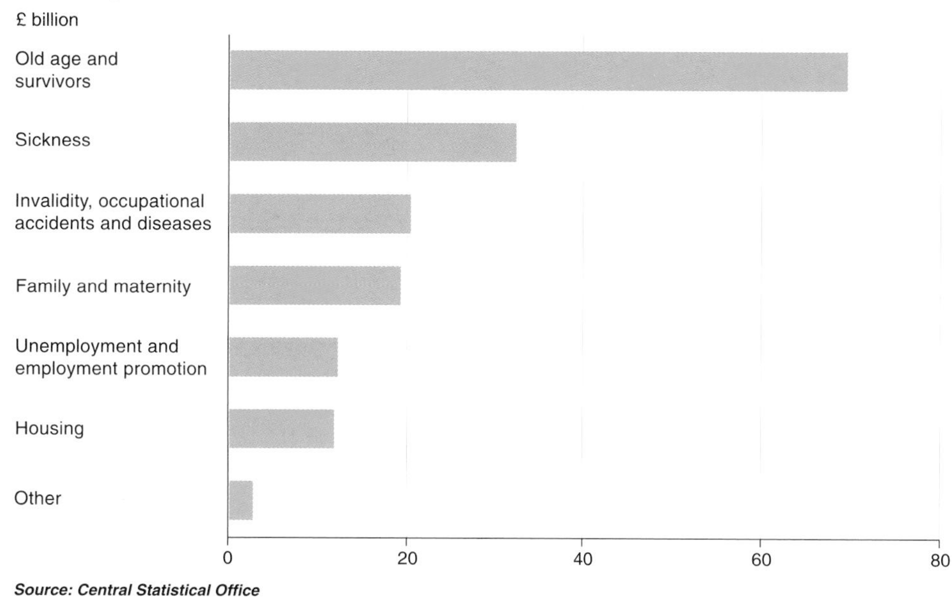

Source: Central Statistical Office

8.3

Expenditure[1] on social protection benefits per head: EC comparison, 1993

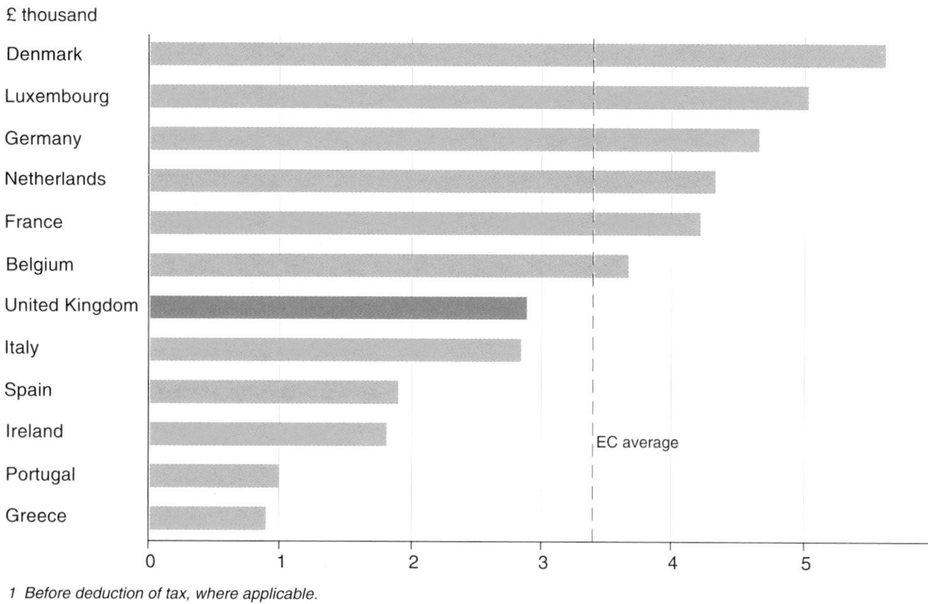

1 Before deduction of tax, where applicable.

Source: Eurostat

This chapter describes the various ways in which central government, local authorities and the private and voluntary sectors act to help people in need. Neediness may arise through ill health, infirmity, inadequate income or through other sorts of misfortune. Generally people who are in need of help or support are identified in other chapters of *Social Trends*. This chapter seeks to analyse the response given to people in need.

General

Some government expenditure programmes are designed specifically to protect people against common sources of hardship such as old age, sickness, unemployment, disability and so on. These programmes can collectively be described as expenditure on social protection, and are those from which households can readily perceive a direct benefit, whether in cash or in kind. Eurostat (the Statistical Office of the European Communities) has designed a framework for the presentation of information on such current expenditure and this has been adopted by member states as the European System of Integrated Social Protection Statistics (ESSPROS).

Although the majority of social protection expenditure comes from government programmes, cash payments of non-governmental benefits such as compulsory occupational pensions are also included. Arrangements made by individuals, such as private medical insurance or a private pension scheme, are not included in this definition of social protection. The sources of hardship or need to which the measures are directed are called 'functions' and data for 1993 for the United Kingdom are given in Chart 8.2.

People are living longer throughout the developed world and changes in employment patterns and family structures are also having an impact on the extent to which people need support. Expenditure on social protection benefits in the United Kingdom increased by about two thirds in real terms between 1980-81 and 1993-94 to reach nearly £170 billion. The largest function in 1993-94 was the combined group of old age and survivors (for example, widowhood) - it claimed just over two fifths of the total. Government expenditure on this function includes cash payments and provision of services such as day care facilities and home helps. Private sector contributions are mainly in the form of occupational pension schemes.

In total, the member states of the European Community (EC) spent 28 per cent of their Gross Domestic Product (GDP) on social protection in 1993. Denmark spent more on social protection per head of population than any other country in the EC and around six times more than Greece, the country which spent the least **(Chart 8.3)**. The United Kingdom spent almost £3 thousand per head of population, a sixth lower than the EC average. However, it would be wrong to make assumptions about the wellbeing of individuals in each country based solely on these data. For example, some benefits in some countries are subject to tax. Comparable data for Austria, Finland and Sweden, which joined the EC in 1995, are not yet available.

One of the major forms that social protection expenditure takes is social security benefit payments. **Table 8.4** shows that three in four households in Great Britain received some type of social security benefit in 1993-94. Some benefits, such as retirement pension, are termed contributory. Eligibility for these is governed by the individual's record of contributions to the National Insurance Fund, including those by their employer on their behalf. Others, such as child benefit, are non-contributory which means that they do not depend on contribution records; some of these, like income support, are income related. Households with children are more likely to receive benefits than those without children, at 99 per cent and 64 per cent respectively. Household income from contributory and non-contributory benefits is shown in Table 5.14.

Not everyone who is entitled to receive a social security benefit claims it. Naturally take-up is higher among the non income-related benefits; for example, take-up of the retirement pension and child benefit is believed to be close to 100 per cent.

Chart 8.5 shows how benefit expenditure is distributed between the different recipient groups. More than two fifths of all benefit expenditure in Great Britain in 1994-95 was accounted for by the elderly. However, the recipient group on which expenditure increased most between 1981-82 and 1994-95 was the sick and disabled: expenditure almost tripled in real terms to £20.4 billion in 1994-95.

8.4

Benefit recipients: by type of household[1], 1993-94

Great Britain — Percentages

	1993-94
Pensioner	*99.6*
Sick/disabled	*90.0*
Unemployed	*92.2*
Other	*60.3*
All households	*75.8*

1 Classification of head of household.
Source: Family Resources Survey, Department of Social Security

8.5

Benefit expenditure: by recipient group[1], 1994-95

Great Britain
Percentages

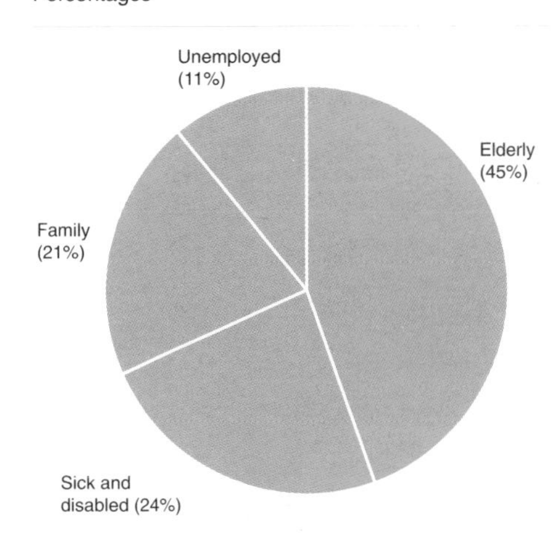

1 See Appendix, Part 8: Benefits to groups of recipients.
Source: Department of Social Security

8.6

Real[1] growth in social security benefit and National Health Service expenditure

United Kingdom

£ billion at 1994-95 prices[1]

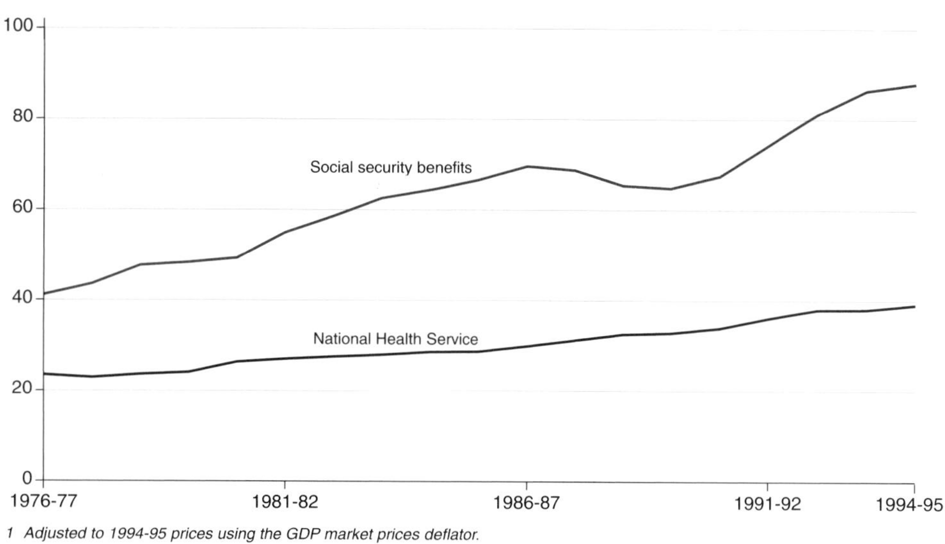

1 Adjusted to 1994-95 prices using the GDP market prices deflator.

Source: Department of Health; Department of Social Security; Department of Health and Social Services, Northern Ireland

Not all health and welfare services are provided from government expenditure. The Charities Aid Foundation, an independent body, is one of the main organisations that aids the flow of funds to charities from individuals, companies and grant-making trusts. Organisations may qualify for charitable status if they are established for purposes such as the relief of poverty, the advancement of education or religion, the protection of health or certain other purposes for public benefit. In 1994 just under 180 thousand voluntary organisations were registered as charities in England and Wales.

Chart 8.6 illustrates government expenditure in real terms on social security benefits and the National Health Service (NHS) since 1976-77. Around a third of general government expenditure in the United Kingdom is spent on the social security programme. In 1994-95 expenditure on social security benefits amounted to nearly £88 billion, more than double in real terms the amount in 1976-77. Over the same period government expenditure on the NHS grew at a slower rate, by only two thirds in real terms, to £39 billion. In 1994-95, three quarters of central government expenditure on the NHS went to the Health Authorities who are responsible for hospitals and community health services. The majority of the remainder was spent by the Family Health Service Authorities whose responsibilities include GPs, dentists and pharmaceutical services. Local authorities in England spent a further £6.3 billion on personal social services in 1993-94.

Table 8.7 shows that the top 500 charities (in terms of voluntary income) in the United Kingdom spent nearly £1.6 billion on health, welfare and housing in 1992-93. These purposes accounted for about three fifths of all charitable expenditure by the top 500 charities. Nearly £1 billion was spent on health which includes expenditure by charities concerned with cancer, heart problems, blindness, AIDS and terminal care, as well as the physically handicapped and mentally ill.

Those employed by central and local government in the health and social service covered in **Table 8.8** accounted for 5 per cent of people in employment in Great Britain in 1994. The NHS, one of the largest employers in the world, directly employed 918 thousand people in Great Britain in 1994 on a whole-time equivalents basis. This figure has fallen by 4 per cent since 1986. (The reduction of the working week for nurses distorts comparisons with earlier years.)

8.7

Charitable expenditure[1] of the top 500[2] charities: by function, 1992-93

United Kingdom	£ million
	1992-93
Health	
Physically handicapped	260
Mentally ill	83
Other	613
General welfare	
Children	177
Elderly	108
Other	328
Housing	8

1 Excludes administrative expenditure.
2 In terms of voluntary income.

Source: Charities Aid Foundation

The composition of the workforce by group has changed since 1986. The proportion of the NHS workforce accounted for by ancillary and maintenance staff fell from 19 to 12 per cent over the period, mainly as a result of competitive tendering exercises. General and senior managers did not exist as a separate group before 1986. The increase in their number is largely due to the reclassification of administrative and professional staff, including many senior nurses, as managers. The number employed in personal and social services occupations rose by 53 thousand between 1981 and 1994. This group includes social work staff, home helps and those working in residential establishments.

In addition to the formal care sector there are a range of informal services provided by people for family, friends and others. In 1990 the General Household Survey asked people in Great Britain if they were carers, that is, looked after anyone who was sick, disabled or elderly. **Table 8.9** shows the type of help given by carers. One in five carers gave help with personal care and just under one in two helped with paperwork or financial matters.

Overall about 15 per cent people aged 16 and over were providing care inside or outside their household. Nearly half of those who were carers were looking after a parent or parent-in-law. More than one in five of carers spent 20 hours or more a week looking after someone although the proportion was higher for those who were looking after someone in the same household.

8.8

Health and personal social services staff[1]

Great Britain — Thousands

	1981	1986	1991	1994
Directly employed National Health Service staff				
Nursing and midwifery[2]	457	472	470	426
Administration and clerical	129	132	152	161
Professional and technical	78	91	103	111
Ancillary and maintenance	238	184	128	108
Medical and dental	48	51	56	60
General/senior managers	.	1	16	26
Ambulance staff	21	22	21	22
Other	7	6	9	4
All health service staff	977	958	954	918
Family health services	27	29	31	32
Family dental services	15	17	18	19
Personal social services	240	270	289	293

1 Whole-time equivalents except family health services and family dental services in Scotland and Wales which are headcounts. Agency and locum staff are excluded.
2 Excludes Project 2000 staff for 1991 and 1994 (in England there were 10.5 thousand and 32 thousand respectively).
Source: Department of Health; Welsh Office; National Health Service in Scotland, Common Services Agency

8.9

Type of help given by carers, 1990

Great Britain — Percentages

	Carers with main dependant: In the same household	Carers with main dependant: In another household	All carers
Keeping company	*62*	*71*	*69*
Keeping an eye on dependant	*54*	*70*	*66*
Taking out	*57*	*55*	*55*
Paperwork or financial matters	*56*	*41*	*45*
Personal care (eg washing)	*55*	*11*	*22*
Physical help (eg with walking)	*48*	*13*	*21*
Giving medicines	*38*	*9*	*16*
Other practical help	*78*	*80*	*79*

Source: General Household Survey, Office of Population Censuses and Surveys

8.10

Voluntary activities undertaken[1], 1992-93

Great Britain		Percentages
	Males	Females
Raising money (except collections)	*8*	*13*
Collecting money	*5*	*9*
Serving on a committee	*8*	*7*
Helping at a club	*5*	*7*
Administration	*4*	*5*
Organising/taking part in entertainment	*4*	*4*
Teaching or training	*4*	*3*
Giving talks/canvassing	*3*	*3*
Visiting people in institutions	*2*	*3*
Giving advice	*2*	*2*
Other practical help	*2*	*3*
Any activity	*21*	*27*

1 In the year before interview; by those aged 16 and over.

Source: General Household Survey, Office of Population Censuses and Surveys

Another way for members of the general public to assist those in need is to carry out organised voluntary activities. In 1992-93 the General Household Survey included questions about voluntary work. This was defined as unpaid work done through a group or on behalf of an organisation. **Table 8.10** shows that the most common activity undertaken in Great Britain was raising money. Overall just over a quarter of women and just over a fifth of men had carried out some voluntary work in the previous 12 months.

Participation varied according to social class, ranging from two in five of those in the professional group to about one in eight in the unskilled manual group in 1992-93. Just over a quarter of those who had undertaken some voluntary work had spent a maximum of five days on it during the year; a half had spent 20 days or more. In 1993 the British Social Attitudes Survey asked people for their opinions on how certain voluntary activities should be organised. While just over half of those questioned felt that youth club outings should be organised exclusively by volunteers, only one in eight thought that work in Citizens Advice Bureaux ought to be unpaid.

As well as the Citizens Advice Bureaux, many other counselling and advisory services exist which between them deal with a wide range of issues. All of the organisations shown in **Table 8.11** experienced large increases in the number of clients during the 1980s - a trend which continued into the 1990s for most of them. Because these organisations record the number of clients or queries in different ways, it is difficult to make direct comparisons between them.

The Citizens Advice Bureaux introduced a new recording system in 1994. Previously the main measurement was enquiries which referred both to a client's problem and also to how often the client sought advice. From April 1994 the number of problems was counted; a single problem may involve more than one enquiry. In 1994-95 the Citizens Advice Bureaux dealt with more than 7.1 million problems.

8.11

Clients of selected advisory and counselling services[1]

United Kingdom				Thousands
	1971	1981	1991	1994
Citizens Advice Bureaux	1,500	4,515	8,278	..
Samaritans	..	1,700	2,500	3,748
Law Centres Federation	1	155	452	525
Youth Access	..	30	113	250
Disablement Information and Advice Lines	.	40	75	137
Cruse Bereavement Care	..	..	55	97
ChildLine	.	.	69	90
Relate	22	38	70	70
Alcoholics Anonymous	6	30	45	48
Turning Point	..	..	..	27
Al-Anon	1	7	13	11
Catholic Marriage Advisory Council	3	3	17	10

1 For details of coverage of individual organisations see Appendix, Part 8: Selected advisory and counselling services.

Source: Organisations concerned

The sick and disabled

Whereas the Health chapter discusses the nature of health and ill-health amongst the population, this section looks at the response provided for the sick and for people with disabilities.

Table 8.12 shows NHS activity for sick and disabled in-patients. Care should be taken when using this table as, due to changes in the administrative system, hospital in-patient cases are a combination of finished consultant episodes (FCEs) and deaths and discharges as follows: data for England are FCEs throughout; Wales and Northern Ireland are FCEs in later years (1991-92 and 1993-94) and deaths and discharges for earlier years; figures for Scotland are deaths and discharges for all years (see Appendix, Part 8: In-patient activity). In the United Kingdom the number of hospital in-patients cases in the acute sector rose by 1.3 million between 1981 and 1993-94. More patients have been able to be treated because of a reduction in the average length of time each patient spent in hospital. The average time spent in hospital by these patients fell to 5.4 days in 1993-94.

In tandem with the increase in the number of hospital in-patient cases there has been a move towards treating patients on an out-patient or day case basis. The number of day case attendances for the acute sectors doubled in Great Britain between 1986 and 1993-94 **(Table 8.13)**.

Another change to the way in which the NHS delivers its services has been in the creation of NHS trusts. These are self governing and are no longer directly managed by the Regions. In 1993-94, 68 per cent of all finished consultant episodes in England were treated in NHS trust hospitals; this rose to 97 per cent in 1994-95. Similarly the organisation of GP practices has been changing: more than a third of the population of England in 1994-95 was cared for by a fundholding GP. Along with this has come an increase in the provision of clinics within GP surgeries and in the number of minor operations carried out at the surgery.

8.12

National Health Service activity for sick and disabled people: in-patients

United Kingdom

	1981	1986	1991-92	1993-94
Acute[1]				
Finished consultant episodes[2] (thousands)	6,226	6,814	7,341	7,519
In-patient episodes per available bed (numbers)	33.8	40.1	49.8	53.4
Mean duration of stay (days)	7.7	6.5	5.8	5.4
Mentally ill				
Finished consultant episodes[2] (thousands)	244	265	277	294
In-patient episodes per available bed (numbers)	2.2	2.7	3.9	4.8
Mean duration of stay (days)	..	..	116.3	76.9
Mentally handicapped[3]				
Finished consultant episodes[2] (thousands)	34	58	62	61
In-patient episodes per available bed (numbers)	0.6	1.2	2.6	2.8
Mean duration of stay (days)	..	..	553.5	317.1

1 Wards for general patients, excluding elderly, younger disabled and neonate cots in maternity units.
2 All data for Scotland and data for Wales and Northern Ireland in 1981 and 1986 are for deaths and discharges. See Appendix, Part 8: In-patient activity.
3 Excluding mental handicap community units.

Source: Department of Health; Welsh Office; National Health Service in Scotland, Common Services Agency; Department of Health and Social Services, Northern Ireland

8.13

National Health Service activity for sick and disabled people: out-patients and day cases

Great Britain

	1981	1986	1991-92	1993-94[1]
Out-patient services				
Accident and emergency				
New attendances (thousands)	10,962	12,227	9,859	9,969
Average attendances per new patient (numbers)	1.4	1.3	3.5	3.5
Mentally ill				
New attendances (thousands)	230	247	271	301
Average attendances per new patient (numbers)	8.8	8.7	7.6	7.2
Mentally handicapped[2]				
New attendances (thousands)	3	4	4	6
Average attendances per new patient (numbers)	6.6	9.6	11.5	10.8
Day case attendances (thousands)				
Acute[3]	817	1,208	1,840	2,529
Mentally ill	12	13	1	2
Mentally handicapped[2]	1	4	1	2

1 Data for out-patient services in 1993-94 exclude Wales.
2 Excluding mental handicap community units.
3 Wards for general patients, excluding elderly, younger disabled and neonate cots in maternity units.

Source: Department of Health; Welsh Office; National Health Service in Scotland, Common Services Agency

8.14

Percentage of National Health Service patients waiting[1] over 12 months: by region, 1995[2]

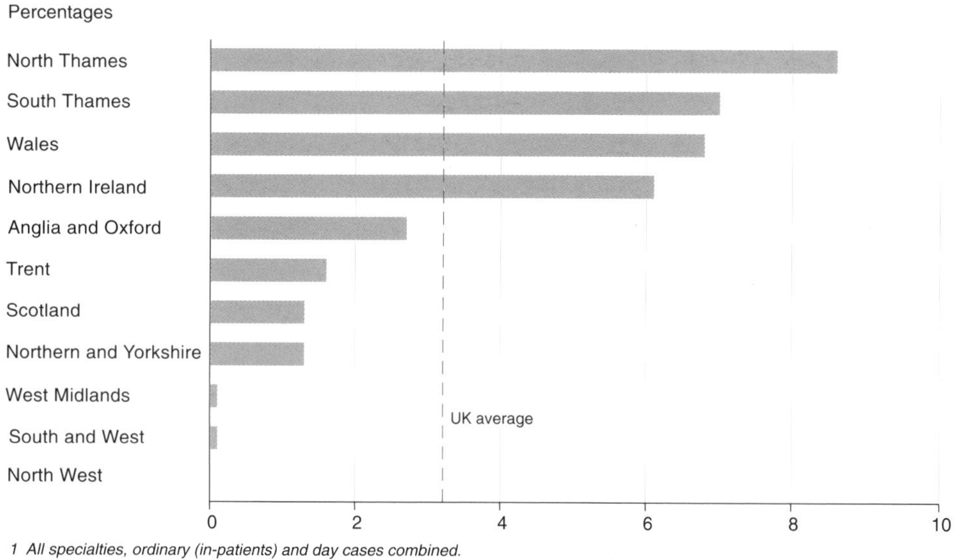

1 All specialties, ordinary (in-patients) and day cases combined.
2 At 31 March.

Source: Department of Health; Welsh Office; National Health Service in Scotland, Common Services Agency; Department of Health and Social Services, Northern Ireland

The length of time spent waiting for hospital treatment varies in different parts of the country. At 31 March 1995 the percentage of patients waiting over 12 months for treatment was highest in the North Thames Regional Health Authority at 9 per cent; in contrast there were no patients waiting over 12 months in the North West Regional Health Authority **(Chart 8.14)**. Waiting times also vary according to the type of treatment sought and the urgency of the treatment: 7 per cent of patients requiring treatment for plastic surgery had been waiting for more than 12 months compared with less than 2 per cent of those awaiting treatment in the obstetrics and gynaecology specialty. From April 1995, under the Patient's Charter, the aim is that no one will have to wait over 18 months for admission.

An important aspect of the services delivered by the NHS is peoples' perceptions of them. Overall 44 per cent of adults questioned in the British Social Attitudes Survey in 1994 said that they were either very or quite satisfied with the NHS compared with 38 per cent who were either very or quite dissatisfied. In 1983, 55 per cent were very or quite satisfied compared with 37 per cent in 1989 and 1990 when public satisfaction was at its lowest over this 12 year period. Interestingly the proportion of respondents who were dissatisfied with hospital in-patient services rose from 7 to 16 per cent between 1983 and 1994. However the proportion who were dissatisfied with out-patient services was the same in 1994 as in 1983, at 21 per cent, although this had risen to 30 per cent in 1989. **Table 8.15** shows that about two in three people thought that the quality of the medical treatment in hospitals was satisfactory or very good; people generally felt that there

8.15

Satisfaction with hospital and community health services[1], 1994

Great Britain — Percentages

	Very good	Satisfactory	In need of some improvement	In need of a lot of improvement	Don't know/ not answered
Hospital services					
Quality of medical treatment	*17*	*48*	*27*	*6*	*2*
General condition of buildings	*9*	*38*	*36*	*15*	*2*
Time spent waiting in out-patient departments	*2*	*25*	*48*	*23*	*2*
Waiting lists for non-emergency operations	*1*	*18*	*43*	*35*	*3*
GP services					
Quality of medical treatment by GPs	*23*	*52*	*18*	*5*	*1*
Being able to choose which GP to see	*18*	*55*	*20*	*7*	*1*
Amount of time GP gives to each patient	*14*	*54*	*24*	*8*	*1*
GPs' appointment systems	*12*	*44*	*32*	*11*	*1*

1 Respondents were asked 'From what you know or have heard, say whether you think the NHS in your area is, on the whole, satisfactory or in need of improvement'.

Source: British Social Attitudes Survey, Social & Community Planning Research

was the greatest need for improvements in the time spent waiting in out-patient departments and in the length of waiting lists for non-emergency operations.

An extensive series of surveys of disability among people in households and communal establishments in Great Britain was carried out between 1985 and 1988, but has not since been updated. An alternative source is the data collected under the terms of the *National Assistance Act 1948*. This requires local authorities in England and Wales to maintain registers of 'persons who are blind, deaf or dumb, and other persons who are substantially and permanently handicapped by illness, injury or congenital deformity'. Data for the disabilities shown in **Table 8.16** are updated by the Department of Health on a rolling triennial basis. As might be expected the numbers registered increase with age. However, registration of disablement with social services departments is voluntary and is not a condition for the provision of certain social services so these figures do not necessarily measure the prevalence of disablement in the population.

In 1994 there were 52 thousand residents aged under 65 in homes in England for people with learning disabilities, mentally ill people and adults with a physical or sensory disability. However, as with other health and social services, the trend is towards providing care in the community. There were 303 thousand attendances at day centres (purchased or provided by local authorities) during the survey week in 1994. A further 42 thousand households where a member was in one of the groups mentioned above had received some form of home help or home care.

8.16

People registered with local authorities as having disabilities: by age

England — Rates per 10,000 population

	Under 18	18-64	65 and over	All ages
Very severely handicapped[1]	5	10	65	18
Severely or appreciably handicapped[1]	10	63	535	126
Other registered persons[1]	10	65	565	132
Blind[2]	3	9	156	31
Partially sighted[2]	3	7	119	24
Deaf[3]	4	9	19	9
Hard of hearing[3]	3	7	129	26

1 Data are for 1993.
2 Data are for 1994.
3 Data are for 1995.
Source: Department of Health

The social security system provides benefits to assist, amongst others, people who are sick or have disabilities. In 1993-94, 1.8 million people, about 4 per cent of the population of working age in Great Britain, were in receipt of invalidity benefit or severe disablement allowance **(Table 8.17)**. This represents two and a half times the number of claimants in 1981-82. The rise in the

8.17

Recipients of benefits for sick and disabled people

Great Britain — Thousands

	1981-82	1986-87	1991-92	1993-94
Long-term sick and people with disabilities				
Invalidity benefit/severe disablement allowance	723	1,092	1,501	1,767
One of the above benefits plus income support	103	136	240	289
Income support only	.	.	229	350
Short-term sick				
Sickness benefit only	369	94	110	112
Sickness benefit and income support	24	16	28	29
Income support only	.	.	79	90
Disability living allowance[1]	617	1,153	1,758	1,320

1 Attendance allowance and mobility allowance before April 1992.
Source: Department of Social Security

8.18

People insured by private medical insurance[1]

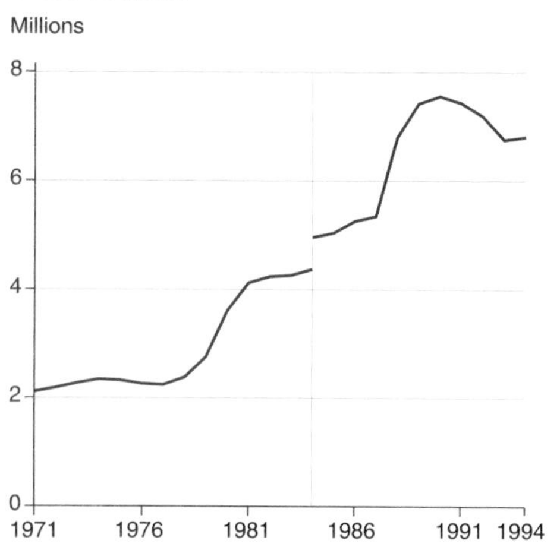

1 Data up to 1976 are from Lee Donaldson Associates; 1977 to 1984 are from BUPA, PPA and WPA; 1984 onwards are from Department of Health.

Source: Lee Donaldson Associates; BUPA; PPA; WPA; Department of Health

8.19

Hospital and local authority expenditure on elderly people in real terms[1]

England	£ million at 1993-94 prices[1]		
	1986-87	1991-92	1993-94
Hospitals[2]	7,295	8,377	8,935
Local authority			
Residential	1,089	1,163	1,322
Non-residential	1,072	1,310	1,560

1 Adjusted to 1993-94 prices using the GDP market prices deflator.
2 Includes community health services.

Source: Department of Health

number of claimants of invalidity benefit, three quarters of whom are male, is partly due to an increase in the length of claims rather than to an increase in the number of new claims. Over the same period expenditure on the long-term sick and disabled tripled in real terms, to more than nearly £18 billion in 1993-94, while spending on the short-term sick remained constant. From April 1995 sickness benefit and invalidity benefit were replaced by incapacity benefit which is paid at three rates depending on the duration of incapacity.

Health care services are, in the main, provided by the state but some people also look to the private sector to deliver services. The number of people with private medical insurance in the United Kingdom increased sharply between 1971 and 1990 to 7.6 million; since then the figure has fallen back slightly **(Chart 8.18)**. However care should be taken in interpreting the chart as figures prior to 1985 are taken from different sources and are not directly comparable with those for later years.

Results from the British Social Attitudes Survey which was carried out in Great Britain in 1994 showed that 36 per cent of households with an annual gross income of £26 thousand or more had private medical insurance compared with only 3 per cent of those with an annual gross income of less than £8 thousand. Those on higher incomes were also more likely to have the majority of the costs of their private medical insurance met by their employer. The survey also showed that the proportion of respondents who thought that people should be able to pay for better health care if they wanted to fell from 53 per cent in 1986 to 43 per cent in 1993, while the proportion of those who thought that health care should be the same for everyone rose from 46 to 55 per cent over the same period.

The elderly

The increase in the number of elderly people and projections for the future are contained in the Population chapter (Chart 1.1) and information on one person households over pensionable age may be found in Chart 2.3 in the Households and Families chapter. This section focuses on services and other forms of help provided to elderly people.

The cost of government expenditure for the elderly has been increasing in recent years and is predicted to grow in the future as the population continues to age. Total benefit expenditure on the elderly in Great Britain rose by almost half in real terms between 1981-82 and 1994-95 to accounted for over two fifths of total benefit expenditure. Hospital and local authority expenditure has also been increasing in real terms. In England between 1986-87 and 1993-94 hospital expenditure on elderly people rose by more than a fifth to just under £9 billion; expenditure by local authorities rose by a third over the same period **(Table 8.19)**. Since 1993 local authorities have been responsible for funding placements for new residents who cannot afford the fees themselves in both residential and nursing homes.

One of the areas in which some elderly people need help in overcoming difficulties is mobility. In 1993-94 the General Household Survey found that nearly one in six people aged 65 to 74 in Great Britain had difficulty in getting about their home or outdoors without some form of assistance. This proportion more than doubled to nearly two in five of those aged 75 and over.

Some information on mobility is also available from the Continuous Household Survey in Northern Ireland. Among those aged 75 and over in the United Kingdom who reported having some form of mobility difficulty, 56 per cent used one aid while 9 per cent used three or more. **Table 8.20** shows the types of aids used. The most common type of aid used was a walking stick; walking frames were the next most common aid.

In 1994 there were 273 thousand residents in homes for the elderly or adults with a physical or sensory disability in Great Britain **(Chart 8.1)** - the last group accounted for only 3 per cent of the total in England. While the number of residents in all homes rose by 11 per cent between 1986 and 1994 the proportion in homes run by the private sector increased at a faster rate, by 77 per cent, to 153 thousand over the same period. In part this reflects the transfer of local authority homes to the independent sector. As the population in general ages so the age distribution of residents in homes for the elderly has also been changing - in England in 1994, 54 per cent were aged 85 or over compared with 47 per cent in 1989. In Northern Ireland in 1993-94 there were 2 thousand residents aged 65 or over in homes administered by local health and social services boards.

Since the community care reforms were implemented in April 1993 local authorities have been responsible for funding placements for people who cannot afford the fees themselves; previously most residents who could not pay the full fee themselves could claim special levels of income support to help pay their fees.

In addition to residential services for elderly people, help is provided to enable them to live in their own homes and as independently as possible. In October 1994 9 per cent of households in England where the oldest member was aged 65 or over were in receipt of home help or home care services which were purchased or provided by their local authority **(Table 8.21)**. Local authorities provided 1.8 million contact hours directly, mainly to the elderly; a further 428 thousand hours were provided by the independent sector under contract from local authorities. As might be expected, the proportion of people receiving services increases with age: 36 per cent of households in the 85 and over group received home help or home care compared with 11 per cent of those aged 75 to 84. This pattern was also reflected in the home help provision in Scotland. In the year to 31 March 1994, 26 per cent of people aged 85 and over received home help or home care compared with 17 per cent of those aged 75 to 84.

8.20

Aids used by elderly people[1] with mobility difficulties, 1993-94

United Kingdom	Percentage of all aids
	1993-94
Walking stick	*62*
Walking frame	*16*
Manual wheel chair	*12*
Trolley	*4*
Electric wheelchair	*1*
Other	*4*
All aids	*100*

1 Aged 75 and over.

Source: General Household Survey, Office of Population Censuses and Surveys; Continuous Household Survey, Department of Finance and Personnel, Northern Ireland

8.21

Households receiving local authority home help or home care services: by sector and age[1], 1994[2]

England — Rates per 10,000 households

		Under contract using		
	Direct	Voluntary sector	Private sector	All sectors
65-74	292	5	25	322
75-84	1,006	15	80	1,101
85 and over	3,270	57	266	3,593
All aged 65 and over[3]	843	19	78	940

1 Of oldest client in the household.
2 Week commencing 3 October 1994.
3 Includes age unknown.

Source: Department of Health

8.22

Health and personal social services for elderly people, 1993-94

England	Rates per 1,000 people aged 65 and over
	1993-94
Hospital in-patients	324
People receiving meals[1]	37
Day centre attendances paid by local authorities[1]	18

1 During survey week in 1994.

Source: Department of Health

There are a variety of other services provided for the elderly by hospitals and local authorities. For example, in 1993-94, 32 per cent of people aged 65 or over in England stayed overnight in a hospital as an in-patient **(Table 8.22)**. As community nursing and rehabilitation services have been promoted, the average time spent has fallen to 17 days in 1993-94.

The ability of elderly people to lead independent lives is enhanced by meals services. Local authorities provided about 56 per cent of the 794 thousand meals served to mainly elderly people in their homes or at luncheon clubs in England in the survey week in 1994. In addition over 300 thousand meals were served to people attending day centres. On average people received three meals per week at home whilst those attending luncheon clubs did so twice a week. Around 7 per cent of meals were provided at weekends, virtually all of which were delivered to people's homes. The proportion of meals provided at weekends has remained broadly constant over time.

The social security benefit system provides financial assistance for elderly people to complement the health and social services provided by the NHS and local authorities. **Table 8.23** shows that over 9 million people were in receipt of a retirement pension in Great Britain in 1993-94. However in recent years there has been a shift away from reliance on state benefits towards provision from private sources. Further information of pensioners' income is given in Table 5.5 in the Income and Wealth Chapter. Retirement pensions may also be paid to beneficiaries outside the United Kingdom under EC regulations, bilateral agreements with other countries or by virtue of UK domestic law. The number of overseas recipients has been increasing at a faster rate than for those living in Great Britain; in 1993-94, 650 thousand pensions were payable overseas, two and a half times the number in 1981-82.

In 1994 for every 100 people of working age there were about 30 over pensionable age (men aged 65 and over and women aged 60 and over) - this is forecast to rise to 38 in 2021. Changing demographic patterns such as these may have an influence on peoples' attitudes towards the way in which pensions should be provided in the future. The findings of the British Social Attitudes Survey in 1993 showed that while there was still a commitment to a basic pension provided by the state, people believed that responsibility should not be borne by the public sector alone. Nearly half of the respondents said that it was mainly the responsibility of the government to ensure that people had an adequate retirement pension, while just under two fifths thought the responsibility should be shared equally

8.23

Recipients of selected benefits[1] for the elderly

Great Britain				Thousands
	1981-82	1986-87	1991-92	1993-94
Retirement pension only	7,205	7,657	8,147	8,074
Retirement pension with income support[2]	1,624	1,592	1,307	1,395
Income support only[2]	113	124	146	167
UK pensions payable overseas	252	372	594	649

1 Retirement pension data are at 31 March except 1981 which is at 30 June. Income support/supplementary benefit data are from annual and quarterly enquiries.
2 Income support replaced supplementary benefit in April 1988.

Source: Department of Social Security

8.24

Attitudes[1] to pension reforms, 1993

Great Britain — Percentages

	In favour	Neither in favour nor against	Against	Don't know/ not answered
Making it compulsory for all medium sized and large employers to set up company pension schemes	*77*	*11*	*9*	*3*
Increasing national insurance contributions for all in work	*42*	*19*	*37*	*3*
Raising the legal retirement age for women to 65	*36*	*9*	*54*	*1*
Lowering the amount of state pension for people with private incomes or pensions	*25*	*15*	*57*	*3*
Raising the legal retirement age for both men and women	*21*	*11*	*67*	*1*
Lowering the amount of state pension for all pensioners	*2*	*3*	*94*	*1*

1 Respondents were asked 'Pensions are taking up a larger and larger part of government spending. Here are some things that might be done about it. Please say how far you are in favour or against each one'.

Source: British Social Attitudes Survey, Social & Community Planning Research

between employers and the government. However **Table 8.24** shows that more than three quarters of those questioned were in favour of making it compulsory for all medium-sized and large employers to set up company pension schemes.

Children and families

In 1993 there were 640 thousand births in England; 98 per cent of these took place in hospital. As with other hospital services in the United Kingdom the number of maternity in-patient cases has been increasing while the number of beds available has been falling and the average length of time spent by women in hospital for childbirth has declined **(Table 8.25)**. Between 1981 and 1993-94 it fell from 5.3 to 2.9 days. In addition to maternity services, longer term help is available to help plan the number and timing of children. In 1992-93 over 4 million visits were made to family planning clinics in England. Family building is covered in more detail in Chapter 2: Households and Families.

8.25

Maternity services

United Kingdom

	1981[1]	1986[2]	1991-92	1993-94
In-patient services				
Finished consultant episodes[3] (thousands)	1,032	1,105	1,209	1,247
In-patient episodes per available bed (numbers)	45	55	69	78
Mean duration of stay (days)	5.3	4.3	3.4	2.9
Out-patient services[4]				
New attendances (thousands)	796	828	828	732
Average attendances per new patient (numbers)	5.6	5.0	4.3	4.1
Contacts with midwives and health visitors (thousands)[5]				
Ante-natal	..	..	3,521	4,052
Post-natal	..	..	6,422	5,980

1 Data for Scotland are for 1981-82.
2 Data for Wales and Scotland are for 1986-87.
3 All data for Scotland and data for Wales and Northern Ireland in 1981 and 1986 are for deaths and discharges. See Appendix, Part 8: In-patient activity.
4 In the 1993-94 column, data for Wales are for 1991-92.
5 Data are England and Scotland only.

Source: Department of Health; Welsh Office; National Health Service in Scotland, Common Services Agency; Department of Health and Social Services, Northern Ireland

8.26

Children looked after by local authorities[1]: by type of accommodation

England, Wales & Northern Ireland — Percentages

	1981	1993
With foster parents	*39*	*61*
In local authority homes	*28*	*13*
Placement with parent regulations[2]	*19*	*11*
Voluntary homes and hostels	*4*	*2*
Schools for children with special educational needs[3]	*3*	*1*
Other accommodation	*7*	*14*
All children in care (=100%) (thousands)	99	56
All children in care per 1,000 population aged under 18	7.6	4.6

1 At 31 March. All data for Northern Ireland and data for 1981 for England and Wales relate to children in care.
2 All data for Northern Ireland and data for 1981 for England and Wales relate to children under the charge and control of a parent, guardian, relative or friend.
3 England and Wales only.

Source: Department of Health; Welsh Office; Department of Health and Social Services, Northern Ireland

8.27

Children on child protection registers: by gender and age, 1994[1]

England, Wales & Northern Ireland — Thousands

	Males	Females
Under 1	1.5	1.4
1-4	6.0	5.5
5-9	6.1	5.6
10-15	4.9	5.7
16 and over	0.4	0.8
All children	19.0	18.9

1 At 31 March.

Source: Department of Health; Welsh Office; Department of Health and Social Services, Northern Ireland

Local authorities are obliged to provide accommodation for children who need it. This may be due to a child having no parent or guardian, because they have been abandoned or because their parents are unable to provide for them. Local authorities also have the power to accommodate children if they consider that to do so would safeguard or promote their welfare and to apply to a court for a care order. The number of children looked after by, or in the care of, local authorities in England, Wales and Northern Ireland fell by 43 per cent between 1981 and 1993 **(Table 8.26)**. At the same time there was a move away from the provision of accommodation in local authority homes (including those controlled or assisted by local authorities); 28 per cent of children were looked after in this way in 1981 compared with only 13 per cent in 1993.

Scotland has a different definition of children in care which means that the data for Scotland are not comparable with those for the rest of the United Kingdom. In Scotland, children who are under a non-residential supervision requirement from a Children's Hearing are considered to be in care whereas in England those under a supervision order are not. In 1993 there were 12 thousand children in care in Scotland.

Personal social services also exist to help children who are considered to be at risk of abuse. All social services departments hold a central register of such children. Registration takes place following a case conference which sets out a protection plan. The registers are not records of child abuse: some children on the register will not have been the victim of abuse but are considered to be at risk, whilst some who have been victims of abuse will not have been placed on the register if there was no case conference. A child may be on the register of more than one authority at a time.

Table 8.27 shows that 38 thousand children in England, Wales and Northern Ireland in March 1994 were on a child protection register. The total number on the registers in England fell from 41 thousand in 1989 to 35 thousand in 1994, although this was due more to an increase in the rate of deregistrations than a decrease in the rate of registrations. The most common reason for children being on a child protection register in 1994 was because they were at risk of physical injury; over a third of boys and over a quarter of girls were considered to be at risk from this type of abuse. Children may be considered to be at risk from more than one form of abuse. Due to changes in the categories of abuse, it is not possible to make direct comparisons with years prior to 1993. In Scotland there were around 2.7 thousand children on child protection registers in 1994.

The social security benefit system also offers support for families with dependent children; around a fifth of benefit expenditure in 1994-95 (see Chart 8.5) was received by such families. The most significant non income-related benefit for families in 1993-94, in terms of both numbers of recipients and expenditure, was child benefit; this was received by 7 million families **(Table 8.28)**. Other benefits received by families include income support and housing benefit.

Benefits are not the sole means by which government provides financial assistance to families. *The Child Support Act 1991* introduced a new system intended to remove discretion from the assessment of child maintenance and to ensure that both parents meet their responsibility towards the support of their children. The Child Support Agency was set up to replace the role of the courts in assessing, collecting and enforcing child maintenance. In 1994-95 it dealt with 568 thousand cases. The system has been reformed since its inception but the general public appear overwhelmingly to back the underlying principles of child maintenance. In 1993 over nine in ten respondents to the British Social Attitudes Survey agreed that if a married couple with a child at primary school divorce, the parent with whom the child does not stay should be made to make maintenance payments to support the child.

8.28

Recipients of benefits for families

Great Britain Thousands

	1981-82	1986-87	1991-92	1993-94
Child benefit				
Number of children	13,079	12,217	12,405	12,662
Number of families	7,174	6,816	6,854	6,960
Lone parent families				
One parent benefit only	469	606	475	535
One parent benefit and income support	146	250	361	379
Income support only	222	360	584	655
Other benefits				
Maternity allowance	115	110	18	15
Statutory maternity pay	.	.	85	85
Family credit	120	215	356	536

Source: Department of Social Security

References and further reading

The following list contains selected publications relevant to **Chapter 8: Social Protection**. Those published by HMSO are available from the addresses shown on the inside back cover of *Social Trends*.

British Social Attitudes, Dartmouth Publishing
Family Resources Survey, Department of Social Security
General Household Survey, HMSO
Health and Personal Social Services Statistics for England, HMSO
Health and Personal Social Services Statistics for Northern Ireland, Department of Health and Social Services, Northern Ireland
Health and Personal Social Services Statistics for Wales, Welsh Office
Health Survey for England, HMSO
Hospital Episode Statistics for England, Department of Health
Hospital Statistics for Northern Ireland, Department of Health and Social Services, Northern Ireland
Individual Giving and Volunteering in Britain, Charities Aid Foundation
On the State of the Public Health, HMSO
Report on Voluntary Work, HMSO
Scottish Health Statistics, National Health Service in Scotland, Common Services Agency
Social Protection Expenditure and Receipts, Eurostat
Social Security Departmental Report, HMSO
Social Security Statistics, HMSO
Social Work Services group of The Scottish Office, Statistical Bulletins
Statistical Publications on aspects of Health and Personal Social Services activity in England (various), Department of Health

Contacts

Telephone contact points for further information relating to

Chapter 8: Social Protection

Department of Health	
Adults' services	0171 972 5582
Children's services	0171 972 5575
Community and environmental health service	0171 972 5536
Financial data	0171 972 5593
General dental and community dental service	0171 972 5536
General medical services manpower	01532 545909
General ophthalmic services	0171 972 5507
General pharmacy services	0171 972 5504
Mental illness/handicap	0171 972 5546
NHS medical Staff	01532 545882
NHS non-medical manpower	01532 545905
Non-psychiatric hospital activity	0171 972 5525
Personal social services budget data	0171 210 5699
Prescription analysis	0171 972 5519
Staffing	0171 972 5595
Waiting lists	01532 545549
Department of Health and Social Services, Northern Ireland	
Health and personal social services activity	01232 522800
Social security	01232 522280
Health and personal social services manpower	01232 522008
Office of Population Censuses and Surveys	0171 396 2327
Department of Finance and Personnel, Northern Ireland	01232 521481
The Scottish Office, Social Work Services Group	0131 244 5431
National Health Service in Scotland, Common Services Agency	0131 551 8899
Welsh Office	01222 825041
Department of Social Security	0171 962 28248
Charities Aid Foundation	01732 520000
Social & Community Planning Research	0171 250 1866 extn 369
Eurostat	00 352 4301 34567

Chapter 9 Crime and Justice

Offences

Many offences are never reported to the police. Almost half of offences in England and Wales involving wounding go unreported as do almost a third of domestic burglaries. (Table 9.2)

Burglary, theft and handling stolen goods accounted for almost three quarters of all notifiable offences recorded by the police in England and Wales in 1994. (Table 9.3)

Rates of recorded crime vary considerably between regions. In 1994 there were over 15 recorded notifiable offences per hundred population in Humberside compared with just 4 per hundred population in Northern Ireland (Chart 9.4)

Offenders

Just over two fifths of offenders in England and Wales in 1994 were aged under 21. (Page 163)

Victims

Young men are more likely to be victims of violence than young women: around one in seven men aged 16 to 29 was the victim of violence in 1993 compared with only around one in twelve women. (Table 9.9)

Police and courts action

The average length of sentence for a male adult sentenced at the Crown Court in England and Wales was 22 months in 1994 compared with 17 months in 1981. (Table 9.16)

Prisons and probation

On average, each female prisoner in Great Britain committed 3.4 offences against prison discipline in 1994, compared with 2.3 offences for male prisoners. (Table 9.22)

Civil justice

There were 41 thousand complaints against the police in England, Wales and Northern Ireland in 1994 of which only 2 per cent were substantiated. (Table 9.26)

9.1

Notifiable offences[1] recorded by the police

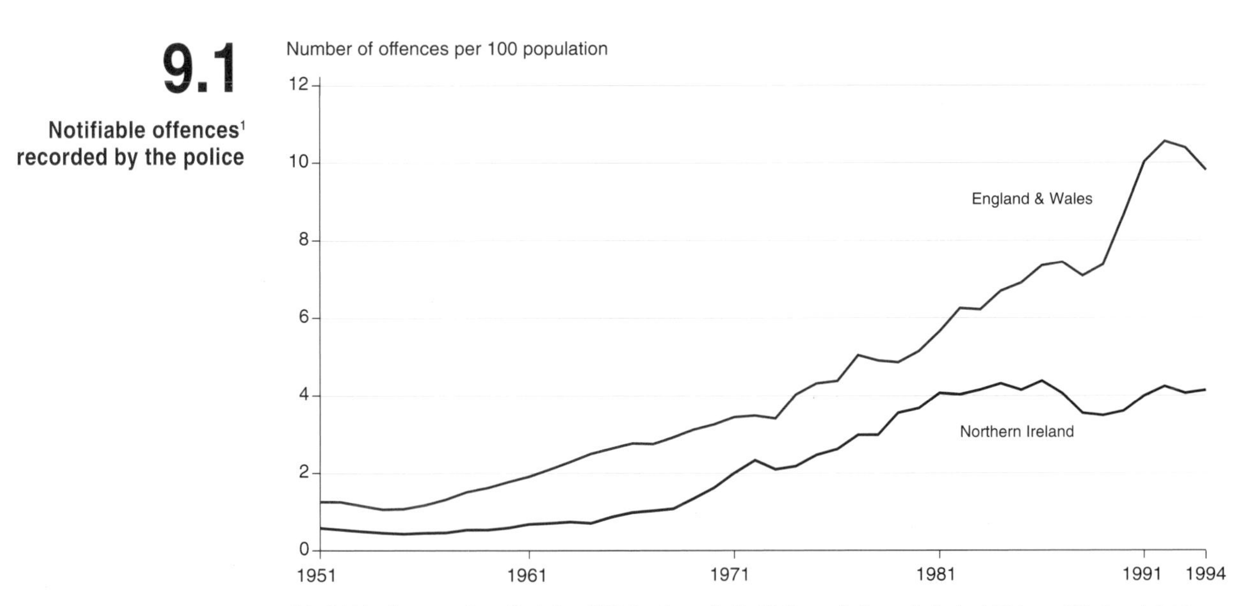

1 *Indictable offences up to and including 1978. See Appendix, Part 9: Types of offences in England, Wales and Northern Ireland.*

Source: Home Office; Royal Ulster Constabulary

9.2

Crimes committed: by outcome[1], 1993

England & Wales				Percentages
	Wounding	Domestic burglary	Vandalism	All offences[2]
Reported	*54*	*69*	*27*	*47*
Recorded	*24*	*41*	*14*	*27*
Cleared up	*19*	*8*	*2*	*5*
Resulting in caution or conviction	*14*	*2*	*2*	*3*

1 As a percentage of offences committed.
2 Offences shown plus theft of, or from, a motor vehicle (including attempts), bicycle theft, robbery and theft from the person.
Source: British Crime Survey, Home Office

Crime and its consequences are a perennial problem for government and society. This chapter explores its nature and impact, and the measures used to deal with it.

England and Wales, Scotland and Northern Ireland are often shown separately in this chapter because of their different legal systems.

Offences

Many crimes are never reported to the police; some may be reported but, for a number of reasons, the police may decide not to record them. For instance, it may be felt that there is insufficient evidence or that the incident reported does not meet the definition of a crime. The best measure of the number of crimes actually committed therefore comes not from police records but from surveys which ask the public about their experiences of crime.

Information on crimes in England and Wales is gathered in the British Crime Survey (BCS). The latest survey, undertaken in 1994, collected information from almost 15 thousand people about their experience of crime in 1993. The survey covers crimes against individuals and their property but excludes those against organisations and people aged under 16 and crimes such as drug abuse where the victim is also the perpetrator. The BCS indicates that in 1993 just under half of the number of offences which were committed were reported to the police while just over a quarter were recorded by them; one in twenty were cleared up and just under one in thirty resulted in a caution or conviction **(Table 9.2)**. Reasons for not reporting a crime are dealt with in Chart 9.12.

9.3

Notifiable offences[1] recorded by the police: by type of offence, 1981 and 1994

						Thousands
	England & Wales		Scotland		Northern Ireland	
	1981	1994	1981	1994	1981	1994[2]
Theft and handling stolen goods,	1,603	2,561	201	235	25	33
of which: theft of vehicles	333	534	33	42	5	9
theft from vehicles	380	844	..	80	7	7
Burglary	718	1,261	96	88	20	17
Fraud and forgery	107	146	21	24	3	5
Violence against the person	100	220	8	14	3	5
Criminal damage[3]	387	930	62	89	5	3
Robbery	20	60	4	5	3	2
Sexual offences,	19	32	2	4	-	1
of which: rape	1	5	-	1	-	-
Drug trafficking	..	18	2	6	-	-
Other notifiable offences[4]	9	25	12	62	3	2
All notifiable offences	2,964	5,258	408	527	62	68

1 See Appendix, Part 9: Types of offences in England, Wales and Northern Ireland and Offences and crimes.
2 No longer includes assault on police and communicating false information regarding a bomb hoax. These offences have been removed from the categories 'Violence against the person' and 'Other notifiable offences'.
3 In Northern Ireland excludes criminal damage valued at £200 or less.
4 In Northern Ireland includes 'possession of controlled drugs' and 'offences against the state'.
Source: Home Office; The Scottish Office Home Department; Royal Ulster Constabulary

A similar survey, the Scottish Crime Survey, is undertaken by the Scottish Office Home Department. The latest survey which was in respect of 1992 suggests that in Scotland a higher proportion of crimes were reported (52 per cent) and recorded (39 per cent) than in England and Wales.

While the number of notifiable offences recorded by the police does not therefore give the full picture, it does give the only available detailed analysis of all offences. However, due to differences in the legal system, recording practices and classification, United Kingdom comparisons should only be made with care: in Scotland the term 'crimes' is used for the more serious criminal acts (roughly equivalent to indictable offences) while less serious crimes are termed 'offences'; in Northern Ireland the definitions used are broadly comparable with those used in England and Wales.

The number of notifiable offences recorded by the police in England and Wales increased steadily from the early 1950s, when there were less than half a million offences per year, up to 1992 when there were 5.6 million - the highest number ever recorded. In 1993 the number fell slightly and then fell again to under 5.3 million in 1994. In Northern Ireland there were 68 thousand recorded notifiable offences in 1994 - around the same amount as in the previous two years. The trend in Scotland since the 1950s has been very similar to that in England and Wales with a peak of 593 thousand crimes in 1991. Since then the number has fallen by 11 per cent to 527 thousand crimes in 1994.

An analysis of the different offences recorded by the police shows that between 1981 and 1994 some offences appear to have increased at a much faster rate than others (**Table 9.3**). For example, in England and Wales recorded offences of robbery tripled while fraud and forgery increased by just over a third. In 1994 almost half of all offences notified to the police were for theft and handling stolen goods and almost a quarter were for burglary.

While trends in the number of offences recorded give some idea of the extent to which people are becoming more or less likely to commit offences, other factors have to be taken into account. For example, it is believed that people are now more likely to report some offences. Hence, while between 1981 and 1993 the number of crimes recorded by the BCS showed an increase of only 77 per cent, for the same types of offences police records showed an increase of 111 per cent.

One of the other factors which should be taken into account is the change in the population size. **Chart 9.1** shows that in England and Wales there were 1.2 recorded offences per 100 population in 1951 compared with a peak of 10.5 in 1992 and 9.8 in 1994. In Northern Ireland the number rose from less than 1 offence per 100 population in 1951 to peak at 4.4 in 1986; the rate was 4.1 in 1994. In Scotland there was a peak of 11.6 crimes per 100 population in 1991 falling to 10.3 in 1994.

An analysis of offences per head of population for each of the police force areas in England, Wales and Northern Ireland is given in **Chart 9.4**. This shows that Humberside had the highest crime rate in 1994 with over 15 recorded notifiable offences per 100 population while the Royal Ulster Constabulary had the lowest rate with just over four. Generally speaking, it is the areas which include large urban conurbations (such as Yorkshire and Cleveland) which have the highest rates.

9.4

Notifiable offences[1]: by police force area, 1994

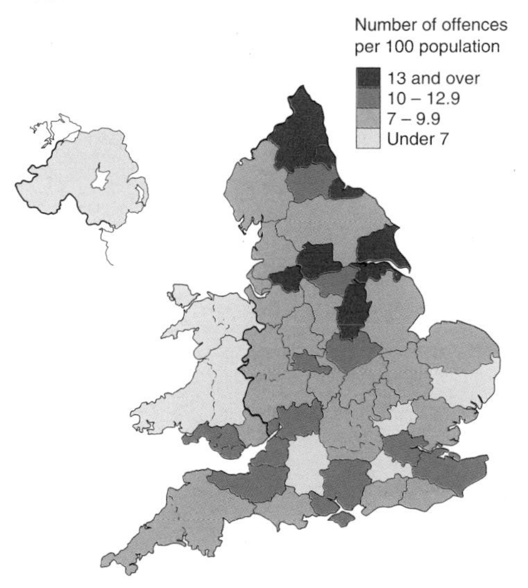

1 See Appendix, Part 9: Types of offences in England, Wales and Northern Ireland.

Source: Home Office; Royal Ulster Constabulary

9.5

Change in number of crimes[1] recorded by the police: international comparison, 1993 to 1994

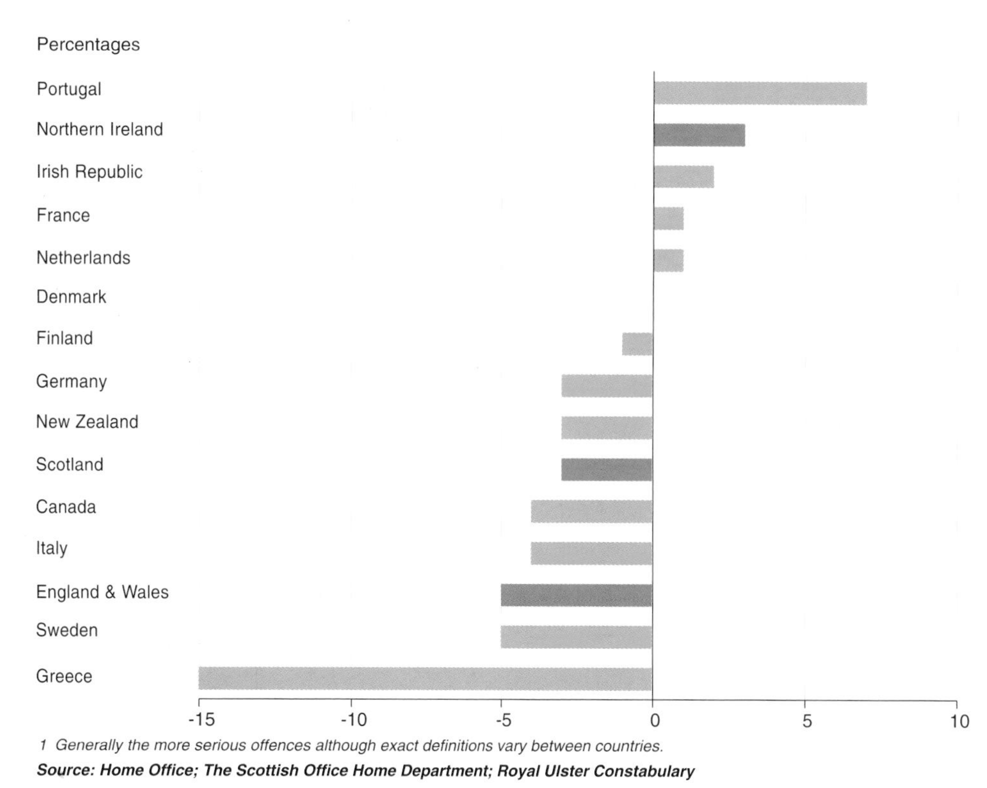

1 Generally the more serious offences although exact definitions vary between countries.

Source: Home Office; The Scottish Office Home Department; Royal Ulster Constabulary

Some other countries have also experienced a rise in recorded crime from the mid-1980s up to the early 1990s but a drop in the most recent years: for example, Finland, Italy and Canada **(Chart 9.5)**. However, in other countries recorded crime has continued to increase: of those countries shown in the chart the biggest rise between 1993 and 1994 was in Portugal at 7 per cent. It must of course be borne in mind that precise comparisons cannot be made because of differing legal systems.

Offenders

In 1994 over 520 thousand people in England and Wales were found guilty or cautioned for an indictable offence **(Table 9.6)**. This compares with a peak of almost

9.6

Offenders found guilty of, or cautioned for, indictable offences[1]: by gender, age and type of offence, 1994

England & Wales — Percentages

	Males					Females				
	10-13	14-17	18-20	21 and over	All aged 10 and over	10-13	14-17	18-20	21 and over	All aged 10 and over
Theft and handling stolen goods	*60*	*47*	*36*	*37*	*40*	*85*	*72*	*62*	*61*	*66*
Other indictable offences	*2*	*6*	*15*	*21*	*16*	*1*	*4*	*14*	*18*	*12*
Drug offences	*1*	*10*	*22*	*16*	*15*	*1*	*4*	*11*	*9*	*7*
Violence against the person	*10*	*13*	*10*	*13*	*12*	*8*	*14*	*9*	*9*	*10*
Burglary	*18*	*17*	*13*	*8*	*11*	*3*	*3*	*2*	*1*	*2*
Criminal damage	*6*	*4*	*3*	*3*	*3*	*1*	*2*	*1*	*1*	*1*
Sexual offences	*1*	*1*	*1*	*2*	*2*	*0*	*0*	*0*	*0*	*0*
Robbery	*2*	*2*	*1*	*1*	*1*	*1*	*1*	*0*	*0*	[illegible]
All indictable offences (=100%)(thousands)	22.8	80.6	75.3	248.1	426.8	9.4	23.0	12.3	51.0	95.7

1 See Appendix, Part 9: Types of offences in England, Wales and Northern Ireland.

Source: Home Office

600 thousand in 1985 - nearly four times the number in 1951. In 1994 two fifths of male offenders and two thirds of female offenders had been found guilty of, or cautioned for, theft and handling stolen goods. However, these proportions vary according to the age of the offender; three fifths of male offenders aged between 10 and 13 had been found guilty or cautioned for theft and handing stolen goods compared with less than two fifths of those aged 21 and over. In Scotland, in 1993, there were 160 thousand people with charges proved for crimes which compares with just under 100 thousand in 1951.

Just over two fifths of offenders in England and Wales in 1994 were aged under 21. Trends in criminal activities can be analysed using the Offender's Index - one of the largest criminal databases in Europe. It covers all indictable offences, triable either way offences and some summary offences in England and Wales from 1963 to 1994 and holds nearly 6 million criminal histories. Data from the index show that 8 per cent of males born in 1958 had made one court appearance before they were 17 compared with just over 3 per cent born in 1973 **(Table 9.7)**. This most likely reflects the increased use of cautioning. In Scotland, 5 per cent of the male population born between July 1975 and June 1976 had a conviction by the time they were 17; less than 1 per cent had four or more convictions by this age. However, since less use is made of cautioning in Scotland, these data should not be directly compared with those for England and Wales.

9.7

Percentage of males who have appeared in court: by year of birth and number of appearances

England & Wales Percentages

	Year of birth				
	1953	1958	1963	1968	1973
Before age 17					
1 court appearance	*7.7*	*8.0*	*7.6*	*6.2*	*3.1*
4 or more	*1.1*	*1.5*	*1.4*	*1.4*	*0.8*
Before age 21					
1 court appearance	*12.8*	*13.4*	*13.2*	*11.3*	..
4 or more	*3.3*	*4.4*	*5.0*	*4.3*	..

Source: Home Office

Any action against an offender taken by the police or courts will, in part at least, be intended as a deterrent against reoffending. The likelihood of reoffending varies according to a number of factors including age, gender and number of previous convictions. Despite the deterrent of one or more previous sentences, of those commencing probation, community service or discharged from prison in England and Wales between 1987 and 1990, nearly three in five males and one in five females were reconvicted within two years. **Chart 9.8** shows the length of time to reconviction for offenders who had been released from prison service establishments in 1991 and had subsequently been reconvicted for a standard-list offence. Almost three quarters of such young male offenders were reconvicted within two years while an eighth were reconvicted within just three months.

9.8

Time to reconviction[1]: by gender and age[2]

England & Wales

Percentages

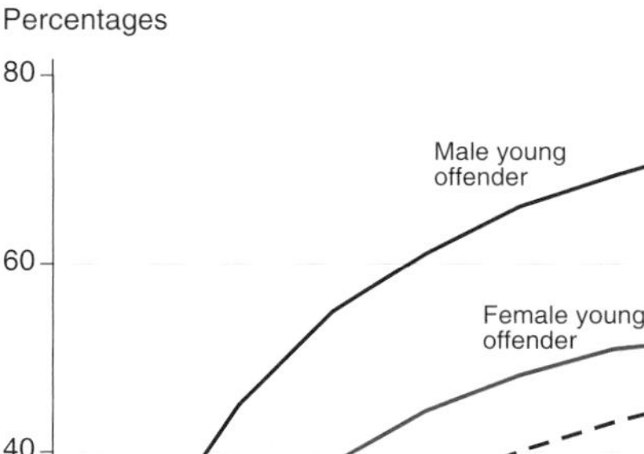

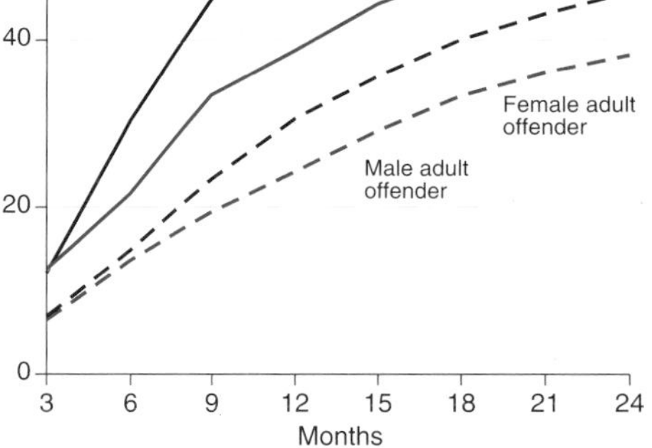

1 Time between discharge from prison in 1991 and first reconviction for a standard list offence. See Appendix, Part 9: Types of offences.
2 Adults are aged 21 and over on the sentencing date; young offenders are aged under 21 on the sentencing date.
Source: Home Office

9.9

Victims of violence[1]: by gender and age, 1993

England & Wales						Percentages
	Males			Females		
	16-29	30-59	60 and over	16-29	30-59	60 and over
Domestic	*1.1*	*0.6*	*0.1*	*3.6*	*1.5*	*0.1*
Mugging	*1.9*	*0.5*	*0.2*	*0.7*	*0.6*	*0.3*
Other	*12.1*	*3.4*	*0.4*	*4.5*	*1.6*	*0.3*
All victims of violence	*14.5*	*4.4*	*0.7*	*8.3*	*3.5*	*0.8*

1 Percentage in each age group who had been a victim once or more.

Source: British Crime Survey, Home Office

9.10

Victims of crime[1]: by ethnic group, 1993

England & Wales				Percentages
	White	Afro-Caribbean	Asian	All ethnic groups
Household offences				
Home vandalism	*4.3*	*3.9*	*4.8*	*4.3*
Burglary	*6.3*	*12.9*	*8.0*	*6.5*
Vehicle crime (owners)				
Vandalism	*8.1*	*12.1*	*9.8*	*8.2*
All thefts	*19.6*	*25.7*	*23.0*	*19.7*
Other	*10.2*	*9.5*	*8.9*	*10.1*
All household offences	*32.6*	*36.2*	*34.3*	*32.6*
Personal offences				
Assaults	*3.8*	*6.6*	*3.1*	*3.8*
Threats	*3.5*	*4.0*	*3.2*	*3.4*
Robbery/theft from person	*1.7*	*2.7*	*3.4*	*1.8*
Other personal theft	*3.7*	*5.2*	*3.2*	*3.7*
All personal offences[2]	*8.5*	*13.2*	*9.3*	*8.6*

1 Percentage in each ethnic group who had been a victim once or more.
2 Excludes sexual offences.

Source: British Crime Survey, Home Office

Victims

An offender may well have to pay some compensation to his or her victim. In 1994, 90 thousand offenders in England and Wales were ordered by a magistrate's court to pay an average of £163 compensation while over 6 thousand offenders were ordered by the Crown Court to pay an average of £2,087 each.

The majority of victims are victims of theft, burglary and criminal damage; only a small proportion of the population is affected by violent crime. **Table 9.9** shows how the likelihood of assault is linked to age and gender, with the greatest risks being for those in the 16 to 29 age group. Almost one in eight males in this age group was the victim of forms of violence other than domestic violence and mugging; these included incidents at various locations including the street, pubs and clubs and the work place. In 1993, one in seven males and one in twelve females in this age group were the victim of a non-sexual assault.

Ethnic origin is another factor which appears to have some effect on the likelihood of being a victim of crime. The BCS shows that in 1993 someone from the Afro-Caribbean group was around twice as likely to be the victim of a burglary as a White person **(Table 9.10)**. These figures should not, however, be interpreted as an indication of the level of racially motivated crime as the risk of being a victim of crime is determined by many factors. For example, the risk of burglary in an inner city area is around twice the national average. Since there is a higher proportion of ethnic minorities in metropolitan districts and London than elsewhere, this alone makes ethnic minorities more vulnerable.

One way in which people feel that they can help reduce the chances of being a victim of damage to, or theft from, their property is by joining a Neighbourhood Watch (NW) scheme. At the end of 1994, 143 thousand schemes were in operation in England and Wales. The aim of the schemes is to promote an awareness of crime prevention methods and encourage people to look out for suspicious behaviour. **Table 9.11** shows how members of a NW scheme appear to be more security minded than those who are not; for example, almost one in three of NW members had security markings on property compared with less than one in six of non-members. In 1994 only an eighth of households in high-risk areas were a member of a scheme compared with a third of households in low-risk areas. However, a greater proportion of elderly households appear to be joining.

While Table 9.2 showed that less than half of offences are reported, **Chart 9.12** shows the reasons why people do not report crime. In just over a third of cases in England and Wales it was because the crime was considered too trivial or because no loss had been suffered. A further third of crimes were not reported because it was thought that the police would not be able to take any action. The reasons for not reporting vary by offence. For example, a higher than average proportion of personal thefts, often taking place at work, were not reported to the police because they would have been reported to an employer. In addition, the loss of comparatively low value property may be reported if an insurance claim is being made. Conversely, when victims know the offender they may decide not to report the matter to the police even if the offence was serious; in 1993 only around two fifths of the most serious assaults were reported, probably because of the victim-offender relationship.

9.11

Actions by members and non-members of Neighbourhood Watch, 1993

England & Wales Percentages

	Members	Non-members
Good door locks[1]	*77*	*68*
Told neighbour when home was empty	*72*	*59*
Good window locks[2]	*70*	*59*
Lights on timers/sensor switches	*40*	*29*
Marked bikes	*33*	*24*
Marked household property	*32*	*15*
Burglar alarm	*26*	*16*
Home security surveyed by police	*11*	*5*

1 Some double locks or deadlocks on outside doors.
2 Some locks that need keys.
Source: British Crime Survey, Home Office

9.12

Reasons for not reporting crime[1], 1993

England & Wales
Percentages

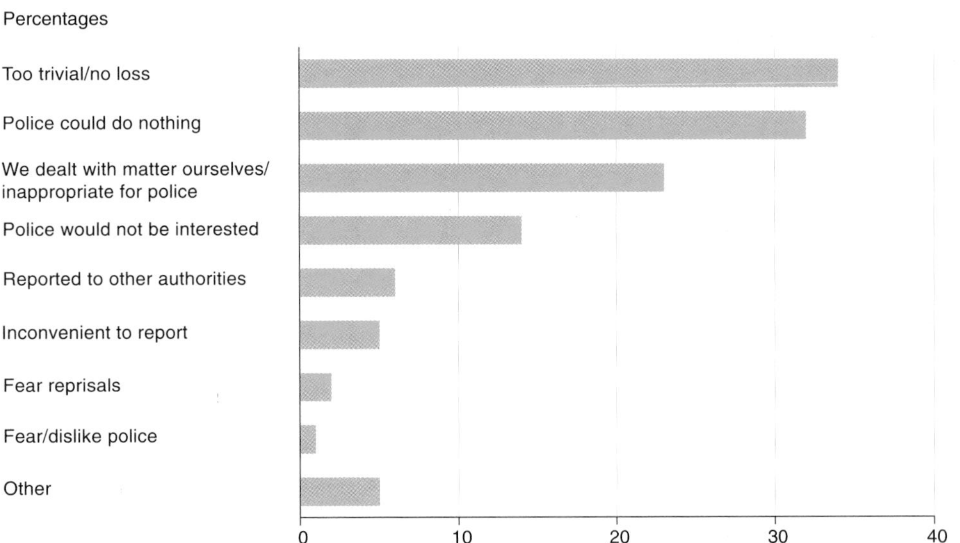

1 As a percentage of those who experienced a crime and did not report it to the police. More than one reason could be given.
Source: British Crime Survey, Home Office

9.13

Offenders cautioned for indictable offences[1]: by type of offence

England & Wales Percentages

	1971[2]	1981	1991	1994
Theft and handling stolen goods	*69.2*	*76.2*	*60.3*	*52.8*
Drug offences[3]	..	*0.3*	*11.8*	*21.1*
Violence against the person	*3.0*	*5.4*	*10.8*	*11.2*
Burglary[4]	*16.0*	*10.8*	*7.4*	*5.5*
Fraud and forgery	*1.3*	*1.3*	*3.1*	*3.6*
Criminal damage	*4.7*	*2.0*	*2.1*	*2.1*
Sexual offences	*5.0*	*2.7*	*1.8*	*1.4*
Robbery	*0.3*	*0.1*	*0.3*	*0.3*
Other[3]	*0.4*	*1.3*	*2.3*	*1.9*
All offenders cautioned (=100%) (thousands)	77.3	103.9	179.9	209.8

1 Excludes motoring offences.
2 Adjusted to take account of the Criminal Damage Act 1971.
3 Data for 1971 are included in 'Other'.
4 See Appendix, Part 9: Offenders cautioned for burglary.

Source: Home Office

Police and courts action

In England, Wales and Northern Ireland, following an arrest the police may: release a suspect without further action; caution, either informally or formally; or charge. In 1994, 210 thousand people in England and Wales were cautioned for indictable offences - a slight fall from the peak of 216 thousand in 1992 **(Table 9.13)**. Prior to this the number had risen steadily from 1979 when only 97 thousand cautions were given. The change in this trend probably reflects the issuing of draft Home Office guidance in 1993 which discouraged the use of cautions for serious offences and for offenders who had been cautioned previously.

In 1994 almost 800 thousand offenders were sentenced (other than for motoring offences) in courts in England, Wales and Northern Ireland. Two fifths of these had been found guilty of an indictable offence. **Table 9.14** shows that just under a third of those

9.14

Offenders sentenced for indictable offences[1]: by type of offence and type of sentence[2], 1994

England, Wales & Northern Ireland Percentages

					Immediate custody			
	Discharge	Fine	Community sentence	Fully suspended sentence	Under 5 years	5 years and over	Other	All sentenced (=100%) (thousands)[2]
Theft and handling stolen goods	*26*	*32*	*29*	*1*	*11*	-	*1*	124.5
Violence against the person	*22*	*17*	*32*	*2*	*20*	*2*	*5*	39.1
Burglary	*11*	*8*	*45*	*1*	*34*	-	*1*	38.9
Motoring	*15*	*53*	*14*	*1*	*12*	-	*5*	38.9
Drug offences	*16*	*52*	*16*	*1*	*12*	*2*	-	28.3
Fraud and forgery	*22*	*25*	*34*	*2*	*14*	-	*2*	19.0
Criminal damage	*29*	*19*	*32*	*2*	*10*	*1*	*8*	11.1
Robbery	*4*	*1*	*24*	*1*	*49*	*16*	*5*	5.1
Sexual offences	*10*	*13*	*27*	*3*	*33*	*11*	*3*	4.6
Other	*7*	*65*	*15*	*1*	*12*	-	*1*	12.3
All indictable offences	*20*	*31*	*28*	*1*	*16*	*1*	*2*	321.8

1 See Appendix, Part 9: Types of offences in England, Wales and Northern Ireland.
2 See Appendix, Part 9: Sentences and orders.

Source: Home Office; Northern Ireland Office

9.15

Court proceedings for persons[1] with charge proved: by type of crime or offence and type of sentence[2], 1993

Scotland								Percentages
	Admonished	Probation	Compensation order	Fine	Community service	Custody	Other	All outcomes (=100%) (thousands)
Crimes								
Crimes of dishonesty	*13*	*9*	*2*	*46*	*7*	*23*	*1*	31.0
Crimes against property	*10*	*4*	*11*	*64*	*3*	*7*	*1*	5.0
Non-sexual crimes of violence	*10*	*10*	*1*	*29*	*11*	*39*	*1*	3.9
Crimes of indecency	*10*	*12*	-	*62*	*2*	*13*	*1*	1.5
Other crimes	*13*	*5*	-	*59*	*5*	*17*	*1*	11.0
All crimes	*12*	*8*	*2*	*49*	*7*	*21*	*1*	52.3
Offences								
Motor vehicle offences	*4*	-	-	*93*	*1*	*2*	-	61.8
Miscellaneous offences	*16*	*3*	*1*	*70*	*2*	*7*	*1*	47.5
All offences	*9*	*1*	-	*83*	*2*	*4*	-	109.3
All crimes and offences	*10*	*3*	*1*	*72*	*3*	*9*	*1*	161.6

1 Includes companies.
2 See Appendix, Part 9: Sentences and orders.
Source: The Scottish Office Home Department

sentenced for an indictable offence were fined while a slightly smaller proportion received a community sentence. The equivalent breakdown for Scotland is in **Table 9.15**; in 1993 almost three quarters of people with a charged proved received a fine.

Custodial sentences will normally be imposed on the most serious, dangerous and persistent offenders. In 1994 the average custodial sentence, excluding life sentences, given to an adult male (aged 21 or over) by the Crown Court was 22 months - an increase from 17 months in 1981 (**Table 9.16**). The equivalent sentence for a woman of the same age was 18 months in 1994 and just 11 months in 1981. In 1993 the average sentence length for an adult male sentenced at the Scottish High Court (the function of which is not directly comparable to the Crown Court in England and Wales) was 52 months. In Northern Ireland the average sentence length for an adult male at the Crown Court in 1994 was 48 months.

9.16

Average sentence length for adults[1] sentenced at the Crown Court: by gender and type of offence

England & Wales						Months
	Males			Females		
	1981	1991	1994	1981	1991	1994
Drug offences	26	33	30	19	37	35
Sexual offences	28	38	39	20	29	33
Robbery	39	48	50	21	34	31
Criminal damage	19	22	28	14	24	30
Violence against the person	17	20	23	13	20	21
Burglary	17	16	17	11	13	15
Fraud and forgery	16	16	15	10	12	11
Theft and handling stolen goods	11	10	11	7	8	9
Motoring offences	6	8	9	4	9	7
Other	11	12	12	11	14	10
All offences	17	21	22	11	18	18

1 Defendants aged 21 and over sentenced to immediate custody; excludes life sentences.
Source: Home Office

9.17

Clear-up rates for notifiable offences[1]: by type of offence, 1981 and 1994

Percentages

	England & Wales		Scotland		Northern Ireland	
	1981	1994	1981	1994	1981	1994[2]
Sexual offences,	73	76	65	80	71	89
of which: rape	68	74	74	79	45	69
Drug trafficking[3]	..	102	99	100	100	87
Violence against the person	75	77	83	77	47	67
Fraud and forgery	70	52	78	79	66	65
Theft and handling stolen goods,	38	24	28	26	27	31
of which: theft of vehicles	28	19	26	24	14	19
theft from vehicles	23	13	..	14	12	8
Criminal damage[4]	27	17	22	20	17	36
Burglary	30	21	20	17	22	20
Robbery	25	22	26	29	15	20
Other notifiable offences[5]	91	94	90	98	33	88
All notifiable offences	38	26	31	37	27	36

1 See Appendix, Part 9: Types of offences in England, Wales and Northern Ireland and Offences and crimes.
2 No longer includes assault on police and communicating false information regarding a bomb hoax. These offences have been removed from the categories 'Violence against the person' and 'Other notifiable offences'.
3 In England and Wales offences cleared up in 1994 may have been initially recorded in an earlier year.
4 In Northern Ireland excludes criminal damage valued at £200 or less.
5 In Northern Ireland includes 'possession of controlled drugs' and 'offences against the state'.
Source: Home Office; The Scottish Office Home Department; Royal Ulster Constabulary

Offences may be cleared-up by primary means when someone is charged, summonsed or cautioned, or by secondary means when a prisoner admits to further offences. **Table 9.17** shows how the overall clear-up rates for notifiable offences vary by type of offence. In Northern Ireland less than one in ten offences of theft and handling stolen goods from a motor vehicle was cleared up compared with almost nine in ten sexual offences. In England and Wales, only just over a quarter of notifiable offences were cleared up in 1994 compared with almost two fifths in 1981. In Scotland and Northern Ireland, rates have risen between these two years.

Rates also vary by police force area. Based on primary rates, the Dyfed-Powys force achieved the highest clear-up rate in England and Wales in 1994, at 46 per cent, while the West Midlands had the lowest rate at 16 per cent. The Royal Ulster Constabulary cleared up over a third of notifiable offences. In Scotland, where the primary and secondary distinction does not exist, the best clear-up rates were achieved by the Central and Northern forces where nearly three fifths of recorded crimes were solved.

9.18

Receptions under sentence[1] into prison service establishments

England & Wales

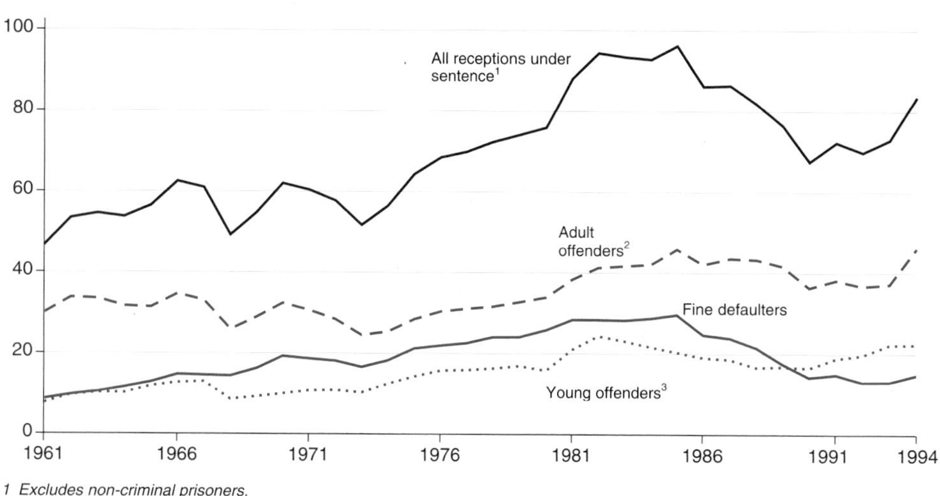

1 Excludes non-criminal prisoners.
2 Includes approved places; excludes fine defaulters.
3 Excludes fine defaulters. See also Appendix, Part 9: Young offenders institutions.
Source: Home Office

Prisons and probation

In 1994, 57 thousand untried and 35 thousand convicted but not sentenced prisoners were received into custody in England and Wales. The remainder were non-criminal prisoners or were received into custody under sentence. There was a 15 per cent increase in the number received under sentence between 1993 and 1994 **(Chart 9.18)**. This sharp rise can partly be attributed to the implementation of the *Criminal Justice Act 1993*. This allows the court to take into account previous convictions or failure to respond to earlier sentences which was previously only allowed in certain circumstances - offending while on bail must now also be taken into account. The rise in receptions also reflects new sentencing guidelines in magistrates' courts. Despite this increase, receptions of sentenced prisoners were still below the record intake of over 96 thousand in 1985. Young offenders aged under 21 (excluding fine defaulters) accounted for nearly a fifth of receptions in 1994 with fine defaulters being just over a quarter of the total.

In Northern Ireland 2.8 thousand people were received into custody under sentence in 1994 - the lowest number since 1984. Over a half of these were fine defaulters which was double the proportion in England and Wales. In Scotland over 21 thousand were received into custody under sentence in 1994 - slightly fewer than in the previous year.

As mentioned above, some of those in custody are on remand; that is they are either untried or convicted but not sentenced. In 1994 there were on average over 12 thousand remand prisoners in England and Wales which was the highest figure ever. Around three quarters of those on remand were untried. The average time spent in prison in England and Wales in 1994 by those who were untried was 59 days for males and 44 days for females **(Chart 9.20)**. In 1977 it was 29 days for a male and 22 days for a female. For those who were convicted but unsentenced in 1994 the average periods in custody were 34 days and 28 days respectively. As can be seen from the chart these times have remained broadly similar for some years. Average time in prison for remand prisoners is much less in Scotland; the average period spent on remand for untried male receptions in 1994 was 16 days.

9.19

Prison population[1] and accommodation[2]

Great Britain

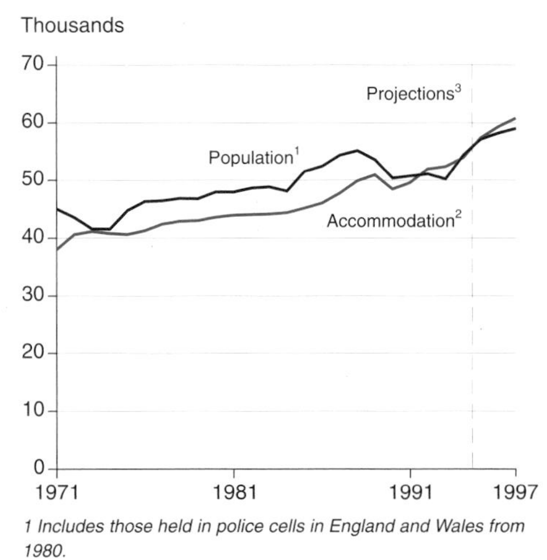

1 Includes those held in police cells in England and Wales from 1980.
2 Certified Normal Accommodation in England and Wales from 1993 excludes accommodation which is not yet operational.
3 At Spring 1995.
Source: Home Office; The Scottish Office Home Department

Mainly as a result of the recent increase in the number of people being taken into custody, the prison population in Great Britain was 8 per cent higher in 1994 than in the previous year and at its highest level since 1988 **(Chart 9.19)**. Hence there were over 54 thousand people in prison service establishments in Great Britain in 1994; the projections produced in Spring 1995 showed a rise to around 59 thousand in 1997. The chart also shows that throughout most of the 1970s and 1980s the prison population exceeded the certified normal accommodation of the prisons. In 1992 and 1993 the reverse was true but in 1994 the increase in the prison population meant that the number in prison service establishments again exceeded the certified normal accommodation. However, in England and Wales in 1994 only 17 per cent of prisoners were sharing two or more to a cell compared with 28 per cent in 1991.

9.20

Average time spent in prison service establishments by remand prisoners: by gender

England & Wales

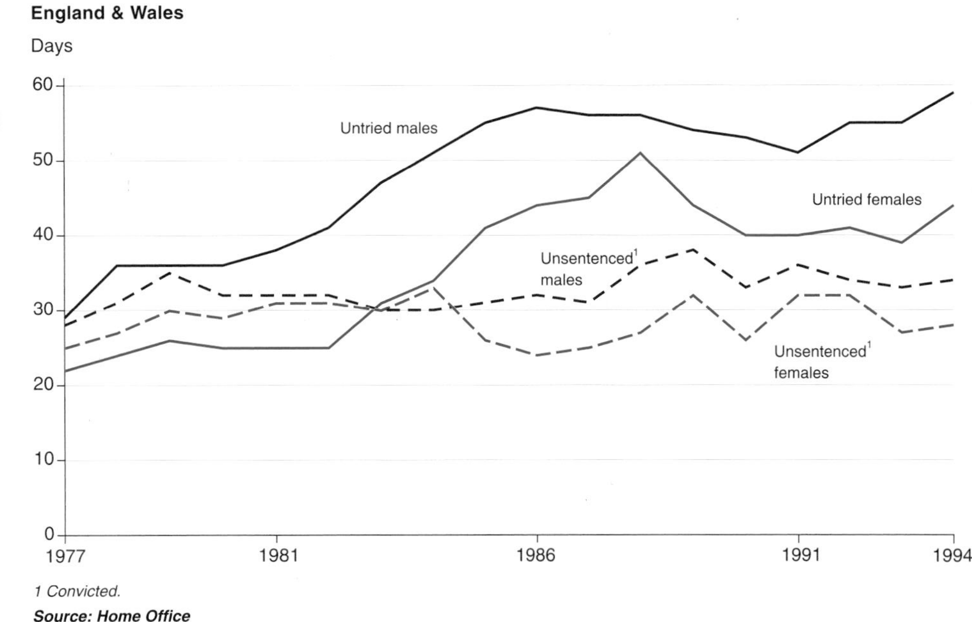

1 Convicted.
Source: Home Office

9.21

Average time spent per prisoner on purposeful activity: by type of establishment[1], 1993-94

England & Wales Hours per week

	Education[2]	Employment	Domestic duties	Other	All purposeful activity
Establishments for males					
Category B	4.8	6.6	6.0	6.1	23.6
Category C	5.7	7.9	6.5	7.8	27.9
Category D	6.5	15.0	5.8	15.5	42.9
Local	2.7	3.4	7.8	5.3	19.2
Dispersal	4.3	4.8	7.0	4.3	20.4
Establishments for females	6.6	4.8	8.2	8.4	28.0
Young offender institutions	6.5	3.4	6.5	8.5	24.9
All prison service establishments	5.3	6.6	6.8	8.0	26.7

1 See Appendix, Part 9: Prison categories.
2 Includes vocational and construction industry training courses.
Source: Home Office

The Prison Service for England and Wales has defined its purpose as 'to look after [prisoners] with humanity and help them lead law-abiding and useful lives in custody and after release'. Table 9.21 shows some of the ways in which it is achieving this while Table 9.22 shows some of the problems encountered along the way.

Prisoners are encouraged to participate in a range of purposeful activities including education, employment and domestic duties. In 1993-94, on average, each prisoner spent over 26 hours per week on such activities **(Table 9.21)**. Over 2 thousand prisoners were registered for National Vocational Qualifications (NVQ) while 375 were taking Open University courses. For the less academically able there are special programmes devised by the Basic Skills Agency. The time that prisoners spend on such activities depends on the type of prison that they are in. Those in high security prisons (Category B), for example, spend less time on most forms of purposeful activity than those in Category D establishments while in young offender institutions there is an emphasis on education rather than on employment.

In Scotland in 1993-94 over four fifths of convicted prisoners were given the opportunity of at least 6.5 hours per working day of programmed activities including education, offence-related counselling, personal development courses and work in prison industries.

In 1994 an average of 129 remand prisoners were held in police cells in England and Wales; this compared with only 13 in 1993 but 715 in 1992. In Scotland there were 142 receptions relating to remand prisoners held in legalised police cells in 1994 compared with just over 80 in each of the previous two years.

9.22

Offences[1] against prison discipline: by type of offence and gender

Great Britain Rates per 100 prison population[2]

	Males			Females		
	1981	1991	1994	1981	1991	1994
Disobedience or disrespect	75	100	111	132	143	142
Violence	8	21	24	16	29	39
Unauthorised transactions/ possessions	19	26	40	29	30	37
Wilful damage	11	13	15	37	12	14
Escapes/absconds	5	4	3	6	9	10
Other offences	47	37	40	98	72	93
All offences	165	200	232	318	295	335

1 Proved at adjudication hearing. Includes attempts.
2 At establishments where punishment is applicable.
Source: Home Office; The Scottish Office Home Department

Maintaining discipline in prisons is a vital but sometimes difficult task. Many of the offences that are committed outside of prison are also committed in prison including assault, criminal damage and drugs-related offences. In 1994, 2.3 offences were committed and proved for every male prisoner in Great Britain and 3.3 offences for

9.23

People commencing criminal supervision orders[1]

England & Wales Thousands

	1981	1986	1991	1993	1994
Community service	28	35	42	48	50
Probation	36	40	45	43	49
Combination	.	.	.	9	12
Under the Children and Young Persons Act 1969	12	6	2	2	2
Other	7	7	8	5	5
All persons commencing supervision orders[2]	79	83	91	100	111

1 Supervised by the probation service. See Appendix Part 9: Sentences and orders.
2 Individual figures do not sum to the total because each person may have more than one type of order.
Source: Home Office

every female prisoner **(Table 9.22)**. This was 40 per cent higher for males and 5 per cent higher for females than in 1981. There are many types of punishment that can be given for offences committed in prison including confinement, forfeiture of privileges, stoppage of earnings, exclusion from work or additional days in custody.

While custody is the sentence given for the most serious offences, crimes such as burglary are more likely to result in the offender receiving a criminal supervision order. In 1994, 111 thousand people commenced a criminal supervision order in England and Wales; this was over 10 per cent more than in 1993 and over 40 per cent more than in 1981 **(Table 9.23)**. The same person may receive more than one order hence the number of orders issued exceeds the number of persons receiving orders. In 1994 over two fifths of the orders issued were probation orders and the same proportion were community service orders. In July 1995 trials began in Manchester, Norfolk and Reading of a new form of community sentence which involves offenders being electronically monitored. If an offender leaves home during a period when he or she is subject to a curfew, electronic equipment will alert a central station which will investigate the matter. In Northern Ireland, 1.8 thousand people commenced a criminal supervision order in 1994.

Civil justice

While this chapter has so far looked at cases where a charge has been made by an organisation which is a part of the official legal system such as the Crown Prosecution Service, a case may also be brought under civil law by others including an individual or a company. The majority of these cases are handled by the county courts and the High Court in England, Wales and Northern Ireland and by the Sheriff Court and court of session in Scotland. The High Court and court of session deal with the more substantial and complex cases. Civil cases may include consumer problems (such as faulty goods), claims for debt, negligence including personal injury, and recovery of land. Following the issuing of a summons or writ many cases will be settled without the need for a court hearing. **Chart 9.24** shows that in England and Wales the total number of writs and summons issued rose sharply from 1.8 million in 1976 to just over 4 million in 1991. This rise may be explained in part by the increase in lending as a consequence of financial deregulation which lead to more cases concerned with the recovery and collection of debt. By 1994 the number of writs and summonses issued had fallen to 2.8 million which in part, at least, reflected more controlled spending by creditors. In Scotland 166 thousand causes were initiated in the Sheriff Court in 1993 which was a fall from the peak of 193 thousand in 1991; just 6 thousand cases were initiated in the court of session in both years. In Northern Ireland just over 20 thousand writs, summonses and civil bills were issued in 1994.

9.24

Writs and summonses issued[1]

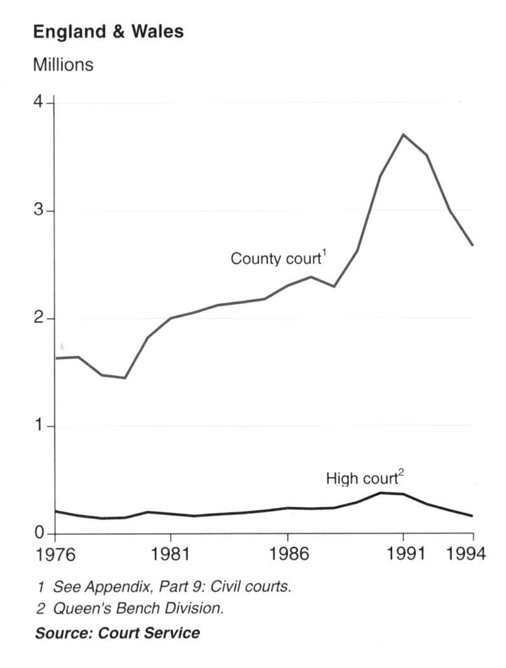

1 See Appendix, Part 9: Civil courts.
2 Queen's Bench Division.
Source: Court Service

9.25

Selected tribunals[1]

Great Britain — Thousands

	Cases received			Cases withdrawn[2]	Cases heard
	1981	1991	1994	1994	1994
General Commissioners of Income tax	..	..	..	..	215
Valuation tribunals	..	194	424	657	101
Social Security Appeal tribunal	.	197	145	22	80
Disability Appeals tribunal	.	.	31	1	28
Industrial tribunals	45	43	88	64	28
Children's Hearings (Scotland)	26	28	27	0	27
Medical Appeals tribunals	..	36	21	3	18
Immigration Adjudicators	..	..	21	..	16
Rent Assessment Committees	15	23	14	2	13
Patents, Design and Trade Marks	8	9	9	1	8
Mental Health Review tribunal	..	8	12	5	6
Social Security Commissioners	..	5	5	-	5
Pensions Appeal tribunal	3	3	8	-	4
Valuation Appeals Committee (Scotland)	7	86	20	15	4
Value Added Tax tribunals	..	5	7	3	2
Immigration Appeals tribunals	..	..	8	..	1

1 For details of coverage of individual tribunals, see Appendix, Part 9: Tribunals.
2 Before hearing.

Source: Tribunals concerned

Not all civil disputes are dealt with by a court; others may be adjudicated over by an ombudsman or by a tribunal. **Table 9.25** lists selected tribunals in Great Britain. Between them, they heard 550 thousand cases in 1994, almost two fifths of which were appeals against assessments for payment of income tax. Almost a fifth were appeals against property valuations which included appeals in connection with non-domestic rates and council tax bandings. The sharp increase in the workload of the valuations tribunals in England and Wales in 1994 was mainly the result of appeals by nearly 920 thousand households in 1992 against the initial valuation of their dwelling for council tax purposes.

Individuals and organisations may sometimes complain about some aspect of the crime and justice system itself. Complaints may be lodged against a solicitor with the Law Society; complaints are also made against the police. In 1994 over 41 thousand complaints were made against the police in England, Wales and Northern Ireland; 5 per cent more than in 1993 and 26 per cent more than in 1986 **(Table 9.26)**. Of all the complaints made in 1994, 41 per cent were withdrawn or not proceeded with and only 2 per cent were substantiated. In England and Wales in 1994 just over half of the substantiated complaints were attributed to failure in duty and nearly a quarter to oppressive behaviour. In Scotland there were just under 3 thousand complaints against the police in 1994 which was 13 per cent less than in 1993 but over half as many as in 1991. However, for the United Kingdom as a whole, the number of complaints was well exceeded by the number of commendations: over 70 thousand commendations and letter of thanks were received in 1994.

9.26

Complaints against the police

England, Wales & Northern Ireland — Percentages

	1986	1991	1993	1994
Withdrawn/not proceeded with	*39*	*42*	*41*	*41*
Informally resolved[1]	*12*	*23*	*27*	*31*
Investigated				
Unsubstantiated	*45*	*33*	*30*	*26*
Substantiated	*4*	*2*	*2*	*2*
All complaints (=100%) (thousands)	32.6	39.7	39.3	41.2

1 Not applicable to Northern Ireland in 1986.

Source: Home Office; Royal Ulster Constabulary

Resources

In 1994 public expenditure on justice and law stood at over £14 billion. Just over half of this was spent on maintaining the police force and a further 15 per cent on the law courts. The proportion spent on legal aid doubled between 1982 and 1994 to 10 per cent. In order to ensure continuing 'value for money' the Audit Commission has undertaken 12 national studies of the police force since 1988. Some £14 million of potential savings were identified of which £10 million have already been achieved. Almost half of these savings came from the reorganisation of the management of vehicles.

Looking in more detail at the expenditure of the police forces, **Chart 9.27** shows how the net cost per head of population of operating the police services in the United Kingdom varied between the different forces in 1994-95. Within England and Wales it ranged from £220 per person for the Metropolitan Police to only £83 per person for the Cambridgeshire force.

These differences should not, however, be interpreted as a measure of efficiency. There are a number of reasons why net expenditure will be higher for some forces than others. The Metropolitan Police, for example, regularly have to deal with marches and rallies which are comparatively rare in other parts of the country. In addition some forces provide specialised training facilities which are used by other forces. Net expenditure for the Scottish police forces in 1994-95 varied from £91 per person for the Grampian force to just over £120 per person for the Lothian and Borders and Stathclyde forces. In Northern Ireland the security situation has contributed heavily to the cost of maintaining the Royal Ulster Constabulary: the cost here, which is on a slightly different basis to that elsewhere, was £366 per person in 1994-95.

Labour costs form the largest component of police force expenditure; in 1994-95 they accounted for over four fifths of the total for England and Wales. In 1994 just over 200 thousand people were employed in the police service (including civilians) in Great Britain - an increase of two fifths since 1971 **(Table 9.28)**. In 1994, 38 thousand were also employed in the prison service in England and Wales. In Northern Ireland over 13 thousand police were employed in the police service in 1994 - almost two and a half times more than in 1971. In 1994, with an additional 3 thousand civilian staff included, there were 98 persons employed in the police service in Northern Ireland for every 10 thousand population.

9.27

Police force net expenditure[1]: by police force area, 1994-95

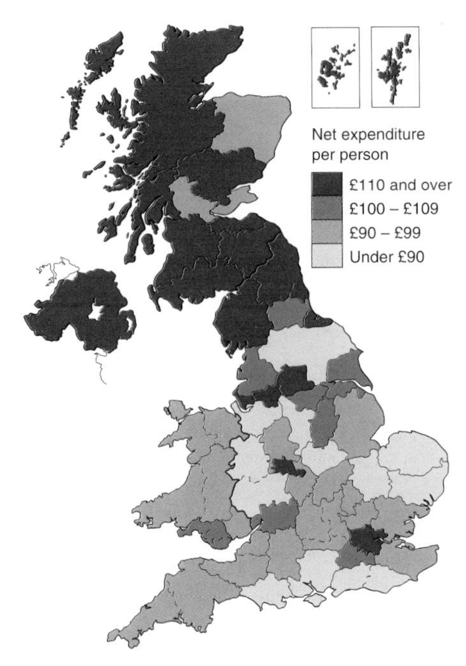

1 Includes loan and leasing charges and excludes revenue contributions to capital.

Source: CIPFA; The Scottish Office Development Department; Royal Ulster Constabulary

9.28

Employment in the criminal justice system[1]

Great Britain

	Thousands				Rates per 10,000 population	
	1971	1981	1991	1994	1971	1994
Police service						
Police	108	133	141	141	19.9	22.8
Civilian staff[2]	36	45	55	60	6.7	9.7
All police service	144	178	196	201	26.6	32.5
Prison service[3]	17	24	33	38	3.5	7.4
Probation service[4]	..	12	18	17	..	3.2

1 At December each year.
2 Includes traffic wardens, clerical and technical staff.
3 England and Wales only. Prior to 1993 excludes headquarters staff and prison officer class trainees.
4 England and Wales only. Full-time plus part-time workers and includes some temporary officers and also some trainees from 1981 onwards. Excludes non-probation officer grade hostel staff.

Source: Home Office; The Scottish Office Home Department

References and further reading

The following list contains selected publications relevant to **Chapter 9: Crime and Justice**. Those published by HMSO are available from the addresses shown on the inside back cover of *Social Trends*.

A Commentary on Northern Ireland Crime Statistics, HMSO

British Crime Survey, Home Office

Chief Constables' Annual Report, Royal Ulster Constabulary

Civil Judicial Statistics, Scotland, HMSO

Council on Tribunals Annual Report, HMSO

Crime and the quality of life: public perceptions and experiences of crime in Scotland, The Scottish Office

Criminal Statistics, England and Wales, HMSO

Criminal Statistics, Scotland, HMSO

Crown Prosecution Service, Annual Report, HMSO

Digest 3: Information on the Criminal Justice System in England and Wales, Home Office

Digest of Information on the Northern Ireland Criminal Justice System 1994, HMSO

Equal Opportunities Commission Annual Report, EOC

Home Office Annual Report and Accounts, HMSO

Home Office Statistical Bulletins and *Research Findings Series*, Home Office

Judicial Statistics, England and Wales, HMSO

National Prison Survey, HMSO

Northern Ireland Judicial Statistics, Northern Ireland Court Service

Police Statistics, England and Wales, CIPFA

Prison Service Annual Report and Accounts, HMSO

Prison Statistics, England and Wales, HMSO

Prisons in Scotland Report, HMSO

Probation Statistics, England and Wales, Home Office

Race and the Criminal Justice System 1994, Home Office

Report of the Parole Board for England and Wales, HMSO

Report of the Parole Board for Scotland, HMSO

Report on the work of the Northern Ireland Prison Service, HMSO

Scottish Crime Survey, The Scottish Office

Statistics of offences against prison discipline and punishments, England and Wales, HMSO

The Offenders Index, Home Office

The Scottish Office Statistical Bulletins Series, The Scottish Office

The Work of the Prison Service, HMSO

Contacts

Telephone contact points for further information relating to **Chapter 9: Crime and Justice**

Home Office	0181 760 8340
Northern Ireland Office	01232 527534/8
Royal Ulster Constabulary	01232 650222 extn 24135
The Scottish Office Home Department	0131 244 2227
CIPFA	0181 667 1144
Court Service	0171 210 1773

Chapter 10 Housing

Housing stock and supply

Owner-occupied housing represented two thirds of the total housing stock in the United Kingdom in 1994 compared with over a half in 1981. (Chart 10.3)

One in seventy new homes in the United Kingdom were built by local authorities and new towns in 1994 compared with nearly one in two in 1976. (Chart 10.1)

Housing standards

Very few households now lack basic amenities: less than 1 per cent do not have an internal flush toilet or a bath or shower. (Page 181)

Housing costs and expenditure

The proportion of new mortgages taken out by women on their own more than doubled between 1983 and 1994 to around 18 per cent. (Chart 10.13)

Households in Great Britain renting furnished accommodation spend a higher proportion of their income on housing costs than those living in other tenures. (Table 10.14)

Characteristics of occupants

Private renters in furnished accommodation tend to be young, single and male. (Page 183)

A higher proportion of households from the Black ethnic group were renting social housing than those from other ethnic groups in the period 1992 to 1994. (Table 10.18)

Homelessness

There were 52 thousand households living in temporary accommodation in Great Britain at the end of 1994, nearly a quarter less than at the end of 1992. (Table 10.25)

10.1

Housebuilding completions: by sector

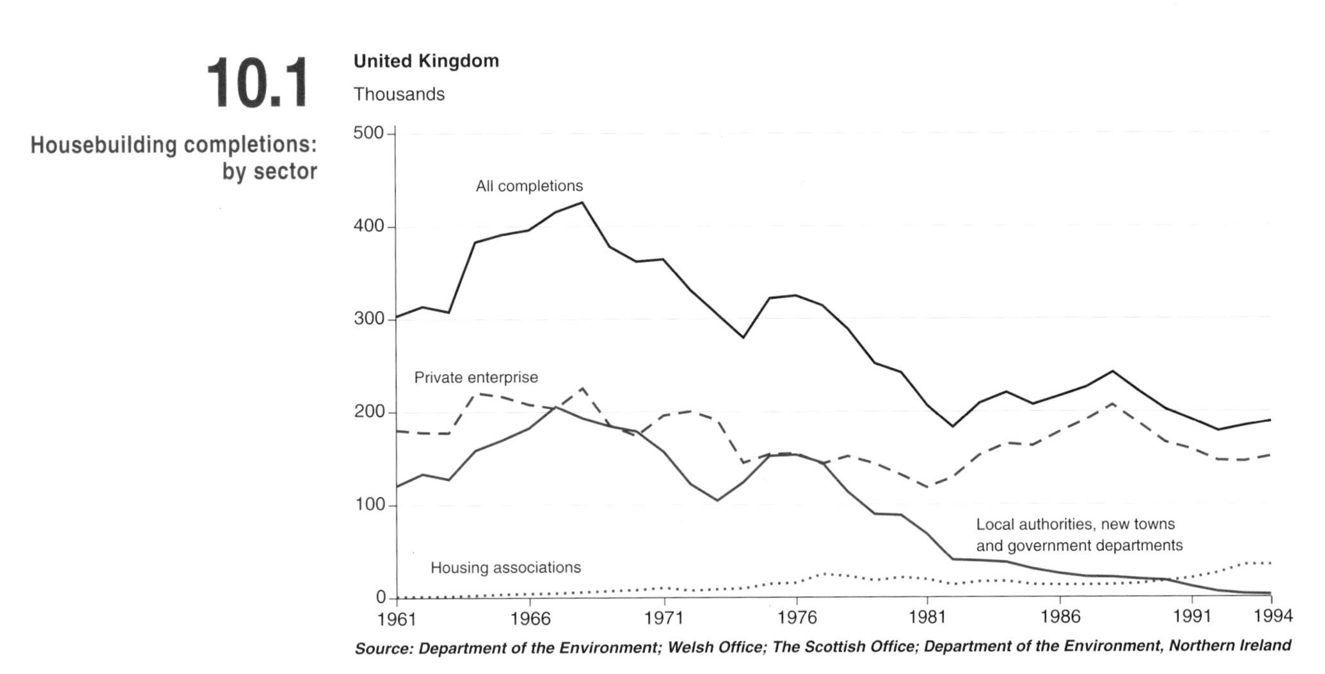

Source: Department of the Environment; Welsh Office; The Scottish Office; Department of the Environment, Northern Ireland

10.2

Dwellings[1] and households

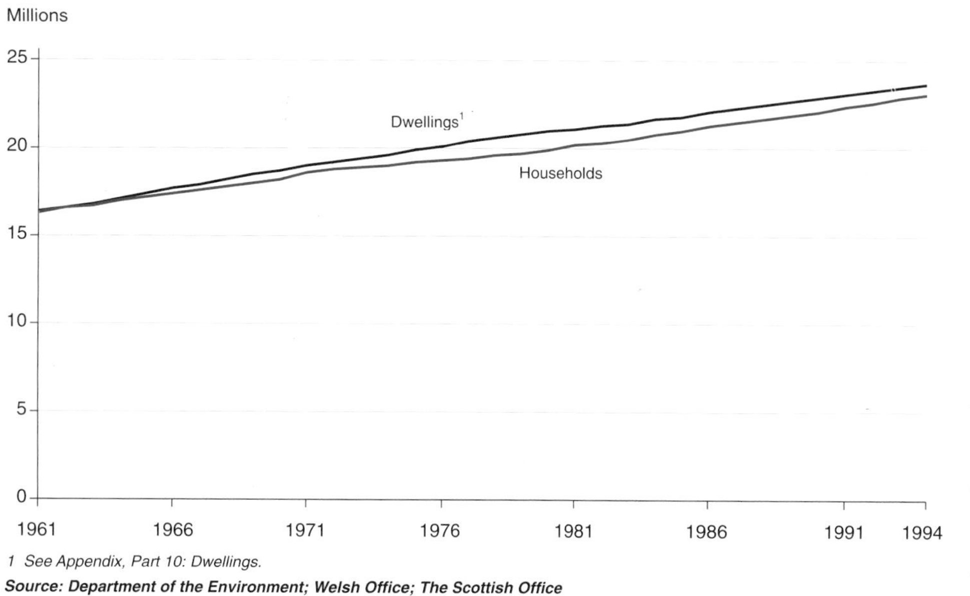

1 See Appendix, Part 10: Dwellings.

Source: Department of the Environment; Welsh Office; The Scottish Office

10.3

Stock of dwellings[1]: by tenure

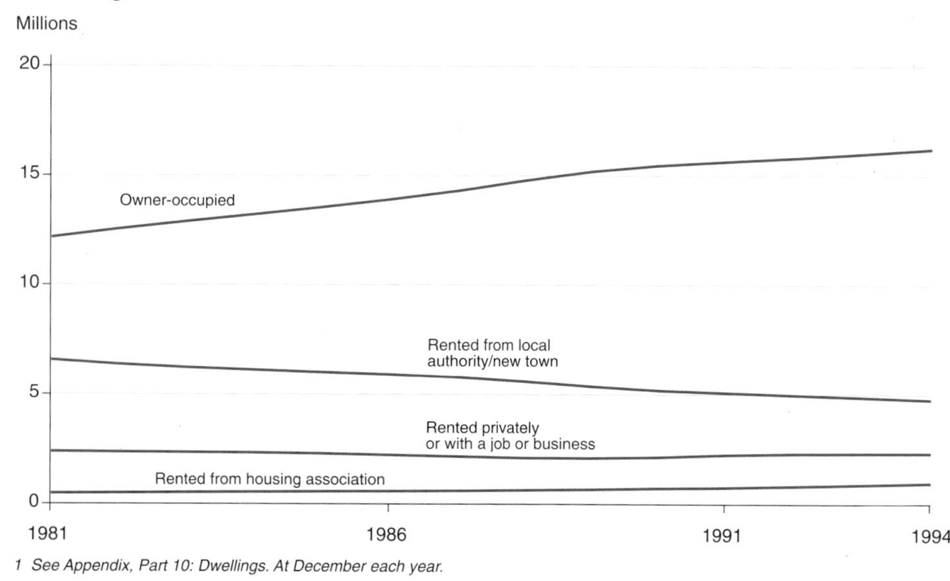

1 See Appendix, Part 10: Dwellings. At December each year.

Source: Department of the Environment; Welsh Office; The Scottish Office; Department of the Environment, Northern Ireland

The need for housing is an essential part of everyone's life. Most people prefer to own their own homes but others rent, either through necessity or choice.

Housing stock and supply

In 1994 there were 23.7 million dwellings in Great Britain and, at 23.1 million, slightly fewer households **(Chart 10.2)**. Some surplus of dwellings is necessary as there is a need for a number of vacant dwellings to allow for mobility in the housing market. Some dwellings are vacant because they are undergoing major repair or refurbishment and are temporarily uninhabitable or are in the process of being sold. In addition, some people have 'second homes' - according to information from the Survey of English Housing 1.2 per cent of households in England owned more than one dwelling for their own use in 1994-95. On the other hand, the number of households excludes 'concealed households', for example, couples or lone parent families who are living as part of someone else's household.

The number of dwellings in the United Kingdom increased by 12 per cent between 1981 and 1994, to 24.3 million. The number of owner-occupied dwellings, owned either outright or with a mortgage, increased by a third over the same period **(Chart 10.3)**. In 1981 owner-occupied housing represented just over half the total dwelling stock but by 1994 the proportion had increased to two thirds. Conversely, the number of dwellings rented from local authorities or new towns has fallen steadily since 1980 to reach the lowest level for 31 years in 1994. This is mainly due to legislation introduced in 1980 which allowed public sector tenants the right to buy their own homes (see Chart 10.7). Housing associations increased their dwelling stock by an average of between 4 and 5 per cent a year between 1981 and 1991 but since then this has doubled to nearly 9 per cent a year. This increase is due to a combination of new building (see Chart 10.1) and acquiring dwellings from local authorities (see Chart 10.8).

There is a wide variation in owner-occupation between the countries of the European Community (EC). About 80 per cent of homes in the Irish Republic were owner-occupied in 1991 which was more than double the proportion in the former Federal Republic of Germany, the country with the lowest percentage of owner-occupied dwellings **(Chart 10.4)**. Just over 70 per cent of rented homes in the United Kingdom were in the social sector, which was the highest proportion of all the EC countries; the Netherlands with 66 per cent and the Irish Republic with 56 per cent were the next highest. At the other end of the spectrum Spain had only 8 per cent of its rental stock in the social sector and Greece had none.

Semi-detached houses are the most common type of dwelling in Great Britain, accounting for three in ten of all dwellings in 1994-95 **(Table 10.5)**. In Northern Ireland terraced houses are the most common, accounting for nearly four in ten of all dwellings, while detached houses are the next most common type. However the type of dwelling occupied varies with tenure. In both Great Britain and Northern Ireland those households renting social housing, that is from local authorities, housing associations, new towns or the Northern Ireland Housing Executive, are more likely to be living in a purpose-built flat or maisonette than other households. Owner-occupiers, particularly those who own their home outright, are the most likely to live in a detached house.

10.4

Owner-occupied dwellings: EC comparison[1], 1991

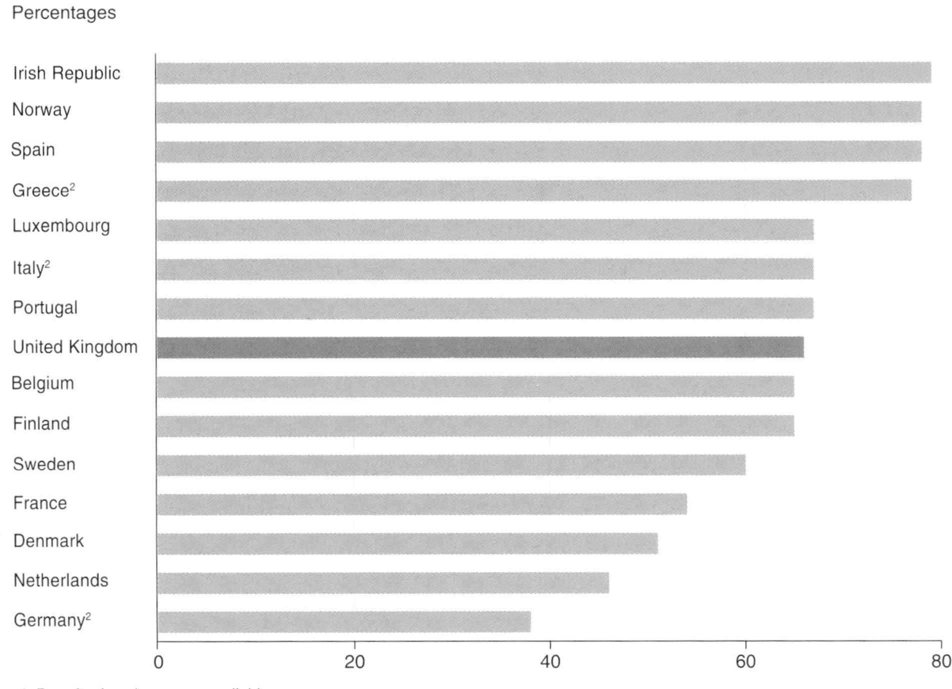

1 Data for Austria are not available.
2 Data are for 1990. Data for Germany relate to the former Federal Republic.
Source: Eurostat

10.5

Tenure: by type of dwelling, 1994-95

Great Britain — Percentages

	House or bungalow			Flat or maisonette			
	Detached	Semi-detached	Terraced	Purpose-built	Con-verted	Other dwellings	All dwellings
Owner-occupied							
Owned outright	*33*	*37*	*23*	*5*	*2*	-	*100*
Owned with mortgage	*26*	*36*	*30*	*6*	*2*	-	*100*
Rented							
Local authority/new town	*1*	*29*	*33*	*37*	*1*	-	*100*
Housing association	*1*	*15*	*25*	*45*	*13*	-	*100*
Other	*10*	*18*	*29*	*16*	*26*	*1*	*100*
All tenures	*20*	*32*	*28*	*14*	*4*	*1*	*100*

Source: General Household Survey, Office of Population Censuses and Surveys

10.6

Housebuilding completions: by region

Rates per 1,000 population

	1981	1991	1992	1993	1994
United Kingdom	3.6	3.3	3.0	3.1	3.3
North	3.1	2.6	2.6	2.4	2.7
Yorkshire & Humberside	3.1	2.6	2.7	2.9	2.9
East Midlands	3.9	3.9	3.5	3.5	4.0
East Anglia	5.1	5.2	4.4	4.9	4.6
South East	3.8	3.1	3.0	2.9	3.0
Greater London	2.9	2.4	2.2	2.0	2.2
Rest of South East	4.3	3.5	3.3	3.4	3.6
South West	4.1	3.7	3.4	3.1	3.3
West Midlands	3.6	3.1	2.8	3.1	3.0
North West	3.3	2.7	2.7	2.9	2.9
England	3.7	3.2	3.0	3.0	3.2
Wales	3.3	3.5	3.4	3.2	3.3
Scotland	3.9	3.7	3.2	4.0	3.8
Northern Ireland[1]	4.5	4.6	4.7	4.4	4.1

1 Data from 1991 relate to financial years.

Source: Department of the Environment; Welsh Office; The Scottish Office; Department of the Environment, Northern Ireland

10.7

Right to buy applications for, and sales of, dwellings owned by local authorities and new towns

United Kingdom

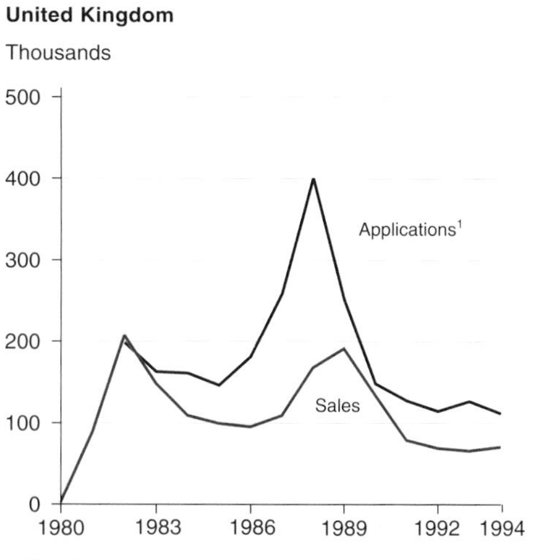

1 Data for 1980 and 1981 are not available.

Source: Department of the Environment; Welsh Office; The Scottish Office; Department of the Environment, Northern Ireland

The number of dwellings built each year in the United Kingdom reached a post-war peak in 1968 at 426 thousand but then fell to 179 thousand in 1992, before rising again to 189 thousand in 1994 **(Chart 10.1)**. In 1994, one in seventy homes was built by local authorities, new towns and government departments compared with nearly one in two in 1976. The number of private enterprise completions fell between 1988 and 1993 but increased slightly in 1994, when they accounted for eight in ten of all completions.

The rate of housebuilding completion varies throughout the United Kingdom. In 1994 East Anglia, where there were 4.6 completions per thousand population, had the highest rate **(Table 10.6)**. This was more than twice the rate in Greater London which, at 2.2, was lower than in any of the regions. Although the completion rate rose in most regions between 1993 and 1994 it fell in East Anglia, the West Midlands, Scotland and Northern Ireland.

While new dwellings are being constructed, others are being demolished. The number of dwellings demolished through slum clearance has been declining since the 1960s and now stands at around 5 per cent of the average for that decade. Figures for England have been collected since before the Second World War. In the 1930s around 30 thousand dwellings were cleared annually. This had tripled to around 90 thousand dwellings a year between 1969 and 1973, but declined sharply to just 4 thousand dwellings in 1993-94.

One reason for the fall in the stock of local authority dwellings is the introduction of *The Housing Act 1980,* and its Scottish equivalent, which gave tenants of local authorities and other public bodies in Great Britain the right to buy their homes, with a discount if they had been a tenant for more than three years. This was subsequently reduced to two years by the *Housing and Building Control Act 1984,* and its Scottish equivalent, which also increased the maximum discount from 50 to 60 per cent. Subsequently in January 1987 the maximum discount for flats was increased again to 70 per cent. In Northern Ireland tenants have had the right to buy their homes since the adoption of *The Housing Order 1983.* However, the Northern Ireland Housing Executive had been selling homes to tenants since 1979. Annual sales in the

Jnited Kingdom peaked at over 200 thousand in 1982 with a slightly smaller peak in 1989 **(Chart 10.7)**. In 1994 sales increased for the first time in five years, although at 70 thousand they only amounted to just over a third of the number sold in 1982.

The Department of the Environment's Survey of English Housing found that in 1994-95, 10 per cent of council tenants expected to buy the home they were renting at the time of the survey, while a further 13 per cent expected to purchase a different property. Those who expected to buy tended to be young and economically active and to have a gross weekly income of at least £300; those living in houses were more likely to be interested in sitting tenant purchase than those living in flats. The proportion of housing association tenants who were expecting to buy was higher at 26 per cent.

Another reason for the fall in the stock of local authority dwellings is the introduction of Large Scale Voluntary Transfers (LSVTs). Under this scheme a local authority can transfer all or part of its housing stock to a new landlord, usually a non-profit making housing association registered with the Housing Corporation or Scottish Homes. For an LSVT to be successful it needs the support of the tenants (via a vote) and the approval of the Secretary of State for the Environment. The number of dwellings transferred in Great Britain peaked at 46 thousand in 1990-91 **(Chart 10.8)**. In England 30 local authorities transferred around 148 thousand dwellings between 1987-88 and 1993-94. The Department of the Environment estimates that a further 140 thousand homes in England will transfer from local authorities to new landlords between 1994-95 and 1996-97. In Scotland 9 thousand homes were transferred between 1986-87 and 1993-94, while in Wales only just over 600 were transferred in the same period.

The letting of local authority homes in the United Kingdom to new tenants is shown in **Table 10.9**. In 1993-94 over half of new tenants came from the ordinary waiting list. The group which has shown the largest increase in allocation of local authority housing is the homeless, which accounted for almost a third of all new tenants in 1993-94 compared with just over a fifth in 1986-87. Further information on homelessness is given in a separate section at the end of this chapter.

10.8

Large scale voluntary transfers[1]

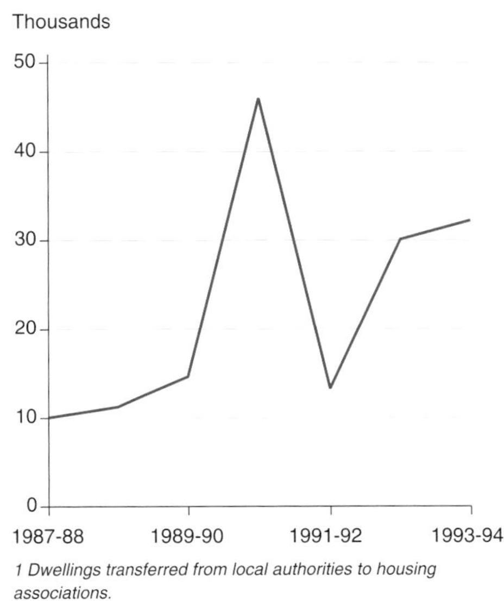

1 Dwellings transferred from local authorities to housing associations.

Source: Department of the Environment; Welsh Office; The Scottish Office

10.9

Allocation of local authority housing

United Kingdom

	1986-87	1990-91	1992-93	1993-94
New tenants (percentages)				
Homeless[1]	*22*	*29*	*33*	*30*
Ordinary waiting list	*65*	*57*	*52*	*57*
Others	*13*	*14*	*14*	*12*
New tenants (=100%)(thousands)	315.6	310.3	293.2	297.6
Tenants transferring or exchanging[2] (thousands)	229.2	205.5	210.7	211.9
All tenants (thousands)	544.9	515.7	503.9	509.6

1 See Appendix, Part 10: Homeless households.
2 Data for Wales include dwellings let to tenants through the 'tenants exchange scheme'.

Source: Department of the Environment; Welsh Office; The Scottish Office; Department of the Environment, Northern Ireland

10.10

Satisfaction with accommodation: by type of dwelling, 1994-95

England — Percentages

	Very satisfied	Fairly satisfied	Neither satisfied nor dissatisfied	Slightly dissatisfied	Very dissatisfied	All households (=100%) (millions)
Self-contained						
House						
Detached	*72*	*23*	*2*	*2*	*1*	4.1
Semi-detached	*60*	*32*	*3*	*4*	*2*	6.3
Terraced	*50*	*37*	*4*	*5*	*3*	5.5
Flat or maisonette						
Purpose-built	*47*	*36*	*5*	*7*	*6*	2.6
Not purpose-built	*37*	*41*	*6*	*9*	*6*	0.8
Caravan/mobile home	*65*	*17*	*4*	*6*	*8*	-
Other	*34*	*42*	*6*	*10*	*8*	-
Not self-contained	*38*	*40*	*5*	*7*	*9*	0.4
All types of accommodation	*57*	*33*	*3*	*5*	*3*	19.7

Source: Survey of English Housing, Department of the Environment

10.11

Under-occupation[1] and overcrowding[2]: by type of household[3], 1994-95

Great Britain

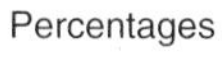

Percentages

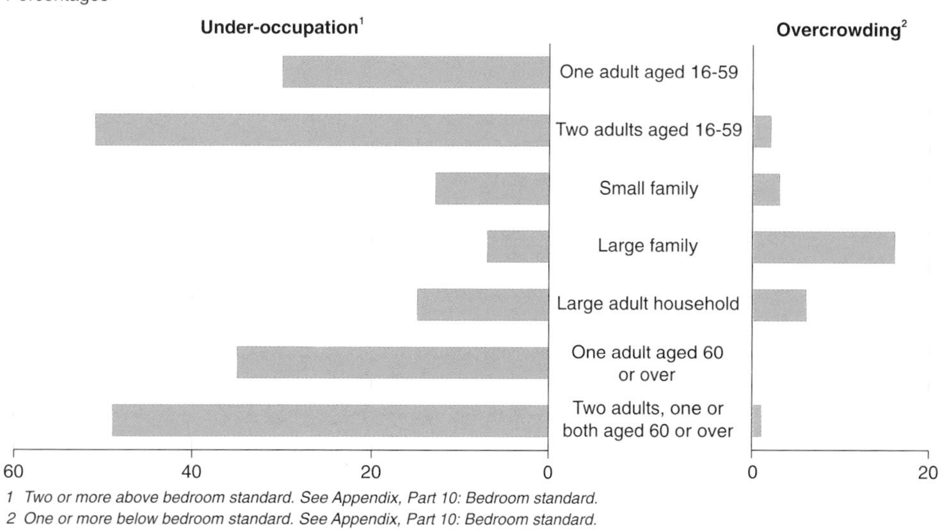

1 Two or more above bedroom standard. See Appendix, Part 10: Bedroom standard.
2 One or more below bedroom standard. See Appendix, Part 10: Bedroom standard.
3 See Appendix, Part 10: Household type.

Source: General Household Survey, Office of Population Censuses and Surveys

Housing standards

The Survey of English Housing found that in 1994-95 most people were satisfied with their accommodation - overall, nearly nine in ten households in England said that they were satisfied (either 'very' or 'fairly') **(Table 10.10)**. As might be expected, satisfaction varies with the type of accommodation people live in. Those who live in houses are more likely to be satisfied than those who live in flats or non self-contained accommodation, that is, they share a kitchen, bathroom or toilet, or a hall or staircase which is needed to get from one part of the accommodation to another. Satisfaction also varies by tenure; more than nine in ten owner occupiers were satisfied with their accommodation.

Overcrowding is another factor which influences satisfaction. In England about a third of households living in rented accommodation below the bedroom standard were dissatisfied. The bedroom standard is a commonly used measure of overcrowding or under occupation. It compares the number of bedrooms available to a household with a calculation of its bedroom requirement (see Appendix, Part 10: Bedroom standard, for a full definition).

Chart 10.11 shows overcrowding varies with household type. Overcrowding is relatively rare in Great Britain; only 6 per cent of households renting from the social sector, and 5 per cent renting privately, were in accommodation below the bedroom standard in 1994-95. Among those who rented privately in England, lone parents with dependent children were more likely than other households to occupy accommodation below the bedroom standard while older people were far more likely to be in accommodation above the standard.

Very few households now lack basic amenities; less than 1 per cent lack facilities such as a bath/shower or an internal flush toilet. Because of this, central heating is a better indicator of a household's standard of accommodation. In 1994-95, over 85 per cent of owner occupiers and just under 80 per cent of households renting from local authorities had full or partial central heating. However, in the private rented sector, this proportion drops to three fifths in unfurnished, and two thirds in furnished, accommodation.

Housing costs and expenditure

House prices vary throughout the different regions of the country. The average dwelling price in the United Kingdom in 1994 was £63,100 **(Table 10.12)**, 3 per cent higher than in 1993. Prices are highest in Greater London where the average of £85,200 is more than double the average house price in Northern Ireland of £38,700.

As the mix of dwellings in the housing market changes over time, a simple comparison of average prices is not a good guide of the change in prices. A better measure of true house price changes over time is the mix adjusted price index. The index shows that between 1985 and 1989 the average dwelling price more than doubled but then, with the recession in the housing market, it fell until 1993 then rose again in 1994.

The council tax was introduced to replace the community charge in England and Wales in April 1993 and in Scotland a year earlier. The amount of council tax payable on a dwelling depends on the valuation band to which it is allocated; the lowest band is A and the highest is H. Sixty eight per cent of dwellings in England were in the lowest three council tax bands in 1994. The North had the greatest percentage in bands A to C, with 86 per cent, while the South East had the lowest at 49 per cent.

Over the last decade or so, there has been a shift in the pattern of those taking out mortgages. The proportion of mortgages taken out in Great Britain by a woman in her own name alone more than doubled between 1983 and 1994, to nearly 18 per cent **(Chart 10.13)**. This change reflects several factors including the increased financial independence for women as they have increasingly moved into the labour market (see Chapter 4: Employment) and higher levels of divorce (see Chart 2.17 in the Households and Families chapter). The proportion taken out by a man and a woman together has fallen, but still accounts for the majority of new mortgages at just over six in ten.

10.12

Average dwelling prices[1]: by region, 1994

£

	First-time buyers	Other[2]	All buyers	Percentage of dwellings in council tax bands A-C
United Kingdom	48,057	65,886	63,077	..
North	37,258	52,838	49,380	*86*
Yorkshire & Humberside	40,508	54,908	53,439	*83*
East Midlands	42,731	56,129	54,618	*81*
East Anglia	46,395	60,028	58,458	*74*
South East	61,708	82,569	80,152	*49*
Greater London	68,890	88,163	85,197	*44*
Rest of South East	57,285	79,894	77,717	*53*
South West	49,592	64,260	62,903	*66*
West Midlands	45,988	61,064	59,128	*78*
North West	42,514	57,672	56,350	*82*
England	50,608	67,749	65,720	*68*
Wales	39,774	53,935	52,144	..
Scotland	35,160	59,666	50,598	..
Northern Ireland	30,468	41,574	38,685	..

1 Building society borrowers' average dwelling price.
2 Excludes local authority sitting tenants.
Source: Department of the Environment

10.13

New mortgages[1]: by gender of borrower

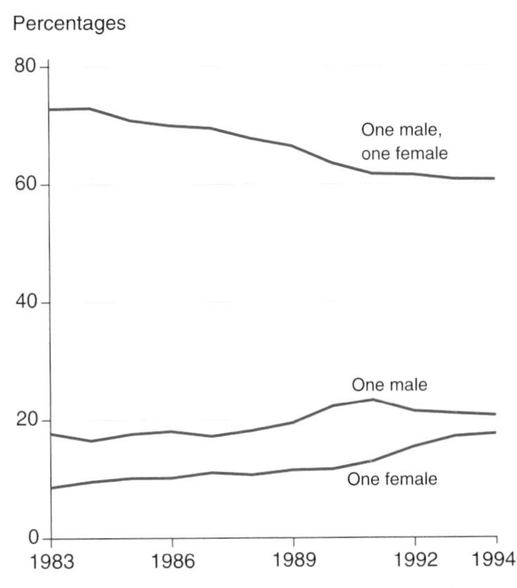

1 New mortgages advanced by building societies, including Abbey National; sitting tenants are excluded.
Source: Department of the Environment

10.14

Household expenditure on housing costs: by tenure, 1994-95

Great Britain £ per week

	Mortgage interest payments	Rent	Council tax	Water and sewerage charges	Repairs, maintenance and decorations	Other housing costs	All housing expenditure	Housing expenditure as a percentage of household income
Owner-occupied								
Owned outright	.	.	8.80	3.92	7.23	3.55	23.51	8
Owned with mortgage	44.20	.	9.68	3.91	9.71	4.00	71.50	13
Rented unfurnished								
Local authority	.	15.57	3.61	2.20	1.43	0.01	22.83	13
Housing association	.	16.05	3.21	2.82	0.79	0.01	22.89	14
Other	.	38.57	5.77	2.39	1.98	0.10	48.81	17
Rented furnished	.	62.63	4.10	1.19	0.56	0.01	68.49	22
Rent free	.	.	6.50	2.36	8.26	1.01	18.12	7
All tenures	19.06	7.54	7.62	3.35	6.47	2.61	46.65	13

Source: Family Expenditure Survey, Central Statistical Office

10.15

Repossession of properties[1]: warrants issued and executed

England & Wales

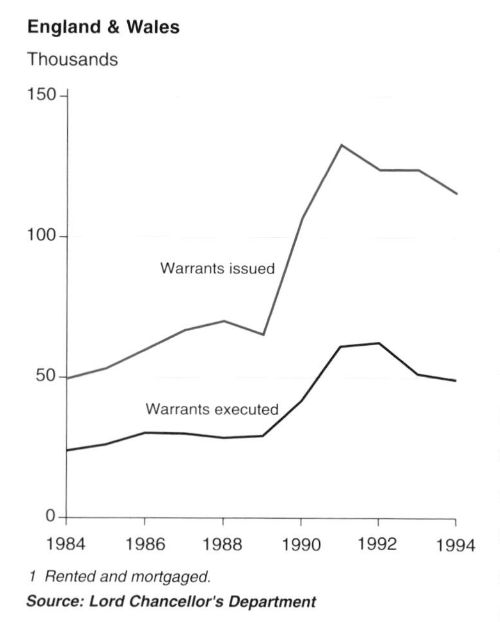

1 Rented and mortgaged.
Source: Lord Chancellor's Department

The amount that people spend on housing costs depends upon many different factors, such as tenure. Households in Great Britain who rent furnished accommodation spend a higher proportion of their income on housing than those living in other tenures; in 1994-95 they spent over a fifth of their income on housing **(Table 10.14)**. However, it was owner-occupiers who are buying with a mortgage that spent the most on housing costs, at just over £71 per week. At around £9 per week, owner-occupiers also spent more on council tax than households in other tenures. This is probably because they are more likely to live in houses than those who rent (see Table 10.5).

In England and Wales, when a household falls significantly behind with its rent or mortgage payments, a county court summons may be issued with a view to obtaining a court order. Not all orders will result in repossession as alternative agreements can often be reached. The number of warrants issued and executed in England and Wales are shown in **Chart 10.15**. The number of warrants issued rose sharply between 1989 and 1991 to a peak of 133 thousand while those executed peaked at 62 thousand in 1992; both have declined since.

In 1993-94 the Survey of English Housing asked owners who were buying with a mortgage if they were having difficulty with their mortgage payments: 6 per cent said that they were in arrears and a further 14 per cent said that they were having difficulty in meeting their payments, but were not actually behind with them. Thus, overall, nearly one in five mortgagors in England, over 1.5 million households, were having some problems with their mortgage payments. The proportion of households in arrears was greatest among those who bought in 1989 and 1990, when house prices were at their highest: about a quarter were either in arrears or having problems. The survey also asked tenants if they were up to date with their rent payments. Nearly

7 per cent of local authority and housing association tenants said that they had been behind with their rent at some time in the year before interview compared with 10 per cent of private sector tenants.

One problem which concerns some owner occupiers is negative equity. This occurs when a mortgage is greater than the value of the home on which it is secured. People who bought property when dwelling prices were at their highest point are more likely to have been left with negative equity as prices have fallen. Research by the Joseph Rowntree Foundation suggests that over 90 per cent of home owners do not have negative equity and, of those who do, the value of their negative equity decreased between late 1993 and early 1995.

Characteristics of occupants

Table 10.16 uses information from the General Household Survey in Great Britain and the Continuous Household Survey in Northern Ireland to show how the tenure of housing in which people live varies with the age of the head of household. It reflects people's life cycle transition. Heads of households aged under 25 are more likely to rent privately than any other age group. This reflects the tendency for private renters in furnished accommodation to be young, single and male. Only a quarter of heads of households in this age group were owner occupiers in 1994-95. However, more than half of 25 to 29 year old heads were buying with a mortgage and this rises to nearly two thirds in the 30 to 44 age group. By the time people retire most of them have paid off their mortgages; over half of household heads aged 60 and over owned their homes outright.

10.16

Tenure: by age of head of household, 1994-95

United Kingdom — Percentages

	Under 25	25-29	30-44	45-59	60-64	65-79	80 and over	All ages
Owner-occupied								
Owned outright	*1*	*1*	*4*	*21*	*49*	*57*	*54*	*25*
Owned with mortgage	*24*	*55*	*65*	*56*	*27*	*7*	*2*	*41*
Rented unfurnished								
Local authority/new town	*25*	*21*	*18*	*15*	*20*	*26*	*27*	*20*
Housing associations	*9*	*5*	*4*	*2*	*2*	*4*	*7*	*4*
Privately	*15*	*6*	*4*	*2*	*2*	*5*	*8*	*4*
Rented furnished	*26*	*8*	*3*	*1*	-	-	*1*	*3*
Rented with job or business	*2*	*3*	*2*	*2*	-	*1*	-	*1*
All tenures	*100*	*100*	*100*	*100*	*100*	*100*	*100*	*100*

Source: General Household Survey, Office of Population Censuses and Surveys; Continuous Household Survey, Department of Finance and Personnel, Northern Ireland

This life cycle effect also means that in Great Britain the group most likely to own their own homes outright is the economically inactive **(Table 10.17)**. Those heads of households in the unskilled manual group are most likely to be renting while those in the professional and employers and managerial groups are the most likely to be buying with a mortgage.

10.17

Socio-economic group[1] of head of household: by tenure, 1994-95

Great Britain — Percentages

	Owned outright	Owned with mortgage	Rented	All tenures
Professional	*11*	*75*	*14*	*100*
Employers and managers	*13*	*74*	*13*	*100*
Intermediate non-manual	*11*	*68*	*21*	*100*
Junior non-manual	*12*	*57*	*31*	*100*
Skilled manual	*14*	*60*	*26*	*100*
Semi-skilled manual	*12*	*42*	*46*	*100*
Unskilled manual	*11*	*32*	*57*	*100*
Economically inactive	*45*	*11*	*44*	*100*
All socio-economic groups	*25*	*42*	*33*	*100*

1 Excludes members of the Armed Forces, economically active full-time students and those who were unemployed and had never worked.

Source: General Household Survey, Office of Population Censuses and Surveys

10.18

Ethnic group of head of household: by tenure, 1992-1994

Great Britain Percentages

	Owned outright	Owned with mortgage	Rented from social sector	Rented privately[1]	All tenures
Ethnic minority group					
Indian	*20*	*64*	*7*	*9*	*100*
Pakistani/Bangladeshi	*13*	*48*	*24*	*15*	*100*
Black	*6*	*34*	*52*	*8*	*100*
Other	*12*	*36*	*33*	*20*	*100*
All ethnic minority groups	*12*	*45*	*31*	*12*	*100*
White	*26*	*41*	*24*	*9*	*100*
All ethnic groups	*25*	*41*	*25*	*9*	*100*

1 Includes rented with job or business.

Source: General Household Survey, Office of Population Censuses and Surveys

The Survey of English Housing found that in 1994-95, 87 per cent of households in England buying with a mortgage were headed by an employed person, usually a full-time worker; almost 60 per cent contained two or more earners. This compares with only 26 per cent of social sector rented tenants being in employment while 39 per cent were retired; 14 per cent were unemployed which is more than double the average for all households. Just over half of those heads of households renting in the private sector were working. There was a high proportion of elderly people renting unfurnished accommodation - about a fifth of those renting unfurnished accommodation were retired. On the other hand more than half of those in furnished accommodation were under 30, and 19 per cent were students.

Tenure also varies with the ethnic group of the head of household. In Great Britain White households were more likely to own their home outright in 1992 to 1994 than those from ethnic minority groups, but this is partly due to the older age structure of the White population. Those from the Black group were the most likely to be renting from the social sector; around half did so compared with a quarter of White, and fewer than one in ten Indian, heads of households **(Table 10.18)**. However, over six in ten Indian heads of households were buying their home with a mortgage compared with only four in ten White households.

The median length of time that households remain in the same home is between five and ten years. The British Household Panel Survey showed that just over one in ten adults in Great Britain moved between 1992 and 1993 **(Table 10.19)**. Households in private rented accommodation were the most likely to have moved. Tenants renting social housing were more likely to have moved than owner occupiers, possibly reflecting the difficulties owners had in selling their own homes. However, 23 per cent of moves by owner-occupiers who had been buying with a mortgage were into rented accommodation, reflecting repossessions, the difficulty of making moves to take up jobs and the consequences of divorce and separation. The survey also found that almost half of moves involved a change of household composition, with only part of the household moving. Further information on housing dynamics is included in the article on the British Household Panel Survey which

10.19

Adults moving house: by tenure before move, 1992 to 1993

Great Britain Percentages

	Whole household	Part of household	All movers[1]
Owned outright	*2*	*3*	*5*
Owned with mortgage	*4*	*5*	*9*
Rented from social sector	*5*	*4*	*12*
Other rented	*13*	*12*	*28*
All tenures	*5*	*5*	*11*

1 Includes households with composition unknown.

Source: British Household Panel Survey, ESRC Research Centre on Micro-social Change

begins on page 27. Further evidence of the greater mobility of those in private rented accommodation is provided by the General Household Survey, which showed that in 1993-94 nearly two thirds of those in rented furnished accommodation had resided at their current address for less than one year.

The 1994-95 Survey of English Housing asked heads of households why they had moved. Among those who had moved in the previous 12 months about a quarter had moved mainly because they wanted larger or better accommodation; this was the most common reason given **(Table 10.20)**. Other common reasons included family or personal ones, wanting to move to a better area, changing job, wanting smaller or cheaper accommodation and accommodation no longer being available; only a small proportion moved because they could not afford the rent or mortgage. About a tenth of those who were outright owners in 1994-95 had moved because they wanted larger or better accommodation but about a quarter of such owners had moved because they wanted smaller or cheaper accommodation. Nearly half of those who had changed tenure to owner-occupation moved because they wanted to buy, whilst the most common reason for moving for those who had changed to private renting was divorce or separation.

The effects of divorce on tenure are examined in Great Britain over the period 1991 to 1993 in more detail in **Table 10.21**. An obvious effect of divorce is that one household could be replaced by two, one or both of which may change tenure. Many married couples require two incomes in order to buy housing and on separation one person may not have the resources to purchase alone. Some divorcees may cease to be householders in their own right by moving into someone else's household.

10.20

Main reason for moving[1]: by current tenure, 1994-95

England — Percentages

	Owner-occupied	Rented from social sector	Rented privately	All tenures
Larger or better house or flat	31	27	18	26
Family/personal reasons	9	17	10	11
To move to a better area	12	10	6	10
Change of job/nearer to job	9	2	15	9
Wanted smaller or cheaper house or flat	8	15	5	9
Accommodation no longer available	1	10	16	9
Divorce or separation	6	4	10	7
Wanted to buy	14	.	.	6
Marriage or cohabitation	4	3	3	3
Could not afford mortgage or rent	-	2	4	2
Other reasons	5	10	14	9
All households (=100%)(thousands)	649	368	542	1,559

1 Continuing household heads who moved in the year before interview.

Source: Survey of English Housing, Department of the Environment

10.21

Tenure one year after divorce: by gender and tenure of former matrimonial home, 1991-1993

Great Britain — Percentages

	Tenure of former matrimonial home		
	Owner-occupied	Rented	All tenures
Tenure one year after divorce			
Males			
Owned outright	6	-	4
Owned with mortgage	55	8	37
Rented from social sector	3	40	17
Other rented	11	20	15
Not a householder	25	32	27
All males	100	100	100
Females			
Owned outright	10	1	6
Owned with mortgage	57	6	37
Rented from social sector	11	67	33
Other rented	5	11	7
Not a householder	18	16	17
All females	100	100	100

Source: General Household Survey, Office of Population Censuses and Surveys

10.22

Owners who traded down[1]: by age of head of household, 1994-95

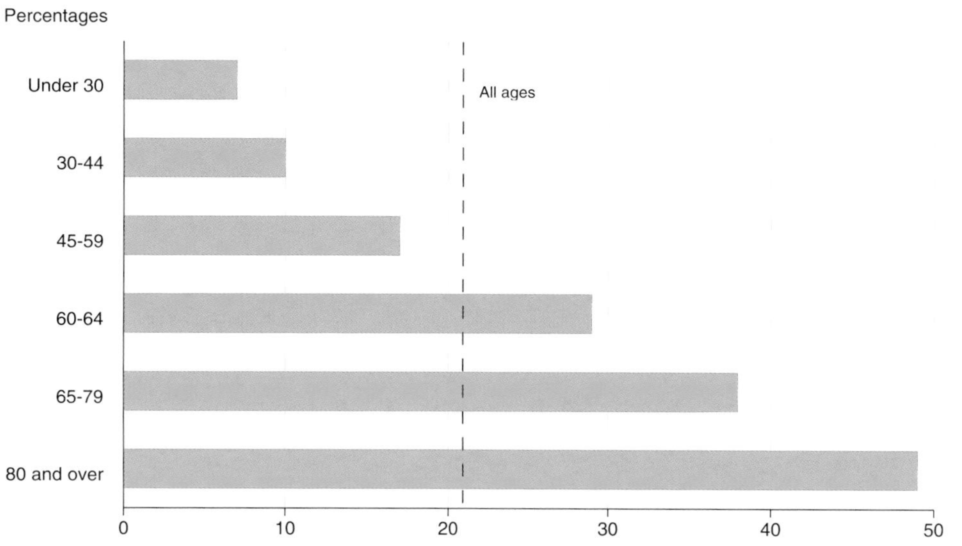

1 Percentage in each age group who paid less for their present property than was received from the sale of their previous property.

Source: Survey of English Housing, Department of the Environment

10.23

Homeless households found accommodation[1] by local authorities

Great Britain Percentages

	1986	1989	1991	1994
Homeless households in priority need found accommodation				
Household with dependent children	*65*	*68*	*65*	*59*
Household member pregnant	*14*	*13*	*13*	*12*
Household member vulnerable because of:				
Mental illness	*2*	*2*	*3*	*6*
Old age	*7*	*6*	*4*	*5*
Physical handicap	*3*	*3*	*3*	*5*
Other reasons[2]	*9*	*7*	*11*	*14*
All in priority need[3] (=100%)(thousands)	107.7	128.7	160.9	135.3
Homeless households not in priority need found accommodation (thousands)	10.2	13.2	9.6	8.3
All households found accommodation (thousands)	117.9	142.0	170.5	143.5

1 Includes 'homeless in emergency'.
2 Includes actions where priority need category is not known.

Source: Department of the Environment; Welsh Office; The Scottish Office

However, the majority of those who had been divorced for at least one year and had not remarried had not changed tenure. Among women this proportion was slightly higher among renters than owner occupiers. Men were more likely than women to have changed tenure following divorce. This is not unexpected as women were also more likely to still be living in the former matrimonial home one year after divorce; 43 per cent were doing so compared with 30 per cent of men.

Owner occupiers who move are said to have 'traded down' when the price they paid for their present property was less than that they received from the sale of their previous property. In 1994-95 the Survey of English Housing asked those owner occupiers who had sold a property in order to buy their present one if there was any difference in the price of the two properties. Just over a fifth of owners, over 1.3 million households, had traded down when they last bought a property **(Chart 10.22)**. The likelihood of trading down increases with age. Much of the trading down among older people will be voluntary, as people find they need less space when their children grow up and leave home. However, the fall in house prices in the early 1990s left those owners who bought when prices were higher with little or negative equity to go towards their next home purchase. In all age groups, those who had purchased after 1984 were more likely to have traded down than those who bought earlier.

Homelessness

Part III of the *Housing Act 1985*, and its Scottish equivalent, requires local authorities to help homeless people in

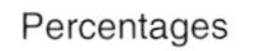

defined categories of 'priority need'. Essentially these are families with young children, women expecting babies and those vulnerable through old age, physical disability, mental handicap or illness. They may help others not in these categories, either by securing accommodation or by providing advice and assistance to enable them to find accommodation themselves.

When a household applies to a local authority as homeless, the council must assess if the household is in fact homeless and then decide if the applicant is in priority need. If this is the case then the local authority must secure suitable accommodation for the household. This may not necessarily be local authority accommodation; it could be that the local authority arranges housing association or private accommodation for the homeless household. Table 10.9, earlier in the chapter, shows that in 1993-94 a third of new local authority tenants in the United Kingdom had been accepted as homeless. In 1994 over 135 thousand households found accommodation in Great Britain were in priority need, 12 per cent less than in the previous year **(Table 10.23)**. Of these 59 per cent were households with dependent children and 12 per cent had a pregnant person in the household. These two categories made up over seven in ten of households in priority need found accommodation. In Northern Ireland there was a slight increase in the numbers applying as homeless to the Northern Ireland Housing Executive between 1993-94 and 1994-95, to just over 10 thousand.

People become homeless for a variety of reasons. Around a third of homeless households who were found accommodation by local authorities in England, Wales and

10.24

Homeless households[1] found accommodation by local authorities: by reason[2] for homelessness, 1994

England, Wales & Northern Ireland

Percentages

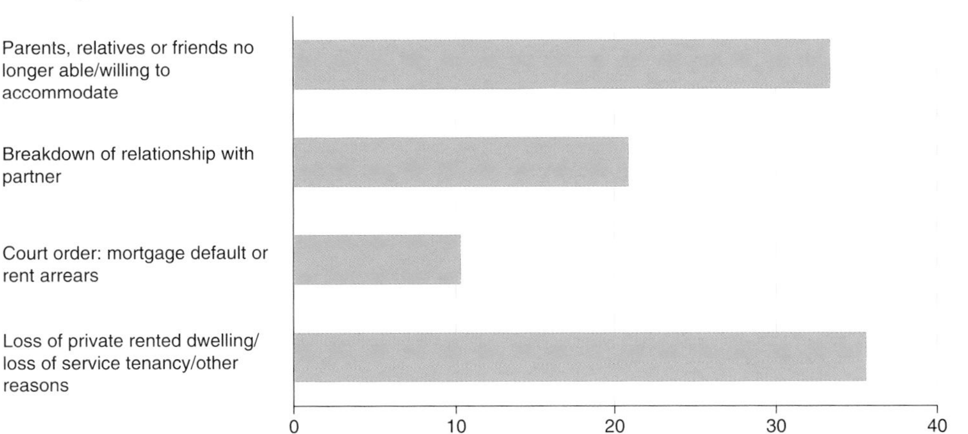

1 See Appendix, Part 10: Homeless households.
2 Categories in Wales and Northern Ireland differ slightly from those in England so cases have been allocated to the closest English category. Data for Wales include priority cases given advice and assistance but exclude those that fall into the non-priority category.
Source: Department of the Environment; Welsh Office; Department of the Environment, Northern Ireland

Northern Ireland in 1994 had become homeless because friends or relatives were no longer able or willing to accommodate them **(Chart 10.24)**. Those households who became homeless due to a break up with their partner accounted for 21 per cent of cases in 1994 compared with 16 per cent in 1981.

When a homeless household is first offered accommodation by a local authority, it is often housed in temporary accommodation until the local authority can find a permanent home for the household. There were 52 thousand households living in temporary accommodation in Great Britain at the end of 1994; nearly a quarter less than at the end of 1992 **(Table 10.25)**. The use of bed and breakfast accommodation has fallen by nearly two thirds since 1991. It accounted for less than one in ten households living in temporary accommodation at the end of 1994, compared with one in five at end-1991. The most common type of temporary accommodation at end-1994 was short-life leasing.

10.25

Homeless households living in temporary accommodation[1]

Great Britain — Thousands

	Bed and breakfast	Hostels	Short-life leasing	All
1982	2.0	3.7	4.8	10.5
1983	3.0	3.6	4.5	11.1
1984	4.2	4.2	5.3	13.7
1985	5.7	5.0	6.7	17.3
1986	9.4	5.0	8.3	22.7
1987	10.6	5.7	10.5	26.8
1988	11.2	6.8	14.2	32.3
1989	12.0	8.6	19.9	40.5
1990	11.7	10.4	27.0	49.1
1991	12.9	11.7	39.7	64.3
1992	8.4	12.6	46.6	67.6
1993	5.4	11.9	40.7	58.0
1994	4.7	11.9	35.7	52.4

1 Data are at end year and include households awaiting the outcome of homeless enquiries. Households made temporarily homeless through flooding in Wales in 1990 and 1993 are excluded.
Source: Department of the Environment; Welsh Office; The Scottish Office

References and further reading

The following list contains selected publications relevant to **Chapter 10: Housing**. Those published by HMSO are available from the address shown on the inside back cover of *Social Trends*.

Changing Households: The British Household Panel Survey, ESRC Research Centre on Micro-social Change
Department of the Environment Annual Report, HMSO
English House Condition Survey, HMSO
Family Spending, HMSO
General Household Survey, HMSO
Housing and Construction Statistics, Great Britain, annual and quarterly, HMSO
Housing Finance, Council of Mortgage Lenders
Housing in England, HMSO
Local Housing Statistics, HMSO
Northern Ireland House Condition Survey, Northern Ireland Housing Executive
Northern Ireland Housing Statistics, CSRB
Our Future Homes, HMSO
Private Renting in England, HMSO
Private Renting in Five Localities, HMSO
Projections of Households in England, HMSO
Regional Trends, HMSO
Rent Officer Statistics, Department of the Environment Statistical Bulletin
Shared Accommodation in Five Localities, HMSO
Social Focus on Women, HMSO
Statistical Bulletins on Housing, The Scottish Office
Statistics on Housing in the European Community, Commission of the European Communities
Welsh House Condition Survey, Welsh Office
Welsh Housing Statistics, Welsh Office

Contacts

Telephone contact points for further information relating to
Chapter 10: Housing

Department of the Environment	0171 276 3496
Department of the Environment, Northern Ireland	01232 540808
Office of Population Censuses and Surveys	
General Household Survey	0171 396 2327
Other inquiries	0171 396 2828
Court Service	0171 210 1773
Central Statistical Office	
Family Expenditure Survey	0171 217 4207
The Scottish Office	0131 244 7232
ESRC Research Centre on Micro-social Change	01206 872957
Eurostat	00 352 4301 34567

Chapter 11 Environment

Environmental concern and conservation

Traffic (including fumes, congestion and noise) is the environmental issue which adults in England and Wales felt was most likely to concern them in 20 years time. (Table 11.2)

Slightly more than half of women and just under half of men claimed to recycle old newspapers on a regular basis in 1993, while just under half of both men and women said that they used bottle banks regularly. (Page 191)

Air quality

Road transport was responsible for over 90 per cent of carbon monoxide emissions and around half of black smoke and nitrogen oxide emissions in 1993. (Table 11.9)

Since 1976 lead emissions from road vehicles have fallen by 85 per cent while petrol consumption has risen by 35 per cent. (Chart 11.10)

Water quality

Over 90 per cent of river and canal water sampled between 1992 and 1994 in England and Wales was of 'good' or 'fair' quality. (Table 11.12)

Land cover and use

There has been a slight fall in the amount of agricultural land used for crops since 1988 mainly as a result of the EC Set Aside Schemes - 728 thousand hectares were set aside in the United Kingdom in 1994. (Table 11.18)

The number of new broadleaved trees planted in the United Kingdom was 13 times higher in 1994-95 than in 1971-72. (Chart 11.19)

Resources

Some commercial fish species are being over-exploited; the weight of plaice in the North Sea capable of breeding fell by 37 per cent between 1990 and 1994. (Table 11.21)

11.1

Air pollutants: emissions of selected gases

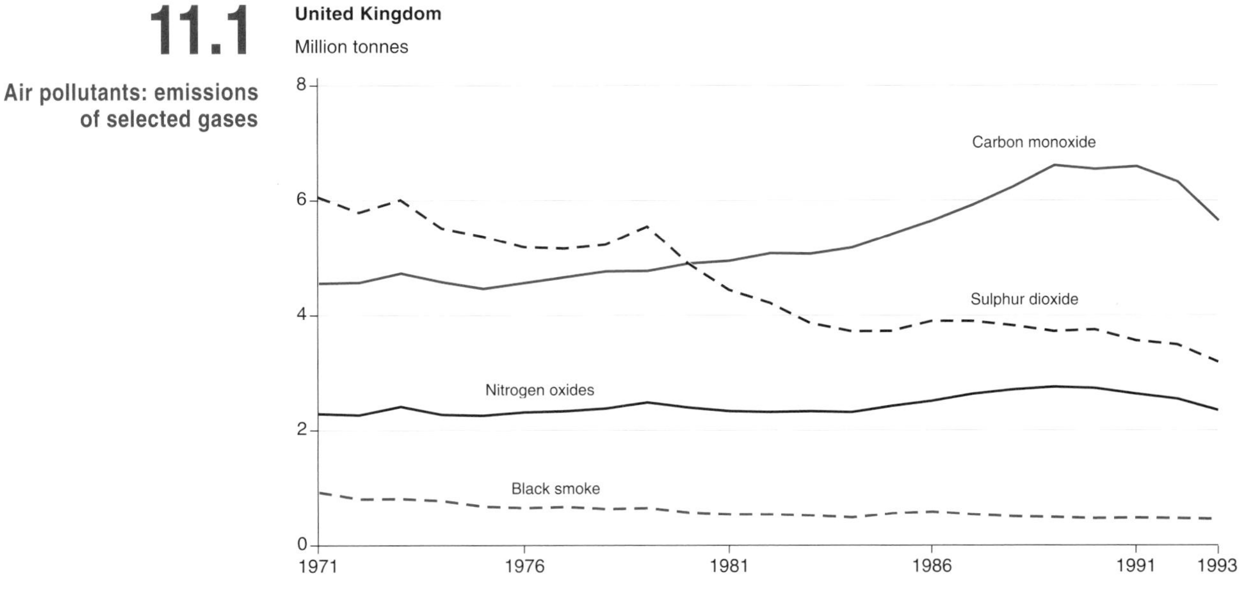

Source: National Environmental Technology Centre

11.2

Future environmental concerns[1]: by age, 1993

England & Wales Percentages

	18-24	25-44	45-64	65 and over	All aged 18 and over
Traffic[2]	*31*	*33*	*42*	*36*	*36*
Level of air pollution	*29*	*31*	*31*	*24*	*29*
Global warming/climate change	*42*	*32*	*21*	*16*	*27*
Level of pollution in lakes, rivers and sea	*24*	*28*	*24*	*16*	*24*
Depletion of ozone layer	*33*	*24*	*17*	*11*	*20*
Radioactive waste	*11*	*17*	*15*	*11*	*15*
Loss of tropical rainforest	*23*	*16*	*14*	*9*	*15*
Toxic waste	*14*	*17*	*12*	*7*	*13*
Population growth	*13*	*12*	*12*	*12*	*12*
Using up the world's natural resources	*18*	*14*	*9*	*6*	*11*
Loss of countryside to urban development	*12*	*12*	*10*	*6*	*10*
Loss of rare species	*17*	*11*	*6*	*3*	*8*
Disposal of household waste	*9*	*10*	*8*	*6*	*8*
Acid rain	*6*	*6*	*4*	*5*	*5*
Decay of inner cities	*5*	*5*	*4*	*5*	*5*
Too many roads/motorways	*3*	*3*	*5*	*5*	*4*

1 Respondents were asked what environmental issues or trends they felt would cause them the most concern in about 20 years time. Respondents were not prompted with suggestions.
2 Includes congestion, fumes or noise.

Source: Department of the Environment

The environment has been an area of increasing interest and concern over recent years, for government, society and the individual. It affects everyone in one way or another and, unlike a great many other important issues, ordinary people can make a contribution.

Environmental concern and conservation

People's attitudes to environmental issues vary with their age. Younger people tend to show more concern than older people on a variety of environmental issues, particularly global ones **(Table 11.2)**. In 1993 the proportion of 18 to 24 year olds who said that global warming and the effect of climate change was one of the issues which would cause them most concern in 20 years time was double that for the 45 to 64 age group; it was the single largest future concern of the younger age group. The biggest concern for those aged 25 and over was traffic congestion and related problems.

A greater understanding of various environmental issues helps to increase awareness. In a survey carried out by NOP Social and Political for the Department of the Environment in 1993, 42 per cent of people in England and Wales picked the correct definition of four offered as the best description of global warming, that is increased gases around the Earth trapping more of the sun's heat. However, 38 per cent chose an incorrect answer: a hole in the ozone layer letting in too much heat. Men were more likely than women to get the answer correct, but women were more likely to admit that they did not know.

One of the success stories in making people aware of environmental issues and in encouraging them to contribute has been

11.3

Recycling levels: by material

United Kingdom Percentages

	1990	1991	1992	1993	2000 (target)
Paper and board	*32*	*34*	*34*	*32*	..
Waste paper used in newsprint	*26*	*26*	*31*	*31*	*40*
Glass	*21*	*21*	*26*	*29*	*50*
Aluminium cans	*6*	*11*	*16*	*21*	*50*
Steel cans	*9*	*10*	*12*	*13*	*37*
Plastics	*2*	..	*5*	..	..

Source: ACRA; BGMC; BP&BIF; BS; SCRIB; PFGB; PPIC

through renewal programmes such as bottle, can and newspaper recycling (**Table 11.3**). This has also become a way for charities to raise extra revenue, with newspaper collection and aluminium can recycling being particularly popular. Recycling levels for glass and cans, particularly aluminium cans, all increased between 1990 and 1993. Slightly more than half of women and just under half of men claimed to recycle old newspapers on a regular basis in 1993 and just under half of both men and women claimed to use bottle banks regularly.

For many years one way in which people have been expressing their environmental concern, and acting upon it, has been through membership of voluntary organisations. The National Trust is now over 100 years old and still has a growing membership with over 2 million members in 1994; in addition the National Trust for Scotland has nearly a quarter of a million members (**Table 11.4**). Friends of the Earth is another high profile organisation; in 1994, at 112 thousand, its membership was over six times higher than in 1981.

Not all facets of environmental concern are material. Noise has become a major concern in recent years and around 3 thousand complaints per million population about noise from domestic premises were received by Environmental Health officers in England and Wales in 1992-93 (**Chart 11.5**). This is over four times the rate for 1981. In 1992-93 only 0.4 thousand complaints per million population were received in Scotland. The government is considering legislation which could mean fixed penalty notices for offenders who exceed proscribed decibel levels at night and, for persistent offenders, the confiscation of the equipment making the noise.

11.4

Membership of selected voluntary organisations

United Kingdom — Thousands

	1971	1981	1991	1994
National Trust	278	1,046	2,152	2,219
Royal Society for the Protection of Birds	98	441	852	870
Greenpeace[1]	..	30	408	300
Wildlife Trusts[2]	64	142	233	263
National Trust for Scotland	37	110	234	235
Civic Trust[3]	214	..	222	222
World Wide Fund for Nature	12	60	227	187
Woodland Trust	..	20	150	170
Friends of the Earth[4]	1	18	111	112
Ramblers Association	22	37	87	100
Council for the Protection of Rural England	21	29	45	46
British Trust for Conservation Volunteers[5]	1	..	9	10
British Trust for Ornithology	5	7	9	9
National Council for the Conservation of Plants and Gardens	..	..	7	7
Campaign for the Protection of Rural Wales	..	2	4	4

1 Data for 1994 are not comparable with earlier years.
2 Includes Royal Society for Nature Conservation
3 Members of local amenity societies registered with the Civic Trust.
4 Data are for England, Wales and Northern Ireland only.
5 Data for 1971 and 1991 relate to two years earlier.
Source: Organisations concerned

11.5

Complaints about noise from domestic premises received by Environmental Health Officers

England & Wales

Number per million population

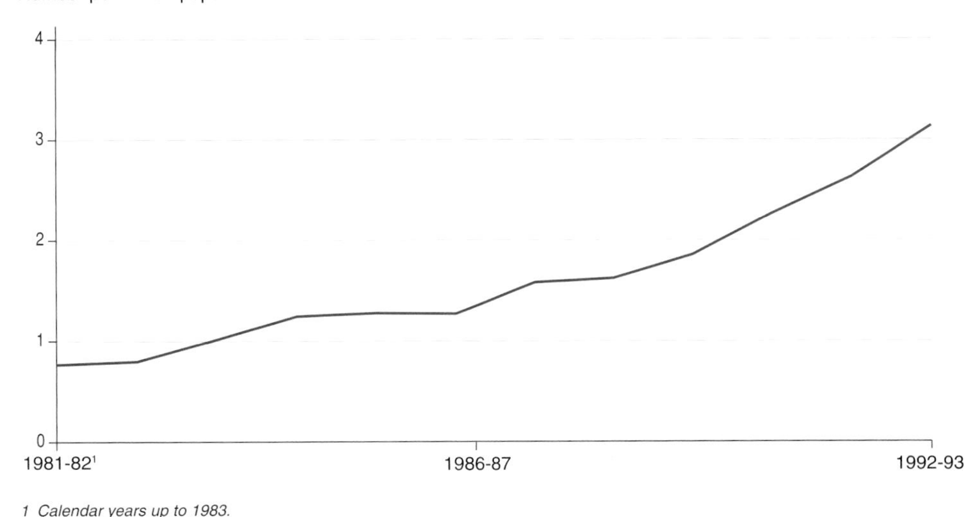

1 Calendar years up to 1983.
Source: Chartered Institute of Environmental Health Officers

11.6

Selected native species at risk[1], 1994

Great Britain — Numbers

	Native species	Extinct	En-dangered	Vulnerable	Rare	Nationally scarce
Plants						
Fungi	20,000	..	72	284	..	..
Seed plants	2,230	19	48	91	151	244
Lichens	1,700	33	44	62	163	263
Liverworts/mosses	1,000	16	31	64	103	271
Animals						
Spiders/harvestmen/ pseudoscorpions	687	0	22	32	27	145
Non-marine molluscs	208	0	10	7	13	19
Larger non-marine crustaceans	70	1	2	1	3	49
True bugs	540	7	9	3	38	159
Caddis flies	199	2	7	7	8	16
Dragonflies/damselflies	41	3	1	2	3	11
Flies	6,000	12	188	196	302	639
Beetles	4,000	68	164	69	155	1,039
Butterflies/moths	2,600	35	126	61	114	370
Bees/wasps/ants	542	17	41	20	57	106
Birds	523	6	..	..	..	..

1 See Appendix, Part 11: Native species at risk.

Source: Joint Nature Conservation Committee

11.7

Designated areas: by region, 1994

Percentages

	National Parks	Areas of Outstanding Natural Beauty[1]	Green Belt areas[2]	Defined Heritage Coasts (kilometres)[3]
North	*23*	*15*	*3*	114
Yorkshire & Humberside	*20*	*6*	*16*	82
East Midlands	*6*	*3*	*4*	.
East Anglia	*0*	*7*	*2*	121
South East	*0*	*24*	*22*	72
South West	*7*	*29*	*3*	638
West Midlands	*2*	*10*	*19*	.
North West	*1*	*11*	*33*	0
England	*7*	*15*	*12*	1,027
Wales	*20*	*4*	*0*	496
Scotland	*0*	*13*	*2*	7,546
Northern Ireland	*0*	*20*	*16*	-

1 National Scenic Areas in Scotland.
2 Data are for 1993.
3 Preferred Coastal Conservation Zones in Scotland, including mainland and islands.

Source: Department of the Environment

The purpose of the organisations listed in Table 11.4 is to help protect and conserve our environment. This can be a difficult task and there is a continual threat to both plants and wildlife. In the United Kingdom there are around 30 thousand species of animals, excluding marine and microscopic groups and other less well known groups such as roundworms of which there are thousands. There are also nearly two and a half thousand species and sub-species of flowering plants, at least 20 thousand fungi, between 15 and 20 thousand algae, 1.7 thousand lichens and about 1 thousand liverworts and mosses.

Table 11.6 shows the numbers and rarity of certain species in mainland Britain. Around 6 per cent of species of both butterflies and moths and beetles are either extinct or endangered; in addition a similar proportion of butterflies and moths are either vulnerable or rare. Species of bees, wasps and ants are at even greater risk: one in four are at least rare, if not extinct.

The countryside may be protected by declaring an area to be National Park, an Area of Outstanding Natural Beauty or a site of special scientific interest. The North, which contains the Lake District, has a greater proportion of its area designated as National Park (almost a quarter) than any other region while the South West has the largest proportion of area (over a quarter) designated as Areas of Outstanding Natural Beauty **(Table 11.7)**. In August 1995 the Tamar Valley, on the Devon and Cornwall border, was added to the list of Areas of Outstanding Natural Beauty.

The global atmosphere

The importance of global warming to all nations has become evident in recent years and the 'Earth Summit' was held in Rio in 1992. More recently there has been the Berlin conference and, inspired by the Earth Summit's resolution to listen to the views of children, a Children's Environmental Global Conference for children from around the world was held in Eastbourne in October 1995. Many other resolutions came out of the Rio conference, particularly the aim of stabilising greenhouse gas emissions at 1990 levels by the year 2000. The main contributing gas is carbon dioxide and the emissions by end user are given for the United Kingdom in **Chart 11.8**. There has been a decrease in emissions for domestic and industrial use while emissions due to transport have increased. Between 1971 and 1993 emissions as a result of domestic use fell by around 18 per cent while those resulting from industrial use fell by around 36 per cent; emissions due to transport use rose by about 63 per cent over the same period. However, industry is still the main producer of carbon dioxide emissions, accounting for over a third in 1993.

11.8

Emissions of carbon dioxide: by end user

United Kingdom

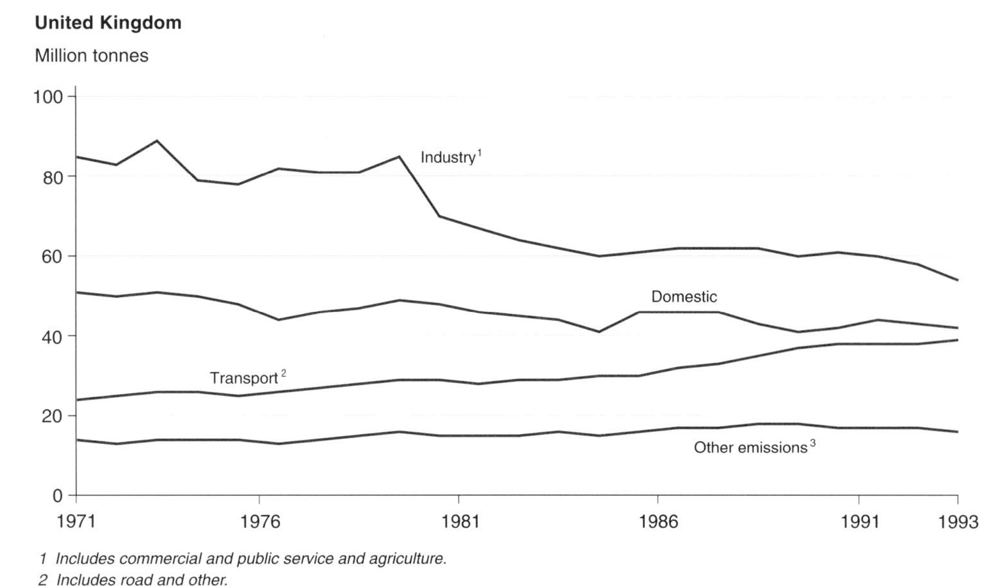

1 Includes commercial and public service and agriculture.
2 Includes road and other.
3 Includes exports and miscellaneous.
Source: National Environmental Technology Centre

There are many ways in which the Government seeks to control unnecessary vehicle emissions. The checking of exhaust emissions is part of the annual roadworthiness test for vehicles, and examiners from the Vehicle Inspectorate enforce the legal levels of emissions either at the roadside or, in the case of heavy commercial vehicles, at operators' premises.

Air quality

There has been concern about the effects of air pollutants on human beings and ecosystems for many years. Recent concern has been focused on the rise of asthma, particularly among children (see Chart 7.9 in the Health chapter), with increased vehicle emissions being a possible contributor. **Table 11.9** shows the source of major air pollutants in the United Kingdom in 1993. Road transport was responsible for over 90 per cent of carbon monoxide emissions and around half of black smoke and nitrogen oxide emissions.

11.9

Air pollutants: by source, 1993

United Kingdom Percentages

	Carbon dioxide	Carbon monoxide	Sulphur dioxide	Nitrogen oxides	Volatile organic compounds	Black smoke
Road transport	*20*	*91*	*2*	*49*	*38*	*51*
Electricity supply	*31*	*1*	*66*	*24*	-	*5*
Domestic	*16*	*5*	*4*	*3*	*1*	*29*
Other	*34*	*4*	*29*	*24*	*60*	*16*
All air pollutants (=100%) (million tonnes)	151.0	5.6	3.2	2.4	2.4	0.4

Source: National Environmental Technology Centre

11.10

Consumption of petrol and emissions of lead from petrol-engined road vehicles

United Kingdom

Indices (1976 =100)

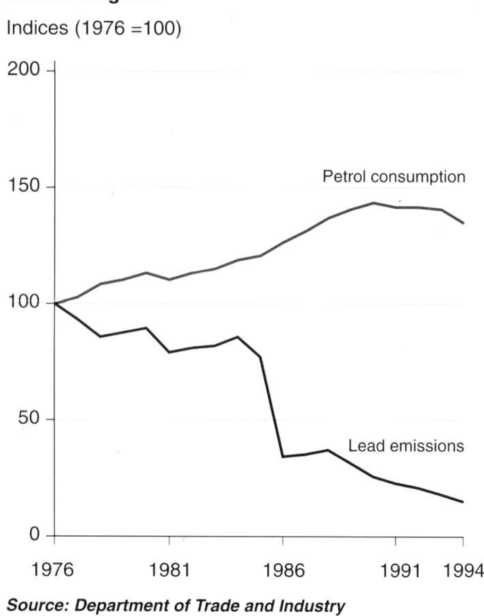

Source: Department of Trade and Industry

11.11

Radon Affected Areas, 1993

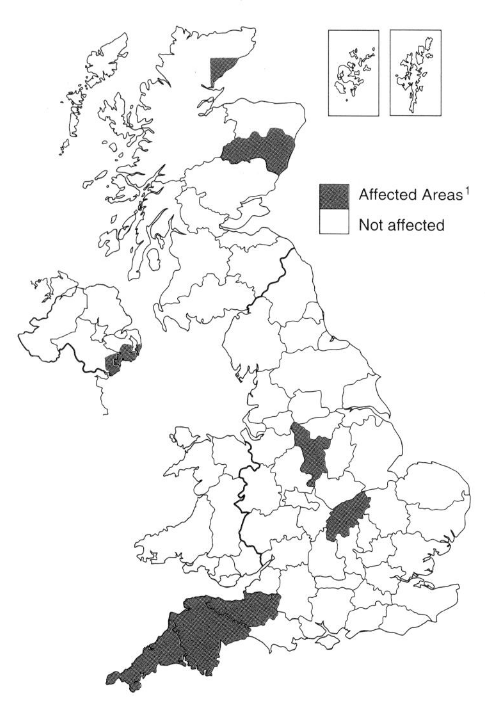

1 Areas where at least 1 per cent of homes have radon concentrations above 200 Bq/m³.

Source: National Radiological Protection Board

In either case users of vehicles found to be exceeding emission limits are issued with a prohibition notice and face prosecution if they fail to take the necessary remedial action. Members of the public can report sightings of excessively smoky heavy commercial vehicles to the Vehicle Inspectorate 'Smoky Diesel Hotline' scheme. This hotline, created in 1991, received over 12.5 thousand calls in the first half of 1995. The Government has set up monitoring stations for all major air pollutants around the country and is now spending over £4 million a year on this project. The monitoring network is due to be increased by a further 12 stations during 1995 to bring the total to nearly 40. By 1997 the network will include over 50 sites and provide comprehensive coverage on air quality in UK cities.

Chart 11.1 shows that since 1971 emissions of black smoke have fallen by more than half. Sulphur dioxide emissions have also fallen by almost a half over the same period. Much of the sulphur dioxide in the atmosphere comes from natural sources but in highly developed and heavily populated regions the greater part comes from combustion of fossil fuels containing sulphur, such as coal and oil. Emissions of the other major gases shown in the chart have increased over the same period.

One of the more practical and popular solutions for reducing pollutants in our atmosphere has been the introduction of unleaded petrol. In 1981 the lead content of petrol was reduced from 0.45 grammes per litre to 0.40; a further reduction, to 0.15 grammes per litre, took place in 1985. This together with the introduction of, and sharp increase in, the use of unleaded petrol has resulted in a sharp decrease in lead emissions from petrol-engined road vehicles. Since 1976 there has been an 85 per cent fall in lead emissions from road vehicles while petrol consumption has risen by 35 per cent **(Chart 11.10)**.

Unlike car fumes and factory smoke some air pollutants, such as radiation, are totally undetectable by people. Radiation comes from both artificial and natural sources. The majority of radiation exposure from artificial sources comes from medical procedures. Another source is fallout from weapons tests and accidents, such as Chernobyl; these accounted for only 0.2 per cent of all exposure from radiation in 1992.

Natural sources include cosmic radiation, gamma radiation from rocks and soil, and radon. Radon is a gas produced by the decay of trace amounts of uranium that occur in virtually all rocks. The radioactive decay products of radon may damage lung tissue and increase the risk of lung cancer, with current estimates suggesting that around 1 in 20 deaths from lung cancer are attributable to radon.

A Radon Affected Area is one where 1 per cent or more of houses have radon levels above the action level (of 200bq/m³ recommended by the National Radiological Board) for measures to be taken to limit the exposure of householders to high levels of radon. Devon and Cornwall are areas that are particularly affected by radon **(Chart 11.11)**; Northamptonshire, parts of Somerset and Derbyshire, parts of Grampian and the Highland regions of Scotland and southern parts of County Down and County Armagh in Northern Ireland have also been designated as Affected Areas.

Water quality

The hot summer of 1995 provided a reminder of how valuable a resource water is. Lower than average rainfall and low river flows are likely to have an effect on water quality as there is less water available to dilute waste effluents. However, high rainfall can also adversely affect water quality by causing greater leaching of pollutants from the soil into the water although it can, in turn, have a diluting effect on other sources of pollution.

Since 1990 river and canal quality in England and Wales has been monitored by a system introduced by the National Rivers Authority (NRA), known as the General Quality Assessment scheme. This scheme has been used to assess the chemical qualities of rivers and canals and the results for the period covering 1992 to 1994 are given in **Table 11.12**. Over 90 per cent of river and canal water in England and Wales is of 'good' or 'fair' quality. Between 1990 and 1994 the proportion of rivers in the best chemical water quality classes increased from 48 to 59 per cent of the total; the length of the poorest classes decreased from 15 to 9 per cent. Since 1990 there has been a net upgrading in overall water quality of 26 per cent of the total length of rivers and canals surveyed. The improvements have largely been achieved by continuing pollution control measures, improved performance of sewage treatment works and better control of farm wastes. The most notable improvements in water quality were achieved in the NRA's Thames, Anglian, Welsh and South Western regions.

Chemicals are one of many substances that are illegally put into our rivers and seas. Other substances include oil and sewage: in 1994 oil and sewage pollution accounted for just over half of the 25 thousand substantiated water pollution incidents in England and Wales **(Table 11.13)**. The total number of reported incidents has increased in recent years. This is partly due to heightened public awareness and concern about pollution and encouragement from the NRA to report incidents. In 1994 there were a total of 348 prosecutions in England and Wales for all types of water pollution, around 23 per cent less than in the previous year.

11.12

River and canal quality: by region, 1992-1994

Percentages

	Good	Fair	Poor	Bad
Welsh[1]	*89*	*9*	*2*	-
South Western	*74*	*23*	*3*	-
Northumbria & Yorkshire	*63*	*22*	*14*	*1*
Southern	*55*	*38*	*6*	-
Thames	*54*	*42*	*4*	-
North West	*53*	*31*	*13*	*3*
Severn Trent	*43*	*45*	*10*	*1*
Anglian	*35*	*52*	*12*	*1*
England & Wales	*59*	*32*	*8*	*1*

1 Regional boundaries are based on river catchment areas.

Source: National Rivers Authority

11.13

Substantiated water pollution incidents: by region and type of pollutant, 1994

Percentages

	Oil	Sewage	Organic wastes	Chemicals	Other	All incidents (=100%) (thousands)
North West	*25*	*25*	*14*	*11*	*25*	3.5
Northumbria & Yorkshire	*22*	*31*	*9*	*8*	*31*	3.2
Severn Trent	*31*	*27*	*8*	*6*	*28*	4.9
Anglian	*36*	*21*	*11*	*11*	*21*	2.8
Thames	*45*	*20*	*5*	*9*	*22*	2.0
Southern	*37*	*25*	*8*	*10*	*21*	1.3
South Western	*20*	*21*	*22*	*5*	*32*	4.3
Welsh	*16*	*25*	*18*	*4*	*37*	3.3
England & Wales	*27*	*25*	*12*	*7*	*28*	25.4
Northern Ireland[1]	*19*	*27*	*27*	*17*	*11*	1.9

1 Data are for reported incidents in 1993.

Source: National Rivers Authority

11.14

Concentrations[1] of selected heavy metals in freshwater

Great Britain

Micrograms/litre

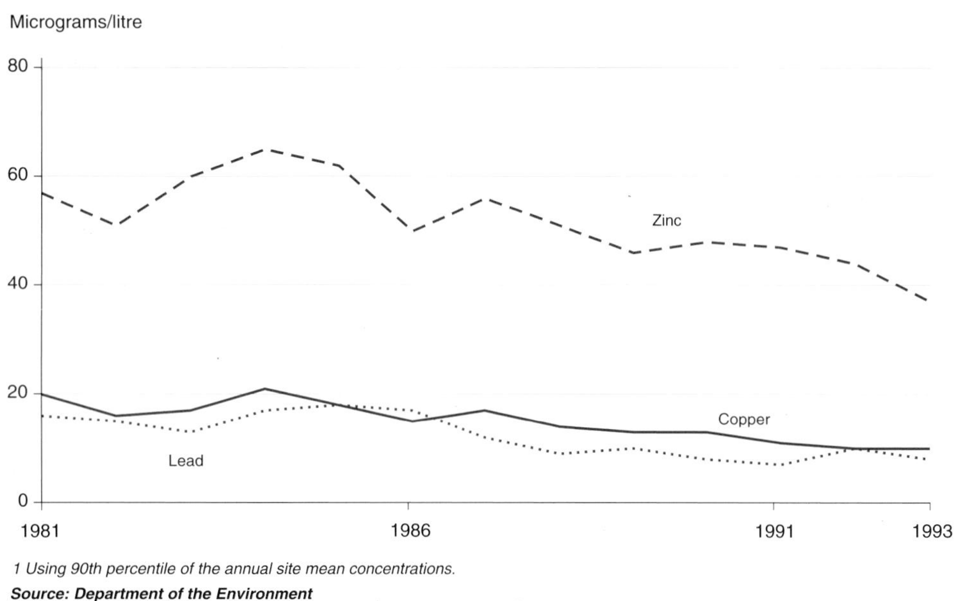

1 Using 90th percentile of the annual site mean concentrations.

Source: Department of the Environment

The EC Dangerous Substances Directive requires member states to reduce the pollution in rivers from a number of listed dangerous substances. These include heavy metals such as zinc, lead, copper, nickel, chromium and arsenic. High concentrations of metals can result from naturally occurring mineral deposits or from industrial pollution incidents. **Chart 11.14** shows that levels of copper, lead and zinc have declined since the early 1980s at the sites monitored by the Harmonised Monitoring Scheme. Levels of nickel and chromium have also declined while for the sixth metal, arsenic, the already low level in 1993 was similar to that of the early 1980s. For all of these metals, average concentrations at most of the sites remained very low and well within Environmental Quality Standards throughout the period.

Critical loads are a method of assessing the impact of acid deposition on environmental ecosystems. For both soils and freshwaters they are defined as levels below which significant harmful effects do not occur. **Chart 11.15** shows the areas in the United Kingdom where critical loads for acidity of soils and freshwaters were exceeded over the period 1989 to 1992. It is estimated that around 18 per cent of freshwaters sampled exceeded the critical load at current levels of sulphur dioxide and nitrogen dioxide emissions. The areas where soils are most affected by acid rain are generally those experiencing high rainfall, including hills close to the west coast of Scotland, the Pennines, the Lake District, parts of Cheshire and the Welsh mountains.

11.15

Exceedence of critical load for acidity of soils and freshwaters, 1989-1992

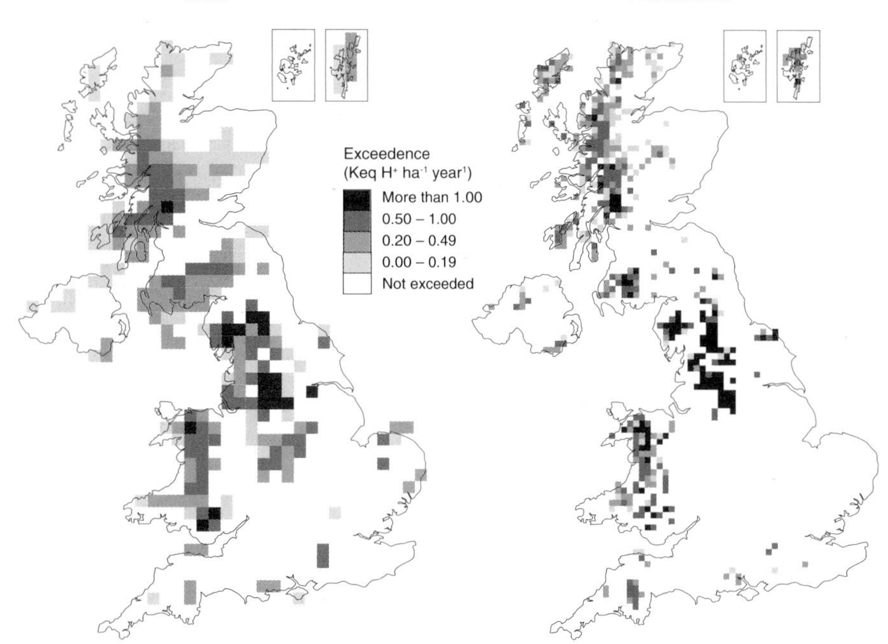

1 Areas where critical loads for acidity of soils are exceeded by annual mean total non-marine sulphur deposition.

2 Areas where critical loads for acidity of freshwaters are exceeded by annual mean total non-marine sulphur and nitrogen deposition.

Source: Warren Spring Laboratory; Institute of Terrestrial Ecology; National Environmental Technology Centre

11.16

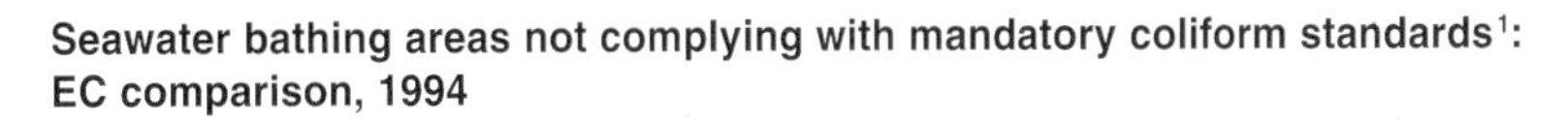

Seawater bathing areas not complying with mandatory coliform standards[1]: EC comparison, 1994

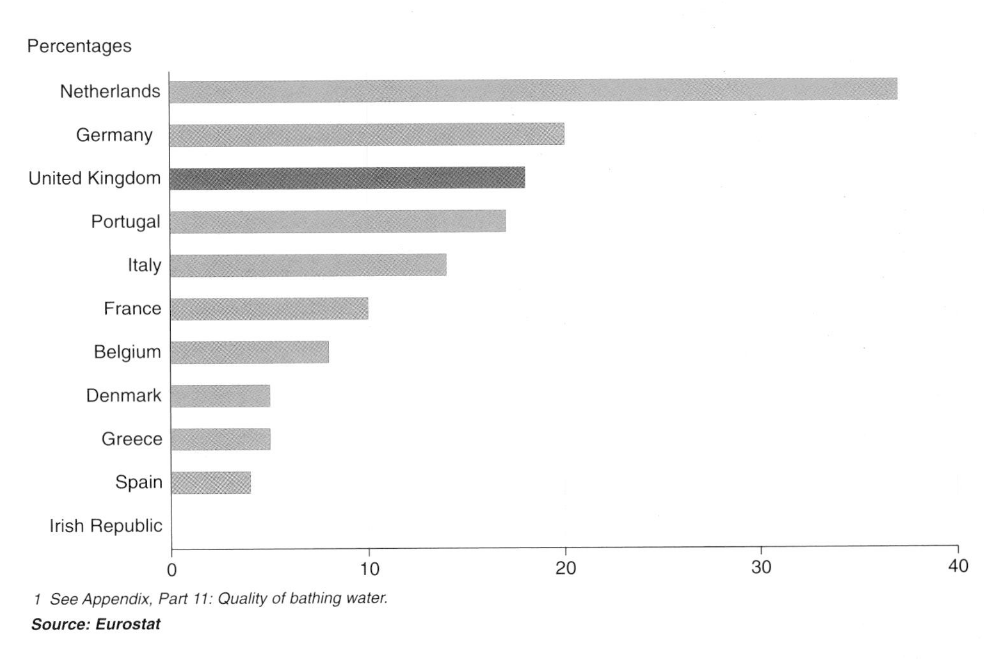

1 See Appendix, Part 11: Quality of bathing water.

Source: Eurostat

Water quality is also an issue affecting our coastal and marine waters. Under the EC Bathing Water Directive, 11 chemical, physical and microbiological factors are measured, including coliforms which are generally seen as the most important indicators of the extent to which water is contaminated by sewage. Bathing water samples are taken at regular intervals just before and then during the bathing season. The Directive requires that at least 95 per cent of samples taken over the bathing season for each of the total and fæcal coliforms do not exceed the mandatory values. **Chart 11.16** shows the percentages of seawater bathing areas failing to reach the required standard across the EC in 1994. In 1994, 18 per cent of seawater bathing areas failed to meet the standard in the United Kingdom, which was one of seven countries who improved between 1993 and 1994. The worst country was the Netherlands where 37 per cent of seawater bathing areas failed to meet the standard in 1994. In the Irish Republic they all met the standard.

11.17

Land use, 1993

United Kingdom Percentages

	England	Wales	Scotland	Northern Ireland	United Kingdom
Agricultural					
Crops and fallow	*30*	*3*	*7*	*5*	*19*
Grass and rough grazing	*39*	*76*	*66*	*73*	*52*
Other[1]	*8*	*3*	*3*	*2*	*6*
Forest and woodland[2]	*7*	*12*	*15*	*6*	*10*
Urban land and land not elsewhere specified	*16*	*6*	*9*	*14*	*13*
All land (=100%) (thousand square kilometres)	129.7	20.6	77.1	13.5	240.9
Inland water (thousand square kilometres)	0.8	0.1	1.7	0.6	3.2

1 Land on agricultural holdings not elsewhere classified eg farm roads, yards, buildings, gardens, ponds, derelict land, land in set aside schemes, woodland etc.
2 All forest land and private woodlands including woodland on agricultural holdings.

Source: Ministry of Agriculture, Fisheries and Food; Ordnance Survey; Forestry Commission; Department of Agriculture, Northern Ireland

Land cover and use

Land and its changing use affects both urban and rural environments. A balance has to be sought between a number of increasing demands including social and industrial developments, conservation and agriculture. Around three quarters of land in the United Kingdom was used for agriculture in 1993 **(Table 11.17)**. In the 1980s, forest and woodland cover increased by an average of 24 thousand hectares a year. By 1993 it accounted for around a tenth of all land use.

11.18

Agricultural land use[1]

United Kingdom Thousand hectares

	1961	1971	1981	1991	1994
Crop areas, of which:	4,276	4,838	4,995	4,956	4,469
Wheat	739	1,097	1,491	1,980	1,811
Barley	1,549	2,288	2,327	1,393	1,106
Other cereals (excluding maize)	768	424	161	127	124
Rape grown for oil seed[2]	..	5	125	440	404
Sugar beet not for stockfeeding	173	190	210	196	195
Potatoes (early and maincrop)	285	256	191	176	164
Other crops	761	577	490	644	665
Bare fallow	123	74	76	64	44
Grasses	7,999	7,240	7,013	6,846	6,758
Sole right rough grazing[3]	7,359	5,550	5,021	4,685	4,551
Woodland	..	154	277	368	428
Set aside[4]	.	.	.	97	728
All other land on agricultural holdings	..	131	211	248	280
Common rough grazing	..	1,128	1,214	1,233	1,224
All agricultural land[5]	19,757	19,115	18,808	18,498	18,482

1 Includes estimates for minor holdings in England and Wales and Northern Ireland for all years and in Scotland prior to 1991.
2 Data are for England and Wales only in 1971 and 1981.
3 The 1961 figure includes common rough grazing.
4 Data are for England only in 1991.
5 Excludes woodland and all other land on agricultural holdings in 1961.

Source: Ministry of Agriculture, Fisheries and Food; Welsh Office; The Scottish Office Agriculture and Fisheries Department; Department of Agriculture, Northern Ireland

11.19

New tree planting

United Kingdom

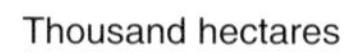

Thousand hectares

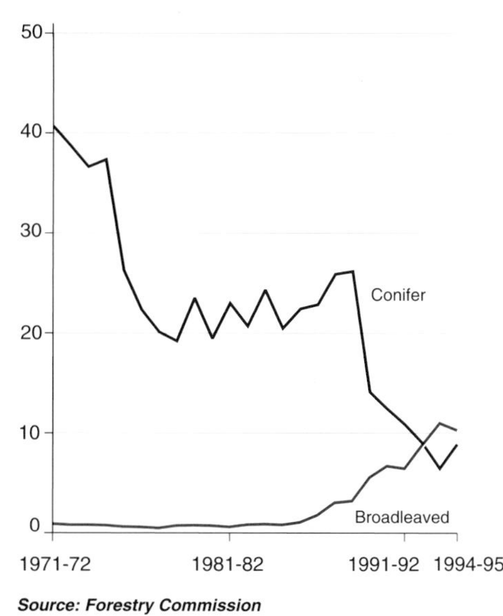

Source: Forestry Commission

The majority of agricultural land is used for grass and rough grazing - around 11 million hectares in 1994 **(Table 11.18)**. This represents just over 60 per cent of total use. Crop areas accounted for almost a quarter of agricultural land, with wheat being the predominant crop. There has been a fall in the amount of agricultural land used for crops over recent years. This is mainly the result of EC Set Aside Schemes established to reduce the amount of agricultural land in arable production. The first scheme was introduced in 1988 and ran for five years. In 1993 the Arable Area Payments scheme was introduced and this required a minimum of 15 per cent of the arable area of a farm to be set aside under rotational set aside. This resulted in nearly 728 thousand hectares being set aside in the United Kingdom in 1994. This land may be used for growing non-food crops but the majority is left to green cover, either sown or established through natural regeneration.

Table 11.17 showed that around a tenth of the land in the United Kingdom was covered by forest and woodland. **Chart 11.19** shows the increase in forests and woodland cover in each year since 1971-72. The importance of trees to the environment is well known with their ability to absorb carbon dioxide and thereby contribute to an overall reduction in global warming. The amount of conifer trees planted in the United Kingdom in 1994-95 was only a fifth of the amount planted in 1971-72. The removal of tax reliefs for conifer planting in the late 1980s resulted in a particularly steep decline in new plantings although there has been a stabilisation in coniferous forest cover. In 1971-72 the Forestry Commission accounted for just over half of all new conifer planting, compared with less than a tenth in 1994-95. While new planting (that is, planting of areas not previously afforested) by the Forestry Commission has gradually fallen, planting by other sources began to pick up in the early 1980s, reaching a peak of just over 22 thousand hectares in 1988-89. It then declined, before increasing again in 1994-95.

For broadleaved trees, new planting was more than 13 times higher in 1994-95 than in 1971-72. The peak figure was in 1993-94 when nearly 11 thousand hectares were planted. One of the main contributors to this increase has been the introduction of the Broadleaved Woodland Grant Scheme and its successor the Broadleaves supplement to the Woodland Grant Scheme, which was started in 1988. There are also strategies to enhance two of the main road gateways into London, the M1 and the M4 with green corridors of trees and shrubs. A pilot scheme announced in September 1995 has hopes of planting more than 300 acres of open land on the M4 corridor from the M25 motorway to Hyde Park Corner, using native oak, ash and field maple along with sycamores, poplars and London planes.

One control over land use is the town and country planning system in England and Wales which, according to Department of the Environment guidance, is designed to 'regulate the development and use of land in the public interest'. The planning system serves to protect and enhance the environment and has a positive role to play in guiding appropriate development to the right place, as well as preventing development which is not acceptable. Under the *Planning and Compensation Act 1991*, all local planning authorities must prepare development plans which set out their policies and proposals for the development and use of land in their area. Planning permission is required to develop or change the use of land. For certain types of small-scale development this is granted by the General Development Order made by the Secretary of State for the Environment. For all other types of development, such as the building of new dwellings, offices or industrial premises, changes of use and significant alterations to existing residential properties, an application must be made to the local planning authority.

In 1994-95, local planning authorities in England decided 451 thousand planning applications (excluding applications relating to minerals and waste developments). Planning permission was granted in 88 per cent of cases. Around 37 per cent of all decisions related to householder developments and 13 per cent to new dwellings. The number of applications decided in 1994-95 was 1 per cent higher than in 1993-94, but 27 per cent below the figure of 618 thousand recorded in 1988-89.

Resources

There are many natural resources at our disposal and their responsible use and maintenance is vital to our welfare. Water resources are of crucial importance as is the regulation of their use. The NRA license all abstractions for domestic and agricultural use in excess of 20m^3 per day and all abstractions for other purposes from surface, tidal and non-tidal water and groundwater in England and Wales. **Table 11.20** shows that 54 thousand megalitres (Ml) per day were abstracted in 1994, a fall of 21 per cent since 1992, but slightly more than in 1993. Over half of this abstracted water is used by the electricity supply industry; they removed 28 thousand Ml per day in 1994 but this was 28 per cent less than in 1992. This fall occured mainly in the Welsh NRA region as a result of the closure of the Trawsfynydd power station in North Wales. In addition, there were also closures of some coastal power stations in the South East.

11.20

Actual abstractions from all surface and groundwater sources: by purpose

England & Wales — Ml/day

	1991	1992	1993	1994
Public water supply[1]	17,563	17,957	16,651	16,735
Spray irrigation	365	284	163	285
Agriculture[2]	134	127	140	119
Electricity supply industry	30,361	38,304	26,579	27,732
Other industry	5,472	4,716	3,895	4,292
Mineral washing	172	212	198	223
Fish farming	3,883	4,475	3,817	3,983
Private water supply	..	51	82	85
Other	1,254	1,795	93	196
All abstractions	59,203	67,921	51,618	53,650

1 Includes some private water supply for 1991.
2 Excludes spray irrigation.
Source: National Rivers Authority; Department of the Environment

11.21

Fish stocks[1]: by sea area and selected species

United Kingdom					Thousand tonnes
	1990	1991	1992	1993	1994
North Sea					
Cod	63	62	60	57	59
Haddock	69	62	103	133	158
Sole	93	81	82	58	82
Herring[2]	1,154	998	775	492	792
Whiting	303	259	256	249	256
Plaice	398	340	325	284	252
West of Scotland					
Cod	18	16	13	15	15
Haddock	25	23	31	50	49
Western English Channel					
Sole	3	3	3	3	3
Mackerel[3]	2,684	3,028	2,937	2,474	2,035

1 Spawning stock biomass.
2 Includes Eastern English Channel.
3 Western stock.

Source: International Council for the Exploration of the Sea

The levels of fish stocks in the sea are largely determined by the intensity of fishing and by natural factors such as breeding success and the extent to which species prey on each other. The largest threat to fish stocks remains over-fishing. The North Sea herring stocks were seriously affected by this in the 1970s but closure of the North Sea Fishery between 1978 and 1982 meant that stocks recovered. However, they have since declined again. **Table 11.21** shows that the spawning stock biomass (the weight of fish capable of reproducing) of herring in the North Sea was nearly 800 thousand tonnes in 1994; this was only just over half the amount in 1989 but ten times the amount in the mid to late 1970s. Most other commercial species are fully exploited and in some cases over exploited. Cod stocks in the North Sea were 59 thousand tonnes in 1994 and have remained stable since 1990.

Since the 1960s two other important products of the waters around the United Kingdom have been oil and gas. At the end of 1994 there were 20 onshore and 73 offshore oilfields in production with a total output of 127 million tonnes of crude oil and natural gas liquids. Just under half of discovered reserves of oil and around a third of those of gas had been recovered from the United Kingdom continental shelf **(Table 11.22)**. For both oil and gas this may represent between a half and a fifth of the estimated total recoverable reserves.

11.22

Oil and gas reserves, 1994

United Kingdom continental shelf	Oil (million tonnes)	Gas (billion cubic metres)
Fields already discovered		
Proven reserves	2,360	1,640
Probable reserves	920	855
Possible reserves	580	400
Total initial reserves in present discoveries	3,860	2,895
of which already recovered	1,786	983
Estimates of potential future discoveries	1,160-4,580	430-1,600
Total recoverable reserves	3,520-8,440	2,070-4,495
Potential additional reserves	150-380	130-300

Source: Department of Trade and Industry

Around 256 million tonnes of oil equivalent of primary fuels were produced in the United Kingdom in 1994, which represents a more than doubling of production in 20 years **(Chart 11.23)**. Apart from gas and oil, primary fuel production also includes primary electricity and coal production. Coal production has been declining and in 1994 production levels were just under 30 million

tonnes of oil equivalent, around two thirds less than in 1971. The big dip in coal production in 1984 was due to industrial action by coal miners and in 1993 and 1994 to pit closures. Conversely, primary electricity production (that is hydro-electric, nuclear and other renewable primary electricity sources such as wind power) nearly tripled over the same period to almost 22 million tonnes of oil equivalent in 1994.

Energy demand for the whole world is forecast to rise by nearly half between 1991 and 2010 according to the International Energy Agency in July 1994. Of this energy demand, non-hydro, non-nuclear renewable forms of energy are expected to be the fastest growing forms, increasing by just over 8 per cent a year on average compared with a 2 per cent average annual increase in total energy use.

In January 1994 the United Kingdom published a 20 year national strategy for sustainable development, following on from the 'Earth Summit' in Rio in 1992. The aim of the strategy is to reconcile economic development with the protection and enhancement of the environment to ensure that growth is sustainable. Progress on this is given every year in a Government White Paper. Action to ensure sustainability involves central and local government, business and other organisations and individuals.

Government expenditure on environmental research and monitoring is shown in **Table 11.24**. Efforts to help provide global protection have seen an increasing amount of money spent on them since the early 1990s with nearly £17 million being spent in 1994-95, more than twice the amount in 1990-91. Another area where spending has grown is air quality: spending increased by nearly 60 per cent between 1990-91 and 1994-95 to just over £9 million. Although other areas such as Her Majesty's Inspectorate of Pollution have experienced falls in expenditure, the overall picture is of growth with an increase of over a quarter in overall expenditure since 1990-91.

11.23

Production of primary fuels

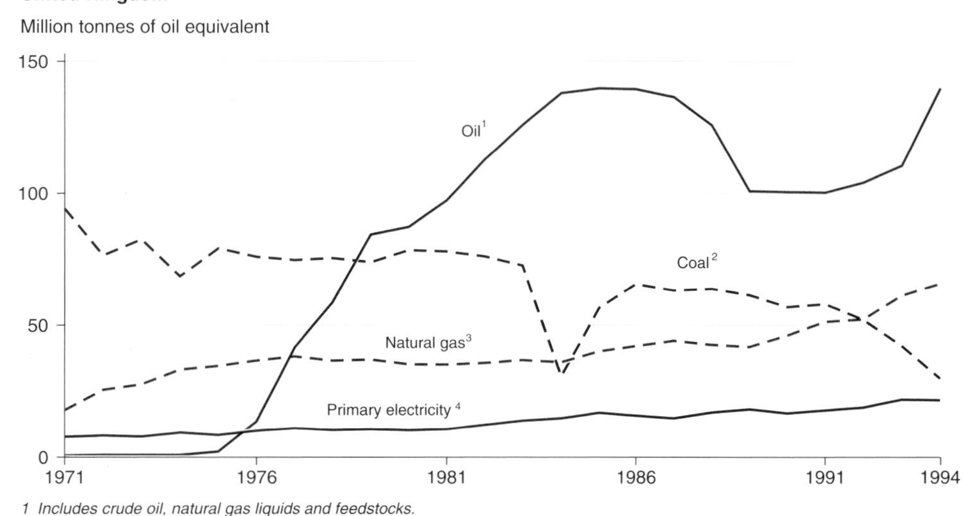

1 Includes crude oil, natural gas liquids and feedstocks.
2 From 1988 includes solid renewables (wood, straw, waste, etc).
3 Includes colliery methane and, from 1988, landfill gas and sewage gas.
4 Nuclear, natural flow hydro-electricity and, from 1988, generation at wind stations.

Source: Department of Trade and Industry

11.24

Government expenditure on environmental research and monitoring

United Kingdom					£ million
	1990-91	1991-92	1992-93	1993-94	1994-95
Global protection	7.7	8.7	12.5	14.3	16.9
Air quality	5.9	8.6	10.1	9.7	9.3
Her Majesty's Inspectorate of Pollution[1]	8.6	7.9	7.5	5.7	4.2
Water	4.5	4.5	4.5	3.8	3.5
Waste management and contaminated land	3.2	5.1	5.5	3.8	3.4
Toxic substances	2.6	3.1	3.9	3.4	2.6
Radioactive substances policy	-	4.1	2.6	2.4	2.2
Noise	0.6	0.6	0.6	0.6	0.3
Other[2]	1.1	1.6	1.3	0.7	0.8
All expenditure on environmental research and monitoring	34.2	44.3	48.5	46.2	43.2

1 Data for 1990-91 include radioactive substances policy.
2 Includes North sea expenditure, environment and health expenditure and environmental economics expenditure.

Source: Department of the Environment

References and further reading

The following list contains selected publications relevant to **Chapter 11: Environment**. Those published by HMSO are available from the addresses shown on the inside back cover of *Social Trends.*

Bathing Water Quality in England and Wales, HMSO
Biodiversity: The UK Action Plan, HMSO
Contaminants Entering the Sea, HMSO
Development of the Oil and Gas Resources of the United Kingdom, Department of Trade and Industry
Digest of Agricultural Census Statistics, HMSO
Digest of Environmental Statistics, HMSO
Environmental Digest for Wales, Welsh Office
Environment Statistics, Eurostat
Forestry Facts and Figures, Forestry Commission
National Radiological Protection Board Statement on Radon in Homes, HMSO
OECD Environmental Data Compendium, Eurostat
Radon Affected Areas, HMSO
Report of the International Council for the Exploration of the Sea's Advisory Committee on Fisheries Management 1995, ICES
Scottish Environmental Statistics, The Scottish Office
Survey of Public Attitudes, Department of the Environment
Sustainable Development, the UK Strategy, HMSO
The Energy Report, Volume 2: Oil and Gas Resources of the United Kingdom, HMSO
The Householder's Guide to Radon, Department of the Environment
The UK Environment, HMSO
This Common Inheritance, HMSO
Water: Nature's Precious Resource, HMSO
Water Pollution Incidents in England and Wales, HMSO

Contacts

Telephone contact points for further information relating to **Chapter 11: Environment**

Department of the Environment	0171 276 8422
Department of Trade and Industry	0171 215 5187
Ministry of Agriculture, Fisheries and Food	01904 455100
Forestry Commission	0131 334 7235
National Rivers Authority	01454 624400
Eurostat	00 352 4301 37286

Chapter 12 Transport

Passenger transport use Between 1992 and 1994 people in Great Britain spent an average of 359 hours a year travelling. (Page 204)

Road A third of households in the South East outside of London had two or more cars in 1993 - the highest proportion of all the regions. (Table 12.8)

In 1994 people in Great Britain cycled around 4 billion kilometres on public roads - about a fifth of the distance cycled in 1951. (Chart 12.1)

Rail London residents each made 13 times more rail journeys (including those by London Underground) than people from the rest of Great Britain (outside the South East) between 1992 and 1994. (Table 12.11)

In its first year of operation, up to November 1995, Eurostar carried almost 3 million passengers. (Page 210)

Water and air Just over 51 million people passed through Heathrow airport in 1994; 86 per cent of these were international passengers making it the world's leading international airport. (Table 12.14)

Transport accidents The risk of death as a passenger in a bus or coach per kilometre travelled was around an eighth of that in a car between 1983 and 1993. (Page 211)

Around half of all car driver casualties in 1994 were aged 22 to 39. (Table 12.17)

12.1

Cycle traffic[1]

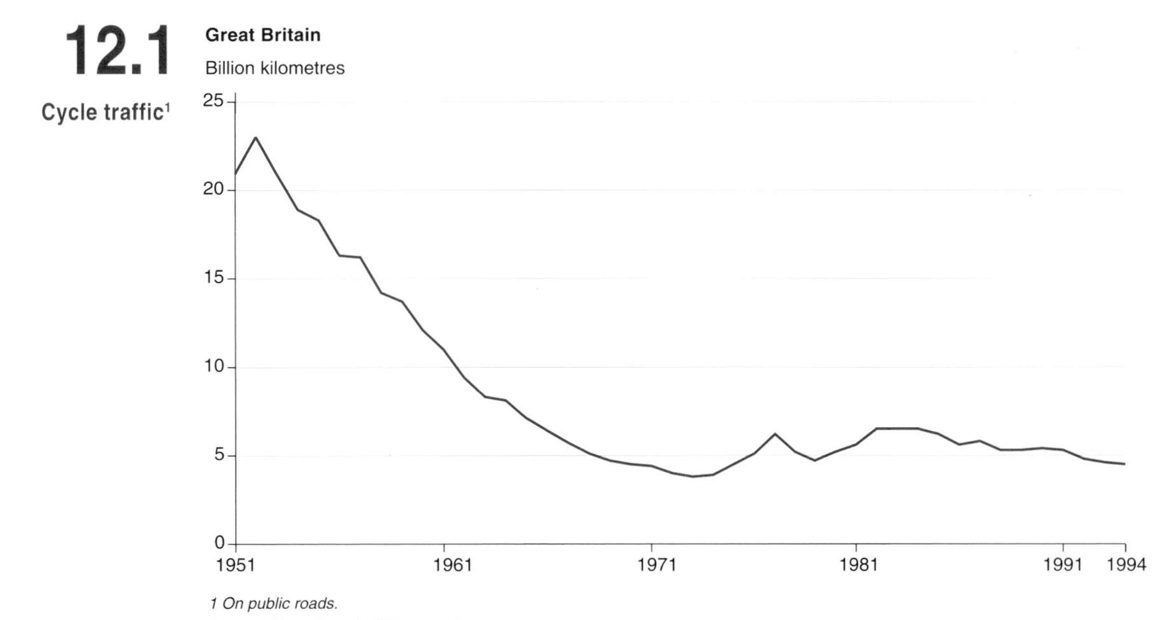

1 On public roads.

Source: Department of Transport

12.2

Passenger traffic: by mode, EC comparison, 1993

Thousand kilometres per head

	Cars and taxis	Buses and coaches	Rail[1]	All these modes[1]
Austria	8.4	1.7	1.2	11.4
Belgium	8.6	0.5	0.7	9.8
Denmark	10.9	1.8	0.9	13.5
Finland	9.8	1.6	0.6	12.0
France	11.0	0.7	1.0	12.7
Germany	8.8	0.9	0.7	10.3
Great Britain	9.6	0.7	0.5	10.9
Greece	..	0.5	0.2	..
Irish Republic	..	..	0.4	..
Italy	10.6	1.5	0.8	12.9
Luxembourg	..	..	0.7	..
Netherlands	9.2	0.8	1.0	11.0
Portugal	7.7	1.2	0.5	9.4
Spain	5.3	0.8	0.4	6.5
Sweden	10.4	1.2	0.7	12.3

1 Excluding metro systems.

Source: Department of Transport

12.3

Passenger journeys: by mode

Great Britain

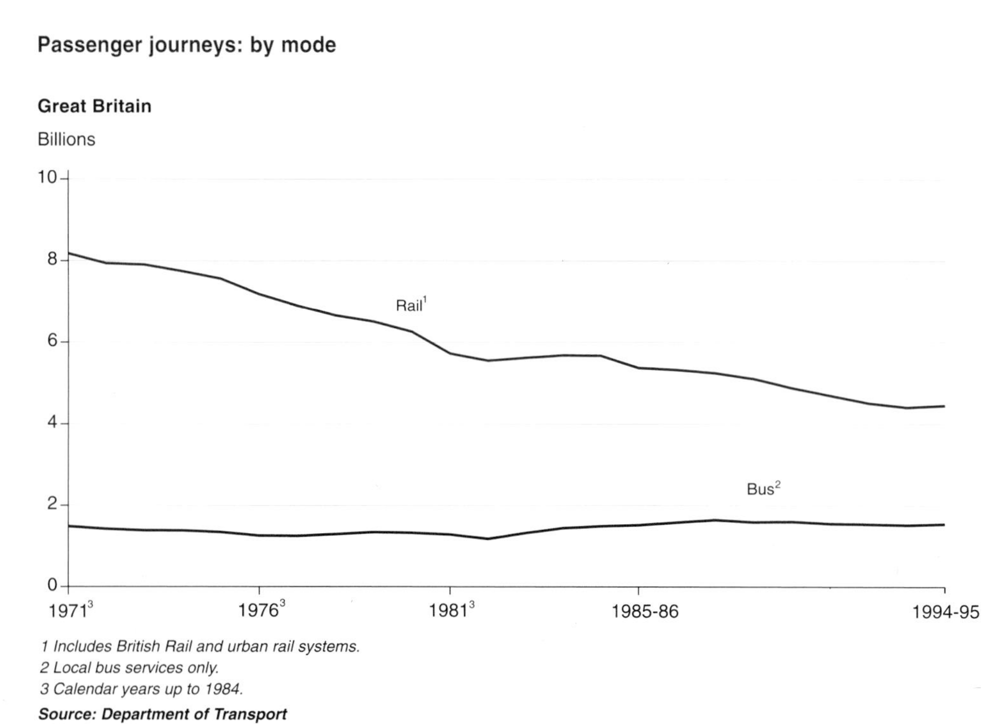

1 Includes British Rail and urban rail systems.
2 Local bus services only.
3 Calendar years up to 1984.

Source: Department of Transport

Increased access to transport, particularly the growth in car use, has had a profound impact on our society, economy and environment during the course of this century.

Passenger transport use

In common with most other European Community (EC) members, Britons travelled more kilometres per head of population by car (including taxis) in 1993 than by any of the other main modes of transport **(Table 12.2)**. Among those member states for whom car usage data are available, Great Britain is ranked around the middle; the French travelled the furthest by car. The Austrians have the highest passenger kilometres per head in rail travel, at more than twice the level in Great Britain. In bus and coach travel we rank in the bottom half of the table, travelling less than half as much by this mode as the Danes, who have the highest usage of all the EC countries. The largest proportionate increase between 1983 and 1993 in the number of cars and taxis was in Portugal where the number more than doubled. The United Kingdom has seen a rise of around a third.

Nearly four and a half billion passenger journeys were made by local bus while just over one and a half billion were made by rail in Great Britain in 1994 **(Chart 12.3)**. Since 1971 the number of journeys made by local bus has almost halved while the number made by rail was virtually the same in 1994 as in 1971. Information from the National Travel Survey shows that over the period 1992 to 1994 each person in Great Britain travelled an average 10.4 thousand kilometres per year - the equivalent of 359 hours or 15 days. Around four fifths of this was travelled by car. Men aged between 30 and 59 travelled the most, averaging 17.4 thousand kilometres a year; they drove a car for three quarters of this distance. Women travelled just under two thirds the distance of men. However, between the periods 1989 to 1991 and 1992 to 1994, the gap between the average mileage travelled by men and women narrowed slightly. In 1992 to 1994 people (including children) travelled an average of around 417 kilometres per year by local bus (including London buses) and 560 kilometres by British Rail and London Underground.

Commuting accounted for nearly a fifth of the total distance travelled in Great Britain in 1992 to 1994 at an average of 1.9 thousand kilometres per person each year. For men aged between 16 and 29, commuting accounted for 30 per cent of all journeys compared with 23 per cent for women in the same age group **(Table 12.4)**. On average, people made 139 journeys a year for commuting purposes in 1992 to 1994, a fall from 1989 to 1991 where the average was 154 journeys. The average number of shopping trips each year between 1992 and 1994 was 144 per person. For 16 to 29 year olds of both genders, shopping was the third largest of all the categories shown in the table, but for women aged between 30 and 59 it was the most common purpose, accounting for nearly one in four of all their journeys. It was also the most common purpose for those aged 60 and over; over a third of their journeys were for shopping.

Social and entertainment journeys, such as visiting friends or participating in sport, was the most common reason for the journeys by those aged under 30. For all ages, it represented an average of around 190 journeys per person per year in the period 1992 to 1994.

12.4

Journey[1] purpose[2]: by age and gender, 1992-1994

Great Britain Percentages

		16-29		30-59			
	Under 16	Males	Females	Males	Females	60 and over	All persons
Commuting	*1*	*30*	*23*	*29*	*21*	*6*	*19*
Business	-	*5*	*2*	*11*	*4*	*2*	*5*
Education	*21*	*6*	*5*	-	*1*	-	*5*
Escort education	*4*	-	*2*	*2*	*5*	-	*2*
Shopping	*14*	*12*	*18*	*15*	*23*	*35*	*19*
Other personal business[3]	*24*	*12*	*14*	*18*	*19*	*20*	*19*
Social/entertainment	*30*	*30*	*31*	*20*	*22*	*27*	*25*
Holiday/other	*7*	*4*	*4*	*5*	*5*	*9*	*6*
All purposes (=100%) (journeys per person per year)	545	892	826	988	865	519	742

1 Excludes journeys under one mile.
2 See Appendix, Part 12: Journey purpose.
3 Includes other escort journeys.
Source: National Travel Survey, Department of Transport

12.5

Mode of transport[1]: by purpose, 1992-1994

Great Britain Percentages

	Car/van	Rail[2]	Local bus	Walk	Motor-cycle	Bicycle	Other	All modes
Commuting	*18*	*49*	*20*	*9*	*48*	*38*	*11*	*19*
Business	*6*	*7*	*1*	*1*	*4*	*3*	*4*	*5*
Education	*2*	*7*	*14*	*10*	*1*	*10*	*19*	*5*
Shopping	*19*	*9*	*33*	*23*	*12*	*11*	*10*	*20*
Other personal business	*24*	*7*	*12*	*14*	*8*	*9*	*14*	*21*
Leisure	*31*	*21*	*20*	*44*	*27*	*29*	*41*	*31*
All purposes	*100*	*100*	*100*	*100*	*100*	*100*	*100*	*100*

1 Percentage of journey stages; see Appendix, Part 12: Journey stages. Excludes journeys under one mile.
2 Includes London Underground.
Source: National Travel Survey, Department of Transport

Commuting represented almost half of all rail journeys in 1992 to 1994 **(Table 12.5)**. On average each person travelled 195 kilometres a year by train when commuting compared with 1,466 kilometres by car or van. For those whose usual place of work was Central London, 43 per cent used British Rail as their usual means for getting to work and 26 per cent used the London Underground. However, the train was used by only 6 per cent of those working in Outer London; 54 per cent were car drivers and a further 6 per cent were car passengers. Outside the conurbations, seven in ten people used a car to get to work (either as a driver or passenger) with walking the second most popular mode which was used by one in seven people.

The predominant use of the car or van was for leisure, around a third of total usage being for this purpose. In order to visit friends at home, people travelled an average of nearly 1,600 kilometres per year by car compared with only 80 kilometres by rail, as their main mode of transport, although leisure still represented around a fifth of all rail use.

One factor which influences the time taken to get to work is the volume of people heading in the same or a similar direction. In 1994 the number of people entering Central London daily between 7am and 10am increased slightly to 989 thousand, breaking the downward trend since 1988 **(Chart 12.6)**. However, this was still around 15 per cent fewer than in 1988. Slightly more people used British Rail, London Underground and the Docklands Light Railway in 1994 than in 1993. The biggest increase though since 1971 has been in the use of coaches and minibuses which has more than doubled - 23 thousand people used these each day during the morning peak in 1994.

12.6

People entering Central London daily during the morning peak[1]

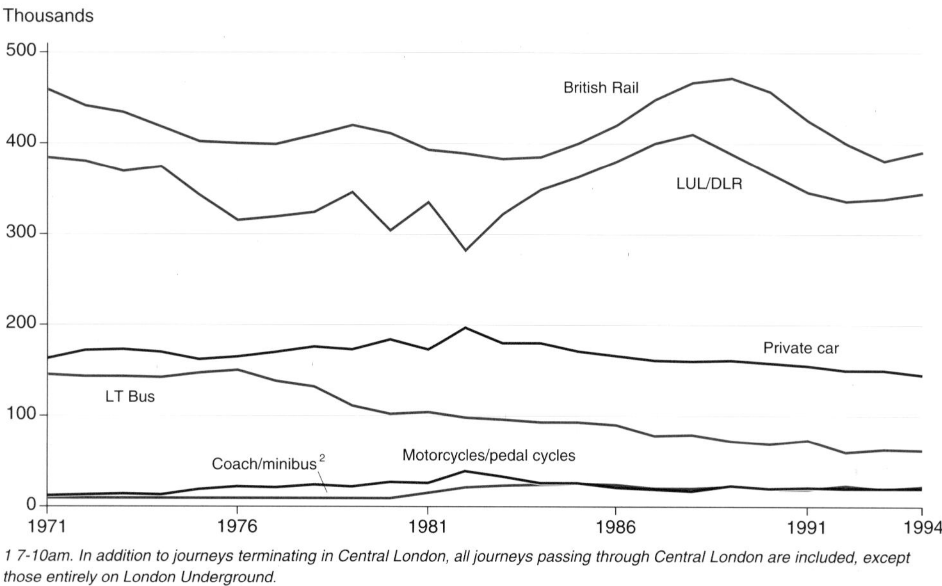

1 7-10am. In addition to journeys terminating in Central London, all journeys passing through Central London are included, except those entirely on London Underground.
2 Includes commuter and tourist coaches.
Source: Department of Transport

Road

In 1994-95 around two thirds of households in Great Britain had a car or van available to them, with over half of households headed by a professional having access to two or more cars **(Table 12.7)**. Households headed by someone who was economically inactive were the least likely to have a car; over half had no car or van available to them. Overall, car ownership has increased by around a half since 1975-76 and for some groups in society it has increased even more markedly. For example, in the period 1992 to 1994, 35 per cent of women owned a car compared with only 13 per cent in 1975-76. This represents nearly a threefold increase compared with a rise of only a quarter for men over the same period. This trend is also reflected in the increase in the proportion of women with full driving licences, which rose from 29 per cent in 1975-76 to 54 per cent in 1992 to 1994. However, women are still far less likely than men to own a car, but are more likely to own a small car.

There were 369 cars per thousand population in England in 1993. The South East outside of London had the highest proportion of households owning at least one car (or van) at around three quarters **(Table 12.8)**. It also had the highest proportion of households owning two or more cars, with a third of households in this category. Households in Scotland were the least likely to have a car. There were also clear differences between urban and rural areas of Great Britain; in 1992 to 1994, 22 per cent of rural households had no car or van, compared with 34 per cent in urban areas. Households in rural areas were also more likely to have two or more cars with one in three households having two or more cars compared with only one in five in urban areas.

12.7

Households with regular use of a car[1]: by socio-economic group[2], 1994-95

Great Britain — Percentages

	None	One car only	Two or more cars
Professional	*5*	*40*	*55*
Employers and managers	*4*	*40*	*55*
Intermediate non-manual	*15*	*56*	*29*
Junior non-manual	*28*	*54*	*18*
Skilled manual and own account non-professional	*14*	*54*	*32*
Semi-skilled manual and personal service	*33*	*53*	*14*
Unskilled manual	*45*	*47*	*8*
Economicaly inactive	*55*	*38*	*7*
All groups	*31*	*45*	*24*

1 Or van.
2 Of head of household. Excludes members of the Armed Forces, economically active full-time students and those who were unemployed and had never worked.
Source: General Household Survey, Office of Population Censuses and Surveys

12.8

Cars[1] and car ownership: by region, 1993

	Percentage of households with		
	One car only	Two or more cars	Cars per 1,000 population[2]
North	*43*	*17*	300
Yorkshire & Humberside	*46*	*19*	326
East Midlands	*47*	*22*	350
East Anglia	*53*	*22*	410
South East	*44*	*27*	386
Greater London	*42*	*20*	333
Rest of South East	*45*	*32*	412
South West	*46*	*28*	410
West Midlands	*43*	*23*	392
North West	*43*	*21*	340
England	*45*	*24*	369
Wales	*46*	*24*	336
Scotland	*44*	*15*	303
Northern Ireland	*47*	*18*	326

1 Includes cars and vans normally available to the household.
2 See Appendix, Part 12: Car ownership.
Source: Department of Transport

12.9

Average daily flow[1] of motor vehicles: by class of road

Great Britain			Thousands
	1981	1991	1994
Motorways[2]	30.6	53.9	57.4
Built-up roads			
Trunk	13.6	18.5	18.7
Principal	12.3	15.2	15.0
Non built-up roads			
Trunk	9.0	15.0	15.1
Principal	4.5	6.8	7.1
All minor roads	1.0	1.3	1.4
All roads	2.2	3.1	3.2

1 Flow at an average point on each class of road.
2 Includes principal road motorways.
Source: Department of Transport

The increase in the volume of traffic can be measured by looking at the average daily flow of vehicles. Between 1981 and 1994 there was an increase of just under half in the average daily flow of vehicles on roads in Great Britain. Motorways continue to carry the majority of traffic, with an average flow of around 57 thousand vehicles in 1994 **(Table 12.9)**. In 1993 the average speed of cars on motorways turned out to be the same as the legal limit at 113 kilometres per hour, but 56 per cent of cars were driven in excess of this limit. In 1992 to 1994 the National Travel Survey collected information which compares the average speeds of journeys between three and five miles which started between 7am and 7pm. For Great Britain overall, the average speed for this type of journey was just over 24 kilometres per hour. However, there are notable regional variations: within Central London the average was 14 kilometres per hour compared with 27 kilometres per hour in East Anglia.

Along with increased vehicle usage has come an increased concern about their impact, both on the environment and on society. In 1993 the British Social Attitudes Survey asked people in Great Britain for their views about certain policy options for cars. The most attractive option among those on which views were sought was that 'many more streets in towns and cities should be reserved for pedestrians only', with nearly seven in ten people supporting this option **(Table 12.10)**. The second most popular option was 'banning company cars except where they are essential for employees in their work'; just over half supported this idea.

There are alternatives to motorised transport, one of the main ones being the bicycle. In 1951 people in Great Britain cycled nearly 21 billion kilometres on public roads, which accounted for around a quarter of all road traffic **(Chart 12.1)**. This fell rapidly to a low of 3.7 billion kilometres in 1973 and the trend remains downwards. In 1994 people cycled around 4.4 billion kilometres, but this was only just over a fifth of the amount in 1951 and represented only 1 per cent of all road traffic. There is a growing awareness of the value of cycling, particularly as a local mode of transport. Many local authorities are taking up Government initiatives designed to encourage cycling by providing cycle facilities such as cycle lanes on the carriageway and cycle networks. There are proposals to establish a London cycle route, as well as proposals for a National Cycle Network by the charity Sustrans which incorporates the 1,000 mile Inverness to Dover Cycle Route.

12.10

Attitudes to policy options for cars, 1993

Great Britain				Percentages
	Agree	Neither agree nor disagree	Disagree	Can't choose/ not answered
Many more streets in towns and cities reserved for pedestrians only	*69*	*17*	*10*	*3*
Banning company cars except where they are essential for employees in their work	*53*	*19*	*24*	*5*
The Government should spend money on campaigns to persuade people to cut back on driving	*39*	*28*	*25*	*8*
The Government should build more motorways to reduce traffic congestion	*37*	*24*	*35*	*5*
Drivers charged tolls on all motorways	*24*	*21*	*51*	*5*
Motorists charged for each mile they drive in city centres in working hours	*18*	*21*	*57*	*4*

Source: British Social Attitudes Survey, Social & Community Planning Research

Rail

Commuting is the main reason why passengers use rail transport (see Table 12.5). In addition, region of residence is a major influence on rail usage. In 1992 to 1994 female full-time workers in London undertook the most journey stages by rail (including the London Underground) at just over 166 per person per year, almost 14 times the number made by their counterparts who lived outside the South East **(Table 12.11)**. Among London residents as a whole, rail usage was almost three times higher than for those living in the rest of the South East. It was also more than 12 times the amount for people in the rest of Great Britain but still represented a fall of just over a fifth since 1989 to 1991 which may be partly due to the economic recession of the early 1990s.

Since 1986-87, performance targets for the railways have been agreed between the Government and British Rail, Northern Ireland Railways and London Underground. The two main aspects of these targets are punctuality and reliability (based on the percentage of the timetable operated). In Great Britain in 1994-95, 62 per cent of route groups met their punctuality targets, with the best performance being by Cornwall, part of the South Wales and Western Operator group. However, only 40 per cent of route groups met their performance targets for reliability; the best performance was by Highland, part of the Scotrail Operator group.

Water and air

Passenger car traffic between UK ports and all major destinations is shown in **Table 12.12**. This passenger traffic doubled between 1981 and 1994, while the amount of traffic passing to and from France more than tripled. The opening of the Channel Tunnel should enhance the prominent position that France holds as a gateway for travellers between the United Kingdom and the rest of Europe. However, it is too early yet to see what effect the Channel Tunnel will have on sea traffic.

An HGV freight service started operating through the tunnel on 19 May with an invitation service; the full service began on 25 July. By the end of 1994, 65 thousand HGVs and 82 thousand cars had been carried through the tunnel, the latter service beginning in a limited way in October of that year. Eurostar services started on 14 November 1994 and by the end of the year

12.11

Rail journeys[1] per person per year: by type of employment and region of residence, 1992-1994

Great Britain — Numbers

	London	Rest of South East	Rest of Great Britain	All regions
Males				
Full time	153	57	11	38
Part time	..	..	..	19
Females				
Full time	166	46	12	44
Part time	70	10	4	11
Not working	32	14	4	9
All persons	76	27	6	19

1 Journey stages. See Appendix, Part 12: Journey stages.

Source: National Travel Survey, Department of Transport

12.12

Passenger car arrivals at, and departures from, UK ports: by overseas country

Thousands

	1981	1986	1991	1993	1994
By ship					
France	1,402	1,944	3,329	4,058	4,575
Irish Republic	378	345	611	621	634
Belgium	591	478	514	413	404
Netherlands	259	325	399	410	328
Spain and Portugal	20	27	47	70	79
Germany	22	21	34	44	48
Scandinavia and Baltic	62	67	56	53	42
Denmark	50	45	44	32	39
All overseas routes	2,784	3,252	5,034	5,701	6,148
By hovercraft					
France	287	218	189	158	181
All overseas routes	3,071	3,470	5,223	5,859	6,330

Source: Department of Transport

12.13

International passenger movements: by mode

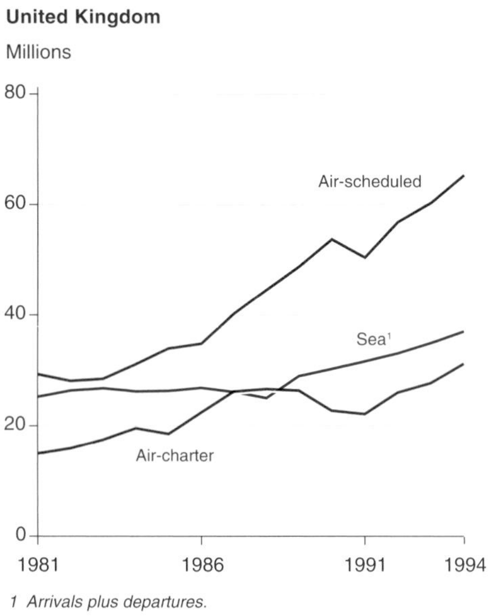

1 Arrivals plus departures.

Source: Department of Transport

approximately 700 trains had passed through the tunnel. The number of commercial (fare-paying) passengers (including freight shuttle drivers, Eurostar passengers and tourist shuttle drivers and passengers) passing through the tunnel in 1994 was 391 thousand. However, during the first 12 months of operation, Eurostar alone had carried almost 3 million passengers.

In 1994 there were just over 21 million visitors to the United Kingdom by all modes of transport from all over the world; this represents around an 8 per cent increase over the previous year. Of these, around 63 per cent came from Western Europe and around 17 per cent from North America.

More overseas residents come to the United Kingdom for a holiday than for business, although between 1993 and 1994 the number coming for business purposes increased by 8 per cent. The majority of both these types of travellers and general holidaymakers arrive and depart by air. There were around 96 million international passenger movements by air in 1994, an increase of nearly 10 per cent on the previous year **(Chart 12.13)**. Scheduled flights accounted for two out of every three air passengers movements in 1994. Sea passenger movements, at just over 37 million in 1994, were 6 per cent higher than in the previous year.

London's Heathrow airport handles more passengers (both international and domestic) than any other airport in the United Kingdom. In 1994 just over 51 million people passed through Heathrow; over 86 per cent were international passengers **(Table 12.14)**. This makes Heathrow the world's leading airport in terms of the number of international passengers who pass through it. It is dwarfed on the domestic front however by Chicago O'Hare International which handled over 59 million domestic passengers in 1993. Conversely, Chicago handled only a seventh of the international passengers of Heathrow. Between 1991 and 1994 there was an increase in the number of passengers passing through nearly all the airports in the United Kingdom with the total increase being around a quarter. The exception was Luton airport which had 8 per cent fewer passengers in 1994 than in 1991.

12.14

Domestic[1] and international air passengers: by selected airport

United Kingdom — Thousands

	Domestic				International			
	1972	1981	1991	1994	1971	1981	1991	1994
Heathrow	2,947	3,867	6,714	7,106	13,437	22,543	33,531	44,261
Gatwick	588	1,011	1,012	1,628	4,143	9,714	17,679	19,417
Manchester	707	983	1,906	2,269	1,419	3,729	8,196	12,064
Birmingham	303	378	720	838	553	1,091	2,526	3,946
Glasgow	1,411	1,426	2,289	2,586	415	839	1,865	2,870
Stansted	3	11	253	475	475	253	1,432	2,782
Luton	49	33	210	111	2,668	1,938	1,748	1,692
Newcastle	320	378	544	699	155	564	983	1,718
East Midlands	190	221	342	280	172	518	802	1,335
Bristol	58	44	141	223	150	202	641	1,053
Aberdeen	188	1,037	1,317	1,461	-	515	703	701
Cardiff	..	62	56	74	141	232	457	923
Belfast	1,115	1,220	1,785	1,407	68	170	384	632
Other	2,930	3,368	5,701	6,847	1,332	1,423	1,839	2,966
All airports	10,809	14,039	22,990	26,005	25,128	43,731	72,786	96,359

1 Passengers are recorded at both airport of departure and arrival. Includes British Government/armed forces on official business and travel to/from oil rigs.

Source: Civil Aviation Authority

Transport accidents

With transport usage come certain inherent dangers. However, Great Britain has one of the best overall road safety records in Europe. The number of road deaths in Great Britain in 1994 was the lowest since records began nearly 70 years ago at 3,650. In terms of deaths per billion kilometres travelled, air travel is the safest form of transport, whilst travel by motorcycle carries the highest risk **(Table 12.15)**. However, the occasional occurrence of major disasters can cause year to year fluctuations, so care should be taken when comparing one year with another. For example, the 1983 to 1993 average for water transport is heavily influenced by the accidents involving the 'Herald of Free Enterprise' (193 deaths) in 1987 and the 'Marchioness' (51 deaths) in 1989.

With recent public concern about the safety of coaches and minibuses, the Government announced proposals in March 1995 that would require every coach and minibus used for carrying children under 16 to be fitted with seat belts. However, in terms of deaths per passenger kilometre travelled, buses and coaches are the safest form of road passenger transport. Over the period 1983 to 1993, the risk of death in a bus or coach was only about an eighth of that in a car.

12.15

Passenger death rates[1]: by mode of transport

Great Britain — Rates per billion passenger kilometres

	1981	1986	1991	1992	1993	Average 1983-1993
Motorcycle	115.8	100.3	94.4	97.0	94.6	102.9
Foot	76.9	75.3	62.5	58.5	56.2	68.8
Pedal cycle	56.9	49.6	46.8	43.4	41.3	48.5
Water[2]	0.4	0.5	0.0	0.5	0.0	9.2
Car	6.1	5.1	3.7	3.5	3.0	4.3
Van	3.8	3.8	2.2	2.2	1.7	2.6
Rail	1.0	0.9	0.8	0.4	0.4	0.9
Bus or coach	0.3	0.5	0.6	0.4	0.8	0.5
Air[2]	0.2	0.5	0.0	0.1	0.0	0.2

1 See Appendix, Part 12: Passenger death rates.
2 Data are for United Kingdom.
Source: Department of Transport

One of the contributory factors affecting road accident death rates is drinking and driving. Campaigns have been running for many years in an effort to reduce the incidence of drinking and driving and have been largely successful. The number of fatalities in the United Kingdom resulting from accidents involving illegal alcohol levels fell by around half between 1986 and 1994, to just over 500 **(Chart 12.16)**. Total casualties, including those seriously and slightly injured, fell by 42 per cent over the same period. Nearly three in ten car drivers who were involved in accidents in Great Britain in 1993 were breath tested, more than double the rate ten years previously. However, whereas 30 per cent failed the breath test in 1983, this figure had fallen considerably to just 7 per cent in 1993.

12.16

Casualties resulting from accidents involving illegal alcohol levels

United Kingdom

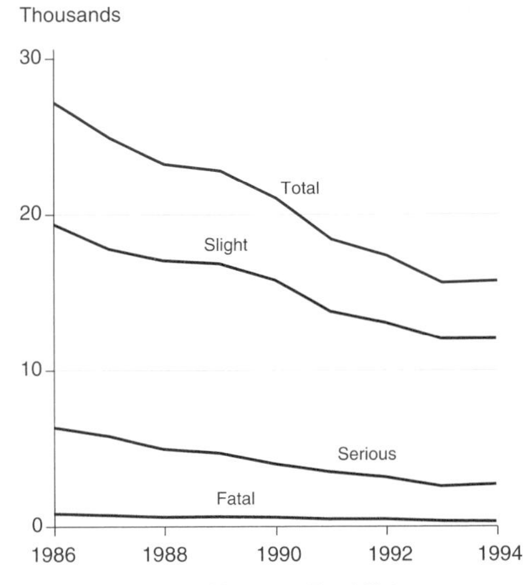

Source: Department of Transport; Royal Ulster Constabulary

12.17

Car driver casualties: by gender and age

United Kingdom			Percentages
	1986	1991	1994
Males			
17-21	*23*	*22*	*18*
22-39	*45*	*46*	*47*
40-59	*22*	*22*	*23*
60 and over	*11*	*11*	*11*
All males[1] (=100%) (thousands)	61.1	66.4	70.1
Females			
17-21	*20*	*20*	*16*
22-39	*49*	*50*	*53*
40-59	*24*	*24*	*25*
60 and over	*7*	*6*	*7*
All females[1] (=100%) (thousands)	32.5	45.5	54.7

1 Excludes cases where age of casualty was unknown.

Source: Department of Transport; Royal Ulster Constabulary

Although the road death rate fell between 1986 and 1994, there was an increase of nearly a half in the number of car driver casualties in the United Kingdom to almost 125 thousand **(Table 12.17)**. The number of car driver casualties has increased at a faster rate among women than men, reflecting the increase in the number of women drivers. Around half of all car driver casualties in 1994 were aged 22 to 39. Among females, the 17 to 21 age group was the only group where there were fewer casualties in 1994 than in 1993 and among males the over 60s was the only age group to experience a fall.

The Department of Transport has recently carried out a special analysis comparing older road casualties (that is, those aged 60 and over) with other adults and children in Great Britain. In 1993 the majority of older road user casualties were car users; at 57 per cent this was lower than for other adult road user casualties, which was around 70 per cent, and probably reflects lower car ownership rates. However, a quarter of older road user casualties were injured whilst walking; this compares with only 9 per cent for other adults and 43 per cent of children.

Resources

The proportion of household expenditure devoted to transport in the United Kingdom remained fairly stable between 1984 and 1994-95, at around 15 per cent. In 1994-95 motoring accounted for just over 84 per cent of expenditure on transport, the majority being on maintaining and running vehicles. Motoring expenditure is highly dependent on income: households in the highest gross income quintile group spent over 14 times more on motoring than households in the lowest quintile group and over six times more on fares and other travel costs **(Table 12.18)**.

Since 1981 motoring costs have doubled but this is slightly below the general rate of inflation **(Table 12.19)**. The largest price rises have taken place in vehicle tax and insurance which more than trebled between 1981 and 1995. The largest increase between 1994 and 1995 was in the cost of

12.18

Household expenditure on transport: by income grouping, 1994-95

United Kingdom						£ per week
	Bottom fifth	Next fifth	Middle fifth	Next fifth	Top fifth	All households
Maintenance and running of motor vehicles	4.11	11.71	21.77	30.31	40.13	21.60
Net purchases of motor vehicles, accessories and spares	1.16	5.16	11.32	20.95	34.26	14.57
Bus and coach fares	1.02	1.39	1.43	1.41	1.40	1.33
Air fares	0.14	0.26	0.96	0.73	3.76	1.17
Rail fares[1]	0.23	0.39	0.90	1.27	2.59	1.07
Other travel and transport[2]	0.95	1.61	2.19	3.18	7.38	3.06
All expenditure on transport	7.60	20.51	38.57	57.85	89.51	42.81

1 Includes tube fares.
2 Includes purchase and maintenance of other vehicles and boats.

Source: Family Expenditure Survey, Central Statistical Office

petrol and oil which rose by 6 per cent. The cost of rail and bus fares has risen steadily since 1981 and by 1995 they had increased by 150 per cent. Changes in local bus fares have shown wide variations in different areas over this period. Between 1982 and 1985-86, certain metropolitan areas in England held prices well below inflation, the 'Fares Fair' policy of the Greater London Council being an example of this. However these fares rose in subsequent years to similar levels found in other areas of the country.

Public expenditure on transport in Great Britain was £7.3 billion in 1994-95, representing an increase of a fifth in real terms since 1971-72 **(Table 12.20)**. About a third was spent on the national roads system, at around £2.5 billion in 1994-95. This includes construction, reconstruction and re-surfacing of national roads, as well as maintenance of bridges. Expenditure on local roads (including net expenditure on car parks) fell by around 5 per cent in real terms over the same period.

In recent years the private sector has been actively encouraged to invest in transport schemes, such as the Channel Tunnel. In 1993-94, of the nearly £8 billion invested in transport, around £1 billion came from the private sector. This figure included £500 million by Eurotunnel. Other projects involving private sector funding include the Skye Bridge which opened in 1995 and the proposed Birmingham Northern Relief road which will become Britain's first privately funded and operated motorway.

12.19

Passenger transport prices[1]

United Kingdom — Indices

	1981	1986	1991	1995
Fares and other travel costs				
Bus and coach fares	100	139	198	252
Rail fares	100	137	201	246
Other	100	107	136	157
Motoring costs				
Vehicle tax and insurance	100	146	220	320
Maintenance of vehicles	100	138	195	242
Petrol and oil	100	145	156	202
Purchase of vehicles	100	116	144	161
Retail prices index (all items)	100	137	185	208

1 At January each year based on the retail prices index.

Source: Central Statistical Office

12.20

Public expenditure on transport in real terms[1]: by type of expenditure

Great Britain — £ million at 1994-95 prices[1]

	1971-72	1981-82	1991-92	1994-95
National roads system				
Capital[2]	1,795	1,359	2,209	2,259
Current[3]	238	185	207	238
Total	2,033	1,544	2,416	2,497
Local transport				
Capital				
Roads and car parks	1,947	1,021	1,379	1,541
Public transport	279	485	143	147
Ports	..	30	12	9
Airports	..	68	156	86
Current				
Roads and car parks[4]	1,791	1,845	2,203	2,026
Revenue support to public transport	26	874	419	562
Concessionary fares	45	370	467	461
All local transport[5]	4,551	4,693	4,778	4,832
Total[5]	6,120	6,236	7,194	7,329

1 Adjusted to 1994-95 prices using the GDP deflator.
2 From 1981-82 includes new construction, reconstruction, new road surface, maintenance of bridges and other road structures and some VAT.
3 From 1981-82 includes minor repairs, routine and winter maintenance.
4 Net of car park receipts.
5 In 1971-72 includes £464 million for administration not shown separately above.

Source: Department of Transport

References and further reading

The following list contains selected publications relevant to **Chapter 12: Transport.** Those published by HMSO are available from the addresses shown on the inside back cover of *Social Trends.*

British Social Attitudes, Dartmouth Publishing

Family Spending, HMSO

International Comparisons of Transport Statistics, Parts I, II and III, HMSO

International Passenger Transport, HMSO

London Area Transport Survey, London Research Centre; Department of Transport

London Journey Times Survey, Department of Transport

London Traffic Monitoring Report, HMSO

National Travel Survey, HMSO

New Motor Vehicle Registrations, Department of Transport

Quarterly Road Casualties Great Britain, Department of Transport

Quarterly Transport Statistics, Department of Transport

Regional Trends, HMSO

Road Accidents Great Britain - The Casualty Report, HMSO

Road Accidents, Scotland, Scottish Office

Road Accidents Statistics English Regions, HMSO

Road Accidents: Wales, Welsh Office

Road Lengths in Great Britain, HMSO

Road Traffic Accident Statistics Annual Report, The Royal Ulster Constabulary

Road Traffic Statistics Great Britain, HMSO

Scottish Transport Statistics, Scottish Office

Traffic in Great Britain, Department of Transport

Transport of Goods by Road in Great Britain, HMSO

Transport Statistics for London, HMSO

Transport Statistics Great Britain, HMSO

Travel Trends, HMSO

UK Airports - Annual Statement of Movements, Passengers and Cargo, Civil Aviation Authority

Vehicle Licensing Statistics, HMSO

Vehicle Speeds in Great Britain, Department of Transport

Welsh Transport Statistics, Welsh Office

Contacts

Telephone contact points for further information relating to

Chapter 12: Transport

Department of Transport	0171 276 8211
Department of the Environment, Northern Ireland	01232 540808
Central Statistical Office	
Family Expenditure Survey	0171 217 4207
Retail prices	0171 217 4310
Office of Population Censuses and Surveys	0171 396 2327
Royal Ulster Constabulary	01232 650222 extn 24135
Social & Community Planning Research	0171 250 1866 extn 369

Chapter 13 Lifestyles

Time use

At weekends in May 1995, men in full-time employment had around two more hours per day of free time than women in full-time employment. (Table 13.2)

In eight out of ten married or cohabiting couples the washing and ironing is usually done by the woman whereas in around half of couples the shopping is either shared equally or done together. (Table 13.3)

Home-based activities

Trade deliveries of compact disc albums reached over 116 million in 1994, representing two thirds of all albums compared with under half in 1991. (Chart 13.8)

Social and cultural activities

The number of people who said that they would attend or had attended a ballet performance in Great Britain increased by nearly 30 per cent between 1986-87 and 1994-95. (Table 13.15)

Sporting activities

In 1993-94, 27 per cent of those in professional occupations had been swimming in the previous four weeks compared with only 8 per cent of those in the unskilled manual group. (Table 13.18)

Holidays

The proportion of adults taking two or more holidays a year has increased by three quarters between 1971 and 1994. (Chart 13.1)

Around eight in ten holidays abroad were taken in Europe in 1994, while the United States was the most common non-European destination. (Page 226)

Political participation

Thirty six per cent of the UK electorate voted at the last European election compared with 91 per cent in Belgium and 87 per cent in Luxembourg - the countries with the highest proportions. (Page 226)

13.1

Holidays[1]: by number taken per year

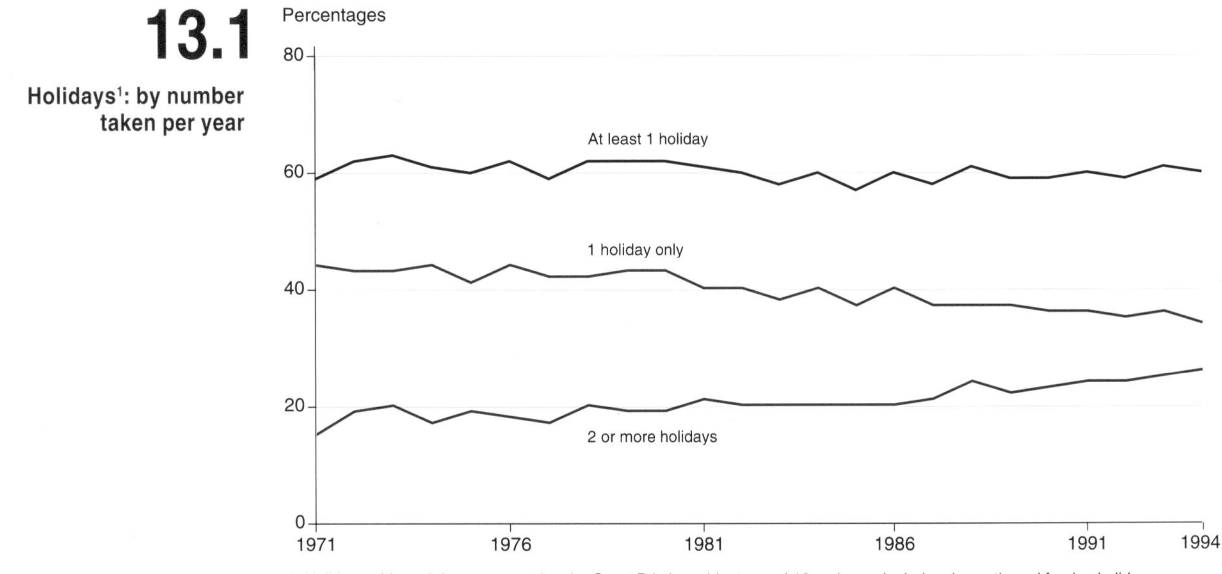

1 Holidays of four nights or more taken by Great Britain residents aged 16 and over. Includes domestic and foreign holidays.

Source: British National Travel Survey, British Tourist Authority

13.2

Time use: by employment status and gender, May 1995

Great Britain Hours

	In full-time employment		In part-time employment		Retired		
	Males	Females	Males	Females	Males	Females	All adults
Weekly hours spent on							
Sleep	57	58	62	60	67	66	61
Free time	34	31	48	32	59	52	40
Work, study and travel	53	48	28	26	3	4	32
Housework, cooking and shopping	7	15	12	26	15	26	16
Eating, personal hygiene and caring	13	13	13	21	15	17	15
Household maintenance and pet care	4	2	6	3	9	3	4
Free time per weekday	4	4	6	4	8	7	5
Free time per weekend day	8	6	8	6	10	8	8

Source: ESRC Research Centre on Micro-social Change, from Omnibus Survey

This chapter reflects just some of the many facets which contribute to the diversity of lifestyles in the United Kingdom today, from what sort of television programmes people watch to whether they exercise their right to vote.

Time use

People's lifestyles are shaped by, amongst other things, the amount of time they spend on various tasks and activities. Men working full time spent 53 hours a week in Great Britain in May 1995 on either work, travel or study which was five hours more than women in full-time work **(Table 13.2)**. However these women spent eight hours more than their male counterparts on housework, cooking and shopping each week. As a result of these differences, at weekends men in full-time employment have around two more hours a day of free time than women who work full time, although on weekdays they have the same amount at nearly four hours of free time each a day. The presence of dependent children in these households reduces the amount of free time each week for men by around 10 per cent and, at around 20 per cent, by even more for women. This is because both men and women with dependent children spend more time on the eating, personal hygiene and caring category than those without dependent children; these women also spend around 70 per cent more time on housework, cooking and cleaning than those women without dependent children.

It seems that in the majority of couples household tasks are still done by women. In 1994 the British Social Attitudes Survey, which is carried out by Social and Community Planning Research, asked married and cohabiting couples about who did certain tasks around the home. In eight

13.3

Division of household tasks[1], 1994

Great Britain Percentages

	Always the woman	Usually the woman	About equal or both together	Usually the man	Always the man	All couples[2]
Washing and ironing	*47*	*32*	*18*	*1*	*1*	*100*
Deciding what to have for dinner	*27*	*32*	*35*	*3*	*1*	*100*
Looking after sick family members	*22*	*26*	*45*	..	..	*100*
Shopping for groceries	*20*	*21*	*52*	*4*	*1*	*100*
Small repairs around the house	*2*	*3*	*18*	*49*	*25*	*100*

1 By married couples or couples living as married.
2 Includes those who did not answer and where the task was done by a third person.
Source: British Social Attitudes Survey, Social & Community Planning Research

out of ten couples the woman usually, or always, did the washing and ironing while in three quarters of couples small repairs around the house were usually, or always, done by the man **(Table 13.3)**. On the other hand grocery shopping is most commonly shared either equally by both partners or done together.

When people do get some free time, they spend it in a variety of different ways. The most common use of free time is watching television or listening to the radio, with people spending an average of 19 hours a week on these activities in May 1995 **(Table 13.4)**. Those in the 60 and over age group spent more time on these activities than younger people. However, this only includes the time spent watching television or listening to the radio when they were not doing anything else simultaneously. For example, if the television was watched whilst visiting friends, this would be recorded as visiting friends and not watching television. The 16 to 24 age group spent the most time on eating or drinking out whilst those in the 60 and over age group spent the least. On the other hand the amount of time people spend reading increases with age.

Home-based activities

The type of television programme that people in the United Kingdom watch also varies with age. Unsurprisingly, children's programmes are most popular with 4 to 15 year olds accounting for a quarter of their week's viewing **(Table 13.5)**. Overall, drama is the most frequently watched type of television programme and the viewing figures reflect this: 'Coronation Street' or 'EastEnders' usually have more viewers than any other programmes. Over recent years there has been an increase in the

13.4

Use of free time: by age, May 1995

Great Britain — Hours per week

	16-24	25-34	35-44	45-59	60 and over	All aged 16 and over
Television or radio	14	15	13	17	26	19
Visiting friends[1]	7	5	4	4	4	5
Reading	1	1	2	3	6	3
Talking, socialising and telephoning friends	3	3	3	4	4	3
Eating and drinking out	6	4	4	4	2	3
Hobbies, games and computing	2	2	1	3	3	2
Walks and other recreation	2	2	1	2	3	2
Doing nothing (may include illness)	1	1	1	2	2	2
Sports participation	3	1	1	1	1	1
Religious, political and other meetings	-	1	1	-	1	1
Concerts, theatre, cinema and sports spectating	1	1	-	-	-	-
Other	1	-	-	-	-	-
All free time	40	37	33	40	52	42

1 This may include eating.

Source: ESRC Research Centre on Micro-social Change, from Omnibus Survey

13.5

Types of television programme watched: by age, 1994

United Kingdom — Percentages

	4-15	16-24	25-34	35-44	45-54	55-64	65 and over	All aged 4 and over
Drama	*19*	*28*	*28*	*26*	*25*	*23*	*24*	*25*
Light entertainment	*20*	*19*	*18*	*18*	*17*	*16*	*17*	*18*
Films	*13*	*17*	*16*	*17*	*17*	*16*	*12*	*15*
Documentaries and features	*7*	*11*	*13*	*13*	*14*	*15*	*15*	*13*
News	*6*	*6*	*8*	*10*	*11*	*13*	*14*	*11*
Sport	*7*	*10*	*10*	*10*	*11*	*12*	*13*	*11*
Children's programmes	*25*	*6*	*4*	*3*	*2*	*1*	*1*	*5*
Other	*3*	*3*	*3*	*3*	*2*	*3*	*4*	*3*
All programmes	*100*	*100*	*100*	*100*	*100*	*100*	*100*	*100*

Source: Broadcasters' Audience Research Board; British Broadcasting Corporation; AGB Limited; RSMB Limited

13.6

Radio listening: by age, 1994

United Kingdom	Hours and minutes per week
	1994
4-15	5:54
16-34	17:19
35-64	18:17
65 and over	18:07
All aged 4 and over	16:07
Reach[1] (percentages)	
Daily	*67*
Weekly	*84*

1 Percentage of the population aged 4 and over who listened to the radio for at least half a programme a day.

Source: British Broadcasting Corporation

number of alternatives to the four main terrestrial television channels. The proportion of those aged four and over who watch cable and satellite television each week has gone up by over three quarters from 5.4 million in 1991 to 9.7 million in 1994. Viewers' choice will be further widened with the introduction of Channel 5 by January 1997.

Those in the 4 to 15 age group watched around 18 hours of television a week in 1994. However, they spent less time listening to the radio, at under six hours per week; those in the 35 to 64 age group listened to three times as much at over 18 hours per week **(Table 13.6)**. On average, people listened to just over 16 hours of radio a week, around two thirds of the amount of time they spent watching television. The most popular time for people to tune into the radio is at breakfast time: the number of listeners rapidly reaches a peak at around 8am and then generally declines throughout the rest of the day, with a much smaller peak at around 4pm to 5pm.

Although watching television is the most popular home-based leisure activity for both men and women, they show different preferences for other activities. For example, in Great Britain only 3 per cent of men admitted to doing dressmaking, needlework or knitting in the four weeks before interview in 1993-94 compared with 38 per cent of women **(Table 13.7)**. On the other hand the proportion of women who carry out DIY has grown to 30 per cent compared with 57 per cent of men. Interestingly, across all ages, women are much more likely to spend time reading than men. Participation in some activities vary more with age than others; for example, gardening is much more popular with those aged 25 and over, while people are less likely to listen to records or tapes as they get older. For all the activities shown in Table 13.7, the participation rates in Northern Ireland were lower than those in Great Britain. For example, only 38 per cent of men and 16 per cent of women carried out DIY and 59 per cent of men and 60 per cent of women listened to records or tapes.

Trade deliveries of compact discs (CDs) in the United Kingdom continued their remarkable upward trend in 1994, breaking the 100 million barrier and reaching 116.4 million **(Chart 13.8)**. In 1994 CDs represented two thirds of trade deliveries of all albums; the proportion accounted for by LPs fell from nearly 90 per cent in 1973 to just under 3 per cent. The top selling CD album in 1994 was 'Cross Road' by Bon

13.7

Participation[1] in home-based leisure activities: by gender and age, 1993-94

Great Britain — Percentages

	16-19	20-24	25-29	30-44	45-59	60-69	70 and over	All aged 16 and over
Males								
Watching TV	*99*	*100*	*99*	*99*	*99*	*99*	*97*	*99*
Visiting/entertaining friends or relations	*96*	*97*	*97*	*97*	*94*	*94*	*91*	*95*
Listening to radio	*93*	*95*	*95*	*94*	*91*	*86*	*83*	*91*
Listening to records/tapes	*96*	*96*	*93*	*86*	*76*	*66*	*50*	*79*
Reading books	*55*	*58*	*56*	*60*	*61*	*59*	*58*	*59*
Gardening	*24*	*22*	*37*	*52*	*62*	*65*	*55*	*51*
DIY	*34*	*44*	*61*	*68*	*65*	*58*	*35*	*57*
Dressmaking/needlework/ knitting	*2*	*3*	*3*	*3*	*3*	*3*	*4*	*3*
Females								
Watching TV	*99*	*99*	*99*	*99*	*99*	*99*	*98*	*99*
Visiting/entertaining friends or relations	*98*	*98*	*99*	*98*	*96*	*95*	*94*	*96*
Listening to radio	*97*	*95*	*92*	*91*	*88*	*84*	*77*	*88*
Listening to records/tapes	*97*	*96*	*92*	*88*	*75*	*62*	*42*	*75*
Reading books	*75*	*70*	*70*	*71*	*71*	*74*	*67*	*71*
Gardening	*11*	*23*	*34*	*51*	*57*	*54*	*39*	*45*
DIY	*16*	*35*	*39*	*40*	*34*	*23*	*10*	*30*
Dressmaking/needlework/ knitting	*19*	*30*	*30*	*37*	*44*	*48*	*38*	*38*

1 Percentage in each age group participating in each activity in the four weeks before interview.

Source: General Household Survey, Office of Population Censuses and Surveys

Jovi, with Beautiful South and Pink Floyd in second and third places respectively. The market share of CD singles has also seen a dramatic increase, from 6 per cent of all singles in 1989 to over 47 per cent in 1994. The share of trade deliveries of singles made up by 7" singles has dropped from over 61 per cent in 1989 to just 7 per cent in 1994. Conversely, the number of cassette singles has increased over 17 times since 1989, to represent nearly a third of all singles in 1994. Although CDs are bought by a roughly equal proportion of men and women, tapes are more likely to be bought by women while the vinyl format is more likely to be bought by men. Among album buyers, 'pop' continues to be the most common type of music they last bought, with 'rock' the next most common. The most popular music magazine continues to be Smash Hits which had an average circulation of 325 thousand per issue in 1994.

On average over 27 million people read at least one national daily newspaper in Great Britain in 1994-95; the most popular daily paper was still The Sun, with a readership of over ten million **(Table 13.9)**. The Times has seen the biggest increase in readership over the previous year, with a rise of around 375 thousand, whilst the Daily Mirror saw the largest decrease of around 650 thousand. More people read Sunday papers than daily ones. Over 30 million people read a national Sunday newspaper in 1994-95; the most popular remained the News of the World which was read by over a quarter of adults.

13.8

Trade deliveries of LPs, cassettes, CDs and singles[1]

United Kingdom

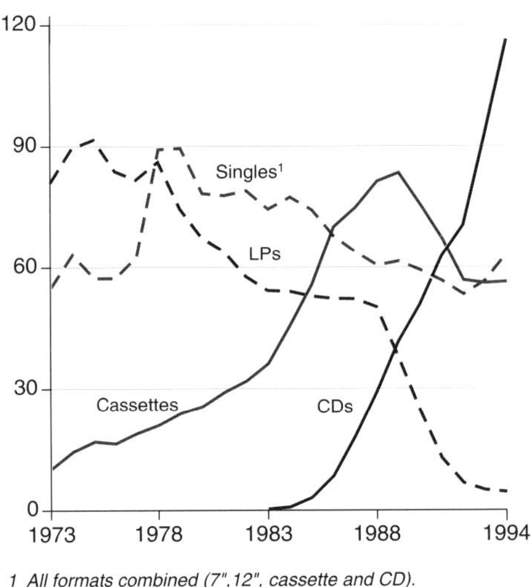

1 All formats combined (7",12", cassette and CD).

Source: British Phonographic Industry

13.9

Reading of national daily newspapers: by age and gender, 1994-95[1]

Great Britain — Percentages

	Percentage reading each paper								
	15-24	25-44	45-64	65 and over	Males	Females	All adults	Readership[2] (millions)	Readers per copy (numbers)
The Sun	30	24	20	16	26	19	22	10.1	2.5
Daily Mirror	15	13	15	15	16	12	14	6.5	2.6
Daily Mail	8	8	12	11	10	9	10	4.4	2.5
Daily Express	5	5	8	10	7	7	7	3.2	2.5
The Daily Telegraph	4	5	9	7	7	6	6	2.8	2.7
Daily Star	6	6	3	2	6	3	4	2.0	2.8
Today	4	4	4	2	5	3	4	1.7	3.0
The Times	4	3	4	3	4	3	4	1.7	2.7
The Guardian	4	4	3	1	3	2	3	1.3	3.5
The Independent	2	2	2	1	2	2	2	0.9	3.3
Financial Times	1	2	2	-	2	1	2	0.7	4.3
Any national daily newspaper[3]	58	56	63	62	64	55	60	27.2	..

1 Data are for the 12 month period ending in June 1995.
2 Defined as the average issue readership and represents the number of people who claim to have read or looked at one or more copies of a given publication during a period equal to the interval at which the publication appears.
3 Includes the above newspapers plus the Daily Record, Sporting Life and Racing Post.

Source: National Readership Surveys Ltd

13.10

Reading of the most popular magazines: by social grade[1] and gender, 1994-95[2]

Great Britain Percentages

	Percentage reading each magazine							Readership[3] (millions)	Readers per copy (numbers)
	AB	C1	C2	DE	Males	Females	All adults		
General magazines									
Reader's Digest	*15*	*14*	*12*	*9*	*13*	*13*	*13*	5.7	3.3
Radio Times	*17*	*13*	*8*	*6*	*11*	*10*	*11*	4.9	3.3
Sky TV Guide	*9*	*11*	*13*	*9*	*13*	*8*	*10*	4.8	..
TV Times	*7*	*9*	*10*	*11*	*9*	*10*	*9*	4.3	4.2
AA Magazine	*16*	*10*	*8*	*4*	*11*	*7*	*9*	4.2	..
What's on TV	*5*	*8*	*9*	*11*	*7*	*10*	*9*	3.9	2.4
Viz	*6*	*8*	*7*	*5*	*10*	*3*	*7*	3.0	5.2
TV Quick	*3*	*6*	*6*	*6*	*4*	*7*	*5*	2.5	..
Women's magazines									
Take a Break	*5*	*11*	*13*	*15*	*5*	*16*	*11*	5.0	..
Bella	*5*	*9*	*10*	*10*	*3*	*14*	*9*	4.0	..
Woman's Own	*6*	*9*	*10*	*10*	*2*	*15*	*9*	4.0	4.6
M & S Magazine	*14*	*10*	*6*	*3*	*4*	*12*	*8*	3.6	..
Woman	*4*	*7*	*7*	*8*	*2*	*11*	*7*	3.1	3.5

1 See Appendix, Part 13: Social grade.
2 Data are for the 12 month period ending in June 1995.
3 Defined as the average issue readership and represents the number of people who claim to have read or looked at one or more copies of a given publication during a period equal to the interval at which the publication appears.
Source: National Readership Surveys Ltd

13.11

The most popular magazines and newspapers read[1] by children: by age and gender, 1995

United Kingdom Percentages

Aged 7-10		Aged 11-14	
Males		**Males**	
Beano	*28*	The Sun	*22*
Match	*25*	Match	*18*
Shoot!	*22*	Shoot!	*18*
Sonic the Comic	*18*	News of the World	*17*
Dandy	*17*	Beano	*15*
Females		**Females**	
Smash Hits	*16*	Just Seventeen	*41*
Barbie	*13*	Sugar	*39*
Girl talk	*13*	Big!	*34*
Beano	*12*	It's Bliss	*34*
Live and Kicking	*12*	Smash Hits	*32*

1 For 7 to 10 year olds data are the percentage of children who said they read the publication; for 11 to 14 year olds data are the average issue readership.
Source: Youth TGI, BMRB International

The most popular general magazine in Great Britain in 1994-95 was Reader's Digest with 5.7 million readers, just under 1 million more than the Radio Times and Sky TV Guide which both had just under 5 million readers **(Table 13.10)**. The general magazine category is dominated by television-related magazines, reflecting television viewing as the most popular home-based leisure activity. The Radio Times was read by 17 per cent of those in social grade AB whilst TV Times was more commonly read by those in social grade DE. Take a Break was the most commonly read weekly women's magazine, with a readership of 5 million per issue it was read by 16 per cent of women but also by 5 per cent of men, making it the most popular women's magazine with men too.

For boys aged 7 to 10 in the United Kingdom, the top five magazines are split between comics and football magazines, with 28 per cent reading the Beano, the most popular magazine in 1995 **(Table 13.11)**. Among girls in the same age group, music magazines are more popular: the top magazine, Smash Hits, is read by 16 per cent of girls of this age. The proportion of girls who read Smash Hits in the 11 to 14 age group is double that for those aged between 7 and 10 at 32 per cent. However, this is only sufficient to put it into fifth place, 9 percentage points behind the most commonly read magazine among girls of this age, Just Seventeen. The Sun is the most commonly read newspaper or magazine among 11 to 14 year old boys, followed by two football magazines, Match and Shoot!

There were over 100 million fewer books borrowed from public libraries in 1993-94 than in 1981-82, a fall of 16 per cent to just over 550 million **(Table 13.12)**. The average number of books issued per head of population also fell over the same period, to an average of 9.5. However, it is not just books that libraries lend. While book issues fell, the average number of audio-visual issues per head more than doubled between 1981-82 and 1993-94 although they still accounted for only a twentieth of book issues. A survey undertaken by Book Marketing Ltd in 1994 found that seven in ten people who borrowed books from libraries also used additional facilities such as borrowing records, tapes or CDs, photocopying, obtaining information on careers, business and the community, and studying facilities. Of those people who held a library ticket, nearly a third borrowed books at least fortnightly. Overall nearly six in ten of the population claimed to have a library ticket.

13.12

Public library issues

United Kingdom — Percentages

	1981-82	1991-92	1992-93	1993-94
Adult fiction	*62*	*56*	*56*	*55*
Adult non-fiction	*22*	*24*	*24*	*25*
Junior	*16*	*20*	*20*	*20*
Books borrowed (=100%)(millions)	655.0	576.0	561.8	550.6
Book issues per head of population	11.6	10.0	9.7	9.5
Audio-visual issues per head of population	0.3	0.5	0.5	0.6

Source: Library and Information Statistics Unit, Loughborough University

Social and cultural activities

The most common free-time activity outside the home amongst adults in 1994-95 was a visit to the pub **(Table 13.13)**. Among those activities shown in the table, the greatest difference in participation between men and women was in those who attended a spectator sports event, with 31 per cent of men but just 13 per cent of women attending an event in the three months before interview in Great Britain. In general people

13.13

Participation[1] in leisure activities away from home: by gender, 1994-95

Great Britain — Percentages

	Males	Females	All persons
Visit a public house	*70*	*68*	*64*
Meal in a restaurant (not fast food)	*60*	*64*	*62*
Drive for pleasure	*47*	*47*	*47*
Meal in a fast food restaurant	*45*	*40*	*42*
Library	*36*	*43*	*40*
Cinema	*35*	*32*	*34*
Short break holiday	*32*	*28*	*30*
Disco or night club	*29*	*22*	*25*
Historic building	*27*	*24*	*25*
Spectator sports event	*31*	*13*	*22*
Theatre	*19*	*22*	*21*

1 Percentage of the population aged 16 and over participating in each activity in the three months prior to interview.

Source: The Henley Centre

13.14

Cinema attendance[1]

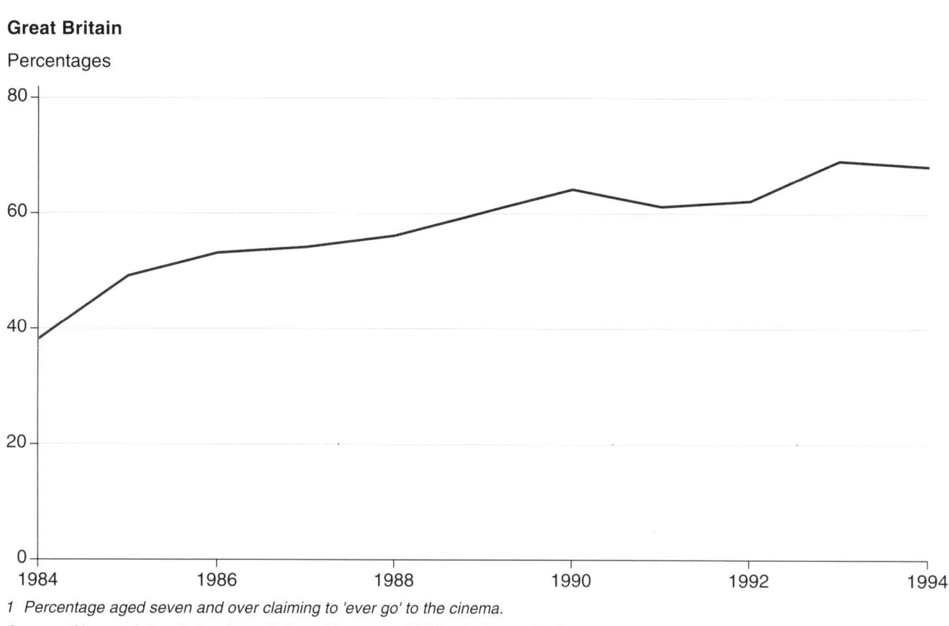

1 Percentage aged seven and over claiming to 'ever go' to the cinema.

Source: Cinema Advertising Association; Cinema and Video Industry Audience Research

13.15

Attendances at arts events

Great Britain			Indices
	1986-87	1991-92	1994-95
Ballet	100	111	129
Opera	100	112	126
Plays	100	102	108
Classical music	100	100	107
Art galleries	100	102	104
Jazz	100	82	89
Contemporary dance	100	77	89

Source: TGI, BMRB International

in the non-manual social classes take part more frequently in leisure activities away from home than those in the manual social classes; for example, eight in ten people in social class AB had visited a restaurant in the previous three months, compared with only around three in ten in social class E. Age also affects participation in some leisure activities; for example, nearly three quarters of 16 to 24 year olds had eaten a meal in a fast food restaurant in the previous three months compared with only one in eight of those aged 60 and over. As would be expected, going to a disco, nightclub or to the cinema were also much more common pastimes with the younger age groups than the older ones.

Sixty eight per cent of people aged seven and over claimed to ever go to the cinema in 1994, which was 30 percentage points higher than in 1984 **(Chart 13.14)**. At 124 million in 1994, admissions to cinemas increased by nearly 10 per cent over 1993. Those people in the non-manual social classes go to the cinema more often than those in the manual social classes. In 1994 over three quarters of people in the non-manual social classes had ever visited the cinema, compared with just under half ten years previously. Among these people, 9 per cent visited the cinema twice a month or more in 1994, which was nearly double the proportion for those in the manual social classes. Four Weddings and a Funeral was the most popular film of 1994, with Mrs Doubtfire and The Flintstones next; around 8 million people had seen each of them in the previous 12 months. Up until the end of November, the top films of 1995 were Batman Forever, Casper and Braveheart.

The number of people who said that they either would attend or have attended ballet performances in Great Britain rose by nearly 30 per cent between 1986-87 and 1994-95 **(Table 13.15)**. In England nearly 3 million people said they would attend or have attended ballet performances in 1994-95, but plays remained the most popular arts event with 9.7 million people saying they would attend or have attended. Up to 31 March 1994 the main funding and development agency for the arts in Great Britain was the Arts Council of Great Britain which was established to develop and improve the knowledge, understanding and practice of the arts, to increase their accessibility to the public and to advise and co-operate with government departments, local authorities and other organisations. From April 1994 the Scottish Arts Council and the Arts Council of Wales were made autonomous bodies alongside a new Arts Council for England and all inherited the responsibilities of the former organisation.

In 1993-94 around 10 per cent of adults in Great Britain visited a betting shop and a similar proportion played bingo in the three months prior to interview. Another form of gambling takes place in casinos where nearly £2.5 billion was staked in 1994-95 **(Table 13.16)**. The amount staked in casinos was around the same in real terms as in 1976-77. In 1993-94 lotteries only accounted for 5 per cent of the amount staked at bingo clubs. The National Lottery, which began in November 1994, is played by the majority of adults. When interviewed by BMRB/Mintel in the last week of November 1994, 71 per cent of adults claimed to have participated and more recent market research by a number of companies has confirmed that this level of participation in the draw has been maintained. Around 15 to 20 per cent of adults claimed to buy 'Instants Scratchcards', which were introduced in March 1995. Information on household expenditure on the National Lottery in the first three months of 1995 is given in Chart 6.4 in the Expenditure chapter.

Sporting activities

Throughout the period 1987 to 1993 men have consistently been more likely than women to participate in sports and other physical activities, but the gap has narrowed over time. In 1993-94, 72 per cent of men and 57 per cent of women in the United Kingdom took part in at least one activity in the four weeks before being interviewed for the General Household Survey and Continuous Household Survey. Walking a distance of two miles or more was the most popular physical activity for men and women of all ages, with the exception of men in the 16 to 19 age group, who were more likely to have participated in cue sports **(Table 13.17)**. Men were over four times more likely to participate in cue sports or golf than women whilst, on the other hand, women had higher participation rates in swimming and keep fit/yoga. In general participation in sports and physical activities decreases with age for both genders; in 1993-94, 86 per cent of those aged between 16 and 19 had participated in at least one physical activity in the previous four weeks compared with only 33 per cent of those aged 70 and over. If walking, which was by far the most popular activity with the older age groups, is excluded, there is an even greater difference in participation rates: 81 per cent for those aged 16 to 19 compared with just 16 per cent for those aged 70 and over.

13.16

Gambling: money staked in lotteries, casinos and bingo clubs

Great Britain — £ million at 1994-95 prices[1]

	Lotteries[2]	Casinos[3]	Bingo clubs[4]
1976-77	..	2,380	1,148
1981-82	113	1,901	885
1986-87	32	2,382	816
1987-88	31	2,437	886
1988-89	28	2,296	789
1989-90	29	2,329	765
1990-91	31	2,178	746
1991-92	60	2,063	771
1992-93	49	2,154	822
1993-94	44	2,291	811
1994-95	39	2,461	..

1 Adjusted to real terms using the retail prices index.
2 Excludes lotteries promoted under local authority registration and the National Lottery.
3 Money exchanged for chips.
4 Licensed clubs only. Prior to 1988-89 includes dutiable bingo played at non-licensed clubs. Figures relate to the year to August.
Source: Gaming Board for Great Britain

13.17

Participation[1] in the most popular sports, games and physical activities: by gender and age, 1993-94

United Kingdom — Percentages

	16-19	20-24	25-29	30-44	45-59	60-69	70 and over	All aged 16 and over
Males								
Walking	45	46	48	48	47	45	33	45
Snooker/pool/billiards	56	47	34	23	14	8	3	21
Swimming	23	19	19	21	12	8	3	15
Cycling	37	19	21	16	11	6	5	14
Soccer	44	27	19	9	2	0	0	9
Golf	15	13	12	11	9	7	3	9
Females								
Walking	40	41	41	41	42	36	20	37
Keep fit/yoga	29	28	26	22	14	8	6	17
Swimming	26	25	22	24	14	8	3	16
Cycling	14	12	8	9	7	4	2	7
Snooker/pool/billiards	26	17	6	4	2	1	0	5
Tenpin bowls/skittles	9	9	5	4	2	1	0	3

1 Percentage in each age group participating in each activity in the four weeks before interview.
Source: General Household Survey, Office of Population Censuses and Surveys; Continuous Household Survey, Department of Finance and Personnel, Northern Ireland

13.18

Participation[1] in sports, games and physical activities: by socio-economic group[2], 1993-94

Great Britain Percentages

	Professional	Employers and managers	Intermediate and junior non-manual	Skilled manual and own account non-professional	Semi-skilled manual and personal service	Unskilled manual	All socio-economic groups[3]
Walking	*57*	*46*	*42*	*39*	*36*	*31*	*41*
Swimming	*27*	*19*	*18*	*10*	*11*	*8*	*15*
Snooker/pool/billiards	*11*	*12*	*8*	*17*	*10*	*9*	*12*
Keep fit/yoga	*13*	*12*	*18*	*6*	*9*	*8*	*12*
Cycling	*14*	*9*	*9*	*10*	*8*	*9*	*10*
Darts	*6*	*5*	*4*	*8*	*6*	*6*	*6*
Weightlifting/training	*7*	*5*	*5*	*6*	*4*	*3*	*5*
Golf	*9*	*10*	*5*	*6*	*2*	*2*	*5*
Running/jogging	*11*	*6*	*4*	*3*	*2*	*2*	*5*
Soccer	*6*	*3*	*3*	*6*	*3*	*3*	*4*

1 Percentage participating in the four weeks before interview.
2 Socio-economic group is based on the person's current or most recent job.
3 Includes full-time students, members of the armed forces, those who have never worked and those whose job was inadequately described.
Source: General Household Survey, Office of Population Censuses and Surveys

13.19

Provision of sports centres[1]: by region, 1995

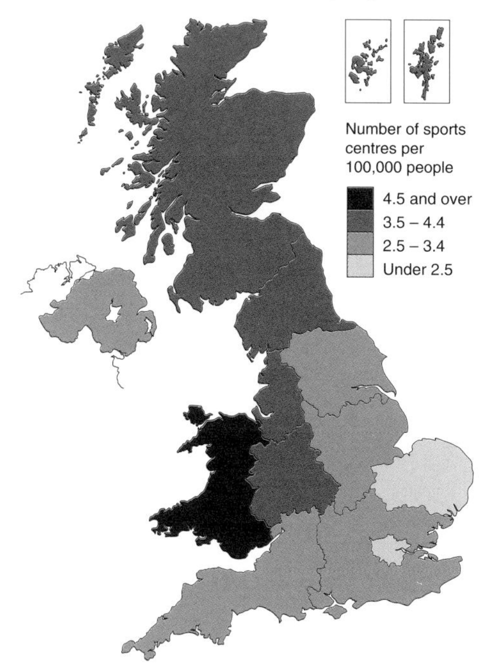

1 The definition of a sports centre may vary between sports councils.
Source: The Sports Council; Sports Council for Wales; Scottish Sports Council; Sports Council for Northern Ireland

Participation in sports, games and physical activities also varies with socio-economic group, with participation rates generally being higher among non-manual than manual workers **(Table 13.18)**. Of those in professional occupations in Great Britain, 82 per cent had taken part in at least one physical activity in the previous four weeks in 1993-94 compared with only 48 per cent of those in the unskilled manual group. However, this was not the case for all activities. Whilst those in the non-manual occupations were much more likely than manual workers to participate in swimming or running/jogging, there were smaller differences in the participation rates for cycling and soccer. On the other hand, those in manual groups were more likely to participate in darts and cue sports than those in the non-manual groups.

Participation in physical activities can be affected by, amongst other things, the availability of sports facilities. In 1995 Wales had a better provision of sports centres than any of the English regions, Scotland or Northern Ireland **(Chart 13.19)**. In Wales there were nearly five sports centres for every 100 thousand people. Wales also had the best provision of swimming pools with over four swimming pools for every 100 thousand people. This compares very favourably with Greater London, which had the lowest provision of facilities: two sports centres and just under two swimming pools per 100 thousand people. Greater London also had the least provision of public access sports pitches in England in 1994, with around five pitches per 10 thousand people, whilst the East Midlands had the best with over 12 pitches per 10 thousand people.

Religious activities

Many people devote part of their free time to some form of religious activity. In 1994, 6.5 million adults were active members of Trinitarian churches in the United Kingdom, which was a quarter fewer than in 1970 **(Table 13.20)**. However, the change in adult membership varied between the different denominations: Orthodox and other free churches both gained members, by just under half and over a quarter per cent respectively over the same period. The Roman Catholic church continues to have the highest membership, but this has also fallen by just over a quarter since 1970, to 2 million. Membership of Non-Trinitarian churches rose by over three quarters between 1970 and 1994, while the number of members of the Muslim religion was four and a half times greater in 1994 than in 1970.

In the 1991 British Social Attitudes Survey over a third of people described themselves as 'somewhat religious' with a further 7 per cent saying they were 'extremely' or 'very religious'; a third said that they never prayed. In the same year, the British Household Panel Survey asked people how much difference religious beliefs made to their lives; four in ten people said they made no difference. In 1993 the British Social Attitudes Survey again included questions on religion. Over one in ten of those questioned said that they attended their church, or meetings associated with their religion, once a week or more. Nearly a quarter said that they never, or practically never, attended.

Holidays

The proportion of British adults taking at least one holiday has fluctuated around 60 per cent, the figure reported for 1994, for at least the last 20 years. However, the proportion of adults taking two or more holidays each year has nearly quadrupled since 1966, to 26 per cent **(Chart 13.1)**. Those in the non-manual social classes were most likely to have gone on two or more holidays in 1994: 45 per cent of those in the AB group went on two or more holidays compared with only 15 per cent of those in the DE group. Britons took a total of nearly 58 million holidays in 1994, 45 per cent of which were abroad. In addition, they took around 32 million holidays in Great Britain which was roughly the same level as in 1966. August remains the most popular month for the British to go on holiday, both at home and abroad. Of those main holidays taken in Great Britain, 27 per cent were begun in August, with 22 per cent being started in the next most popular month, July. Second holidays are not so biased towards these two summer months, with 41 per cent being taken out of the main season (between October and April). Holidays abroad are also more evenly distributed over the year. Data from the International Passenger Survey suggest that winter holidays have increased, both absolutely

13.20

Church membership[1]

United Kingdom — Millions

	1970	1980	1992	1994
Trinitarian churches				
Roman Catholic[2]	2.7	2.4	2.1	2.0
Anglican	2.6	2.2	1.8	1.8
Presbyterian	1.8	1.4	1.2	1.1
Methodist	0.7	0.5	0.4	0.4
Baptist	0.3	0.2	0.2	0.2
Other free churches	0.5	0.5	0.6	0.7
Orthodox	0.2	0.2	0.3	0.3
All Trinitarian churches	8.8	7.4	6.6	6.5
Non-Trinitarian churches				
Mormons	0.1	0.1	0.2	0.2
Jehovah's Witnesses	0.1	0.1	0.1	0.1
Other Non-Trinitarian	0.1	0.2	0.2	0.2
All Non-Trinitarian churches	0.3	0.4	0.5	0.5
Other religions				
Muslims	0.1	0.3	0.5	0.6
Sikhs	0.1	0.2	0.3	0.3
Hindus	0.1	0.1	0.1	0.1
Jews	0.1	0.1	0.1	0.1
Others	0.0	0.1	0.1	0.1
All other religions	0.4	0.8	1.1	1.2

1 Adult active members.
2 Mass attendance.
Source: Christian Research

13.21

Holidays[1] taken at home by Great Britain residents: by destination, 1994

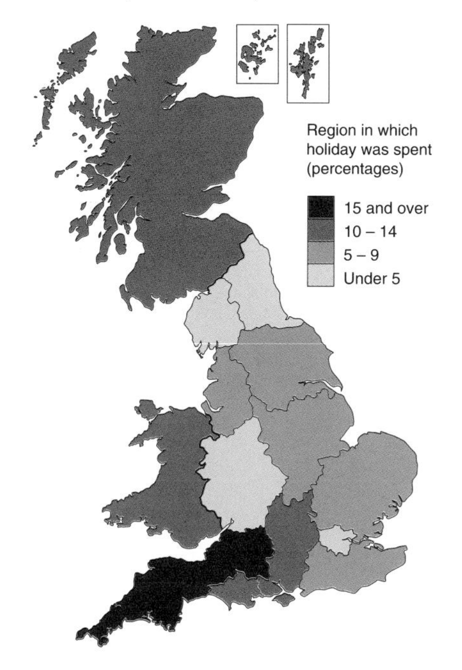

1 Holidays of four nights or more taken by adults aged 16 and over.

Source: British National Travel Survey, British Tourist Authority

13.22

Destination of holidays[1] abroad

Percentages

	1971	1981	1991	1994
Spain[2]	*34.3*	*21.7*	*21.3*	*26.4*
France	*15.9*	*27.2*	*25.8*	*22.2*
Greece	*4.5*	*6.7*	*7.6*	*7.6*
United States	*1.0*	*5.5*	*6.8*	*5.7*
Portugal	*2.6*	*2.8*	*4.8*	*3.9*
Italy	*9.2*	*5.8*	*3.5*	*3.9*
Cyprus	*1.0*	*0.7*	*2.4*	*3.3*
Irish Republic	..	*3.6*	*3.0*	*2.7*
Netherlands	*3.6*	*2.4*	*3.5*	*2.6*
Turkey	..	*0.1*	*0.7*	*2.4*
Germany	*3.4*	*2.6*	*2.7*	*2.0*
Austria	*5.5*	*2.5*	*2.4*	*1.8*
Other countries	*19.0*	*18.4*	*15.6*	*15.4*
All destinations (=100%) (thousands)	4,201	13,131	20,788	27,336

1 A visit made for holiday purposes. Business trips and visits to friends or relatives are excluded.
2 Excludes the Canaries prior to 1981.

Source: International Passenger Survey, Central Statistical Office

and proportionately, since 1980 with visits abroad by United Kingdom residents in December 1994 and January 1995 (for all purposes) representing 11 per cent of total visits, compared with just under 9 per cent in the corresponding months in 1980-81.

When Britons holiday at home, the West Country is the most common destination for holidays of four or more nights **(Chart 13.21)**, accounting for nearly a quarter of such holidays in 1994. Scotland and Wales were the next most popular destinations; Greater London accounted for only 2 per cent of these holidays. Car travel is still the preferred mode of transport for holidays in this country, with nearly three quarters using cars to get to their destination. Self-catering accommodation is more common on British holidays of four nights or more than serviced accommodation, with self-catering used on 51 per cent of holidays in 1994 and serviced accommodation on 30 per cent. The residual is accounted for by holidays at the homes of friends or relatives. In 1994 the average total cost of a holiday in Britain of four or more nights was £146 per person.

In 1994 Spain regained its position as the most popular destination for United Kingdom residents taking a holiday abroad. Over a quarter of people holidaying abroad visited Spain, although the proportion was 8 percentage points lower than in 1971 **(Table 13.22)**. France also remains a very popular destination: over a fifth of UK residents went there in 1994. In recent years France has become increasingly popular as a day trip destination, especially since the relaxation of customs regulations on duty paid goods. Europe is still much more popular with British holidaymakers than other parts of the world. Around eight in ten of all holidays abroad were taken in Europe, while the United States was the most popular non-European destination.

Political participation

The highest intake of women Members of Parliament (MPs) in the United Kingdom at a general election was in 1992 when 60 women were elected to Parliament **(Chart 13.23)**. This has since risen to 63 in September 1995, representing just 9.7 per cent of MPs in the House of Commons; just under two thirds of women MPs are members of the Labour party. Among European Community countries the proportion of MPs who are women varies considerably. After their latest general elections, France and Greece had the lowest proportion of female MPs with around 6 per cent each while Sweden and Finland had by far the highest proportion, with 40 and 38 per cent respectively. The other Scandinavian countries also had high proportions of women MPs.

Turnout for elections to the European Parliament varies considerably among member countries. In 1994, 91 per cent of Belgians and 87 per cent of Luxembourgers voted in the European elections, but less than 36 per cent did so in the Netherlands and Portugal; in the United Kingdom 36 per cent voted. This compares with over 76 per cent of the electorate who voted in the latest general election in the United Kingdom **(Table 13.24)**. Whilst the turnout has stayed between 73 and 76 per cent for the last four general elections in the United Kingdom, far fewer people vote at by-elections and the proportion has been falling. The average turnout was only 53 per cent for the by-elections held between April 1992 and September 1995, which was well down on the average turnout of 61 per cent for the May 1979 to June 1983 by-elections. In the last general election the Conservative party had 42 per cent of the votes, Labour had 35 per cent and the Liberal Democrats 17 per cent. However, at by-elections since then, the proportion of votes for the Conservative party has dropped to 18 per cent; the Liberal Democrats share of the vote has increased to 29 per cent whilst Labour's share was up just 1 per cent on the general election. In general, it seems that people are more likely to vote for the smaller parties in by-elections than in general elections. In addition, in the 1994 British Social Attitudes Survey, 53 per cent of people said that in a general election they would vote for a party regardless of the candidate.

13.23

Women MPs in the House of Commons[1]

United Kingdom

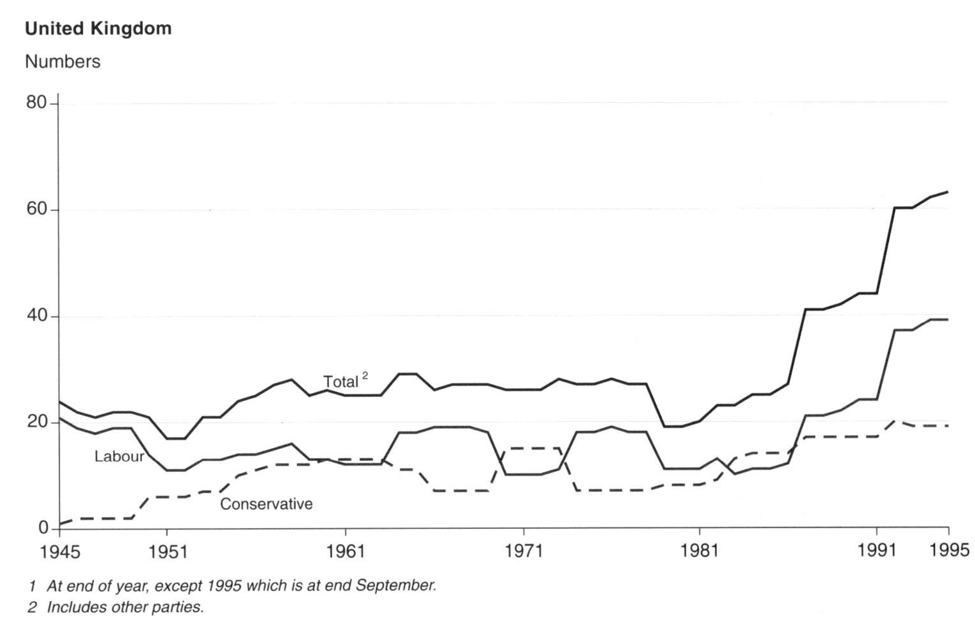

1 At end of year, except 1995 which is at end September.
2 Includes other parties.
Source: House of Commons Library

13.24

Votes recorded in parliamentary general elections and by-elections: by party

United Kingdom

	General election 3/5/79	May 1979 to June 1983	General election 6/6/83	June 1983 to June 1987	General election 11/6/87	June 1987 to April 1992	General election 10/4/92	April 1992 to Sept 1995
Number of by-elections	.	20	.	31	.	24	.	14
Turnout (percentages)[1]	*76.1*	*61.2*	*72.7*	*62.4*	*75.3*	*57.6*	*76.3*	*52.8*
Votes recorded by party (percentage of all votes)								
Conservative	*43.9*	*23.8*	*42.4*	*16.0*	*42.3*	*23.8*	*41.8*	*18.2*
Labour	*36.9*	*25.7*	*27.6*	*14.9*	*30.8*	*38.9*	*35.2*	*36.2*
Liberal Democrats[2]	*13.8*	*9.0*	*13.7*	*15.0*	*12.8*	*19.1*	*17.0*	*29.0*
Social Democratic Party[2]	.	*14.2*	*11.6*	*5.6*	*9.7*	*3.2*	.	.
Plaid Cymru	*0.4*	*0.5*	*0.4*	*0.3*	*0.4*	*2.3*	*0.4*	*0.6*
Scottish National Party	*1.6*	*1.7*	*1.1*	.	*1.3*	*4.8*	*1.9*	*6.5*
Northern Ireland Parties[2]	*2.2*	*23.3*	*2.5*	*47.4*	*2.2*	*3.7*	*2.1*	*5.4*
Green Party[3]	*0.1*	*0.3*	*0.2*	-	*0.3*	*1.8*	*0.6*	*0.1*
Others	*1.1*	*1.6*	*0.5*	*0.8*	*0.2*	*2.5*	*1.1*	*4.0*
All (=100%)(thousands)	31,221	715	30,671	1,979	32,530	877	33,275	494

1 Estimated by dividing the number of votes cast by the number of people on the electoral registers in force at the time of the elections.
2 See Appendix, Part 13: Parliamentary elections and political parties.
3 Known as the Ecology Party before 1987.
Source: Home Office

References and further reading

The following list contains selected publications relevant to **Chapter 13: Lifestyles**. Those published by HMSO are available from the addresses shown on the inside back cover of *Social Trends.*

Annual Report of Department of National Heritage, HMSO
Annual Reports of the Sports Council, Sports Council for Northern Ireland, Sports Council for Wales and the Scottish Sports Council, organisations concerned
Arts Council of England Annual Report and Accounts, Arts Council of England
BBC Handbook, BBC
BPI Statistical Handbook, British Phonographic Industry
British Social Attitudes, Dartmouth Publishing
Cinema and Video Industry Audience Research, CAA
Cultural Trends, Policy Studies Institute
Cultural Trends in Scotland 2, Policy Studies Institute
Digest of Tourist Statistics, British Tourist Authority
Film and Year Book, British Film Institute
General Household Survey, HMSO
Independent Broadcasting Authority Annual Report and Accounts, IBA
Leisure Futures, The Henley Centre
LISU Annual Library Statistics, Library and Information Statistics Unit, Loughborough University of Technology
Scottish Arts Council Annual Report, Scottish Arts Council
Social Focus on Women, HMSO
The UK Tourist, Tourist Boards of England, Northern Ireland, Scotland and Wales
Travel Trends, HMSO
Visits to Tourist Attractions, British Tourist Authority and National Tourist Boards

Contacts

Telephone contact points for further information relating to
Chapter 13: Lifestyles

Central Statistical Office	
Family Expenditure Survey	0171 217 4207
International Passenger Survey	0171 217 4701
Department of Finance and Personnel, NI	01232 252508
Office of Population Censuses and Surveys	0171 396 2327
Arts Council of England	0171 333 0100 extn 250
British Phonographic Industry	0171 287 4422
British Tourist Authority	0181 846 9000
Christian Research Association	0181 294 1989
Cinema Advertising Association	0171 439 9531
ESRC Research Centre on Micro-social Change	01206 872957
LISU, Loughborough University	01509 223071
National Readership Surveys	0171 379 0344
Social & Community Planning Research	0171 250 1866 extn 369
The Gaming Board for Great Britain	0171 306 6200
The Henley Centre for Forecasting	0171 353 9961

Geographical areas of the United Kingdom used in Social Trends

Appendix: major surveys

	Frequency	Sampling frame	Type of respondent	Location	Set sample size (most recent survey included in *Social Trends*)	Response rate (percentages)
Agricultural Census	Annual	Agricultural lists	Occupiers of agricultural holdings	UK	245,000 individuals	86
British Crime Survey	Biannual	Postcode Address File	Adult in household	EW	14,520 addresses[2]	77
British Household Panel Survey[1]	Annual	Postal Addresses	All adults in households	GB	5,500 households	95
British National Travel Survey - Yearly	Annual	Electoral Register	Individual adult	GB	4,283 individuals[3]	63
British Social Attitudes Survey	Annual	Postcode Address File	Adult in household	GB	6,000 addresses	65
Census of Population	Decennial	Detailed local	Household head	UK	Full count	98
Continuous Household Survey	Continuous	Valuation and Lands Agency Property Database	All adults in household	NI	4,500 addresses	80
Family Expenditure Survey	Continuous	Postcode Address File in GB, Rating Lists in NI	Household	UK	10,355 addresses[3]	66[4]
Family Resources Survey	Continuous	Postcode Address File	All adults in household	GB	39,668 households[3]	66
General Household Survey	Continuous	Postcode Address File	All adults in household	GB	11,836	80
Health Survey for England	Annual	Postcode Address File	All adults in household	E	13,104 addresses	82
International Passenger Survey	Continuous	International passengers at ports and airports	Individual traveller	UK	229,000 individuals	85
Labour Force Survey	Continuous	Postcode Address File	All adults in household[5]	GB	60,000 addresses	83[6]
Longitudinal Study[7]	Continuous	Population	All persons	EW	1 per cent	[8]
National Food Survey	Continuous	Postcode Address File	Person responsible for domestic food arrangements	GB	12,353 addresses[3]	63
National Readership Survey	Continuous	Postcode Address File	Individual in home	GB	37,500 individuals	65
National Travel Survey	Continuous	Postcode Address File	Household	GB	4,500-5,000 households per year[3]	76
New Earnings Survey	Annual	Inland Revenue PAYE records	Employee[9]	GB	[9]	[9]
Omnibus Survey	Continuous	Postcode Address File	One adult per household	GB	36,000 individuals	77[10]
Survey of English Housing	Continuous	Postcode Address File	Household	E	28,000 addresses[3]	80
Survey of Personal Incomes	Annual	Inland Revenue	Individuals[11]	UK	80,000 individuals	97
Survey of Psychiatric Morbidity	Irregular	Postcode Address File	One adult in private household	GB	12,730 households	80
Youth Cohort Study	Irregular	DFEE schools records	Young people aged 16-19	EW	27,138 individuals	64

1 See article starting on page 27 for further detail. Response rate refers to wave four.
2 Effective sample only. Set sample includes ineligible households.
3 Basic sample only.
4 Response rate refers to GB.
5 Includes some proxy information.
6 Response rate to first wave interviews quoted. Response rate to second to fifth wave interviews 96 per cent of those previously accepting.
7 See article starting on page 16 for further detail.
8 Linkage rates from Census to Census were 91 per cent for Longitudinal Study members present in both the 1971 and 1981 Censuses and 90 per cent for Longitudinal Study members present for both the 1981 and 1991 Censuses.
9 In the New Earnings Survey employers supply data on a 1 per cent sample of employees who are members of PAYE schemes. For the 1995 sample 214 thousand were selected and there was a 95.1 per cent response but some 42 thousand returned questionnaires did not contain data.
10 The Omnibus Survey changes from month to month. The overall response for 1994 was 77 per cent.
11 In the Survey of Personal Incomes local tax offices supply data on individuals to a central point in Inland Revenue.

Appendix: definitions and terms

Symbols and conventions

Reference years. Where, because of space constraints, a choice of years has to be made, the most recent year or a run of recent years is shown together with the past population census years (1991, 1981, 1971, etc) and sometimes the mid-points between census years (1986, etc). Other years may be added if they represent a peak or trough in the series.

Rounding of figures. In tables where figures have been rounded to the nearest final digit, there may be an apparent discrepancy between the sum of the constituent items and the total as shown.

Billion. This term is used to represent a thousand million.

Provisional and estimated data. Some data for the latest year (and occasionally for earlier years) are provisional or estimated. To keep footnotes to a minimum, these have not been indicated; source departments will be able to advise if revised data are available.

Non-calendar years.
Financial year - eg 1 April 1994 to 31 March 1995 would be shown as 1994-95
Academic year - eg September 1993/July 1994 would be shown as 1993/94
Data covering more than one year - eg 1992, 1993 and 1994 would be shown as 1992-1994

Units on tables. Where one unit predominates it is shown at the top of the table. All other units are shown against the relevant row or column. Figures are shown in italics when they represent percentages.

Germany. Unless otherwise stated data relate to Germany as constituted since 3 October 1990.

Symbols. The following symbols have been used throughout *Social Trends*:

..	*not available*
.	*not applicable*
-	*negligible (less than half the final digit shown)*
0	*nil*

PART 1: POPULATION

Population and population projections

The estimated and projected populations of an area include all those usually resident in the area, whatever their nationality. Members of HM forces stationed outside the United Kingdom are excluded. Students are taken to be resident at their term-time addresses. Figures for the United Kingdom do not include the population of the Channel Islands or the Isle of Man.

The population estimates for mid-1991 were based on results from the 1991 Census of Population and incorporate an allowance for census underenumeration. Estimates for later years allow for subsequent births, deaths and migration. The estimates for 1982-90 have been revised to make them consistent with both the 1981 and the 1991 figures based upon successive censuses.

The most recent set of national population projections for the United Kingdom are based on the populations of England, Wales, Scotland and Northern Ireland at mid-1992. Further details of these were published in *National Population Projections: 1992-based Series PP2 No. 19* (HMSO). Subnational projections are also made. Due to definitional changes, there are minor discontinuities for Scotland and Northern Ireland between the figures for 1971 and earlier years. At the United Kingdom level these discontinuities are negligible.

Area classifications

For summary presentation of population changes, the Office of Population Censuses and Surveys uses a classification of local authority districts in England and Wales divided into six broad area types. The classification is based upon cluster analysis of 1991 Census results for a representative range of variables at local authority district level. Full details of the classification are given in 'A 1991 Socio-economic classification of local and health authorities of Great Britain' *OPCS Studies on Medical and Population Subjects,* HMSO. The classification extends to local authority areas of Scotland (although it is not used for summary presentation of population changes in Scotland) but it does not extend to Northern Ireland.

International migration estimates

Overall migration between the United Kingdom and other countries (Table 1.16) is estimated from three separate sources: the International Passenger Survey (IPS); Home Office data on people who entered as short-term visitors but were subsequently allowed to stay for a year or more; and estimates of migration between the United Kingdom and the Irish Republic. More detailed estimates (as in Table 1.17) are derived solely from the IPS.

The IPS provides information on all migrants into the United Kingdom who have resided abroad for a year or more and stated on arrival the intention to stay in the United Kingdom for a year or more and vice versa. Migrants to and from the Irish Republic, diplomats and military personnel are excluded. It is also highly likely that the IPS migration figures exclude the persons mentioned above who enter the country as short-term visitors (intending to stay for less than 12 months) and are subsequently granted an extension of stay, for example as students, on the basis of marriage or because they applied for asylum after entering the country. After taking account of persons leaving the United Kingdom for a short-term period who stay overseas for periods longer than originally intended, the adjustment needed to net migration ranges from about 10 thousand in 1981 to 50 thousand in 1992, an average of approximately 20 thousand. The adjustment for 1993, the latest year available is about 40 thousand.

'Main reason for migration' data are derived from the IPS question 'what is the main reason for your visit'. This question was designed to cover all types of traveller to and from the United Kingdom, not specifically migrants which constitute a tiny sample. Nevertheless it provides our only source of information on reason for migration. Note that the 'work related' category excludes 'looking for work', 'working holiday' or 'voluntary working': these are included in 'Other'. Also the category 'accompany/join' excludes 'visiting friends and relatives' and is confined to accompanying or joining a partner (including arriving in the United Kingdom to get married).

PART 2: HOUSEHOLDS AND FAMILIES

Households

A household: is a person living alone or a group of people who have the address as their only or main residence and who either share one meal a day or share the living accommodation. Household projections are based on the definition of a household being people living together who share common housekeeping or a living room.

Size of household: is a count of those people who are usually resident in the household irrespective of whether or not they are present on census night. In the General Household Survey the size of the household is the number of people who normally live there.

Families

A family: is a married couple, either with or without their never-married child or children (of any age), or a lone parent together with his or her never-married child or children. A lone parent (in the Census) is a married parent whose spouse does not reside in the same household, or any single, widowed, or divorced parent.

A lone parent family (in the General Household Survey): consists of a lone parent, living with his or her never-married dependent children, provided these children have no children of their own. Married lone mothers whose husbands are not defined as resident in the household are not classified as lone parents because evidence suggests the majority are separated from their husband either because he usually works away from home or for some other reason that does not imply the breakdown of the marriage (see OPCS's *GHS Monitor 82/1*). Couples describing themselves as married (or common-law married) but who are in fact cohabiting are coded and counted as married.

Children: are never-married people of any age who live with one or both parent(s). They also include step-children and adopted children (but not foster children) and also grandchildren (where the parents are absent).

Dependent children: in the 1961 Census, were defined as children under 15 years of age, and persons of any age in full-time education. In the 1971 Census, dependent children were defined as never-married children in families who were either under 15 years of age, or aged 15 to 24 and in full-time education. However, for direct comparison with the General Household Survey (GHS) data, the definition of dependent children used for 1971 in Table 2.6 has been changed to include only never-married in families who were either under 15 years of age, or aged 15 to 18 and in full-time education. In the 1991 Census and the GHS, dependent children are never married children in families who are aged under 16, or aged 16 to 18 and in full-time education.

PART 3: EDUCATION

Qualifications

In England, Wales and Northern Ireland the main examination for school pupils at the minimum school leaving age is the General Certificate of Secondary Education (GCSE) which can be taken in a wide range of subjects. This replaced the GCE O Level and CSE examinations in 1987 (1988 in Northern Ireland). In England and Wales the GCSE is awarded in seven grades, A to G, the highest three (A to C) being regarded as equivalent to O level grades A to C or CSE grade 1. In Northern Ireland it is awarded in eight grades, A* and A to G.

GCE A Level is usually taken after a further two years of study in a sixth form or equivalent, passes being graded from A (the highest) to E (the lowest).

In Scotland pupils study for the Scottish Certificate of Education (SCE) S (Standard) Grade in their third and fourth years of secondary schooling (roughly ages 14 and 15). Each subject has several elements, some of which are internally assessed in school, and an award is only made (on a scale of 1 to 7) if the whole course has been completed and examined. The SCE H (Higher) Grade requires one further year of study and for the more able candidates the range of subjects taken may be as wide as at S Grade with as many as five or six subjects spanning both arts and science. Five SCE highers are regarded as being approximately the equivalent of two GCE A levels

The National Curriculum: assessments and tests

Under the *Education Reform Act (1988)* a National Curriculum has been progressively introduced into primary and secondary schools in England and Wales. This consists of mathematics, English and science (and Welsh in Wales) as core subjects with history, geography, information technology and design and technology, music, art, physical education and (in secondary schools) a modern foreign language as foundation subjects. For all subjects measurable targets have been defined for four key stages, corresponding to ages 7, 11, 14 and 16. Pupils are assessed formally at the ages of 7, 11 and 14 by their teachers and by national tests in the core subjects of English, mathematics and science. Sixteen year olds are assessed by means of the GCSE examination. Statutory boards have been set up for England and for Wales to advise government on the National Curriculum and promote curriculum development generally. Northern Ireland has its own common curriculum which is similar but not identical to the National Curriculum in England and Wales. Assessment arrangements in Northern Ireland are expected to become statutory from September 1996. In Scotland, though school curricula are still the responsibility of education authorities and individual head teachers, in practice all 14 to 16 year olds study mathematics, English, a science and five other core subjects.

NVQ foundation targets

Much of further education is vocational in character, ranging from lower-level technical and commercial courses up to those leading to professional qualifications. Courses and examinations are offered by many bodies including the Business and Technology Education Council (BTEC), the City and

Guilds of London Institute and the Royal Society of Arts Examination Board.
To provide an integrated framework a National Council for Vocational Qualifications covering England, Wales and Northern Ireland was set up in 1986. The Council does not award qualifications itself but those accredited by it are called National Vocational Qualifications (NVQs). As an extension of these for people seeking a wider range of study General National Vocational Qualifications (GNVQs) have been introduced since 1992 as a vocational counterpart to GCSE and A Level. An intermediate level GNVQ is equivalent to five good GCSEs and an advanced GNVQ to two A Levels. The Scottish Vocational Education Council (SCOTVEC) has similar functions to the National Council but also awards qualifications in its own right.

Main categories of educational establishments
Educational establishments in the United Kingdom are administered and financed in several ways. Most schools are controlled by local education authorities (LEAs), which are part of the structure of local government, but some are 'assisted', receiving grants direct from central government sources and being controlled by governing bodies which have a substantial degree of autonomy. In recent years under the Local Management of Schools initiative all LEA and assisted schools have been given delegated responsibility for managing their own budgets and staff numbers. Since 1988 it has also been possible for LEA schools in England and Wales to apply for grant maintained status, under which they receive direct funding from the Department for Education and Employment or the Welsh Office. The governing bodies of such schools are responsible for all aspects of their management, including use of funds, employment of staff and provision of most educational support services.

Outside the public sector completely are non-maintained schools run by individuals, companies or charitable institutions.

Further education colleges and further education courses in other establishments have since 1993 been funded by the Further Education Funding Councils (FEFCs). These also support some higher education courses, as do the Higher Education Funding Councils for England and Wales, the Scottish Office Education and Industry Department and the Northern Ireland Department of Education.

Stages of education
Education takes place in several stages: primary, secondary, further and higher, and is compulsory for all children between the ages of 5 (4 in Northern Ireland) and 16. The primary stage covers three age ranges: nursery (under 5), infant (5 to 7 or 8) and junior (up to 11 or 12) but in Scotland and Northern Ireland there is generally no distinction between infant and junior schools. Nursery education can be provided either in separate nursery schools or in nursery classes within primary schools. Most public sector primary schools take both boys and girls in mixed classes. It is usual to transfer straight to secondary school at age 11 (in England and Wales) or 12 (in Scotland), but in England and Wales some children make the transition via middle schools catering for various age ranges between 8 and 14. Depending on their individual age ranges middle schools are classified as either primary or secondary.

Public provision of secondary education in an area may consist of a combination of different types of school, the pattern reflecting historical circumstance and the policy adopted by the LEA. Comprehensive schools normally admit pupils without reference to ability or aptitude and cater for all the children in a neighbourhood, but in some areas they co-exist with grammar, secondary modern or technical schools. In Northern Ireland, post primary education is provided by comprehensive and grammar schools.

Special schools (day or boarding) provide education for children who are so handicapped, physically or mentally, that they cannot profit fully from education in normal schools.

The term further education may be used in a general sense to cover all non-advanced courses taken after the period of compulsory education, but more commonly it excludes those staying on at secondary school and those in higher education, ie courses in universities and colleges leading to qualifications above GCE A Level, SCE H Grade, BTEC National Diploma or Certificate, and their equivalents.

Pupil/teacher ratios
The pupil/teacher ratio in a school is the ratio of all pupils on the register to all teachers employed on the day of an annual count. Part-time teachers are included on a full-time equivalent basis.

Student grants and loans
Students planning to take full-time or sandwich courses of further study after leaving school may be eligible for grants, funded by central government though paid, except in Scotland, by LEAs. Some grants are mandatory, provided the course leads to a degree or designated equivalent qualification and the student satisfies conditions relating to residence and previous education. Other grants are discretionary, each awarding authority deciding its own policy and criteria. Parental contributions are deductible from grants on a sliding scale except for students over 25 who have been self-supporting for at least three years. All those receiving grants have their fees paid in full, regardless of parental income. The means-tested maintenance grant is intended to cover the Christmas and Easter vacations as well as term time, but not the summer vacation. Additional allowances are available if, for example, the course requires a period of study abroad. Under legislation enacted in 1990, students receiving mandatory grants are eligible for top-up loans, interest-free but indexed, to be repaid over five to seven years, though this can be deferred if income is low.

Adult education
This sector spans a wide range of provision, from recreational courses to some at degree level. Until 1992 the main providers were LEAs but since then the Further Education Funding Councils for England and Wales have been responsible for, and funded, those courses which lead to academic or vocational qualifications, prepare students for further or higher education or provide training in basic skills. Advanced courses are funded by the Higher Education Funding Councils. In Scotland and Northern Ireland all provision is still in the hands of education authorities. Throughout the United Kingdom most courses are part-time but a few are full-time and there are some residential courses, both short and long-term, at colleges. Full-time courses at degree level attract mandatory grants but on other courses all students over the age of 19 must pay a fee, though discretionary grants and bursaries may be available.

PART 4: EMPLOYMENT

Occupational classification
From 1991 the Labour Force Survey has used the Standard Occupational Classification 1990 (SOC) which has

replaced the old Classification of Occupations and Directory of Occupational Titles (CODOT).

Labour disputes
Statistics of stoppages of work caused by labour disputes in the United Kingdom relate to disputes connected with terms and conditions of employment. Small stoppages involving fewer than ten workers or lasting less than one day are excluded from the statistics unless the aggregate number of working days lost in the dispute exceeds 100. Disputes not resulting in a stoppage of work are not included in the statistics.

Workers involved and working days lost relate to persons both directly and indirectly involved (unable to work although not parties to the dispute) at the establishments where the disputes occurred. People laid off and working days lost at establishments not in dispute, due for example to resulting shortages of supplies, are excluded.

There are difficulties in ensuring complete recording of stoppages, in particular near the margins of the definition; for example short disputes lasting only a day or so, or involving only a few workers. Any under-recording would affect the total number of stoppages much more than the number of working days lost.

Unemployment - claimant count
People claiming benefit (that is unemployment benefit, income support, or national insurance credits) at Employment Service local offices (formerly Unemployment Benefit Offices) on the day of the monthly count, who on that day state that they are unemployed and that they satisfy the conditions for claiming benefit. (Students claiming benefit during a vacation and who intend to return to full-time education are excluded.)

Unemployment - ILO definition
The ILO definition of unemployment refers to people without a job who were available to start work within two weeks and had either looked for work in the previous four weeks or were waiting to start a job they had already obtained. Estimates on this basis are not available before 1984, as the Labour Force Survey did not then collect information on job search over a four week period. The former GB/UK Labour Force definition of unemployment, the only one available for estimates up to 1984, counted people not in employment and seeking work in a reference week (or prevented from seeking work by a temporary sickness or holiday, or waiting for the results of a job application, or waiting to start a job they had already obtained), whether or not they were available to start (except students not able to start because they had to complete their education).

Unemployment and unemployment rates - SOEC and OECD concepts
The unemployment figures used in these standardised rates are estimated by the OECD to conform, as far as possible, with the definition of unemployment in the guidelines of the International Labour Organisation (ILO), and the rates are calculated as percentages of the total economically active, again as defined in the ILO guidelines.

According to these guidelines the unemployed covers all persons of working age who, in a specified period, are: without work; available for work in the following two weeks; and were seeking work in the previous four weeks or are waiting to start a job. The total labour force consists of civilian employees; the self-employed; unpaid family workers; professional and conscripted members of the armed forces; and the ILO unemployed. The standardised rates will therefore differ from the unemployment rates published in national sources whenever the national definition of unemployment differs from that indicated above, or the denominator used to calculate the national rates is other than the total economically active.

The data used by Eurostat represent a composite of each country's latest Labour Force Survey (LFS) data and the latest data on each country's registered or claimant unemployment. Eurostat start by taking baseline figures for ILO unemployment and the economically active in each EC country, which they obtain from the most recent community-wide LFS conducted in each member state. These baseline data are extrapolated by Eurostat using the most recent data available in each EC member state relating to either ILO unemployment or administrative sources. Revisions are applied whenever the data are re-benchmarked to the latest available LFS data for each country. OECD's methodology is similar to Eurostat's, but slight differences of approach produce different outcomes.

PART 5: INCOME AND WEALTH

Household sector
The household sector includes private trusts and individuals living in institutions as well as those living in households. It differs from the personal sector, as defined in the national accounts, in that it excludes unincorporated private businesses, private non-profit-making bodies serving persons, and the funds of life assurance and pension schemes. More information is given in an article in *Economic Trends*, September 1981.

Household disposable income is equal to the total current income of the household sector *less* payments of UK taxes on income, employees' national insurance contributions, and contributions of employees to occupational pension schemes. It is revalued at constant prices by the consumers' expenditure deflator.

Equivalisation scales
The Department of Social Security (DSS), the Central Statistical Office (CSO) and the Institute for Fiscal Studies (IFS) all use McClements equivalence scales in their analysis of the income distribution, to take into account variations in the size and composition of households. This reflects the common sense notion that a household of five adults will need a higher income than a single person living alone to enjoy a comparable standard of living. An overall equivalence value is calculated for each household by summing the appropriate scale values for each household member. Equivalised household income is then calculated by dividing household income by the household's equivalence value.

The scales conventionally take a married couple as the reference point with an equivalence value of 1; equivalisation therefore tends to increase relatively the incomes of single person households (since their incomes are divided by a value of less than 1) and to reduce relatively incomes of households with three or more persons. For further information see *Households Below Average Income, A Statistical Analysis, HMSO.*

The DSS and IFS use both before and after housing costs scales, whilst the CSO only use before housing costs scales.

McClements equivalence scales:

	Before housing costs	After housing costs
Household member		
First adult (head)	0.61	0.55
Spouse of head	0.39	0.45
Other second adult	0.46	0.45
Third adult	0.42	0.45
Subsequent adults	0.36	0.40
Each dependent aged:		
0-1	0.09	0.07
2-4	0.18	0.18
5-7	0.21	0.21
8-10	0.23	0.23
11-12	0.25	0.26
13-15	0.27	0.28
16 or over	0.36	0.38

Redistribution of income (ROI)

Estimates of the incidence of taxes and benefits on household income, based on the Family Expenditure Survey (FES), are published by the CSO in *Economic Trends*. The article covering 1994-95 appeared in the December 1995 issue, and contains details of the definitions and methods used.

Households Below Average Income (HBAI)

Information on the distribution of income is provided in the DSS publication *Households Below Average Income: 1979 to 1992/93*. This gives a comprehensive statistical analysis of income relating principally to the lower half of the income distribution; and explains the methodology used to derive the figures from the FES.

Two different measures of disposable income are used in HBAI: before and after gross housing costs are deducted. Gross housing costs consist of rent, water rates and community water rate charges, mortgage interest, structural insurance, ground rent and service charges.

Difference between Households Below Average Income and Redistribution of Income series

These are two separate and distinct income series based on the FES, produced by two different government departments. Each series has been developed to serve the specific needs of that department. The DSS series, HBAI, provides estimates of patterns of personal disposable income in the United Kingdom and of changes over time; as the name suggests, it concentrates on the lower part of the income distribution and shows disposable income before and after housing costs (where disposable income is after deduction of income tax; national insurance contributions; contributions to occupational pension schemes; domestic rates; council tax; repayments of Social Fund loans). The CSO series, ROI, shows how Government intervention through the tax and benefit system affects the income of households; it covers the whole income distribution and includes the effects of indirect taxes like VAT and duty on beer, as well as estimating the cash value of benefits in kind (eg from state spending on education and health care). The ROI results are designed to show the position in a particular year rather than trends in income levels over time, although trends in the distribution of income are given. An important difference between the two series is that HBAI counts individuals and ROI counts households.

Net wealth of the personal sector

Balance sheet estimates of the net wealth of the personal sector are published in the *United Kingdom National Accounts*, 1995 edition. These figures exclude the stock of consumer durables which are no longer available. Quarterly estimates of net financial wealth (excluding tangible and intangible assets) are published in *Financial Statistics*.

Distribution of personal wealth

The estimates of the distribution of the marketable wealth of individuals relate to all adults in the United Kingdom. They are produced by combining estimates of the distribution of wealth identified by the estate multiplier method with independent estimates of total personal wealth derived from the Central Statistical Office personal sector balance sheets. The methods used were described in an article in *Economic Trends* (October 1990) entitled 'Estimates of the Distribution of Personal Wealth'. Net wealth of the personal sector differs from marketable wealth for the following reasons:

Difference in coverage: the CSO balance sheet of the personal sector includes the wealth of non-profit making bodies and unincorporated businesses, while the Inland Revenue estimates exclude non-profit making bodies and treat the bank deposits and debts of unincorporated businesses differently from CSO;

Differences in timing: the CSO balance sheet gives values at the end of the year, whereas Inland Revenue (IR) figures are adjusted to mid-year;

IR figures: exclude the wealth of those under 18 and the very wealthy, to avoid producing misleading estimates.

Funded pensions: are included in the CSO figures but not in the IR marketable wealth. Also the CSO balance sheet excludes consumer durables and includes non-marketable tenancy rights, whereas the IR figures include consumer durables and exclude non-marketable tenancy rights.

Share ownership

Estimates of the value of shares held by individuals and others are obtained from the Share Register Survey, run by the Central Statistical Office. Results of the most recent survey are published in *Share Ownership, The Share Register Survey Report*. The survey results are based on an analysis of the ordinary share registers of a sample of UK companies listed on the London Stock Exchange. A sample of shareholdings on each register are analysed and allocated to one of the categories of beneficial ownership. Results are grossed to stock market totals.

Estimates of the number of individuals holding shares are obtained from a survey run by National Opinion Polls on behalf of HM Treasury.

PART 6: EXPENDITURE

Household expenditure

The national accounts definition of household expenditure, within consumers' expenditure, consists of: personal expenditure on goods (durable and non-durable) and services, including the value of income in kind; imputed rent for owner-occupied dwellings; and the purchase of second-hand goods less the proceeds of sales of used goods. Excluded are: interest and other transfer payments; all business expenditure; and the purchase of land and buildings (and associated costs).

In principle, expenditure is measured at the time of acquisition rather than actual disbursement of cash. The categories of expenditure include that of non-resident as well as resident households and individuals in the United Kingdom. For further details see the article entitled 'Consumers' expenditure' in *Economic Trends*, September 1983.

The Family Expenditure Survey definition of household expenditure represents current expenditure of goods and services. This excludes those recorded payments which are really savings or investments (for example life assurance premiums). Similarly, income tax payments, national insurance contributions, mortgage capital repayments and other payments for major additions to dwellings are excluded. For purchases financed by hire purchase or loans, the amounts paid under the finance agreement are recorded as expenditure as they occur; the full cost of the item is not recorded at the time of the initial transaction. For further details see *Family Spending*.

Pensioner households
The data in Table 6.5 relate to those households where the head of household is a male aged 65 or over or a female aged 60 or over. For the analysis two categories are used:

Mainly dependent on state pensions: where three-quarters of the total income of the household is derived from national insurance retirement and similar pensions, including housing and other benefits paid in supplement to or instead of such pensions. A small proportion of people in these households may be working a few hours a week.

Other households: where more than a quarter of the household's income derives from occupational retirement pension and/or income from investments, annuities, etc.

Student expenditure
The data in Table 6.6 relate to students aged under 26 at the start of their course. The base period for analysis is the academic year, that is the number of weeks of term plus the short vacations; the Summer vacation is excluded. Capital payments are excluded from the definition of expenditure. Food expenditure includes meals bought on college premises as well as food prepared at home. Food bought in restaurants and alcoholic drinks are included in the entertainment category. Essential travel is the cost of daily travel to and from college and the equivalent of three trips home to parents. Any additional trips home are included in leisure travel. Course-related expenses refer to books and equipment which the student was required to purchase as well as photocopying and other expenses directly relevant to the course.

Retail prices
The general index of retail prices measures the changes month by month in the level of the commodities and services purchased by all types of households in the United Kingdom, with the exception of certain higher income households and households of retired people mainly dependent on state benefits. These households are:

(a) the 4 per cent (approximately) where the total household recorded gross income exceeds a certain amount (£960 a week in 1993/94).

(b) those in which at least three quarters of the total income is derived from state pensions and benefits and which include at least one person over the national insurance retirement age.

The weights which are used to calculate the index are based on the pattern of household expenditure derived from the continuing Family Expenditure Survey. Since 1962 the weights have been revised in February of each year.

Expenditure patterns of one-person and two-person pensioner households differ from those of the households upon which the general index is based. Separate indices have been compiled for such pensioner households since 1968, and quarterly averages are published in the CSO *Business Monitor MM23 (Retail Prices Index)*. They are chain indices constructed in the same way as the general index of retail prices. It should, however, be noted that the pensioner indices exclude housing costs.

A brief introduction to the RPI is given in the June 1994 issue of CSO *Business Monitor MM23 (Retail Prices Index)*, also available as a booklet from HMSO. Each month's edition of the RPI *Business Monitor* contains further articles of interest, covering topics such as reweighting and indicator items.

Household saving
Household saving: is the balance of income and expenditure on the current account of households, and is derived from the personal sector account, mainly by subtracting the income and the expenditure (and hence the saving) of the other parts of the personal sector.

The household savings ratio: is household saving expressed as a percentage of household disposable income.

Household income: comprises
Wages and salaries, and forces' pay
Self-employment income
Rent, dividends, and interest
Income in kind
Pensions and benefits paid by life assurance and pension schemes
Social security benefits
Other current transfers

Household disposable income: comprises
Household income less
United Kingdom taxes on income
Social security contributions (excluding employers' contributions)
Employees' contributions to occupational pension schemes

Household expenditure: comprises
Interest payments
Community charge (until March 1993);
Council tax (from April 1993);
Rates (Northern Ireland)
Expenditure on goods and services
Life assurance premiums etc paid by individuals
Other current transfers

(Note: this definition of household expenditure does not accord with that for national accounts purposes - see above.)

PART 7: HEALTH

Standardised death rates
To enable comparisons to be made over time, standardised death rates have been calculated by applying a scaling factor to the base year's rates. For Chart 7.1 the scaling factor is the study year's 1951-based standard mortality rates (SMR) and for Chart 7.22 the scaling factor is the study year's 1971-based SMRs.

Expectation of life
The expectation of life, shown in Table 7.3, is the average total number of years which a person of that age could be expected to live, if the rates of mortality at each age were those experienced in that year. The mortality rates which underlie the expectation of life figures are based, up to 1993, on total deaths occurring in each year and, in the case of subsequent years, on the mortality

rates assumed for those years in the Government Actuary's mid-1992 based population projections.

Body mass index (BMI)
Obesity is linked to ill-health and results in an increased risk of a number of diseases. Body weight is a poor indicator of obesity on its own as it does not take account of skeletal size or body composition. A number of alternative measures of obesity have been developed.

Body mass index (BMI) or Quetelet Index is the most widely used index of obesity which standardises weight for height and is calculated as weight (kg)/height(m)^2. The index can only be calculated on cases where both height and weight measurements are considered to be valid: 10,361 men and 11,467 women in the Health Survey (1991, 1992 and 1993 combined).

While BMI is the most widely used measure of obesity it is not without faults. BMI does not take account of the relative distribution of fat on different parts of the body nor does it distinguish between body fat and muscle. It is known to give misleading measures of obesity on certain physiques, in particular, individuals with muscular physiques.

For the purposes of analysis, BMI is classified according to the following internationally accepted categories:

Level of index	Description
20 or less	Underweight
over 20 to 25	Desirable
over 25 to 30	Overweight
over 30	Obese

Standardised registration ratios (SSR)
The incidence of cancer varies greatly with age. The SRR is an index which enables ready comparison of incidence rates in populations with different age structures. It is calculated by denoting one set of age-specific rates as the standard. These are then applied to each of several index populations of known age structure to see how many registrations would have been expected in these index populations had they, at each, stage, experienced the cancer incidence of the standard population. The 'expected' incidence so found is then compared with the 'observed', their ratio being multiplied by 100 to give an index in which 100 is the value for the standard population.

High stress levels and age standardised ratios
People reporting high stress levels were those who: in the previous four weeks had experienced quite a lot/ a great deal of stress (the other categories were *not at all, slightly,* and *moderately*); and those who said stress or pressure in life had affected their health quite a lot or a great deal.

The age standardised ratio is a means of adjusting for the different age composition of each of the subgroups - in this case, social class. It is calculated on the observed rate for the subgroup divided by the state which would be expected if the subgroup conformed to the age-specific rates in the sample as a whole, multiplied by 100. A ratio of more than 100 indicates a greater likelihood of suffering from stress than would be expected in that group on the basis of age distribution alone. A ratio of less than 100 indicates a reduced likelihood.

Immunisation
Data for 1991-92 and 1993-94 for England, Wales and Northern Ireland relate to children reaching their second birthday during the year and immunised by their second birthday. Data for 1981 for England, Wales and Northern Ireland, and for Scotland in all years, relate to children born two years earlier and immunised by the end of the specified year.

Death rates for breast cancer
The data used in Table 7.15 relate to 1992 and 1994. For England and Wales deaths for 1992 represent the number of deaths registered in that year while deaths for 1994 are deaths which occurred in that year. For this and other reasons, the death rates for the two years are not directly comparable although the effects of these changes are small.

Proportional mortality ratios (PMR)
These are calculated as the number of observed deaths from suicide divided by the number of expected deaths multiplied by 100. The expected deaths are computed by applying the proportion of total deaths due to suicide for all men aged 16 to 64 to the total deaths in the occupation group of interest. Thus a PMR of 200 indicates that the proportion of deaths attributable to suicide was twice as great among the specific occupation group as among a comparable England and Wales population, that is all men aged 16 to 64.

PART 8: SOCIAL PROTECTION

Benefits to groups of recipients

Elderly people
Retirement pension
Non-contributory retirement pension
Christmas bonus paid with retirement pension and other non-disability benefits
Principal income-related benefits and social fund payments to people over 60[1]

Sick and disabled people
Invalidity benefit
Attendance allowance
Mobility allowance
Disability living allowance
Disability working allowance
Industrial disablement benefit
Other industrial injuries benefits
Severe disablement allowance
Invalid care allowance
War pensions
Independent living fund
Motability
Christmas bonus paid with disability benefits
Principal income-related benefits and Social fund payments to disabled people
Statutory sick pay
Sickness benefit

Unemployed people
Unemployment benefit
Principal income-related benefits and payments from the social fund to unemployed and their families

Families, widows and others
Child benefit
One parent benefit
Family credit
Income support
Statutory maternity pay
Maternity allowance
Social fund maternity payments
Principal income-related benefits and social fund payments to lone-parent families[1]
Housing and council tax benefits paid to people in work
Widow's benefits
War widow's pensions
Guardian's allowance and child's special allowance
Industrial death benefit
Social fund funeral payments
Income support paid to people who do not fall within the other client groups

1 Principal income-related benefits are income-support, housing benefit and council tax benefits.

Selected advisory and counselling services
Al-Anon Family Groups: Includes Irish Republic.
Alcoholic Anonymous: Includes branches in the Channel Isles. The 1981 and 1990 figures exclude Northern Ireland.
Catholic Marriage Advisory Council: Figures relate to Great Britain.
Citizens Advice Bureaux: Figures given for 'Clients' represent new enquiries in 1971, and new plus repeat enquiries thereafter.
Relate: Includes England, Wales, Northern Ireland, Channel Isles and Isle of Man. Marriage Guidance Scotland is excluded. Up to 1990, figures given for 'Clients' represented numbers of families (based on new cases during the year). From 1991 it represents all clients using Relate services.
Samaritans: Figures relate to the number of contacts.
Youth Access: Figures given are numbers of young people accessing information, advice and counselling services.

In-patient activity
In-patient data for England and later years for Northern Ireland are based on Finished Consultant Episodes (FCEs). Data for Wales and Scotland and earlier Northern Ireland data are based on Deaths and Discharges. An FCE is a completed period of care of a patient using a bed, under one consultant, in a particular District/Special Health Authority. If a patient is transferred from one consultant to another within the same hospital, this counts as an FCE but not a hospital discharge. Conversely if a patient is transferred from one hospital to another within the same district without changing consultant, this counts as a hospital discharge but not as an FCE.

PART 9: CRIME AND JUSTICE

Types of offences in England, Wales and Northern Ireland
Notifiable offences: are broadly the more serious offences. They include most indictable offences and triable either way offences and certain summary offences (for example, unauthorised taking of a motor vehicle). Excludes criminal damage of value £20 or under in England and Wales and £200 or under in Northern Ireland.

Indictable offences: are those for which an adult must be tried at the Crown Court, for example robbery, arson and rape. Figures for indictable offences given in this chapter include those for offences which are triable either way (see below).

Triable either way offences: are offences triable either on indictment or summarily. They may be tried in a magistrates' court unless either the defendant or the magistrate requests a Crown Court hearing. Thefts including car crime and less serious violence against the person fall into this category.

Summary offences: are those offences which are normally tried at a magistrates' court.

Standard list offences: (not applicable to Northern Ireland) are offences for which the name of the offender and details of each sentence have been collected by the Home Office since 1963. These are linked by name/criminal record number to enable research into criminal histories. The offences include all indictable offences, triable either way offences and some summary offences. The full list is given in Appendices 4 and 5 of *Criminal Statistics 1993*.

Offences and crimes
There are a number of reasons why figures for notifiable offences in England, Wales and Northern Ireland and recorded crime in Scotland cannot be directly compared:

Different legal systems: The legal system operating in Scotland differs from that in England and Wales and Northern Ireland.

Differences in classification: There are significant differences in the offences included within the recorded crime categories used in Scotland and the categories of notifiable offences used in England, Wales and Northern Ireland. Scottish figures of 'crime' have therefore been grouped in an attempt to approximate to the classification of notifiable offences in England, Wales and Northern Ireland.

Counting rules: In Scotland each individual offence occurring within an incident is recorded whereas in England, Wales and Northern Ireland only the main offence is counted.

Burglary: This term is not applicable to Scotland where the term used is 'housebreaking'.

Theft from vehicles: In Scotland data have only been collected from January 1992. The figures include theft by opening lockfast places from a motor vehicle and other theft from a motor vehicle.

Sentences and orders
The following are the main sentences and orders which can be imposed upon those persons found guilty in 1991 and subsequently. Some types of sentence or order can only be given to offenders in England and Wales in certain age groups. Under a new statutory framework for sentencing contained in the *Criminal Justice Acts 1991* and *1993*, the sentence must reflect the seriousness of the offence. The following sentences are available for adults (a similar range of sentences is available to juveniles aged 10 to 17):

Absolute and conditional discharge: A court may make an order discharging a person absolutely or (except in Scotland) conditionally where it is inexpedient to inflict punishment and, before 1 October 1992, where a probation order was not appropriate. An order for conditional discharge runs for such period of not more than three years as the court specifies, the condition being that the offender does not commit another offence within the period so specified. In Scotland a court may also discharge a person with an admonition.

Attendance centre order: Available in England, Wales and Northern Ireland for offenders under the age of 20 and involves deprivation of free time.

Probation/supervision: An offender sentenced to a probation order is under the supervision of a probation officer (social worker in Scotland), whose duty it is (in England and Wales only) to advise, assist and befriend him. A cardinal feature of the order is that it relies on the co-operation of the offender. Probation orders may be given for any period between six months and three years inclusive.

Community service: An offender who is convicted of an offence punishable with imprisonment may be sentenced to perform unpaid work for not more than 240 hours, and not less than 40 hours. In Scotland the *Law Reform (Miscellaneous Provisions) (Scotland) Act 1990* requires that community service can only be ordered where the court would otherwise have imposed imprisonment or detention. Probation and community service may be combined in a single order in Scotland.

Combination order: The *Criminal Justice Act 1991* introduced the combination order in England and Wales only, which combines elements of both probation supervision and community service.

Imprisonment: is the custodial sentence for adult offenders or, in the case of mentally disordered offenders, hospital orders which may include a restriction order such that Home Office consent is needed for release or transfer. The *Criminal Justice Act 1991* abolished remission and substantially changed the parole scheme in England and Wales. Those serving sentences of under four years, imposed on or after 1 October 1992, are subject to Automatic Conditional Release and are released, subject to certain criteria, halfway through their sentence. Those serving sentences of four years or longer are considered for Discretionary Conditional Release after having served half their sentence, but are automatically released at the two-thirds point of sentence. All offenders serving a sentence of 12 months or more are supervised in the community until the three quarter point of sentence. A life sentence prisoner may be released on licence subject to supervision and is always liable to recall. In Scotland the *Prisoners and Criminal Proceedings (Scotland) Act 1993* changed the system of remission and parole for prisoners sentenced on or after 1 October 1993. Those serving sentences of less than four years are released unconditionally after having served half of their sentence, unless the court specifically imposes a Supervised Release Order which subjects them to social work supervision after release. Those serving sentences of four years or more are eligible for parole at half sentence. If parole is not granted then they will automatically be released on licence at two thirds of sentence. All prisoners are liable to be 'recalled on conviction' ie if between the date of release and the date on which the full sentence ends, a person commits another offence which is punishable by imprisonment, then the offender may be returned to prison for the remainder of that sentence whether or not a sentence of imprisonment is also imposed for the new offence'.

Fully suspended sentences: may only be passed in exceptional circumstances. In England, Wales and Northern Ireland, sentences of imprisonment of two years or less may be fully suspended. A court should not pass a suspended sentence unless a sentence of imprisonment would be appropriate in the absence of a power to suspend. The result of suspending a sentence is that it will not take effect unless during the period specified the offender is convicted of another offence punishable with imprisonment. Suspended sentences are not used in Scotland.

Fines: The *Criminal Justice Act 1993* introduced new arrangements on 20 September 1993 whereby courts should take account of an offender's means in setting fines. This system replaced the more formal unit fines scheme included in the Criminal justice Act 1991. The Act also introduced the power for courts to arrange deduction of fines from income benefit for those offenders receiving such benefits. The *Law Reform (Miscellaneous Provision) (Scotland) Act 1990* as amended by the *Criminal Justice (Scotland) Act 1995* provides for the use of supervised attendance orders by selected courts in Scotland.

Offenders cautioned for burglary

In England and Wales offenders cautioned for going equipped for stealing, etc were counted against Burglary offences until 1986 and against Other offences from 1987. Historical data provided in Table 9.13 have been amended to take account of this change. Drug offences were included under Other offences for 1971.

Young offenders institutions

The Criminal Justice Act 1991 made a number of changes to the custodial sentencing arrangements for young offenders in England and Wales. A common minimum age of 15 for boys and girls was set for the imposition of a sentence of detention in a young offender institution thus removing boys aged 14 from the scope of this sentence.

Prison categories

Prisons with security categories: These are A, B, C and D. Prisoners placed in category A accommodation (category A prisoners) are those for whom escape would be highly dangerous to the public. Category A prisoners are held in separate accommodation within other prisons hence there is no separate entry for this group in the table. Category D prisons contain prisoners who have the lowest security rating and are those who can reasonably be trusted in open conditions.

Local prisons: take remand prisoners and convicted prisoners from the courts prior to categorisation.

Dispersal prisons: take prisoners who require high security conditions.

Civil courts

England and Wales: The main civil courts are the High Court and the county courts. Magistrates' courts also have some civil jurisdiction, mainly in family proceedings. Most appeals in civil cases go to the Court of Appeal (Civil Division) and may go from there to the House of Lords. Since July 1991, county courts have been able to deal with all contract and tort cases and actions for recovery of land, regardless of value. Cases are presided over by a judge who almost always sits without a jury. Jury trials are limited to specified cases, for example, actions for libel.

Scotland: The Court of Session is the supreme civil court. As a general rule it has the original jurisdiction in all civil cases and the power to hear and give decisions on appeals over all civil courts unless such jurisdiction is expressly excluded by statute. The sheriff court is the principal local court of civil, as well as criminal jurisdiction. Its civil jurisdiction is generally comparable with that of the county court in England and Wales but is more extensive in certain directions. For example, there is no limit to the sum which may be sued for.

Tribunals

Valuation tribunals: Data relate to England and Wales and are for financial years.
Children's Hearings (Scotland): Data for 1994 relate to 1993.
Industrial tribunals: Includes data from the Industrial tribunals for Scotland.
Immigration adjudicators: Cases heard include cases withdrawn before a hearing. In addition to the cases shown in the table, in 1994, 9 thousand cases were determined without a hearing.
Immigration Appeals tribunal: Data for cases heard include cases withdrawn before a hearing.
Rent Assessment Committee: Includes data from the Rent Assessment Panel for Scotland
Mental Health Review tribunal: Cases withdrawn before a hearing include cases where the patient is discharged by a doctor, the Home Office or a court, patients who have absconded, deaths, transfers to other hospitals, remits to prison and invalid applications.
Social Security Commissioners: Cases withdrawn and heard in 1994 includes cases determined without a hearing.
Valuation Appeals Committee (Scotland): Data for 1994 refer to 1994-95.

PART 10: HOUSING

Dwellings

Estimates of the stock of dwellings are based on data from the Censuses of Population (Great Britain) and Valuation and

Lands Agency listings (Northern Ireland), with adjustments for enumeration errors and for definitional changes. The figures include vacant dwellings and temporary dwellings occupied as a normal place of residence. Privately rented dwellings include dwellings rented with farm or business premises and those occupied by virtue of employment.

Household type
The classification of household type uses the following categories:
one adult aged 16 to 59
two adults aged 16 to 59
small family: one or two persons aged 16 or over and one or two persons aged under 16.
large family: one or more persons aged 16 and over and three or more persons aged under 16, or three or more persons aged 16 and over and two persons aged under 16.
large adult household: three or more persons aged 16 or over with or without one person aged under 16.
two adults, one or both aged 60 or over
one adult aged 60 or over

Homeless households
Great Britain: Households for whom local authorities accepted responsibility to secure accommodation under the *Housing Act 1985* and *Housing (Scotland) Act 1987 Part II.* Data for Wales include some households given advice and assistance only.

Northern Ireland: Households for whom Northern Ireland Housing Executive has accepted responsibility to secure permanent accommodation, not necessarily those for whom permanent accommodation has been found.

Bedroom standard
This concept is used to estimate occupation density by allocating a standard number of bedrooms to each household in accordance with its age/gender/marital status composition and the relationship of the members to one another. A separate bedroom is allocated to each married couple, any other person aged 21 or over, each pair of adolescents aged 10 to 20 of the same sex, and each pair of children under 10. Any unpaired person aged 10 to 20 is paired, if possible with a child under 10 of the same gender: if that is not possible, they are given a separate bedroom, as is any unpaired child under 10. This standard is then compared with the actual number of bedrooms (including bedsitters) available for the sole use of the household, and deficiencies or excesses are tabulated. Bedrooms converted to other uses are not counted as available unless they have been noted as bedrooms by the informant; bedrooms not actually in use are counted unless uninhabitable.

PART 11: ENVIRONMENT

Native species at risk
The data for endangered, vulnerable or rare species are included in Red Data Lists which are based on criteria devised by the International Union for the Conservation of Nature. The table also includes figures, where available, for Nationally Scarce species. These are species which are recorded as present in only 16 to 100 10km squares in Great Britain. Red Data Listed and Nationally Scarce species are used in evaluating the conservation importance of sites; their presence is one of the criteria used to select Sites of Special Scientific Interest

Quality of bathing water
Directive 76/160/EEC concerning the quality of bathing water sets, among other things, the following mandatory values for the coliform parameters:

- for total coliforms 10,000 per 100 ml; and
- for faecal coliforms 2,000 per 100 ml.

The Directive requires that at least 95 per cent of samples taken for each of these parameters over the bathing season must meet the mandatory values. In practice this has been interpreted in the following manner: where 20 samples are taken a maximum of only one sample for each parameter may exceed the mandatory values for the water to pass the coliform standards; where less than 20 samples are taken none may exceed the mandatory values for the water to pass the coliform standards.

PART 12: TRANSPORT

Journey purpose
The purpose of a journey is taken to be the activity at the destination, unless that destination is 'home' in which case the purpose is defined by the origin of the journey. A journey is defined as a one-way course of travel having a single main purpose.

To and from work: journeys to a usual place of work, or from work to home.

In course of work: personal journeys in course of work. This includes all work journeys by people with no usual place of work (eg site workers) and those who work at or from home.

Education: journeys to school or college etc, excluding part-time non-vocational courses.

Escort for work/education: used when the traveller has no purpose of his own, other than to escort or accompany another person to a place of work or education. All other escort purposes are included with the purpose of the person being escorted.

Shopping: all journeys to shops or from shops to home.

Personal business: visits to services eg hairdressers, launderettes, solicitors, churches etc and for medical consultations/ treatment, and eating and drinking unless the main purpose was entertainment/social.

Social and entertainment: meeting friends etc, travelling to all types of entertainment, voluntary work, non-vocational evening classes etc.

Holidays and day trips: journeys (within Great Britain) to or from any holiday (including stays of four nights or more with friends or relatives) or journeys for pleasure (not otherwise classified as social or entertainment) within a single day.

Journey stages
A journey consists of one or more stages. A new stage is defined when there is a change in the form of transport or when there is a change of vehicle requiring a separate ticket.

Car ownership
Car: the figures for household ownership include four wheeled and three wheeled cars, off-road vehicles, minibuses, motorcaravans and dormobiles.

Cars and vans: road motor vehicle other than a motorcycle, intended for the carriage of passengers and designed to seat no more than nine people (including the driver). The term 'passenger car' therefore covers microcars (which need no permit to be driven), taxis and hired passenger cars, provided that they have fewer than ten seats. This category may also include pick-ups.

Passenger death rates

The following rates are used:

Air: World passenger carrying services of United Kingdom airlines for fixed and rotary winged craft over 2,300 kilograms. Passenger kilometres relate to revenue passengers only.

Sea: Domestic and international passenger services of United Kingdom registered vessels.

CHAPTER 13: LIFESTYLES

Social grade

Social grade categories in Table 13.10 are based on the occupation of the chief income earner of his or her household as follows:

A: Higher managerial, administrative or professional
B: Intermediate managerial, administrative or professional
C1: Supervisory or clerical and junior managerial, administrative or professional
C2: Skilled manual workers
D: Semi and unskilled manual
E: State pensioners or widows (no other earners), casual or lowest grade workers or long-term unemployed

Parliamentary elections and political parties

A general election must be held at least every five years, or sooner, if the Prime Minister of the day so decides. The United Kingdom is currently divided into 651 constituencies, each of which returns one member to the House of Commons. To ensure equitable representation, four permanent Boundary Commissions (for England and Wales, Scotland and Northern Ireland) make periodic reviews of constituencies and recommend any change in the number or redistribution of seats that may seem necessary in the light of population movements or for some other reason.

The Social Democratic Party (SDP) was launched on 26 March 1981. In the 1983 and 1987 general elections the Liberals and SDP contested seats as the Liberal-SDP Alliance. In 1988 the Social and Liberal Democrats were formed, after which the Democrats and the SDP contested elections separately. In June 1990 the SDP disbanded.

On 17 December 1985 all 15 Ulster Unionist MPs resigned their seats and sought re-election as a protest against the Anglo-Irish agreement. The 15 by-elections were held on 23 January 1986.

Index

The references in this index refer to table and chart numbers, or entries in the Appendix.

Central
Statistical
Office

Articles published in previous editions

No. 1 1970
Some general developments in social statistics Professor C A Moser, CSO

Public expenditure on the social services Professor B Abel-Smith, London School of Economics and Political Science

The growth of the population to the end of the century Jean Thompson, OPCS

A forecast of effective demand for housing in Great Britain in the 1970s A E Holmans, MHLG

No. 2 1971
Social services manpower Dr S Rosenbaum, CSO

Trends in certificated sickness absence F E Whitehead, DHSS

Some aspects of model building in the social and environmental fields B Benjamin, CSC

Social indicators - health A J Culyer, R J Lavers and A Williams, University of York

No. 3 1972
Social commentary: change in social conditions CSO

Statistics about immigrants: objectives, methods, sources and problems Professor C A Moser, CSO

Central manpower planning in Scottish secondary education A W Brodie, SED

Social malaise research: a study in Liverpool M Flynn, P Flynn and N Mellor, Liverpool City Planning Department

Crimes of violence against the person in England and Wales S Klein, HO

No. 4 1973
Social commentary: certain aspects of the life cycle CSO

The elderly D C L Wroe, CSO

Subjective social indicators M Abrams, SSRC

Mental illness and the psychiatric services E R Bransby, DHSS

Cultural accounting A Peacock and C Godfrey, University of York

Road accidents and casualties in Great Britain J A Rushbrook, DOE

No. 5 1974
Social commentary: men and women CSO

Social security: the European experiment E James and A Laurent, EC Commission

Time budgets B M Hedges, SCPR

Time budgets and models of urban activity patterns N Bullock, P Dickens, M Shapcott and P Steadman, Cambridge University of Architecture

Road traffic and the environment F D Sando and V Batty, DOE

No. 6 1975
Social commentary: social class CSO

Areas of urban deprivation in Great Britain: an analysis of 1971 Census data S Holtermann, DOE

Note: Subjective social indicators Mark Abrams, SSRC

No. 7 1976
Social commentary: social change in Britain 1970-1975 CSO

Crime in England and Wales Dr C Glennie, HO

Crime in Scotland Dr Bruce, SHHD

Subjective measures of quality of life in Britain: 1971 to 1975 J Hall, SSRC

No. 8 1977
Social commentary: fifteen to twenty-five: a decade of transition CSO

The characteristics of low income households R Van Slooten and A G Coverdale, DHSS

No. 9 1979
Housing tenure in England and Wales: the present situation and recent trends A E Holmans, DOE

Social forecasting in Lucas B R Jones, Lucas Industries

No. 10 1980
Social commentary: changes in living standards since the 1950s CSO

Inner cities in England D Allnutt and A Gelardi, DOE

Scotland's schools D Wishart, SED

No. 14 1984
Changes in the Life-styles of the Elderly 1959-1982 M Abrams

No. 15 1985
British Social Attitudes R Jowell and C Airey, SCPR

No. 16 1986
Income after retirement G C Fiegehen, DHSS

No 17 1987
Social Trends since World War II Professor A H Halsey, University of Oxford

Household Formation and Dissolution and Housing Tenure: a Longitudinal Perspective A E Holmans and S Nandy, DOE; A C Brown, OPCS

No. 18 1988
Major Epidemics of the 20th Century: from Coronary Thrombosis to AIDS Sir Richard Doll, University of Oxford

No. 19 1989
Recent Trends in Social Attitudes L Brook, R Jowell and S Witherspoon, SCPR

No. 20 1990
Social Trends, the next 20 years T Griffin, CSO

No. 21 1991
The 1991 Census of Great Britain: Plans for Content and Output B Mahon and D Pearce, OPCS

No. 22 1992
Crime statistics: their use and misuse C Lewis, HO

No. 24 1994
Characteristics of the bottom 20 per cent of the income distribution N Adkin, DSS

Printed in the United Kingdom for HMSO.
Dd.301752, 1/96, C100, 3400, 5673, 340313.